SILK AND STEEL

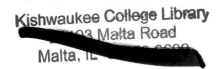
SILK AND STEEL

WOMEN AT ARMS

R. L. WILSON

PREFACE BY ANGIE ROSENBRUCH-HAMMER,
DIRECTOR, ROSENBRUCH WILDLIFE HERITAGE MUSEUM

FOREWORD BY GUY M. WILSON,
MASTER OF THE ARMOURIES, H.M. TOWER OF LONDON (RET.)
DIRECTOR, ROYAL ARMOURIES MUSEUM, LEEDS (RET.)

PHOTOGRAPHY BY PETER BEARD, G. ALLAN BROWN, AND DOUGLAS SANDBERG

RANDOM HOUSE NEW YORK

Front endpapers: Left, Alice H. Bull, a remarkable pioneer in the role of women in competitive target shooting in the United States, was recognized as the person who opened up shooting sports to women in America. In addition to numerous wins in national rifle competitions, she was the first woman elected to the board of directors of the National Rifle Association (1949), and the first woman to receive an honorary NRA life membership. Her achievements, which began on a national level as early as the mid-1930s, were given formal recognition by establishment of the Alice H. Bull Trophy, an annual National Board for the Promotion of Rifle Practice award in the government matches at Camp Perry, Ohio.

Center: Books and art reflecting the diversity of themes in which women have used weaponry. At *right*, fictional defense worker Rosie the Riveter, celebrated Norman Rockwell painting on World War II *Saturday Evening Post* cover; from Norman Rockwell Museum, Stockbridge, Massachusetts; note influence of Michelangelo. *Lower right*, Post-its mark numerous historic houses and sites associated with women shooters and hunters. *Top center*, Sharlot Hall, Arizona pioneer and accomplished outdoorswoman. *Below*, Aldo Uberti with daughter Maria Laura, formerly president of Uberti U.S.A., gunmakers. *Center*, teaching young lady to shoot, scene from Amos Gital's anguished film *Kedma*, from Jewish Museum, New York. *Left center*, former Hermitage (St. Petersburg, Russia) Museum curator of arms and armor Dr. Leonid Tarassuk, with wife, Nina, and children Ilya and Irena, at opening of arms and armor gallery, Art Institute of Chicago, in the 1980s.

California gunmaker Roy Weatherby and his family, all shooters; *bottom center*, in library at Southgate home, from *left*, daughters Diane and Connie, Weatherby, Sr., son Ed, and wife Carmella. The internationally celebrated maker of high performance hunting rifles established the Weatherby Trophy, to this day the most distinguished award in the world of big game hunting. Although several female hunters are among the attendees at this annual event, the Oscar of the hunting world, no woman has received this honor—yet. Among Weatherby clients pictured, Countess Claire d'Acquarone of Verona, Italy, kneeling by 100-pound elephant, taken in Kenya, and actress Jane Powell admiring rifle (*left center*).

Page i: Pen-and-ink drawing by Friedrich A. von Kaulbach of women shooting at men targets. Woman at *right*, firing pinfire revolver of Belgian or French style. Von Kaulbach was best known for his painting of the *Schützenliesl* (see page 215). This drawing was discovered by writer-researcher Tom Rowe, and is one of numerous illustrations in his magnum opus on single-shot rifles.

Frontispiece: Several centuries of women at arms, beginning *upper left*, and sweeping through into modern times, at *right*. Beginning with women warriors, the saga gradually evolved into innumerable disciplines within the umbrella of the shooting sports. These spheres have been primarily target shooting, hunting, and self-defense—on a nearly universal scale. Woman in pagoda at *upper left* is from the nineteenth century (painting is presently in Cleveland Museum of Art). It likely depicts Maharani of Kotah, a family with strong hunting traditions.

Other books by R. L. Wilson

The World of Beretta: An International Legend*
Buffalo Bill's Wild West (with Greg Martin)*
Ruger & His Guns
Steel Canvas: The Art of American Arms*
The Peacemakers: Arms and Adventure in the American West*
Winchester: An American Legend*
Colt: An American Legend*
The Colt Heritage (first edition of *Colt: An American Legend*)
The Paterson Colt Book
The Official Price Guide to Gun Collecting (annual editions)
The Book of Colt Firearms (two editions)
The Colt Engraving Book (three editions)
Winchester Engraving (two editions)
Winchester: The Golden Age of American Gunmaking and the Winchester 1 of 1000
Samuel Colt Presents
The Arms Collection of Colonel Colt
L. D. Nimschke, Firearms Engraver
The Rampant Colt
Colt Commemorative Firearms (two editions)
Theodore Roosevelt, Outdoorsman (two editions)
Antique Arms Annual (1971 edition)
Colt Pistols (with R. E. Hable)
Colt Handguns (Japanese)
Paterson Colt Pistol Variations (with P. R. Phillips)
The Deringer in America (with L. D. Eberhart, two volumes)
The Art of the Gun (with Robert M. Lee, five volumes)
Colt's Dates of Manufacture
Lock, Stock, & Barrel (compiled by Charles F. Priore, Jr.)

*foreign-language editions: French, German, Italian, in addition to English

Copyright © 2003 by R. L. Wilson

Photographs copyright © 2003 by Peter Beard and G. Allan Brown, excepting photographs from other sources

All rights reserved under International and Pan-American Copyright Conventions. Published in the United States by Random House, an imprint of The Random House Publishing Group, division of Random House, Inc., New York, and simultaneously in Canada by Random House of Canada Limited, Toronto.

RANDOM HOUSE and colophon are registered trademarks of Random House, Inc.

Library of Congress Cataloging-in-Publication Data

Wilson, R. L. (Robert Lawrence)
Silk and steel: women at arms / by R. L. Wilson; foreword by Guy M. Wilson; photography by Peter Beard, G. Allan Brown, and Douglas Sandberg.
p.   cm.
Includes bibliographical references and index.
ISBN 0-375-50761-2
I. Title.
TS533 .W57 2003   683.4'0082—dc21   2002068211

Printed in Italy on acid-free paper
Random House website address: www.atrandom.com
Author's website address: www.wilsonbooks.com
Frazier Historical Arms Museum website address:
www.frazierarmsmuseum.org
Royal Armouries Museum website address:
www.armouries.org.uk

98765432

First Edition

The author and publisher are grateful to the Bridgeman Art Library, New York, London, and Paris, for special considerations in supplying James Joseph Jacques Tissot's "The Crack Shot," as well as assistance in supplying other singular images for the body of the book. The oil painting on canvas is from the collection of Wimpole Hall, Cambridgeshire, UK/National Trust Photographic Library/John Hammond Bridgeman Art Library.

To the

countless millions of women

through the centuries

who have mastered

the captivating world of firearms

and know the great pleasure

of marksmanship and wilderness adventure

and the appreciation of works of art, craftsmanship,

and mechanical ingenuity.

T. HOLLES PELHAM

DUKE OF NEWCASTLE.

By Her Majesty the Queen,
Guardian of the Kingdom, &c.

Caroline R C R

THESE are in his Majesty's Name
to Will and Require you to Kill,
or Cause to be Kill'd, within your
Charge, One fat Buck of this Season, and
deliver the Same for the Use of *His Grace
the Duke of Newcastle.* — 'And
for so doing this shall be your Warrant.
Given at the Court at KENSINGTON
this *9th* Day of *June* 1736
In the *ninth* Year of his Majesty's Reign.

*For the Ranger or Keeper
of Windsor little Park*

Sr

I Desire you will Send a Very Good Buck
To Claremont a Thursday Morning Early
for The Use of his Grace The Duke of
Newcastle Yps Tho' Northeast

N.B. My Lord Duke thought the Last
was hunted so I Desire if Possible
you will Shoot it Dead & Not Let
it run as Little as Possible.

Augt 9. 1736

QUEEN CAROLINE
*Queen Consort
to K. Geo. 2d.
B. 2 Mar. 1682
Mar. 1705*

Hunting license for ranger or gamekeeper of Windsor Little Park,
issued by Queen Caroline of England, August 9, 1736, for benefit
of the Duke of Newcastle. Note reference to a quick kill, which
was best for the quality of the meat, and in humane consideration
of the buck.

It's ironic thinking of men and women shooting

out here [Africa]. The women are better shots.

—Philip H. Percival,
dean of Professional Hunters in Africa,
president, East African Professional Hunters Association
(Statement made to Peter Beard in 1961. Among the women
Percival guided in the bush were Lady Delamere, Beryl Markham,
the Duchess of Connaught, Osa Johnson, Karen Blixen, Delia
"Mickie" Akeley, and Lucille Parsons Vanderbilt.)

The deerskin rug on our study floor, the buck's head over the fireplace, what are these after all but the keys which have unlocked enchanted doors, and granted us not only health and vigor, but a fresh and fairer vision of existence.

—Paul (Paulina) Brandreth,
Trails of Enchantment

The return of the most sporting time of the year brings such thoughts to the surface, the promise of what the months as they unfold their treasures may hold for those who find their best pleasures in the worship of Diana and in the trumpet sound of the true keynote of sport.

—Hilda Murray, *Echoes of Sport*

Also, I do not want to be thought to claim credit for being a woman who was doing a man's work. I honestly believe that any healthy woman with a love of sport can hunt through British East Africa today almost, if not quite, as easily as a man.

—Gretchen Cron, *The Roaring Veldt*

I had just obtained a new gun. Nobody knew I owned such a thing. It was a .22, and my most treasured possession.

—Fran Hamerstrom, *Is She Coming Too?*

When you shoot your first pheasant and he comes down . . . , you feel you really are a sportswoman, and a new confidence which brings success in its train, springs up in your heart.

—The Honorable Mrs. Lancelot Lohther,
The Sportswoman's Library

With all due reverence, I defy anyone to deny the importance of such a trinity in life as—God, sex and shooting.

—Marjorie Wiggin Prescott,
Tales of a Sportsman's Wife: Shooting

A fighting force of child-bearers would solve several questions: the question of overpopulation that precedes wars and "shortage of men" that follows them. And the question of how to rid war of its romantic implications: there would be far fewer sentimental gold-star mothers of the next war if there had been disillusioned war-veteran mothers of the last. It might even solve the question of war itself. What nation would plunge into a war in which its men fought not for their wives and sweethearts, but with their wives and sweethearts?

—Clare Boothe Luce, quoted in *Rage for Fame*,
Sylvia Jukes Morris

To the extent that hunting has served both patriarchy and feminism as a root metaphor for men's activity in the world, Woman the Hunter is a necessarily disruptive figure.

—Mary Zeiss Stange, Ph.D., *Woman the Hunter*

*Woman fair and turkeys wild,
In this progressive age we're living,
A woman brings us our Thanksgiving.*

—Anonymous

Only the lack of opportunity and mentors has kept millions of interested women from participating.

—Sue King, *Women on Target* (on hunting and shooting)

The questions as to which of the five big-game animals—elephant, lion, buffalo, leopard, or rhino—is the most dangerous to hunt is one that is constantly being debated by big-game hunters. . . . If a woman may venture an opinion—formed after five strenuous years of big-game hunting, two and a half years of which were spent following elephants for scientific purposes—I would say that the hazards of tracking these mammoth creatures through the vast primeval forests of Central Africa are infinitely greater than the perils attending the hunting of any other kind of so-called big game. . . . In the forest, where but few white men go to hunt, the odds are all in favor of the elephant. . . .

—Delia Akeley, *Jungle Portraits*

CONTENTS

PREFACE

Angie Rosenbruch-Hammer, *director, Rosenbruch Wildlife Heritage Museum*

Coming from a pioneer family in the American West, and one whose life's blood for generations has revolved around hunting, it might be said that the subject of women at arms is one that our family has taken for granted. My mother, MaryAnn Rosenbruch, is a registered guide in Alaska, as is my younger sister, Alisha. We grew up in Utah and in Alaska, and virtually all the girls and women we knew could shoot and hunt—and could do so every bit as well as the men (sometimes better).

A love of the outdoors and dedication to the shooting sports were vital foundations of our life, helping immeasurably to form an essential, indeed, unequaled family bond.

As Alisha relates in her passages in *Silk and Steel,* sometimes her male clients mistakenly assume that as a "girl guide" she is not in the same league as the men, and that hunting and shooting are activities for men only. Some are even so retrograde and chauvinistic that they only reluctantly agree that women *might* be allowed to come along on a field trip!

Silk and Steel challenges conventional assumptions, indeed, vaporizes them as the myths they surely are. This book documents the vital role of women throughout arms history, proving time and again that they have made important contributions to the traditions and achievements in a wide range of subjects in firearms history— among them gunmaking, engraving, engineering, manufacturing, target shooting, hunting—in other words, virtually every *other* aspect of the shooting sports.

At the Rosenbruch Wildlife Heritage Museum, most of our exhibits were collected worldwide by my father, Jim; my mother, MaryAnn; my brother, Jimmie; and by Alisha. In doing so they carried on the traditions of such pioneers in creating natural history museum collections as Carl and Delia Akeley, Jim and Sally Clark, and Martin and Osa Johnson. As long as there has been taxidermy, such collecting trips were often under extremely trying circumstances—so clearly documented in *Silk and Steel.*

We first knew of the author's work through his accompanying our longtime client Bob Lee, with Anne Brockinton, on a Glacier Guides expedition in the Alaskan Archipelago (spring 1997). While Larry was on board our flagship, the *Alaskan Solitude,* we became enamored of how he could bring history alive. With laptop before him whenever on board, he was incessantly recording observations and information; some of his adventures afield appeared in the recently published *Lock, Stock, & Barrel* memoir. We were delighted to learn of the *Silk and Steel* project—and anxious to help.

By focusing on the significance of women in the long and complex chronicle of firearms, *Silk and Steel* stands as a milestone. By convincingly extending the level of scholarship on this vital theme, women are finally being given the credit they so richly deserve. Never again, after studying this book, will we ever think of firearms as a theme "for men only."

With women from our family having braved expeditions and adventures on six continents, the Rosenbruch Wildlife Heritage Museum takes particular pride in launching the traveling exhibition accompanying *Silk and Steel.* Our congratulations to the author, the publisher, and particularly to the women who are celebrated in this landmark book.

FOREWORD

Guy M. Wilson, *Master of the Armouries, H.M. Tower of London (ret.); Director, Royal Armouries Museum, Leeds (ret.)*

This is a book to make us all think again and confront our prejudices. Larry Wilson has gathered together a mass of evidence that shows that the use of arms (and armor) has never been the preserve of men alone. From prehistoric times to the present day, women, too, have been users of weapons. They have fought, they have hunted, and they have defended themselves. Social attitudes toward female involvement with weapons of violence have varied considerably over the centuries and among different cultures, but the evidence here presented shows that women have been far more frequent users of arms than our modern Western prejudices have generally allowed us to believe.

Given what Western culture owes to the classical world, this should not surprise us, but it does. This new book encourages us to remember that in both the Greek and Roman pantheons, there was not a god but a *goddess* of hunting (Artemis, or Diana), and that in Greek mythology Athena was the goddess of war and the Amazons were the most formidable of warriors. There is no reason to believe that these myths developed by chance, and if the historian Herodotus thought it a marvel that a woman, Artemesia, should lead troops against the Greeks in the war with Xerxes, modern science is raising the possibility that female warriors were more common in prehistory than our prejudices have allowed us to appreciate. There is growing evidence that the assumption that when weapons are buried in a grave the associated body will be that of a male may not be entirely true. DNA testing may soon reveal the extent to which the Amazon myth is based on an unexpected reality.

If we test the past against the evidence both of today, when women serve in the front line in many armies and fly warplanes in many air forces, and of the twentieth century, when women served and fought in many theaters, even in covert operations behind enemy lines, we can perhaps judge how much thoughtless prejudice has clouded our collective judgment of the past. Add to this the evidence here presented of the considerable and active involvement of women in hunting, not to mention their frequent use of weapons for self-defense, and a very different perspective is thrust before us.

It is to be hoped that this excellent and intriguing book will help to set the record straight and ensure that future studies of the making and use of arms will treat these simply as human activities without either sexual bias or tokenism. Larry Wilson has shown us all the way to a new and fairer approach and has opened our eyes to hitherto hidden aspects of the history of arms.

V. Cornaro's "A Day's Sport" captures the spirit of adventure enjoyed by two fortunate lady wildfowlers from the nineteenth century. Bridgeman Art Library, New York, London, and Paris.

AUTHOR'S INTRODUCTION

Silk and Steel: Women at Arms sprang forth as a consequence of the first tour of the United States by a party of five, investigating the possibilities of a presence in the Western Hemisphere for the Royal Armouries Museum, Leeds. Leading the tour was an old hand at traveling to arms and museum sites: Guy Wilson. His chief associate was Royal Armouries board of trustees' member Sir Blair Stewart-Wilson, formerly equerry to the Queen (1976–94) and a key adviser to Her Majesty. Nick Thompson, then manager of sales and marketing for the Royal Armouries Museum, was on the expedition, as were Tom Costello, U.S. representative for the RAM, and the author.

During this tour it was decided that the Royal Armouries' presence in America would be best served at first by organizing gallery space in existing (or soon-to-exist) museums.

We traveled from coast to coast, and in the interchange with museums and private collectors, the idea was hatched to do a book, traveling loan exhibition, and television documentary on the subject of women and firearms.

What better way to market the Royal Armouries Museum in the United States than a traveling exhibition celebrating the unique role of women in the world of firearms—particularly in that Her Majesty Queen Elizabeth II is the custodian of several institutions featuring arms and armor subjects including the Royal Armouries Museum and the Windsor Castle Armoury.

Among participating Museums are the Buffalo Bill Historical Center (Cody, Wyoming), the National Cowboy Museum and Western Heritage Center (Oklahoma City), the Tennessee State Museum (Nashville), the New York Historical Association (Cooperstown), and the starting point for the exhibition—the Rosenbruch Wildlife Heritage Museum (St. George, Utah). The Royal Armouries Museum itself was the likely final stop on this ambitious tour. Further, a *Silk and Steel* documentary for television would follow the exhibition.

The story of the role of women in the firearms history of America was lost, in large part because the later generations—those who wrote the story, thought as men, and thought of guns as manly objects—forgot that, in a pioneer nation, which required firearms to survive and to flourish, firearms as the tools of one sex alone was an untenable concept.

In looking back on the gestation period of this book, it is inevitable that a recurring image is foremost: that of resourceful, dedicated, energetic, often intelligent, inspiring, and brave women building their own history, in a field that has been written off as the exclusive purview of men.

Silk and Steel reveals a world of firearms, hunting, shooting, and the outdoor sports that belongs to women, too. In America, particularly, there is a grassroots movement of women, and girls, joining their sisters in the shooting sports—an evolution that has been gaining momentum for centuries. One might say that ever since Queen Elizabeth shot three stags (albeit with a crossbow) in a private game park in the late sixteenth century, women have been embracing the shooting sports with a vengeance. The unique American experience with firearms has given that movement its particular impetus.

The author is especially indebted to Peter Hawkins, Christie's arms and armor specialist for many years, and a sport shooter of wide experience, who had himself conceived of a book along the same lines of *Silk and Steel* more than thirty-five years ago. In the best spirit of friendship and generosity, he has kindly shared a tremendous amount of information and suggestions that have proven invaluable in the research and presentation of *Silk and Steel*. I am hopeful that this book will do justice to his own conception of what a work on this subject should be.

R. L. Wilson
June 20, 2003

SILK AND STEEL

CHAPTER I

Aristocratic Shooters and Collectors
from Queen Elizabeth I to Queen Elizabeth II

Diana, chiseled detail from triggerguard of flintlock pistol from the Musée de l'Armée, Paris; eighteenth century.

Facing page: Original records and the limited number of surviving paintings and prints would suggest that this type of enclosed hunt was popularly and not infrequently conducted by aristocratic men and women. The elaborately costumed women in pagodas are shooting flintlock rifles at wild boar, stag, and other beasts, driven into the enclosure by huntsmen. Residue from black powder made this type of hunt a somewhat polluted experience. Considerations of safety would suggest an occasional wounding of gamekeepers. *Prunkjagd* of Kurfurst Carl Philipp von der Pfalz (1716–42); oil painting by Jacobus Schlachter, Mannheim, 1733.

All the men of quality at Vienna were spectators, but only the ladies had permission to shoot, and the Archduchess Amalie carried off the first prize. I was very well pleased with having seen this entertainment. . . . This is the favourite pleasure of the Emperor, and there is rarely a week without some feast of this kind, which makes the young ladies skilful enough to defend a fort, and they laughed very much to see me afraid to handle a gun. . . .

—Lady Mary Wortley Montagu, after witnessing a target match, writing to her sister, Lady Mar, from Vienna, September 14, 1716

Historians and anthropologists have assumed that, from the earliest of times, men were the hunters and warriors within the social structure while women were the gatherers and nurturers. Recent research, however, is revealing a different picture. Women were sometimes part of a hunting band, even bringing their children along. Driving herds of animals over cliffs, for example, was one means of primitive hunting in which women and children could work together. Even those women left behind had to be armed and ready to defend themselves and their homes from predators—animal and human.

Mary Zeiss Stange, professor of sociology and religion at Skidmore College, has done groundbreaking research into women's role in hunting.

There are surviving hunting-gatherer cultures in which women hunt. Among the Agta people of the Philippines, both men and women go out and hunt, using whatever techniques work for them. Or there's the Tiwi people of Australia, where the men's job is to fish and the women's is to hunt, which they do with stone axes that they make for themselves. . . . There's an assumption that the stone weapons we find from the Paleolithic era must have all been fashioned and used by men. But who knows who used these weapons—women or men? I think you can assume that there were individual women who hunted, just as there were individual men who did not. . . .[1]

It is no coincidence that the patron of hunters in Greco-Roman mythology was a woman—called Artemis, or Diana—or that she has inspired hunters and arms makers to the present. Dr. Stange notes,

Even before I became a hunter, I was very attracted to [Artemis'] image, but also found her very forbidding. She was violent, a hunter, and her worship demanded a lot of blood sacrifice. . . . There's a tendency to forget that she's not only the goddess of childbirth, but of the hunt. . . .[2]

Artemis/Diana: Goddess of Hunting

Gracing some of the finest sporting arms built over the centuries is the lithe, graceful, beautiful, and woods-wise figure of the goddess of hunting. Her image can also be found as a decorative motif in elegant hunting lodges, in palaces of princely hunters, on powder flasks and other accessories, and in paintings, prints, and drawings.

Known to the Greeks as Artemis, her domain was that of animals and fish, and she had power over famine and feast, bad fortune and good.

She was also, though a virgin goddess, the patron of childbirth. Born on Delos, the daughter of Zeus and Leto and the twin sister of Apollo (god of light), her association with the hunt probably stems from her encounter with the hunter Actaeon, who happened upon her when she was bathing. The angry goddess turned Actaeon into a stag, whereupon his own hounds turned on him and tore him to bits.

An authority on deer hunting and its history, Robert Wegner cites a Homeric hymn to Artemis:

I sing of Artemis of the golden shafts, the modest maiden
Who loves the din of the hunt and shoots volleys of
arrows at stags

He goes on to note that Artemis

appeared throughout the ages in deer hunting attire made of deerskin with a silver bow and a quiver of arrows on her back and often in the company of a deer. Dressed in deerskins, Artemis pursued deer in groves called "deer-gardens" (German *Tiergarten*).

In her Roman guise as Diana (from *diviana*, "the luminous one"), the goddess was popular in medieval times as the protector, guide, and inspiration of hunters, though the Church denounced her as demonic. During the Renaissance, she was venerated by hunters, and her classical figure would become a popular subject for painting, sculpture, and the decorative arts, and embellish some of the finest sporting arms.

The Hunting Aristocracy

As weapons for war and the hunt grew increasingly sophisticated, from the development of the first functional firearms until the French Revolution of 1789, they came to be considered the purview of the aristocracy. Allowing such dangerous implements, with their potential for leveling social hierarchies, to fall into the hands of their subjects was not thought to be in the best interests of the ruling classes. The American and French Revolutions were bellwethers that did, in fact, exploit more widely available firearms to effect significant change in the New World and the Old.

Even today, hunting and shooting remain primarily aristocratic pursuits in Europe. Hunting lands are largely in private hands, and are available only to their owners or those with connections. (In America, hunting lands are predominately public, and the enjoyment of the shooting sports has been far more egalitarian.)

Her Majesty Queen Elizabeth I, after felling a stag with a crossbow, accepting a knife for the traditional ceremony of the initial step in the rendering of the fallen beast. From *The Noble Arte of Venerie or Hunting*, 1575, by G. Turbervile. Courtesy of the British Library, London.

If shooting sports have, historically, been restricted to the privileged classes, one may wonder how often a woman, or a girl, even one from the social and aristocratic elite, might have owned a firearm—or had the opportunity to use one. These are challenging questions, because, unfortunately, historians have shown scant interest in the sporting enthusiasms of the prerevolutionary elite—whether American or European. Collectors, on the other hand, have long found shooting sports and their artifacts fascinating. To appreciate and understand firearms and their accessories, they have tried to gain knowledge of those who owned them and those who designed and made them.

Interestingly, one of the first books on the hunt was written by a woman. Dame Juliana Berners was a fifteenth-century English nun, whose treatise *The Boke of St. Albans*, published in 1486, paid eloquent and witty tribute to the chase of the stag.

The Archduke Ferdinand and His Wife, Anna, 1521

A rare weapon combining the power of a crossbow with the trajectory of a gun was made for the Archduke Ferdinand and his wife, Anna, dating from 1521. It is one of the earliest known wheel locks, and boasts heraldic arms with the initials *F* and *A*. The combination weapon is in the Bayerisches National Museum, Munich.

Queen Elizabeth I: A Passionate Huntress

All forms of hunting and shooting were popular at the court of Queen Elizabeth I. Her Majesty particularly enjoyed both the chase (hunting from horseback) and the battue (shooting at game with crossbows in an enclosure). She was often presented with the kill after a hunt. Other ladies of her court also were skilled at hunting, as well as hawking and target shooting.

Howard Blackmore's *Hunting Weapons* notes that when "Duke Frederick of Württemberg vis-

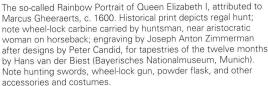

The so-called Rainbow Portrait of Queen Elizabeth I, attributed to Marcus Gheeraerts, c. 1600. Historical print depicts regal hunt; note wheel-lock carbine carried by huntsman, near aristocratic woman on horseback; engraving by Joseph Anton Zimmerman after designs by Peter Candid, for tapestries of the twelve months by Hans van der Biest (Bayerisches Nationalmuseum, Munich). Note hunting swords, wheel-lock gun, powder flask, and other accessories and costumes.

ited Queen Elizabeth in 1592, an English Lord was detailed to escort him to a deer hunt at Windsor." Apparently, Her Majesty also extended to guests the pleasures of the hunt, which she herself so enjoyed.

According to Robert Wegner:

When noblemen entertained the Queen, they took her deer hunting. When Shakespeare aimed to please her, he made references in his plays, especially "The Merry Wives of Windsor," to the deer hunt as sexual pursuit and to deer antlers as signs of cuckoldry.

Queen Elizabeth was passionately fond of deer shooting. . . . The Master of the Buckhounds, the Earl of Leicester, frequently accompanied her on . . . many uproarious, deer-hunting exploits. He reportedly presented her with a richly enameled crossbow which deer hunters used at this time to dispatch the buck after being brought to bay by the hounds.[3]

An eyewitness account of "Good Queen Bess" killing a deer with a crossbow was published by J. Strutt in *Sports and Pastimes of the People of England:*

When Queen Elizabeth visited lord Montecute at Cowdrey in Sussex, on the Monday, August 17, 1591, Her highness tooke horse, and rode into the park, at eight o'clock in the morning, where was a delicate bowre prepared, under the which were her highness musicians placed; and a cross-bow, by a nymph with a sweet song, was delivered into her hands, to shoote at the deere; . . . of which . . . she killed three or four, and the countess of Kildare, one.

In addition to deer driving, Queen Elizabeth also liked to course deer with horses, horns, and hounds. Historians of hunting note that even in her sixty-seventh year, she still engaged in coursing. The deer hunts of Queen Elizabeth I were grand and magnificent extravaganzas. On one hunt in April 1557, she pursued bucks with twelve ladies on horses clad in white satin and twenty yeomen dressed in green. British deer authority G. Kenneth Whitehead describes the colorful scene: "It was all very magnificent, and on entering the Chace she was met by fifty archers in scarlet coats, blue lapels and yellow caps and vests. . . ."

Mrs. Russell Barnett Aitken with firearms treasures in Fifth Avenue apartment, New York City. A member of the Visiting Committee, Department of Arms and Armor, Metropolitan Museum of Art, Irene Aitken ranks among the foremost connoisseurs of fine guns, and of seventeenth- and eighteenth-century French decorative art. Female motifs depicted within decoration of exquisite wheel-lock gun; Adam Vischer stock with bone inlays (engraving attributed to Johannes Sadeler); the metalwork sculpted in steel by Daniel Sadeler.

Mrs. Aitken holds some of the choicest arms: in vignette, musket rest, formerly Rothschild Collection, mate to wheel-lock gun in Royal Armoury, Turin. *Below,* sculpted steel and gilt combination French wheel-lock gun and sword, based on designs by Etienne Delaune (mid–sixteenth century). *Bottom,* exquisite flintlock pistol by Nicholas Noel Boutet.

6

Hunting and Target Shooting on the Continent

Tantalizing references exist referring to the keen pursuit of hunting at the courts of Louis XIII and Louis XIV (the Gun and Sun King, respectively). Certainly, many country estates were built in locations considered prime hunting lands. The royals enjoyed escaping from Paris to indulge in hunting on horseback, and shooting wild game. As noted in the author's *Steel Canvas*, Louis XIII had a well-inventoried, large, and exquisite arms collection. His Majesty took considerable pleasure in the hunt, and in taking apart and reassembling his treasured firearms.

Less well known are the shooting and hunting pursuits of the Austrian court, particularly at Vienna. As early as the seventeenth century, journals and works of art document a passion for these sports, in which girls and women played an active role—often in women-only events, with men and boys serving as gamekeepers, drivers of the intended quarry, and attendants for loading and looking after the firearms.

A number of firearms exist today that were once the property of aristocratic girls and women, particularly from countries where bird shooting and target shooting were popular. In fact, so many examples have been identified that this chapter could easily be expanded into an entire book on the subject.

As firearms became more reliable and cleaner to operate, women and girls became increasingly infatuated with sport shooting. The elegant young lady celebrated in Parisian artist James Tissot's "The Crack Shot" shows the typical social status of a gallery target shooter in Paris. Photographs of women from English country estate shooting parties reveal her counterpart in the field.

It is clear that hunting was the true sport of kings—and queens.

Well-armed Kenau Simonsdaughter Hasselaer (1526–88), leader of a group of three hundred women who fought the Spaniards in the celebrated siege of Harlem; c. 1572–73. The conflict was part of the Eighty Years War (1568–1648), in which the Dutch fought for liberation from Spain. Hasselaer was a shipyard owner and a builder, and was evidently left-handed. By Adam Willaerts (1600–50), from the Rijksmuseum, Amsterdam.

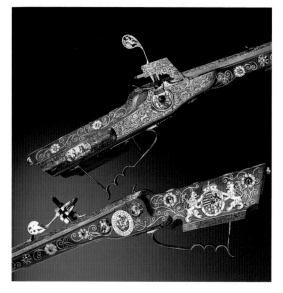

Evolving Devotion to Hunting and Firearms in the Courts of Europe—the Seventeenth, Eighteenth, and Nineteenth Centuries

Beginning with the French, whose tradition of shooting and the hunt continues with particular dedication into modern times, the pomp and splendor of the royal court lent considerable scope to elaborate hunting expeditions. Hawking, battue, the chase, and shooting were all popular, and were often patronized by queens.

Some court shoots were lavish spectacles, and were organized as state events, whether in celebration of a marriage, a festival, or in honor of distinguished guests. The royal families of Europe competed to see who could put on the most spectacular show. Some of the hunting lodges were more like palaces: Nymphenburg, near Munich; Hubertusburg, near Dresden; and the most famous of them all, Versailles.

Spectators were allowed to watch, from stands, and hunting scenes were recorded in word, song, and in works of art. Melchior Kussell (1622–83) executed a half-dozen etchings, in commemoration of the wedding of Emperor Leopold I and Margarita of Spain (1666). Yet another such spectacle honored the marriage of Duke Karl of Wurtemberg to Elisabeth, Countess of Brandenburg-Bayreuth (1748).

Left: From the Staatliche Kunstsammlungen, Dresden: pair of wheel-lock rifles by Christian Herold, Dresden, 1669; barrel of iron, engraved, blued, partly gilded. Signed CHRISSTIANUS HEOLD DRESDA; lock of iron, engraved, gilded, and with enamel; stock of wood, with silver inlay, colored enamel medallions, and colored stones. Note female figures within decoration.

Facing page: "Kenau Hasselaer and the Battle of Harlem," by Egenberger en Wijnveld, from the Frans Hals Museum. Graphic painting depicts the ferocity and determination of women during the sixteenth-century siege, especially after they had heard how badly the Spaniards treated women following the fall of the towns of Mechelen, Zutphen, and Naarden.

Their Majesties Louis XVI and Marie Antoinette

King Louis XVI was a keen huntsman. He took part in all forms of the hunt, pursuing most species of game—stag, roebuck, boar, and birds, both shot and hawked. Marie Antoinette was a noted equestrian and frequently hunted with him. A brief account of Louis's hunting appears in Campan's *Private Life of Marie Antoinette.*

> [The King's] only passion was for hunting. He used himself to select the meets, and kept notes of the stags hunted, of their age, and of the circumstances of their capture. He also very often went out shooting, and although short-sighted shot very well, and often came back with his face blackened with powder. He was a bad rider and wanting in confidence. The Queen, on the other hand, rode on horseback with much eloquence and boldness.[4]

Fowling pieces exist that were made for Marie Antoinette—for her own use or for her to give as gifts. The most exquisite of these arms is pictured on page 17.

The German States

Empress Amalia, consort of the Holy Roman Emperor Joseph I (1705–11), took part in elaborate target shoots, which were staged for the ladies of the court in Vienna. The quotation that begins this chapter is from the eyewitness account of Lady Mary Wortley Montagu, in a letter to her sister. She also noted that

> the Empress sat on a small throne at the end of a beautiful alley in her garden, and two groups of young ladies were posted one on either side of her, headed by two arch-duchesses. All were finely clad and wearing their jewels, and each had a light gun in her hands. The ladies had to fire at three oval targets and the winners were presented with the most handsome prizes, including jewelled rings, gold snuffboxes, porcelain etc.[5]

Among firearms known to have been used by an Austrian woman is a wheel-lock target rifle, custom-made for Maria Theresa, the Holy Roman

Empress and wife of Franz von Lothringer. The arm is of small proportions, and likely dates from when she was a young lady. In most instances, these guns were made in sets, or garnitures, some composed of longarms and pistols together.

Scandinavian Huntresses

Queen Christina of Sweden (1632–54) and Queen Marie Sophie von Frederikke of Denmark, wife of King Frederick VI (1808–39), both had a practical interest in the firearms of

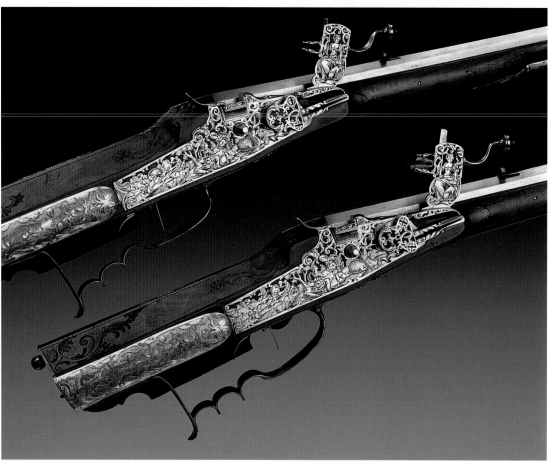

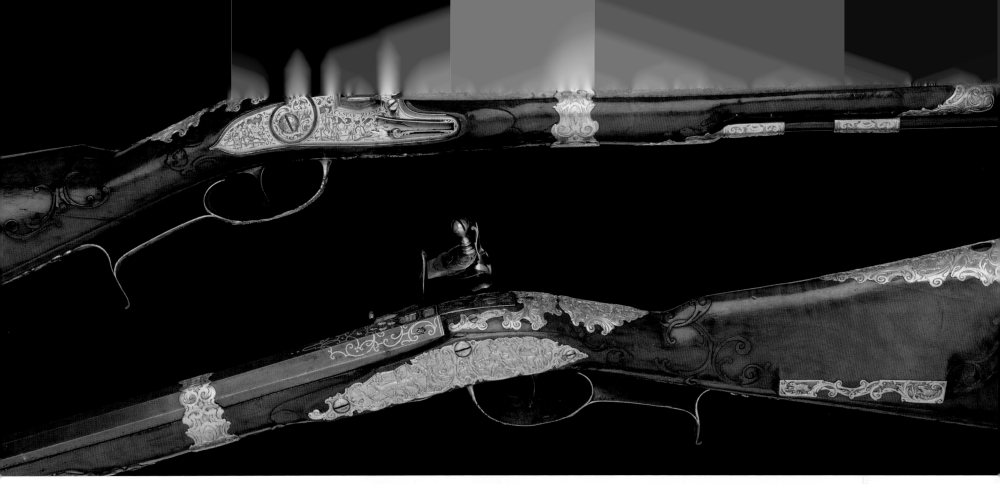

Facing page, top: Wheel-lock rifle by Johann Leopold Milotta, Dresden, 1752. Iron lock, marked LE MILOTTA A DRESDE 1752. Exquisitely engraved, and featuring women in hunting costume, with falcon. The lock including woman with hunting horn and spear, surrounded by game motifs. From Staatliche Kunstsammlungen.

Facing page, bottom: A pair of wheel-lock rifles by Franz Joseph Marr, Prague, c. 1760; barrel and lock iron and brass; engraved and chiseled in relief. Stock of richly carved walnut. Note armed figures of women in hunting attire on hammers. These elegant pieces were likely made specifically for women. Staatliche Kunstsammlungen, Dresden.

Pair of ladies' guns made for court shoots, in Vienna, by Caspar Zelner, c. 1720. Zelner (1661–1745) was master of the Vienna Guild of Gunmakers in 1695. Lock of gun at *top* with figures and hunting scene; note decoration of sideplate of mate, *below*. *Top* view shows detail of mounts, with hunter carrying the dead game, then the tables turned, with the game carrying the dead hunter. Buttplate with additional refinements.

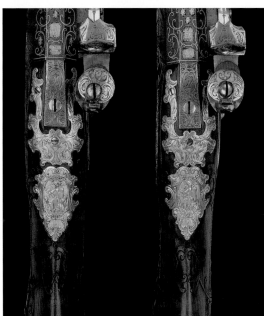

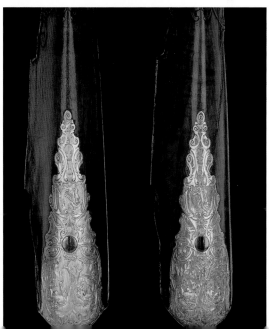

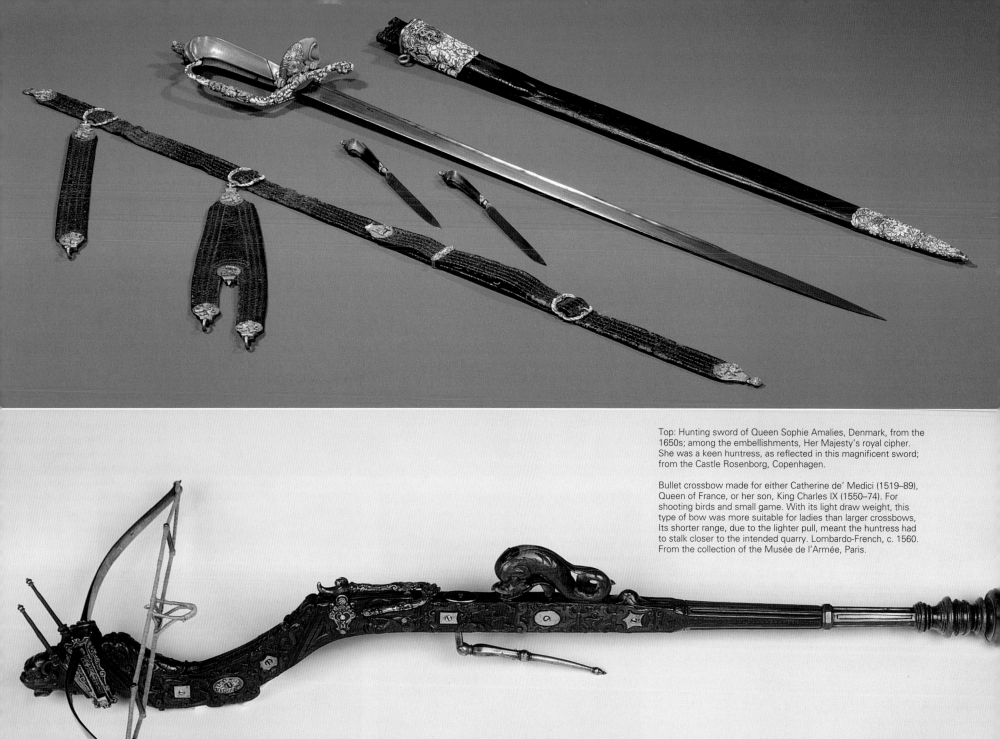

Top: Hunting sword of Queen Sophie Amalies, Denmark, from the 1650s; among the embellishments, Her Majesty's royal cipher. She was a keen huntress, as reflected in this magnificent sword; from the Castle Rosenborg, Copenhagen.

Bullet crossbow made for either Catherine de' Medici (1519–89), Queen of France, or her son, King Charles IX (1550–74). For shooting birds and small game. With its light draw weight, this type of bow was more suitable for ladies than larger crossbows. Its shorter range, due to the lighter pull, meant the huntress had to stalk closer to the intended quarry. Lombardo-French, c. 1560. From the collection of the Musée de l'Armée, Paris.

their times, and had pieces specially commissioned for their pleasure.

The memoirs of Prince Raimund Montecuccoli state that Queen Christina had requested him (in December 1653) to order a repeating carbine capable of firing thirty or forty shots from the Salzburg gunmaker Klett. A deluxe crossbow was also made for Queen Christina. Decoration on the bow, with which she hunted, reveals that it was also used for target practice. In addition, there were no less than fifty-eight sporting guns in her private armory. She was painted by Sebastien Bourbon in 1653 astride a favorite horse, with hawk and hounds and accompanied by a gamekeeper.

Anne of Denmark—Wife of King James I of England

Alongside her husband, Queen Anne enjoyed the chase, and was also keen on shooting with the crossbow. During James's reign, attempts were made to enforce the statutory practice of longbow hunting, which maintained it as a sporting weapon after its military use was eclipsed by firearms.

Above: Breech detail of three flintlock fowling pieces by Johann Christoph Stockmar, active c. 1719–47, with stocks by Johann Stephan Seeber, 1708–92. The barrel breech details, sculpted with gold and silver background, rank among the most exquisite and beautiful of any known flintlock sporting guns. From the Historisches Museum, Dresden.

Left: Flintlock gun by Philip Muller, Dresden, 1754. Iron barrel, in-the-white; marked PHILIP MULLER A DRESDE. The barrel breech superbly engraved with woman and dog, the huntress holding her flintlock gun. Carved walnut stock. Staatliche Kunstsammlungen, Dresden.

Blackmore's *Hunting Weapons* describes an accident on a hunt (1613), which caused some consternation by His Majesty:

> The Queen, shooting at a deer, mistook her mark, and killed Jewel, the King's most principal and special hound; At which he stormed exceedingly awhile, but after he knew who did it, he was soon pacified and with much kindness wished her not to be troubled with it, for he should love her never the worse; and the next day sent her a diamond, worth £2,000, as a legacy from his dead dog. . . .

Details of the firearms and hunting interests of Hedvig Sofia, favorite sister of King Karl XII, were chronicled in the Swedish historical journal *Livrustkammaren*. Headlined "A Princess Out Hunting," the article described a handsome painting of her, with a sporting gun:

> [The princess stands] erect, her slender, supple figure placed asymmetrically on the left in a forest, clearly outlined against the pale reddish-yellow skies showing through the sparse vegetation behind her. Apart from a precious ornament in her hair she is suitably dressed in a dark, tight-fitting coat of the same cut as the uniform of her brother's soldiers. . . . In the right half of the picture the forest is dense and steeped in brown shadows, housing the intended prey (caperzeailzie). The princess is holding her gun demonstratively in front of her with both hands . . . , clearly displaying the flintlock, which on closer inspection is found to be engraved with the place of manufacture, *Stockholm*. It is worth noting that Hedvig Sofia started to accompany her father on his hunts when she was only 11 years old. Her interest in hunting lasted until her untimely death [from smallpox, at age twenty-seven, in 1708].[6]

Russian Empresses

The Empresses Elizabeth (1741–62) and Catherine the Great (1762–96) were both deeply interested in Russia's firearms, the manufacturer of which was centered in the city of Tula. Both were responsible for importing foreign craftsmen, mainly from Scandinavia, Ger-

13

many, and France, to work there. Several special arms were made for the empresses, both of whom were keen on shooting and hunting.

A fascinating and rare image, published in V. Berman's *Masterpieces of Tula Gun-Makers*, shows a woman shooting game from an ornate balcony. A footman is nearby, holding a gun to hand to her for the next shot.[7]

Dueling—Personal Warfare of the Upper Class

Discouraged, reviled, and even outlawed, the duel was a unique institution, thought by the upper classes to be a privilege of theirs—a means of asserting status—that lasted up to the twentieth century. Though women were often the cause of such affairs of honor, it is difficult to imagine them actually participating. But they did, and not infrequently.

V. G. Kiernan, in *The Duel in European History: Honour and the Reign of Aristocracy*, covers duels fought over women, as well as duels between women.

> . . . [In France a] baroness was contemptuous of a bourgeoise who declined the honor of a duel with her. . . . In 1650 a fight between two sisters, near Bordeaux, was followed by their husbands fighting; in each case one died of wounds. . . . Actresses were the best known for their prowess; they were among the first liberated, self-reliant women, along with prostitutes. . . . Two French actresses fought with swords in the theatre, and one was wounded; another pair with pistols, at which Louis XIV is said to have condescended to be amused. . . .
>
> Usually women fought over a man, as men so often did over a woman; doubtless men appreciated the flattering tribute as much as women did, though some might balk at a mistress of such militant disposition. . . . But about [1715] two *grandes dames*, the Comtesse de Polignac and the Marquise de Nesle, fought with pistols, one being grazed by a bullet, to decide their claims on that thoroughbred duellist the Duc de Richelieu, whom they could expect to be suitably impressed. . . .

Facing page: Lady Teresia Shirley with her Scottish all-metal pistol, in portrait by an English artist, c. 1624–27. Holding the pistol in a prominent way is indicative of her intent that the artist capture an object of which she was very proud—and which was symbolic of her substantial social rank. Collection of Berkeley Castle, Gloucestershire.

Above: Exquisite pistols of the Empress Catherine the Great, by Johan Adolph Grecke (Swedish-born master gunmaker). Built in St. Petersburg, 1786; soon thereafter presented by her, as part of a garniture, to King Stanislaw August of Poland. Of chiseled steel, engraved, gilded, and blued; the stocks of ivory, engraved with green-tinted foliation; the mounts of steel and brass chiseled, engraved, and gilded. Overall length 14¼ inches. Metropolitan Museum of Art, gift of John M. Schiff, 1986 (1986.265.1-.2). Photograph © 1982 Metropolitan Museum of Art.

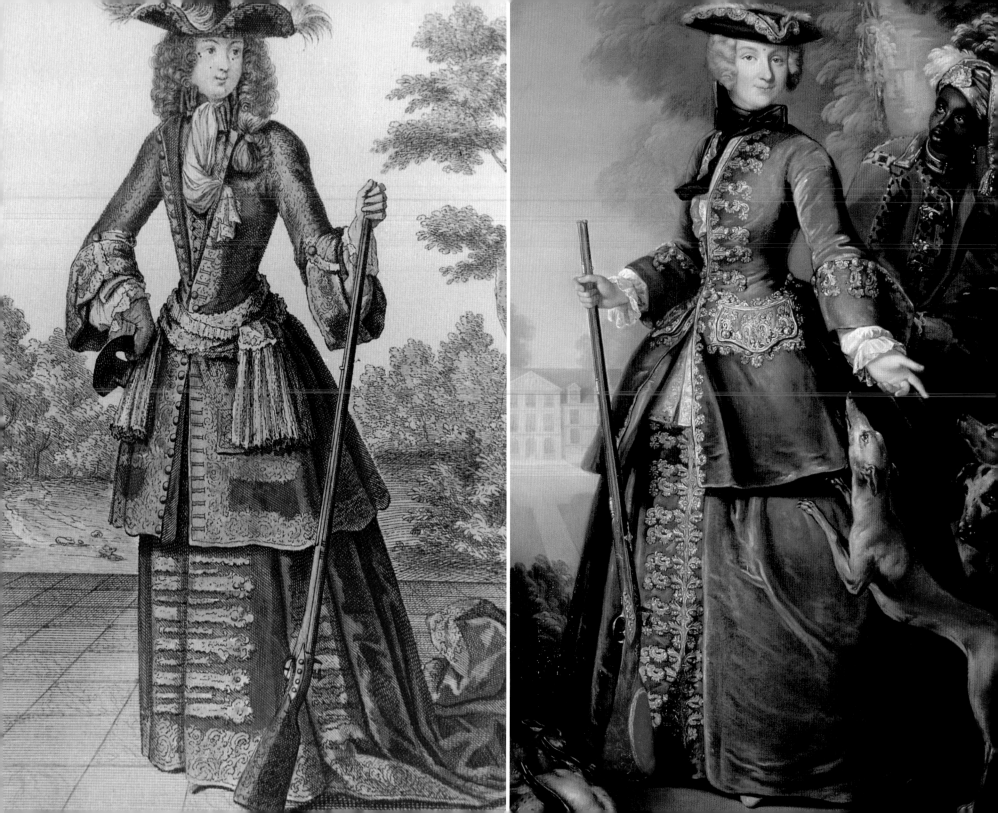

Facing page, left: Marquise de Heutefeuille, ready for the hunt. Late-eighteenth-century print from the Musée de la Chasse, Chateau de Gien.

Facing page, right: Oil painting by French portrait artist depicts Bavarian princess, in hunting costume and with favorite flintlock fowling piece. Late eighteenth century. From the Musée de la Chasse, Chambord, France.

Top left: Flintlock gun by Pierre de Sainte, active 1747–88, and "gunmaker in ordinary to the King at Versailles" under Louis XVI from 1763. Number V from set of twelve ladies' sporting arms, originally a gift from Archduke Albert of Sachsen-Teschen to his niece Empress Maria Ludovica Beatrix d'Este (1787–1816), the third wife of Emperor Franz II (1768–1835; reigned from 1792). At some point in their history, the set is believed to have been sent by Marie Antoinette to Vienna, where ten examples remain in the

Waffensammlung. Number V became a part of the Liechtenstein Collection in 1925. De Sainte was father-in-law to French gunmaker Nicholas-Noel Boutet.

Oil painting depicting Her Majesty hunting on horseback; in the background, King Louis XVI, also in pursuit of stags; by Louis-Auguste Brun, 1783.

Bottom left: Pair of flintlock pistols by Harrison & Thompson, London, 1782. Silver mounts with maker's mark of MB, for Michael Barnett. One of only two known marquetry cases of the period, of which this is the best specimen. Penelope Harrison

was the widow of John Harrison; James Thompson was their son-in-law. The firm was at 18 Swan Street, Minories, c. 1779–1803, and was a contractor to Ordnance and to the East India Company.

Right: Also by de Sainte, believed made for Marie Antoinette, this flintlock fowling piece boasts light weight and small proportions, sculpted steel décor, gilding, and silver wire inlay, mounts, and sights. Velvet-covered cheekpiece and buttplate; 49½-inch overall length. An elegant gun befitting the Queen of France, one of history's most famous women.

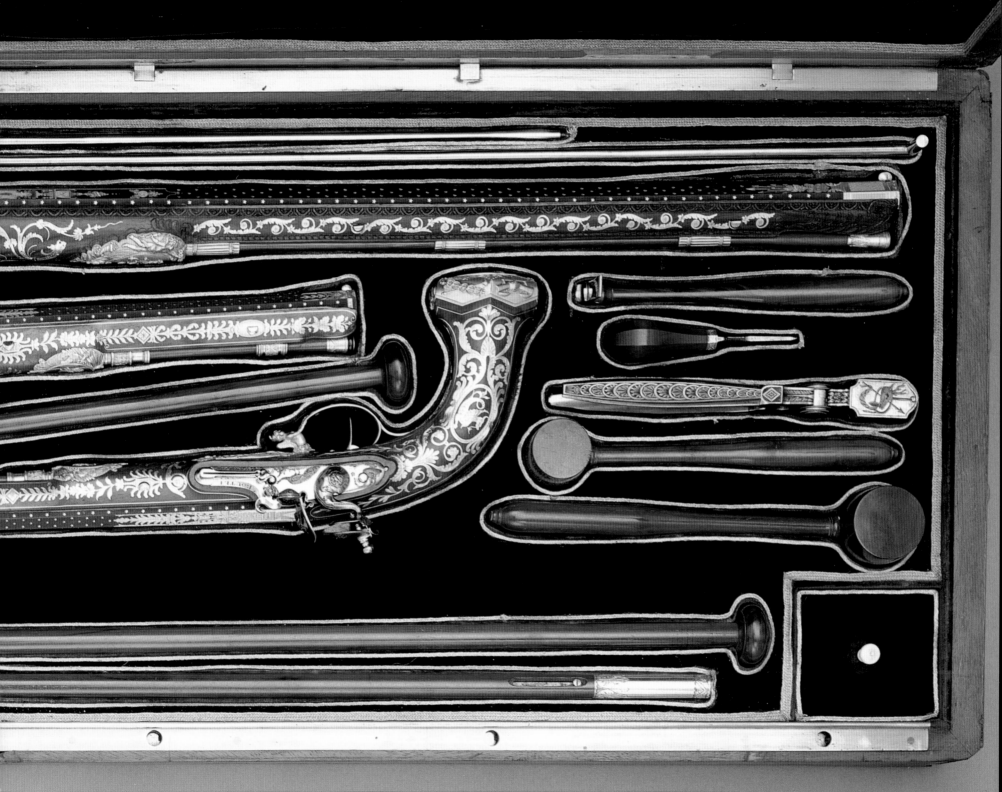

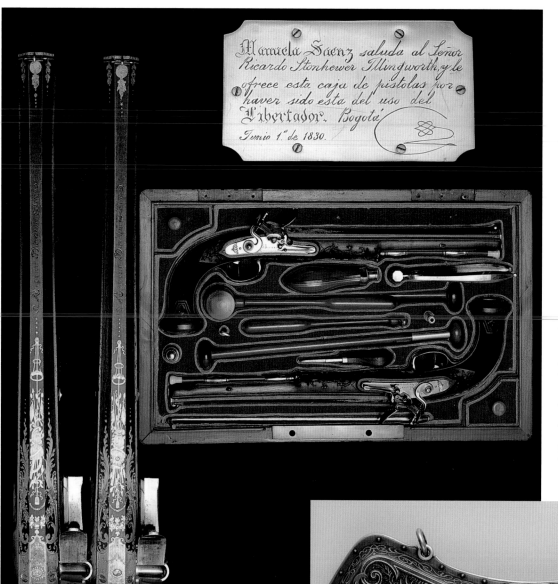

Preceding pages: From Napoléon Bonaparte to the Marquisa de Santa-Cruz, c. 1803–04, this magnificent cased presentation garniture of flintlock firearms is symbolic of the significance of fine arms in diplomacy, as well as the important role of women in such matters. One of history's most distinguished gunmakers, Nicholas Noel Boutet—holder of the official title *Directeur Artiste,* from the Emperor Napoléon Bonaparte—was accustomed to creating exquisite arms. Set delivered on behalf of the emperor to the Spanish marquise early in the Napoleonic period.

The rifle, and pairs of holster- and pocket-size pistols, are encrusted and inlaid with gold, with gilt silver mounts. Garniture documented in the gunmaker's own records as the most elaborate set ever made. The rifle of approximately .60 caliber; holster pistols, .50 caliber; pocket pistols of .45. Case measures 47¼ inches × 16 inches and is 4½ inches thick. Within lid, visible when the velvet lining has been removed: documents giving the set's history of being transported to its regal destination in Spain. Boutet's unsurpassed artistry spanned the years from before the French Revolution (1785) through the Revolution, Directory, Consulate, Empire, Restoration, and Paris periods.

Silver lid plaque and set of Boutet pistols, presented to Simón Bolívar, the "George Washington of South America," later a gift by his mistress, Manuela Saenz, to Ricardo Stonehewer Illingworth. Also known as "the Liberator," Bolivar had befriended John Illingworth, a Horatio Hornblower–type British naval hero, who served on various vessels under the flags of rebels in Chile, Peru, and Colombia. The recipient of the presentation set from Manuela was a brother of John Illingworth.

Manuela Saenz (1797–1856) had met Bolívar in 1822, just after the liberation of Ecuador. She became his great passion, and he hers. She shared in his triumphs thereafter, but also in his failures. Saenz saved him from conspirators when in Bogotá, Colombia, and upon learning of his death (December 17, 1830), she attempted to commit suicide.

Exquisite powder flask by renowned Parisian gunmaker LePage, decorated in relief with Diana, a hound at her feet and stag at her head. Signed, and dated 1838. Of anodized copper, gold inlaid, with silver rivet borders; monogram FPO surmounted by a crown. Note ivory on spout. Not visible are viewing ports of blue glass in nozzle. From a cased set, and made for an elaborate over-and-under rifle. 9⁵⁄₃₂ inches overall length.

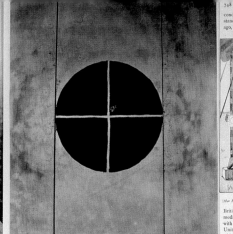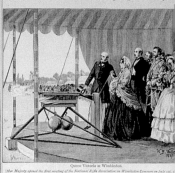

conditions to which they are habituated are allowed ; but at long ranges, notwithstanding the excellent results the American shots achieved twenty to twenty-five years ago, they are far behind the standard of shooting ruling in this country and

Queen Victoria at Wimbledon.

(Her Majesty opened the first meeting of the National Rifle Association in Wimbledon Common on July 2nd.)

British Colonies. As a sport, long-range rifle-shooting is dead in America ; medium range is that now practised. Recent triangular competitions at short range with '22-calibre rifles, between representatives of Great Britain, Australia, and United States of America, have resulted in decisive victories for the British team, which would point either to their greater skill with the "low power" rifles, or to the superior accuracy of the British-made rifles.

Left: Images as adapted from Kurt G. Bluchel's *Game & Hunting,* a lavish two-volume treatise celebrating European game and the Continent's culture of hunting. A vital part of the book's content was drawn from Munich's Hunting and Fishing Museum (Deutsches Jagd- und Fischereimuseum). Hunting party, *below,* from nineteenth century, "Departure for the Hunt." *Bottom center,* Meissen porcelain figures depicting armed huntresses. Remaining vignettes primarily as depicted in fashion magazines, from as early as the late eighteenth to the mid–twentieth centuries—including the Italian edition of *Vogue.* Hunting costumes, though sometimes immune to changes and whims in fashion, are a study in themselves. Throughout *Silk and Steel* are depictions of women in a variety of hunting attire—a subject worthy of volumes.

Top: For decades the standard work on firearms was British gunmaker W. W. Greener's *The Gun and Its Development,* published in numerous editions, from 1835 (first by his father, William Greener). Pages 748–49 of the ninth edition document Queen Victoria's firing of the first shot at the British National Rifle Association's initial meeting at Wimbledon, July 2, 1860.

To quote from Greener's description of this historic event:

. . . The first shot was fired by Queen Victoria, from a Whitworth rifle on a machine rest, at 400 yards, and struck the bull's-eye at 1¼ inches from its centre. The Whitworth muzzle-loading rifle won most of the important prizes at it, and at subsequent meetings until 1871—for its use was compulsory in the Queen's Prize, except in the years 1865–66–67. . . .

21

The Whitworth rifle fired by Her Majesty is pictured on its secure rest, with the cord attached for her to pull. The target is also shown. Photographs taken in 1860 by Roger Fenton. Courtesy The Royal Archives © 2001, Her Majesty Queen Elizabeth II.

Bottom: Fashionable French lithograph, for New York journal, as indicated in engraved description. Except for the muzzle-loading percussion pistol being fired by lady targetshooter, and its mate in hands of gentleman at *left,* all guns shown are pinfires.

Women fought for other reasons as well. Two aristocratic ladies, Princess Metternich and Countess Kilmannsegg, had words over arrangements for an exhibition to be held in Vienna and attempted to settle their differences in a duel. They both suffered injuries in the encounter.

Dueling in America, especially in the South, had its own special history. As in London and Paris, certain locations were established as dueling grounds. In New Orleans, considered the capital of southern chivalry, the most renowned of these was the "Dueling Oaks," where one would find a refined etiquette, and an audience to observe what transpired.

During the Civil War, a New Orleans actress, Adah Menken, was playing the role of Naked Lady in *Mazeppa* on the New York stage. When her loyalty to the Union was questioned, she responded by challenging any man from the audience to a duel—with sword or pistol. She then put on a display of her skills with each. Apparently, there were no takers.

Catherine the Great—Arms and Art Collector and Patroness of Gunmakers

Besides her keenness for fine guns and other weaponry, and for hunting, the Empress Catherine II was founder of the Hermitage Museum and a keen collector of art. More generally known as Catherine the Great, her interest in arms even extended to miniatures, some of which she presented at holiday time to her favorite grandson, Grand Prince Alexander. The empress's affection for arms and her patronage of their makers is evident in observations by the late Dr. Leonid Tarassuk, Department of Arms and Armor, the Metropolitan Museum of Art:

Enjoying the patronage of the monarch and the no-

bility, foreign armorers produced excellent decorated weapons and provided training for Russian craftsmen and decorators.

One of these immigrant masters was Johan Adolph Grecke, son of a Stockholm court gunmaker. . . . In 1780 Grecke made for the empress a splendid hunting garniture of a fowling piece (blunderbuss), a rifle, and a pair of pistols . . . , all marked in Saint Petersburg and dated. Another fowling piece and a rifle made by Grecke for Catherine II are dated 1783. . . .

Soon the master was rewarded for his skill and appointed Master Armorer of the Imperial Hunt. This title, in French, first appears after his name on a magnificent ivory-stock fowling piece dated 1786. . . . The pair of ivory-stocked pistols was designed and decorated *en suite* with [a fowling piece and a rifle]. On the grips [of the pistols] is an oval steel escutcheon formed by two swags and a laurel wreath, which encloses Catherine II's monogram under the Russian imperial crown.[8]

The magnificent set of guns was presented by Catherine to King Stanislaw August Poniatowski of Poland, for many years a personal favorite of the empress. However, since the garniture had originally been made for Catherine herself, the decoration of the locks and steel mounts included garlands and vases, flowers and classical figures, along with the elegant scrollwork.

Spanish Royalty and the Hunt

King Philip V (1700–46), grandson of another hunting enthusiast, King Louis XIV, took part with his queen in daily hunts, at first for birds, later concentrating on large game. On one such occasion, as recorded by an aristocratic observer—the Duke of Saint-Simon—the Duke del Orco oversaw the events, even choosing the site where the royal couple would stand at the ready. Accompanied by the captain of the guards and the grand Ecuyer, the party was armed with some twenty guns and loading paraphernalia.

The Duke of Saint-Simon was in a nearby shooting enclosure, with the Prince of the Asturias, the Duke de Popoli, the Marquis del Surco, the Marquis de Santa Cruz, the Duke Giovenazzo, and a handful of others. Between two hundred and four hundred peasants beat the countryside "with hue and cry," driving the game to the hunters. As the animals ran by at top speed, "the King and the Queen banged away in good earnest. . . . And this is the daily diversion of their Catholic Majesties. . . ."[9]

Shooting Sports and Queen Victoria—the Nineteenth Century in Great Britain

Queen Victoria had relatively little interest in the shooting sports. She was not a huntress, and generally disapproved of ladies who fired guns, stating it was the pursuit of "fast women." Despite her disapproval—or perhaps because of it—her daughter, Princess Victoria, was a frequent participant at shooting party weekends.

On the other hand, Her Majesty was a patron of shooting: she fired the inaugural shot of the National Rifle Association's first competition at Wimbledon, in 1860. And although there is no evidence of her personally firing a gun again, a few guns were made for her. These stand as works of art and craftsmanship, and proof of Victorian technical superiority and mechanical ingenuity. Victoria's personal journals contain no references to shooting or to hunting, but she clearly enjoyed the performances of Buffalo Bill's Wild West, in which gunfire played a prominent role. Her admiration for Annie Oakley was such that she remarked she was "a very clever little girl."

Deer hunting, long regarded as the greatest of sports, has had a long and regal history in Britain. Chasing deer on horseback reached its height during the reign of Elizabeth I—the golden age of sport—when seven hundred deer parks were scattered about the countryside. Interest subsequently declined until, by 1910, there were fewer than half that number—and even those were disappearing. Deer shooting, also popular in the Elizabethan period, became more so with the advent of accurate and reliable firearms. The stalking of deer came fully into its own in Britain in the second half of the nineteenth century, when vast tracts were opened in the Scottish Highlands for this purpose.

Many of the original English deer parks continued to be maintained through the centuries, including several owned by women at the end of the nineteenth century. That the relationship between the parks and hunting in England was still strong, there is no doubt. Many of the lady owners may well not have been interested in hunting by this time, but at least some would have hosted stag hunts or shoots, and participated themselves.

As deer hunting became confined to parks and Highland stalking, foxhunting rose in popularity for those who enjoyed the unbridled chase across open country.

Deer Stalking and the Determined Lady Breadalbane

Deer stalking in the nineteenth century was decidedly a man's sport, in contrast to shoots in parks or forests. Women were not even likely to come along as spectators, and if they chose to find amusement by walking the countryside, they had to be careful not to venture where deer stalking might be in progress.

James Joseph Jacques Tissot's "The Crack Shot," one of the finest paintings by the distinguished French artist, part of whose career was spent in England. 1882. Collection of Wimpole Hall, Cambridgeshire, UK/National Trust Photographic Library/John Hammond. Courtesy Bridgeman Art Library. Among his French contemporaries, the illustrator and caricaturist Henry Somm (1844–1907) celebrated the elegant women of *La Belle Époque* in a series of watercolors. Among these was a fashionably attired young lady aiming a pistol.

23

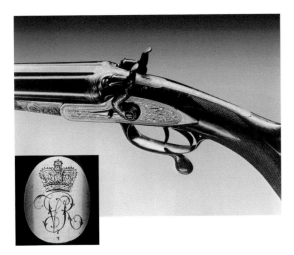

For decades Sandringham Estate in Norfolk has been a favorite shooting property of the British royal family, enjoyed by the original purchaser Edward, Prince of Wales (1862), and many descendants, of both genders, since. The Royal Collection there has only one firearm made for Her Majesty Queen Victoria: an Alexander Henry double-barrel rifle, serial number 6440, .450 caliber, with 28-inch barrels. Note Celtic engraving style, with the added touch of a royal cipher engraved on the stock escutcheon. Since Her Majesty was seventy-one years old at the time of the rifle's manufacture, it is thought to have been produced to reveal the craftsmanship of the maker. Courtesy The Royal Archives © 2001, Her Majesty Queen Elizabeth II.

Facing page: Most of these shooting ladies were clients of Gastinne Renette; they ranked among the most distinguished sportswomen of Continental Europe—and their descendants still do. Note several women present observing imperial pheasant shooting, Compiegne, during which Renette played a key role in aiding the Emperor Napoléon himself. From the English-speaking African safari contingent, at *upper left,* Florence Baker in 1865, daring and adventurous wife of Sir Samuel; bought by Baker at a slave market, she was believed to be the first woman to hunt the Dark Continent on safari. At *right center,* Mary Kingsley, c. 1895, wore a revolver and Bowie knife while in the African bush. Kipling said of her: "Being human, she must have been afraid of something, but one never found out what it was." *Top center,* the cousins Cecily and Agnes Herbert; on safari they generally outshot and outhunted parties of men they encountered, and ran camps that were better organized. Agnes left the fly of her tent open, and felt secure with a 12-bore Howdah pistol at the ready beside her bed.

D. Harte-Davis, in *Monarchs of the Glen,* notes:

For them to go stalking, even in the role of spectator, was most unusual. Still rarer was it for a lady to shoot, and apart from a single reference in Lord Malmesbury's memoirs to Lady Seymour stalking in 1845 at Achnacarry, the Marchioness of Breadalbane stands on her own as the only lady who regularly took a rifle to the hill in the nineteenth century.

Alma Graham, a daughter of the fourth Duke of Montrose, was introduced to shooting at an early age, and she soon made herself expert, in spite of the formidable handicap of a squint so pronounced that people could not tell whether she was looking at them or at some object in the vicinity. In 1872 she married Gavin, the seventh Earl of Breadalbane. . . . The couple had no children, but by her marriage Alma became mistress of immense sporting estates, of which the 100,000-acre Black Mount was only one.[10]

Lady Breadalbane did not stand on convention, and took pleasure in visiting her tenants. On one such occasion she came to visit the home of the estate's deer stalker. She was so taken by the gamekeeper and his family (all girls, except one son), that she soon found herself deer stalking. She wrote of her pleasure in the hunt. She said that "the stag is the least part of it all," and added:

The real enjoyment and pleasure consist in the close intercourse with nature—the solitude, the apartness, the constant variation of light and shade, the mystic vagaries of the fleecy clouds, the grandeur of the passing storms, the tender sadness of the setting sun leaving his last rosy kiss on the brows of the peaks, and the quiet peace of evening as we turn towards home.

Lady Breadalbane developed into an accomplished shot. Her practice was to leave for the hunt at 7 A.M., dressed in boots, a skirt of ankle length, a jacket, and a cap. She wrote of firing her rifle:

Slowly I raise the rifle and cover him as he steps along. He stops a moment to look back at his neighbours and gets the shot in the right place. He is quickly followed by a fine ten-pointer a few yards further back. Two barrels have now accounted for two stags, and the rifle is quickly reloaded. . . .

Rifles and ammunition had an impact on the presence of women stalking in the Highlands. Lady Breadalbane herself had experienced the punishing recoil of express rifles.

A rifle was taken at haphazard from the gun-room. . . . In those days I had eyes to see through a stone wall, and fortunately a pair of arms long enough to get over most of the other difficulties. That rifle did not hide its light under a bushel. . . . It bumped me on the nose, and kicked me in the shoulder till I was black and blue, and four or five shots at the target sent me home with a headache for the rest of the day. Its report was like a peal of thunder.

When, at the turn of the century, express rifles gave way to smokeless powder bolt-actions, technology helped to pave the way for women in the Highlands. Black-powder rifles had been heavier, and the cartridges more punishing to the shooter. Such new ammunition as .303 or even .256 was more than adequate for stalking. Lady Breadalbane's new rifle, a .303 by Purdey, was regarded by her as, "for lightness, quickness in handling, and noiseless report, unsurpassed." She was also more inclined to practice target shooting, since "there is no recoil and no concussion to give headaches."

The Edwardian Shooting Parties

Nothing on so grand a scale—before or since—has captivated the public interest in hunting more than the gala shooting parties that epitomized the reign of Victoria's son Edward, both as Prince of Wales and as the monarch Edward VII in the years preceding the First World War. Ladies were invariably present at these gatherings, and some were noted for taking an active part in the shooting, rather than merely spectating. Among these shooting women—and in spite of the disapproval they would have received

From Peter King's *The Shooting Field*, celebrating the 150th anniversary of Holland & Holland, Ltd. From *upper left*, fashion print (gentleman astonished to see a lady attired *"en habit de chasse a pied"*). *Lower left*, youthful lady shooter, believed one of Holland's European clients. The Comtesse de Paris, with gun afield and accompanied by two of her dogs. Aiming from tree, "A Sportswoman in India," captioned "With my last barrel I fired." With felled hippopotamus, taken in Portuguese East Africa, H & H client the Princess Helene d'Orleans, on her safari tour of 1910. Seated with poodle at her feet, the Duchess of Bedford, a pioneer lady gun at Edwardian house parties. H.M. the Queen on a shikar in India, attending a rhino shoot (1961), in a day when these were not endangered. Norman Clarke, renowned shooting coach, had a special knack for teaching children. *Upper right*, members of the Holland family, gathered at time of publication of the book. Color image of H & H instructor for many years, Ken Davies, coaching lovely lady shooter.

from the late Queen—were the Princess of Wales, the Princess Radziwill, the Duchess of Bedford, Lady MacCalmont, Miss Queenie Robinson, Hwfa Williams, William Garnier, and Willie Jameson.

The most delightful book on this period of excess is Jonathan Ruffer's *The Big Shots*, reviewed by *The Guardian* as "disgraceful" and welcomed by the Prince of Wales (author of the book's foreword) as "splendid"—reflecting extremely polarized views of the sport. Ruffer notes that the "Duchess of Bedford was a very keen shot, and she reported that 'it is impossible for a woman to do a long day's walking in comfort over the moors or in turnips in a skirt which is longer than eight inches below the knee.'" The shooting season opened on the twelfth of August—known as the "Glorious 12th"—at which time virtually everyone who was anyone was on the grouse moors. As to the participation of women, it was Lady Warwick who summed up the attitudes of most men, her husband included: "No women exist, wives or mistresses, after August 12th."

Despite prevailing British attitudes on women shooters, game books show that:

Mrs. William Garnier shot three partridges as early as 1845. Princess Radziwill shot regularly with Sir Frederick Milbank at Barningham. On 6 September 1889 she was the lowest scorer. She also shot less than anybody else on 13, 15 and 16 August 1890. By 10 September 1891 she had improved—bottom equal with the vicar! One of the best, on the other hand, was Mrs. Willie Jameson, the wife of the millionaire yachtsman and a close friend of King Edward VII. Her specialty was driven partridges, and, whenever she was out, she took with her a little King Charles spaniel as retriever. It could manage partridges satisfactorily, but could only struggle with the size of a dead pheasant. Hares seem to have been altogether beyond it.[12]

Women on the Continent shot more than did their British counterparts. A client of the finest London gunmakers was Daisy of Pless, who shot frequently at her estate at Fursenstein, Germany. But when she and her husband were guests at Chatsworth, it was he who shot, while she was at hand watching. It was Mrs. Hwfa Williams who proudly commented on her own skill while shooting at Monaco: "I was so successful at the *tir au sanglier* that the people at the Casino gave me a medal. . . . You can imagine how proud I was."

On the subject of gamekeepers, who were almost exclusively men, Ruffer notes one exception: Polly Fishbourne, from the Holkham estate, in the 1820s. He describes her as

an imposing woman whose flashing eyes and close-cropped hair intimidated the North Norfolk countryside, including, it seems, the cattle. She once saved a man from a bull which was goring him. She approached it, and, as it saw her, it cowered away. The animal had apparently once attempted to charge her, but she lodged a charge of small shot in its muzzle! Her aggression was generally directed against the local poachers whom, no doubt, she treated with equal consideration. . . .

The annual shooting parties at Windsor Castle and Sandringham estate prior to the First World War regularly attracted many European monarchs and heads of state. Of course, for the royalty present these events were often very much a family gathering.

Lady Grace Lowther, Adventurous Wife of the Yellow Earl

Born in 1856, one of twelve children of the aristocratic Gordon family of Scotland, Grace was an active child who enjoyed playing tennis, cricket, and billiards with her brothers. She was also keen on hunting and shooting, and was a notably fine horsewoman. It was through these pursuits that she first met Hugh Lowther.

Hugh, the younger brother of St. George, the fourth Earl of Lonsdale, married Grace in 1878. Four years later Hugh became the fifth earl, upon his brother's untimely death. An adventurous, outgoing personality, Hugh became known as the Yellow Earl, since that color was predominant in many of his trappings, and his reputation as a sportsman was of international proportions.

The couple enjoyed hunting and shooting together. In 1879 they visited the United States and hunted big game with friends who had emigrated to Wyoming Territory. Their adventures came at a time not long after Custer's Last Stand, and the property of their friends in Wyoming was not far from where the event took place. The territory was overrun with buffalo, and there were grizzly bear and other sporting species to hunt. Among the trophies they took back to England were "tomahawks which had seen service before bullets from the United States carbines laid their owners low" and thirty-one grizzly bear skins.

During the months spent in the Big Horn country, they ran the risk of Indian uprisings, and the threat of rustlers, thieves, and prairie fires. After surviving all this—and enjoying the great West—on returning east in November 1879, the couple were "met by a battery of press-men" and welcomed by "socially conscious New York," which was "delighted with them." Grace was praised extravagantly. In one such tribute, the *New York World* challenged American womanhood to step up to the challenge of Lady Lowther's talents afield: "It is time for the American votaresses of Diana to be up and doing."

Their carefree life continued until 1881, when Grace, then pregnant, was badly injured in an accident while foxhunting. Her horse fell and rolled onto her, causing the loss of their child and rendering her incapable of bearing another. She continued to be a patroness of hunting to the hounds for the rest of her life, but was never

H.R.H. DUKE OF CONNAUGHT ON SAFARI

again well enough to participate—though she could still shoot.

Between the two world wars, many of the finest shots in the British Isles came to the Lowther estate for shooting weekends, including King George V. During some of these occasions Grace also took an active part, enjoying the shoot as she had before. In 1942 Lady Lowther died at the age of eighty-six; her husband died two years later, at eighty-seven.

The Lure of Painted Targets

A charming array of hand-painted targets was created over a four-hundred-year period in Germanic-speaking countries. Generally oil or tempura on wood, they appear in a variety of sizes from about 24 to 45 inches in diameter, with a number of square configurations ranging from about 24-by-24 inches up to 48-by-48 inches, and in rectangular variations from as small as 17-by-16 inches to as large as 48-by-44 inches. Most were by folk painters, and were generally for *schuetzenfests* or for use by the numerous shooting societies.

Although the early sixteenth century is the accepted period for the introduction of painted targets, earlier examples are known, such as a steel plate from Esslingen, 1413, and a tableau of 1545, in Luneburg, Lower Saxony.

Facing page: From British royalty to East African pioneers—some of them also bluebloods—on safari, from the early twentieth century. *Center* and *bottom left*, Princess Mary, with black rhinoceros and Cape buffalo, in Kenya with hunter Philip Percival. Her daughter Princess Elizabeth was in Kenya on safari, at Treetops, when news came of her father's death, and she assumed the throne (1953). Karen Blixen at *center left* (with two lions) and at *center bottom*, with rifle and zebra trophy. *Top left*, Kathleen Seth-Smith, with a reedbuck, shot only a week after she survived the charge of a black rhino. *Top center*, Vivienne de Watteville on safari. *Left center*, Theodore Roosevelt with Mrs. Philip Percival, during historic 1909–10 East African expedition. At *top right*, the Cottar children, from an expatriate American family from Oklahoma—all of whom enjoyed extensive safari experience.

Historical Targets, by Anne Braun, is the standard text on what has become a collectible.

Even on early target pictures one finds animals, plants and landscapes, views of towns, fortresses and castles, interiors, depictions of courtly life and from the everyday lives of the people. There are paintings of shooting, hunting, riding, fencing and angling, scenes depicting various working processes, festivals and local events. Eventually subjects from the world of allegory, symbolism and fable appeared on targets in considerable measure, as well as satirical contemporary portraits which were, indeed, astonishingly accurate.

As they evolved, targets showed the influence of artistic periods, such as the Baroque of c. 1600–1750; the Rococo, c. 1710–60; the Romantic, from c. 1800; the Classicist of c. 1760–1830; and other influences, into the twentieth century. At that point target painters were isolated, such as in the Alps and Switzerland, and the practice was in decline. Toward the end of the twentieth century, with the flowering of the demand for collectibles, the genre made a comeback.

Often targets bore inscriptions, which might be of a poem, dates to commemorate the shooting match, a wedding or other festive occasion, or a sponsor, as well as space for the name of the match's winner—the *Schuetzenkonig*. Sometimes a pair of targets was created, one to be shot at, the other as a prize for the winner.

The artists-craftsmen were generally skilled, passed down the trade through generations, and, according to Braun, likely also "embellished the interiors of churches, painted house gables and facades, produced religious statues, furniture, tasteful trade signs or shop-signs."

Women in the decoration of painted targets took many forms. Among known examples are "Women Shooting Men from Trees," an erotic target of Junker Hans Vilhelm von Streitberg (1629; aiming points of such targets were the

breasts, navel, or pubic area), Diana (a common theme), Venus on a swing, three maidens, a maiden with birds, the two Graces, and a shooter's marriage.

Princess Elizabeth Leading the Field

The sport of hunting on horseback, so popular during the reign of Elizabeth I, is practiced today as foxhunting, and remains a popular country sport in Great Britain—despite unrelenting pressure from mostly urban animal rights activists. Innumerable female members of the British aristocracy have been dedicated foxhunters, as well as devotees of the shooting sports. An exciting childhood foxhunting adventure of Queen Elizabeth II is a subject of *Monarchy and the Chase*, in a captivating vignette told by Captain George Drummond of Pitsford Hall, Northampton:

Her Majesty the Queen is the only monarch in history who has ever led the whole field of a crackpack out fox-hunting on foot, and, what is more, done it across a heavy plough. . . . At the time of this occurrence [April 18, 1931, with the Duke of Beaufort's Hunt] H.R.H. Princess Elizabeth was three days short of being five years old. . . .

The Princess Elizabeth with her mother holding her pony was in a corner of Boughton Covert and the fox which was there found could not have given a better performance even if commanded or . . . 'if we had had him on a string,' for after he went away he passed right under the nose of the Princess's pony and jumped on to a wall and after giving his royal audience the once-over, made straight across the middle of the adjoining ploughed field, circling to the right before disappearing from view. Freeman [huntsman] laid his hounds on in a flash, coming straight to the royal and other holl'as. When the field debouched from the covert they saw to their amazement and probably to the annoyance of the hard thrusters that they were being led by a small child on a pony, going best pace across the plough in the wake of hounds. The occasion [marked the] initiation of our most important little lady to the joys of the Chase. . . .[12]

To this day, hunting and sport shooting remain popular pastimes among Europe's aristocrats. Two modern factors have impacted these hunts: one is that some families no longer have the wherewithal to indulge, while the other is that women are more active than ever before. Much of this socially oriented shooting takes place in privacy, away from the prying eyes of tabloid journalists.

"A Lady Out Shooting," watercolor by British artist S. A. May, late nineteenth century. Among keen participants in mid-twentieth-century shooting parties were the Duke and Duchess of Windsor, in an annual duck shoot with friends Edith Baker and her son George, at Horse Shoe Plantation, Tallahassee, Florida.

"A Hawking Party," colored engraving, F. Taylor, Pinxt., C. Cousen, sculpt., late eighteenth century. Like hunting and shooting, falconry was immensely popular at all the royal courts throughout Europe and Great Britain. Ladies enjoyed the sport, and among those known to partake were Queen Elizabeth I, whose Grand Master was a lady, Mary of Canterbury. A print in Turberville's *Book of Falconerie* depicts Her Majesty on horseback in the open countryside, attended by her falconers, hunting herons with her hawks. Although beyond the scope of *Silk and Steel,* falconry continues to be a popular sport into modern times, with such exclusive resorts as Gleneagles operating a falconry school—under charge of a woman.

FIRST BLOW FOR LIBERTY
To the Memory of the Patriots of 1775

This lithograph captures the courageous dedication of American rebels from the early stages of the Revolutionary War. Woman at *right* grasps the musket of a fallen comrade, taking on British adversaries.

CHAPTER II

Women at War

I don't know how long before I shall have to go into the field of battle. For my part I don't care. I don't feel afraid to go. I don't believe there are [sic] any Rebel's bullet made for me yet.

—Private Lyons (Sarah Rosetta) Wakeman, 153rd Regiment, New York State Volunteers

"More deadly than the male" is a long-standing claim for the female of any species. For the human species, the female has proven to be capable, effective, and deadly in battle, though the role women have played in combat through the ages has received far less attention than is warranted by their contributions.

Tales have been told, legends formulated, and, more recently, histories have been written about courageous women defending their homes. But only very recently has their active participation as aggressors in war been studied. Much of this information can now be found on the World Wide Web.[1] While woman as defender is more understandable, the concept of woman as aggressor forces a serious reconsideration of the heretofore male stereotype of the warrior.

Though giants of the past have certainly been lauded in story and song—the legendary Amazons, who fought the Greeks; the historical Boadicea, Britain's Icenian queen who took on the Roman legions; and Countess Matilda of Tuscany, an eleventh-century warrior who led troops in the service of three popes—we still consider them anomalies, if not outright fabrications. Yet DNA evidence has been added to other scientific tools to show that female warriors were far more prevalent in all cultures than previously believed.

Plutarch, describing a battle in 102 B.C. between Romans and Celts, observed, "The fight had been no less fierce with the women than with the men themselves . . . the women charged with swords and axes and fell upon their opponents uttering a hideous outcry."

It is not difficult to understand the belligerent spirit that might lead a woman to defend hearth and home (or even homeland), taking arms against an aggressor. But it is clear that her fascination with, and skill at, the art of war has, in all periods, gone well beyond the requirements of necessity.

In A.D. 200, Emperor Alexander Severus issued an edict prohibiting women gladiators from the arena—a sure indication, even if there weren't paintings and frescos to provide additional proof, that they were there in numbers. The medieval equivalent to gladiatorial contests, the tournament, also drew women. A fourteenth-century British chronicle describes a band of women warriors who "came on excellent chargers or other horses splendidly adorned, to the place of tournament. And in such manner they spent and wasted their riches and injured their bodies with abuses. . . ."

Joan of Arc's position in history is unique, a story celebrated in art and in words for centuries, and an example of spirituality and courage to women of all cultures. At the time of her death, in 1431, firearms were not a factor in warfare, and thus her armaments would have been sword and dagger, and perhaps the mace. She stands as the sole warrior woman to have achieved sainthood from the Catholic Church.

Spain's Doña Catalina de Erauso traveled to Peru in the seventeenth century as a soldier of fortune, where she was noted for her proficiency with sword, pistol, and knife. Robert Baldrick, in his book *The Duel*, tells of a Madame de Saint-Belmont who disguised herself as a man and fought a duel with a cavalry officer after he ignored a letter she had sent complaining of his discourtesy.

"Men's Clothing I'll Put On . . ."

Women who took part in the battles of Western Europe and the Americas during the seventeenth, eighteenth, and nineteenth centuries usually disguised themselves as men. Some went to stay close to husbands or lovers, but others, surely, went for combat itself. An amazing number served aboard naval vessels, at a time when conditions at sea were so brutal that men were

frequently duped or doped to fill vacancies in a ship's crew. And many of these male impersonators were, quite literally, exposed when they were stripped for flogging—a common punishment for even minor offenses.

According to Suzanne Stark, in her book *Female Tars*, in June 1690 one Anne Chamberlyne dressed in men's clothing and fought in a six-hour battle against the French on board her brother's ship. And an unidentified gentlewoman petitioned the Queen for payment for serving aboard HMS *St. Andrew* in a battle with the French in the summer of 1691. During the English Civil War (1642–49), so many women were fighting with the armies that King Charles issued a proclamation banning them from wearing men's clothing.

It was the English Civil War, perhaps, and certainly the many rebellions and revolutions that followed during the eighteenth and nineteenth centuries, that set the stage for the widespread participation by women in battle, carried on through the twentieth century into the present. That war has frequently served to better women's position in society was noted by Field Marshal Montgomery of Alamein in *A History of Warfare*. Speaking of the Crimean War (1854–56), he says, "It was not the least important consequence of this war that the emancipation of women was considerably advanced. Every war since then has seen a marked gain for women in social emancipation and public responsibility."

Certainly, over hundreds of years of rebellion in Scotland, women played dramatic and pivotal roles. In the fourteenth century, Isobel, Countess of Buchan, stole her husband's best warhorses and went to fight for Robert the Bruce. The earl, who did not support the Bruce, issued a warrant for her death. Isabelle, the French-born wife of England's King Edward II, was so converted to the Scottish cause that she took arms against her husband and his followers. When Edward III took over the throne, Isabelle fled to Scotland, where she joined a troop of women warriors that included Isobel of Buchan and the Bruce's sister, Christian.

Lady Agnes Randolph ("Black Agnes") was another of the Bruce's warrior women. Later in life she successfully defended her castle at Dunbar for more than five months against England's Earl of Salisbury and his sophisticated siege force. Salisbury is purported to be the author of a ballad about her: "She kept a stir in tower and trench, / That brawling, boisterous Scottish wench, / Came I early, came I late / I found Agnes at the gate." Sir Walter Scott wrote, "From the record of Scottish heroes, none can presume to erase her."

Scotland apparently had a tradition of husbands and wives who differed forcefully over political issues. During the Jacobite rebellion in 1745–46, Lady Anne Macintosh sided with Prince Charles Edward Stewart's forces to the dismay of her husband, the Laird of Macintosh, who was a staunch Hanoverian. According to Maggie Craig in *Damn Rebel Bitches—Women of the '45*, "Colonel Anne" is credited with raising several hundred men for the cause, though she never led them in battle. Lady Lude fired the first shot in the Jacobite counterattack on Blair Castle, her family home, after it had been captured by the Hanoverians. Jean (Jenny) Cameron of Glendessary raised and led three hundred men in Bonny Prince Charlie's cause.

In the American colonies, there were many cases of women who fought heroically, both colonials and Native Americans. Awashonka, a female sachem of the Saconnets in Rhode Island, was among several women tribal leaders who helped the colonists defend their homes during King Philip's War in 1675.

French priest Father Joseph Francois Lafitau wrote of the Iroquois:

Nothing is more real than the women's superiority. . . . It is they who really maintain the tribe, the nobility of blood, the genealogical tree, the order of generations, and conservation of the families. In them resides all the real authority; the lands, fields, and all their harvest belong to them; they are the soul of the councils, the arbiters of peace and war; they hold the taxes and the public treasure; to them the slaves are entrusted; they arrange the marriages; the children are under their authority; the order of succession is founded on their blood. The men . . . are isolated and limited to themselves. Their children are strangers to them. Everything perishes with them.[2]

A barricade in 1830, gouache by P. Manguin (1815–69), 1834. From the Musée de la Ville de Paris, Musée Carnavalet, Paris.

35

Nancy Ward (née Nanye'hi), the teenage wife of a Cherokee warrior, accompanied her husband on a military expedition. He was killed in combat, whereupon she fought on, using his gun. For this she became known as "War Woman," an exalted status. With her new position, she had the power to spare captives. She did so when a white woman was about to be burned at the stake. In return, the spared captive taught War Woman to make butter. She was also remarkable in supporting the cause of the Patriots during the Revolutionary War. Although her position of authority remained undiminished in her tribe, she warned white pioneers of planned attacks by Cherokee warriors. A diplomat of the Cherokee, she stated at a treaty conference with the newly formed United States (1781): "This peace must last forever. Let your women's sons be ours; our sons be yours. Let your women hear our words."[3]

In 1697, a band of Abnaki raiders from Canada abducted Hannah Duston and Mary Neff from their homes in Haverhill, Massachusetts, and began the long trek north with their captives. After a forced march of a hundred miles, they camped on an island in New Hampshire. During the night, Hannah, with the aid of Mary and a young boy who had been captured previously, stole the Indians' tomahawks, killed and scalped ten of them, and escaped in a canoe after destroying the rest to prevent pursuit. A monument was dedicated to Hannah Duston in Haverhill in 1861—the first in the United States to commemorate a heroic woman.

Women Fight for American Liberty

About one half of the white population of the thirteen colonies remained loyal to the British crown, or neutral. From that other half were more than a few women who were fearsome, determined, and diligent in their efforts on behalf of the cause of independence. Not many actually took up arms or played a frontline role, but there are documented cases of women doing so. Among the first who braved arrest, and probable execution, was the sixteen-year-old daughter of a militia commander, Sybil Ludington of Fredericksburg, New York. Termed "the female Paul Revere," she sped some forty miles at night on horseback to awake the militia, warning them that the British were marching on Danbury, Connecticut.

Donna M. Lucey's *I Dwell in Possibility* noted several of the ways women supported the Revolution:

[They] . . . sewed uniforms and bandages for the soldiers and donated their pewter dishes, cutlery, and candlesticks to be melted into cannon balls and shot. One New England woman was so eager to supply bullets for the troops that she even pilfered from her ancestors—melting down the nameplates accompanying her family's graves. A women's group in Litchfield, Connecticut, managed to obtain most of the monumental equestrian statue of King George III that had been torn down by angry patriots on Bowling Green in New York City. Ingeniously, they melted the hated statue down for its lead, which they poured into moulds to make musket cartridges (over 42,000 of them) for use by patriot troops.[4]

Perhaps the best-known woman in America's War of Independence is also the most controversial. "Molly Pitcher," so the story goes, was married to a man who joined an artillery regiment. Following her husband into the field, as many wives did at the time, she provided assistance to his gun crew. During the Battle of Monmouth, New Jersey, on June 28, 1778, she carried water on the field of battle to the sweltering soldiers. They supposedly called out "Molly—pitcher" when they wanted water, and the nickname stuck. (Actually, it appears that "Molly Pitcher" was a frequent nickname for water carriers during the time, and it is not clear, nor may it ever be proven, when the term actually came into general use.) When her husband collapsed at his gun, either from heat or because he was wounded, "Molly" took up his place and helped keep the gun firing. A woman named Mary Ludwig, daughter of a New Jersey dairy farmer, is widely believed to be the famous Molly Pitcher. She was married to John Hays, a cannoneer. A soldier present at the battle wrote as an eyewitness, and was greatly impressed by her courage:

A cannon shot from the enemy passed directly between her legs without doing any other damage than carrying away all the lower part of her petticoat. . . . Looking at it with apparent unconcern, she observed that it was lucky it did not pass a little higher. . . .[5]

Yet another battlefield heroine was Margaret Corbin, who, in 1776, took *her* husband's place at an artillery piece when he fell during the attack on Fort Washington. Severely wounded in the action, Corbin was awarded a pension and a suit of clothes by Congress, and was the only woman appointed to the Invalid Regiment, posted at West Point. In the 1920s, the Daughters of the American Revolution reinterred her remains and erected a monument to her behind the Old Cadet Chapel at West Point. A plaque in Fort Tryon Park, New York City, near where the battle took place, proclaims Corbin "the first American woman to take a soldier's part in the War for Liberty."

Facing page: Not only used by women serving surreptitiously in the U.S. military in the War of 1812, Mexican War, Civil War, and various Indian wars, these arms were also wielded by pioneer women. Surplus arms were often supplied to settlers, at little or no cost, and spread all over the United States as wagon trains and other means of transportation relocated families in early America. From *top*, Model 1808 contract flintlock musket in .69 caliber, made by Sutton, Millbury, Massachusetts; Model 1841 "Mississippi Rifle," .54 caliber, by Robbins, Kendall and Lawrence, Windsor, Vermont; Model 1863 Remington "Zouave" contract rifle; Model 1861 Colt Special musket, and Model 1861 Springfield rifle-musket. *Bottom* three in .58 caliber. Note treacherous saber and triangular bayonets.

Other women served as well. Deborah Samson, of Plymouth, Massachusetts, disguised herself as a man and enlisted as Robert Shirtliffe in Captain Nathan Thayer's company. In over three years' service, she was wounded twice, receiving a sword cut to the head, and being shot through the shoulder. Her sex was not discovered until she contracted brain fever. She later received a pension and a land grant.

Donna Lucey notes other brave women who "rose up to defend their home ground":

> When news reached the residents of Groton, Massachusetts, that the British were en route, local women promptly organized a female militia. Wielding muskets and pitchforks, the women successfully dispersed a detachment of British soldiers. A handful of women actually joined up with the regular army, drawn perhaps by economic need. They bound their breasts and disguised themselves as men to do so. At least one, a young Creole woman named Sally St. Clair, was killed in battle; another woman rose to the rank of sergeant before her sex was discovered and she was discharged.[6]

Rachel and Grace Martin disguised themselves as men and captured a British courier, stealing his dispatches and delivering them to General Nathanael Greene. Anna Warner Bailey, the "Heroine of Groton," aided the wounded during the massacre at Fort Griswold in Connecticut, and Angelica Vrooman calmly sat in a tent throughout a battle, pouring lead into molds to make bullets for the rangers.

Abigail Adams Admonishes Her Husband to Remember the Ladies—1776

In many ways as heroic as her husband, John, Abigail Adams penned innumerable letters so powerful that Adams often showed them to his colleagues at the Continental Congress. In one such missive, with her characteristic imaginative grammar and spelling, she wrote:

> Remember the Ladies, and be more generous and favourable to them than your ancestors. Do not put such unlimited power into the hands of the Husbands. Remember all Men would be tyrants if they could. If particular care and attention is not paid to the Laidies we are determined to foment a Rebelion, and will not hold ourselves bound by any Laws in which we have no voice, or Representation.[7]

John Adams later remarked that "these were times . . . which tried women's souls, as well as men's."

Elizabeth Shell Loads Muskets and Fights the Enemy with an Ax

When the Shell family of upstate New York were under siege by Loyalist and Indian forces (1781), Elizabeth Shell responded with indignation, bravery, and ferocity. The fight lasted from early in the afternoon until just after dark. She was loading guns for her husband, aided by their sons, when five of the enemy aimed through the walls with their muskets. She attacked them with an ax, damaging the barrels. The attackers abandoned the fight, beating a retreat with their ruined muskets.

Nancy Hart—Revolutionary War Heroine

On November 11, 1931, a monument was unveiled near Hartwell, Georgia, honoring Revolutionary War heroine Nancy Hart. Senator Richard B. Russell, Jr., told the story of how she took on a group of Tories, bravely responding to an invasion of her home. The earliest published description of the event appeared in the Milledgeville *Southern Recorder*:

> One day six Tories paid Nancy a call and demanded a meal. She soon spread before them smoking venison, hoe-cakes, and fresh honeycomb. Having stacked their arms, they seated themselves, and started to eat, when Nancy quick as a flash seized one of the guns, "cocked it, and with a blazing oath declared she would blow out the brains of the first mortal that offered to rise or taste a mouthful!" She sent one of her sons to inform the Whigs of her prisoners. Whether uncertain because of her cross-eyes which one she was aiming at, or transfixed by her ferocity, they remained quiet. The Whigs soon arrived and dealt with the Tories "according to the rules of the times."[8]

Over the years the story became embellished somewhat, to the point that the image pictured opposite shows her having killed one of her adversaries. It has been determined that she was born c. 1735, and died c. 1830. Accounts of her heroism were widely known in Georgia's Elbert, Oglethorpe, and Wilkes counties, following the war. But they did not appear in print until the occasion of the Marquis de Lafayette's visit to Georgia in 1825. At that time the *Southern Recorder* ran its article, as part of promoting the patriotic record of the state.

Helping the Cause of the American Revolution

A variety of sources prove that women played important roles as noncombatants in the American Revolution. Sarah Cribbs made some 22,000 musket cartridges. Another cartridge maker was Betsy Ross, better known for sewing the flag. She built ammunition in the basement of her Philadelphia home, now a museum, known as the American Flag House and Betsy Ross Memorial. Edith Steward produced 37,000 cartridges between February 11 and May 25, 1780.

The War of 1812 and the Mexican War

When the USS *Constitution*, "Old Ironsides," defeated HMS *Guerrière* during the War of

1812, a U.S. Marine serving aboard as "George Baker" was actually a woman named Lucy Brewer. She is credited with being the first woman in the Marine Corps.

As in the Revolutionary War, the manufacture of ammunition was a task willingly assumed by not a few women and girls. Among them was Elizabeth Sexton Ferguson, eleven, who assisted her mother in molding lead balls for use by troops in the war.

During the Mexican War, in the late 1840s, Sarah Borginis enlisted with her husband in the army, and was the principal cook at Fort Texas. When the Mexicans began bombarding the fort, Sarah was issued a musket. Supposedly, she never missed either hitting a target or preparing a meal, and was brevetted to colonel by General Zachary Taylor. Upon her death in 1866, she was buried with full military honors at Fort Yuma, the first woman to be a ranking U.S. Army officer.

More widely known from that conflict, at least at the time, was Eliza Allen, of Eastport, Maine. She followed her beloved, then serving in the U.S. forces, to Mexico. Subsequently she enlisted, served in several battles, was wounded, and then set sail for California to participate in the Gold Rush. These exploits, and more, were published in her illustrated work, *The Female Volunteer; or, the Most Strange, Wonderful, and Thrilling Narrative of the Life and Adventures of Eliza Allen*. The book ends with "marriage and [the] happy termination of all her trials and sorrows."

The Civil War
Private Lyons Wakeman, 153rd Regiment, New York State Volunteers

According to continually evolving research, the Civil War saw as many as 750 women serving, under the guise of men, as soldiers, for both Union and Confederate forces. (The numbers who actually did so are no doubt higher—but this figure is generally accepted at this writing. With the numbers of young men and boys serving, and for various other reasons, identifying these women was difficult then, and nearly impossible now.) Likely more than sixty of them were either wounded or killed during the conflict.

The only one of these courageous women presently known to have left a body of letters concerning her service was Sarah Rosetta Wakeman. Her story is told in Lauren Cook Burgess's *An Uncommon Soldier*. Burgess has recorded over 150 Civil War women soldiers, and her research has been the basis for much new information on women in the Civil War.

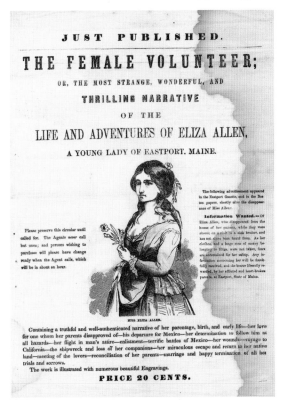

Broadside on the adventurous Eliza Allen, c. 1848. Backside printed in German.

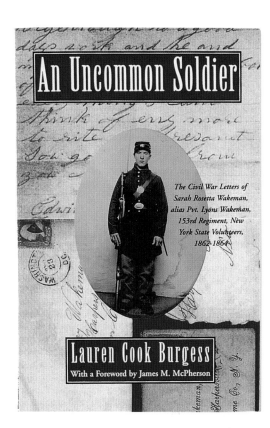

Cover of monograph of Sarah Rosetta Wakeman, based on letters she sent to her parents as Private Lyons Wakeman. Pulitzer Prize–winning historian James M. McPherson, author of *Battle Cry of Freedom*, said of this moving book: "With the publication of *An Uncommon Soldier*, an important facet of the Civil War has finally gotten in the books."

The survivor of two pitched battles, Private Wakeman expressed a sentiment common among many Civil War troops, a literate lot who wrote millions of letters during the conflict. From *An Uncommon Soldier*:

Wakeman's letters provide a rare glimpse of what life was like for a woman fighting as a common soldier in the Civil War under the guise of a man. The letters (the only such correspondence known to exist) tell of army life in the defenses of Washington D.C. and on the march and in battle during the 1864 Louisiana

Red River Campaign. In them, Private Wakeman expresses her determination to perform honorably the duty required of a soldier, and her pride in being able to "drill just as well as any man" in her regiment. Although Wakeman did not survive the war, her letters remain as a singular record of female military life in the ranks, a phenomenon largely ignored by historians and researchers. This unique collection of letters offers a firsthand look at the personality and character of women who defied convention to take a man's place in the Union army.

Sacrifices by Both Union and Confederate Women

Sarah Emma Edmonds, who masqueraded as Franklin Thompson, was both a nurse and a spy for the Union Army. Jennie Hodgers served in combat for three years as Albert Cashier, and it wasn't until 1913 that her true identity was made known. These, with Sarah Wakeman, are among the growing number of women who were known combatants.

One who died was reported in Frank Moore's book *Women in War*. In 1863, a nineteen-year-old woman known only as Emily joined the drum corps of a Michigan regiment. During the battle at Chattanooga, Tennessee, she was struck in the side by a musket ball. As she lay dying, her sex was discovered, and at first she refused to tell her real name. Finally, she dictated a telegram to her father in Brooklyn: "Forgive your dying daughter. I have but a few moments to live. My native soil drinks my blood. I expected to deliver my country but the fates would not have it so. I am content to die. Pray forgive me. Emily."

Dr. Mary Walker became a suffragette and championed more comfortable clothing for women, and was also one of the pioneer female physicians and served as a surgeon in the Civil War. She attended sick and wounded soldiers and suffered for four months as a prisoner of war. She was awarded the Congressional Medal of Honor, the nation's highest award for valor, by President Andrew Johnson.

Clara Barton, founder of the Red Cross, was so accustomed to tending to the wounded and sick at or near the front lines that her dress was once shot through by a bullet, which killed a soldier for whom she was caring. When she discovered that one of the wounded in her care was actually a woman, she persuaded her to return to her family.

Women of the Confederacy

Although loyal to the South, many Confederate white women were often troubled by the institution of slavery. Since they were frequently outnumbered by black slaves, some of whom might revolt if the opportunity presented itself, a logical conclusion is that these women were skilled in the use of firearms.

Donna M. Lucey's *I Dwell in Possibility* devotes two chapters to southern white women and Civil War heroines, and to enslaved women. When the Civil War began, many Confederate women "wanted to join in the battle themselves."

> "O if I was only a man!" wrote Louisianan Sarah Morgan in her diary. "Then I could don the breeches and slay them with a will!" Indeed, a number of women—perhaps as many as 250—disguised themselves as men and fought for the Confederacy. At least one woman soldier died at Shiloh and another at Gettysburg, probably as part of Pickett's ill-fated charge. In a letter to his father, a Union soldier described an 1864 battle near Dallas, Georgia:

> One Secesh woman charged . . . waving the traitor flag and screaming vulgarities at us. She was shot three times but still on she came. . . . Another She-Devil shot her way to our breastworks with two large revolvers dealing death to all in her path. . . . If Gen. Lee were to field a brigade of such fighters, I think the Union prospects would be very gloomy indeed for it would be hard to equal their ferocity and pluck.[9]

A woman of the South who became famous as a Confederate spy was Belle Boyd. Well educated, and a member of an old and wealthy Virginia family, Boyd killed a Union soldier who had dared to curse her mother. While treating the wounded, she listened carefully to the conversations of Union soldiers. Information she gleaned was passed on to General Thomas J. "Stonewall" Jackson. She was rewarded with a captain's commission, and given the title of honorary aide-de-camp. To the Yankee press, she was "The Secesh Cleopatra."

Yet another heroine of the South was the socialite and confidante of numerous powerful figures of her time, Rose O'Neal Greenhow. Suspicioned as part of a Confederate ring of spies, she was kept under surveillance by detectives in her Washington, D.C., residence, soon after the war broke out. Prior to the Battle of Bull Run, she had been able to advise the Confederacy of movements by Union troops. For some five months she and her eight-year-old daughter were under house arrest—though she was still able to pass on information. Soon they were incarcerated at the Old Capitol Prison. She grew concerned about the health of her daughter, which led to their release in June 1862. The *Richmond Dispatch* observed: "If the tyrant has released her, it was because that even he quailed before the might of her power as representative of the feelings of every true Southern lady."

In 1863 Greenhow visited Europe, representing President Jefferson Davis. She met with Napoleon III and Queen Victoria. On behalf of Davis, she smuggled gold and documents back to the Confederacy. When a Union patrol sighted her ship off the coast of North Carolina, she attempted to escape in a rowboat, accompanied by two other agents. The boat was capsized, and, weighted down by the gold, Greenhow drowned. Her body was recovered, and she was buried in Wilmington, North Carolina, with military honors due a heroine.

Supplying Guns and Ammunition for the Civil War Effort: Lieutenant General Thomas J. "Stonewall" Jackson Honors Mrs. Captain Bradley T. Johnson

As the Civil War began, Maryland's Mrs. Captain Bradley T. Johnson was instrumental in supplying 500 Mississippi rifles, 10,000 cartridges, and 3,500 caps for the Confederacy. She was recognized for her achievement by Stonewall Jackson, whose officers had resolved "That the thanks of the Maryland Line be tendered to Mrs. Captain Bradley T. Johnson for her earnest, patriotic and successful efforts in arming and equipping the Maryland Line." Further, they pledged "that the arms she has obtained shall at the close of the war be returned . . . without stain or dishonor." The guns were not returned, at war's end, or ever.[10]

Harriet Tubman—the Moses of Her People, Armed with a Handgun

A remarkable woman who courageously escaped from her slave masters on a Maryland plantation, Harriet Tubman vowed to help save her people, and became a conductor on the Underground Railroad. She was responsible for saving hundreds, including members of her own family. Tubman's story is one of the most inspiring from the Civil War period.

As a Maryland plantation field hand, Tubman suffered cruel punishments as a child. She regularly "prayed to God to make me strong and able to fight." On the death of her master, in 1849, she learned that she and her brothers were to be sold into the Deep South. She decided to escape, but neither her husband nor her brothers dared to flee. Hiding during the day and walking at night, she left on her own. She made it to Pennsylvania, and freedom: "I felt like I was in heaven."

Putting together a war chest by working menial jobs, she decided to attempt to help others escape to the North. In 1850 she went back south, surreptitiously rescuing her sister and her two children. Next she saved a brother and two other men. She became active on the Underground Railroad, and saved over three hundred slaves—even her own mother and father. All the while she carried her own gun, a reasonable precaution, since there was a $40,000 reward for her capture.

Tubman also served the Union in the Civil War, as both spy and scout, behind Confederate lines. Thought to be a freed woman, she traveled widely, in the process determining locations of cotton storage, as well as ammunition dumps, and places where slaves were awaiting rescue. Several raids in coastal South Carolina, Georgia, and Florida made by guerrilla fighter Colonel James Montgomery were based on information from Tubman. Sometimes Tubman herself led these raids. By their actions, over eight hundred slaves were released from Combahee River (South Carolina) plantations in the summer of 1863.

World War I

While the thorough organization of forces in the United States during the First World War effectively eliminated the opportunity for women to go to war disguised as men (at least in a combat role—some thirty thousand of them served, in uniform, in noncombat capacities), in other countries they quite openly took their places in the thick of the action.

Flora Sandes, the daughter of a Scottish clergyman, went to Serbia at the outbreak of the war as a nurse with an ambulance unit. In November 1915, the Serbian Army was forced to retreat into Kosovo, and Sandes, though nearly forty, joined the Serbian peasant women who were serving in the trenches. In December 1916, she was promoted to the rank of sergeant-

Believed made for J. Diaz, wife of Mexican president Porfirio Diaz, this 6.35mm pistol by N. Pieper, of Liège, Belgium, is inlaid with gold, including a Mexican eagle motif. Serial number P11527. From the Douglas Arms Collection of the Royal Military College of Canada, Kingston, Ontario, c. 1908–10. Diaz was a keen collector of firearms. This pistol was part of an elaborate cased set with a larger automatic, in 7.65mm; on the case lid escutcheon, the monogram JD.

Facing page: Accompanied by tools of the trade, a Mauser Model 1898 bolt-action (with bayonet) and a Model 1894 Winchester, these Mexican revolutionaries took no prisoners. Note bandoliers, handguns, rifles, and the youthful faces of several. Not much uniformity is evident in the models of firearms, though Winchesters, Mausers, and Colts prevail. At *left,* none other than Pancho Villa, with his wife, Luz (1914); the *lower* image shows her in 1977, when she sold worn-out copies of Colt handguns to naive tourists (at a tidy profit), claiming each one to have been used by her husband. At *lower right* a well-heeled young lady who appears to have stepped out of Sam Peckinpah's *The Wild Bunch,* a powerfully evocative film in which women were correctly depicted as armed and dangerous. Pictures of Mexican revolutionary women are not uncommon.

Above: The Imperial War Museum, housing unequaled collections from World Wars I and II, and images and objects from intervening and later conflicts. Photographs from the museum's archives.

major. She published *An English Woman-Sergeant in the Serbian Army* that year to raise funds for the army. She was seriously wounded by a grenade, hospitalized, and was awarded the Kara George Star, the country's highest military decoration. Sandes recovered and returned to

the front. After the war she remained in the army and retired with the rank of major.

In France, an artist, Madame Arno, organized a regiment of Parisian women in 1915 to fight the Germans. Emilienee Moreau fought in a number of frontline actions, killing two snipers, and was awarded the Croix de Guerre, the British Red Cross Medal, and the St. John Ambulance Society Medal. (In 1940, she was again in combat, and earned a second Croix de

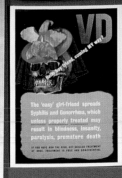

Guerre.) Another French woman, Marcelle Semer, braved German bullets to open a drawbridge across the Somme River. J. David Truby says she "pinned down their engineers with gunfire for several hours prior to exhausting ammunition for her rifle." Her actions caused the enemy a day's delay.

Eastern European women were especially inclined to fight on the battlefield, and as insurgents. Among examples of these were Sophie Jowanowitsch, Stanislawa Ordynska, and more than two hundred others who fought in the Polish Legion.

Nineteen-year-old Helen Ruz was a corporal in the Voluntary Ukraine Legion, and fought in the Carpathian Mountains and during the Galacian campaigns, winning two medals. Sophie Haletchko was a decorated sergeant-major in the Ukranian cavalry.

In the Russian Army, twelve teenage girls disguised themselves as boys and fought in Galacia and the Carpathians. Zoya Smirnow was the only survivor. Captain Olga Kokovtseva fought with the 6th Regiment of the Ural Cossacks in Serbia (most Cossack regiments included some women). She was twice wounded and received the St. George Cross. Lieutenant Marie Baktscharow led the first Russian women's battalion in 1917, while Maria (Yashka) Botchkareva led a crack women's battalion known as the "Battalion of Death."

During the Revolution of 1917, a recently formed women's battalion stood among the troops defending the Winter Palace, St. Peters-

burg, as remaining members of the provisional government were secured inside. The palace was overtaken after lengthy but unproductive negotiations, followed by a battle of short duration.

The use of combat aircraft was pioneered in World War I, and women were active as pilots from the start. Princess Eugenie Shakhovskaya was the first Russian woman to become a military pilot when she flew reconnaissance missions for Tsar Nicholas II in 1914, and Princess Sophie Alexandrovna Dolgorunaya, who was awarded her pilot's license that same year, began flying missions with the 26th Corps Air Squadron in 1917. In France, Helene Dutreux was the first of a number of Parisian women to become military pilots during World War I.

As the war drew to a close, Germany pressed women into armed service as rear-area security guards, but some saw more active duty as well. J. David Truby notes that a Canadian journalist who had been captured by the Germans in 1918 witnessed women working in Maxim machine-gun crews.

World War II

From the outset of hostilities, Britain began drafting women as well as men into its armed forces, a policy that was considered but rejected by the United States. During the course of the war, 2 percent of Britain's female population, more than a half million women, were serving in the armed forces, though most did not see combat.

A number of the gunners who shot down Nazi aircraft and buzzbombs in the Battle of Britian and the aftermath were women. When Germany began launching buzzbombs against the beleaguered island, the bombs had a fatal characteristic—their trajectory could not be changed once launched—which the British quickly ex-

ploited. At a facility staffed largely by women, trajectories were calculated and coordinates fed to antiaircraft positions; the bombs became easy targets.

Mary Cox notes in *British Women at War:*

The A.T.S. (Auxiliary Territorial Service) was originally recruited to replace soldiers as clerks, cooks, drivers of light cars, mess and telephone orderlies, messengers, store-keepers, etc. All these duties they have performed so well that many others have been added to the list. . . .

Perhaps the most interesting form of A.T.S. work is that done in connection with the Anti-Aircraft Command. Over 200 A.T.S., including cooks, clerks, telephonists and operational members, are included in the personnel of a heavy A.A. battery, serving with an approximately equal number of men. Women wireless operators work on radiolocation instruments, others man the predictors which calculate the position of enemy aircraft by the movement of dials and control the direction and fire of the guns; three women work each height-finder by which the correct timing of the fuses is determined, while spotters with powerful binoculars and other instruments decide whether an approaching aircraft is hostile or friendly.

Edith Summerskill, aka "Flossie Bang-Bang," and Britain's Home Guard

A leading socialist politician and member of the Socialist Medical Association, Dr. Edith Summerskill was an early advocate of women's rights. Her 1941 pamphlet "Women Fall In" explained conditions of service in sundry auxiliary and civilian organizations for women. According to Imperial War Museum curator David Penn, "The Home Guard was a particular concern of hers. Women were allowed to join, but only as non-combatant Auxiliaries (all the women's Auxiliary services were non-combatant, with the exception of the First Aid Nursing Yeomanry, which is why female SOE agents were FANYs), and Edith Summerskill

Russian snipers, *left* and *right,* with Russian volunteer women on
the march in Moscow, many of them carrying rifles with fixed
bayonets. Angola's Organization of National Defense, in 1976,
included women, all equipped with assault rifles; the corps was
intended for defense and labor.

47

Service and sniper bolt-action rifles widely used by the Germans (*top* two) and the Russians in World War II. From the *top,* Model 98K sniper rifle with low turret scope, with standard-issue Model 98K Mauser infantry rifle; both arms in 7.92mm (8mm Mauser) caliber. Third from *top,* Model 38 Moisin-Nagant carbine, in 7.62 × 54mm, with Model 91/30 Moisin-Nagant sniper rifle with side-mounted PE scope. The sniper rifles gained special notoriety, used by skillful and daring male and female sharpshooters—with the Russian arms particularly celebrated in the book and film *Enemy at the Gates.* Note Model 91/30 reversed on paperback book jacket, to better fit cover design.

was determined that this should change with regard to the Home Guard."

Summerskill herself wrote in her book, *A Woman's World*:

> It seemed logical that these women should be taught to use a rifle even if there were not, as we were told repeatedly, enough to go round. In the event of a male Home Guard being killed then his rifle should be used by whoever was near him at the time, irrespective of sex. We could not in these circumstances expect the enemy to be scrupulous about the sex of his opponents. . . . While the capacity of the women was indisputable and they became first-class shots, we were not unaware of our incongruous appearance. Lying on their tummies in the Coventry Street room, handling vintage rifles, were women of all ages, fat and thin, blondes, brunettes and grey, married and single, clad in breeches, trousers or skirts, yet all fully determined that "they shall not pass" if they could help it.

Penn's mother had known Summerskill from her own wartime service:

> Dr. Summerskill spent much of her career at Charing Cross Hospital close by Trafalgar Square in London. My late mother, who was Casualty Sister there during the war, told me that Dr. Summerskill had the tendency to treat her colleagues as a political audience, a trait that did not always endear, and her oft-expressed support for women's rifle shooting earned her the nickname of "Flossie Bang-Bang."

Array of submachine guns, all used by women in combat and sometimes in police situations—the former primarily as partisans, resistance fighters, or revolutionaries. From *top,* U.S. M1A1 Thompson by Auto Ordnance Corporation, .45ACP, with 30-round magazine. At *top left,* 50-round drum from the Colt-made Model 1928A1 Thompson. Below it, the Liberator single-shot pistol, also in .45ACP. *Top right,* U.S. M3A1 "grease gun" in .45ACP. *Left center,* British MK II Sten gun, *above* Sterling MK 6 Patchett, both in 9mm. Angled at *right,* the Russian PPSh-41 in 7.62mm Tokarev. *Bottom center,* German MP40 Schmeisser in 9mm parabellum. *Lower left,* folding-stock model Uzi in 9mm, famous from use by Israeli forces. *Right,* U.S.-made Mac 11/9 by Cobray with a suppressor/silencer attached; 9mm—this gun is occasionally seen in films and TV.

Left: Most of these postcards are from the Imperial War Museum shop, and primarily reflect the British effort in World War II. At *top center,* Princess Elizabeth in ATS war uniform, in front of vehicle she drove. Classic Churchill photograph depicts the PM with a Thompson submachine gun. Of somewhat later vintage, "Social Security," wielding an AK-47!

49

Most arms accompanied by bayonets, from *top:* U.S. M16A1 military rifle, in 5.56 (.223) caliber; U.S. M1 Carbine, .30 caliber; U.S. M1 Rifle, the Garand, in .30 (.30-06) caliber; the U.S. M14 Rifle, in .308 caliber (7.62mm NATO). At *bottom,* Model 700 Remington in M40 sniper rifle configuration, also in .308 caliber, with 3-9 power Redfield scope. All of these arms have seen service use by women, though not necessarily in combat, and have appeared on rifle ranges in both training and in organized competitions—including the U.S. mecca for competitive shooting, Camp Perry, Ohio.

King George VI and Queen Elizabeth (later the Queen Mother) were well prepared to fight a guerrilla war, should Britain be overrun. They were also aware of plans by the Nazis to kidnap the royal family. Elizabeth Longford told the story in *The Queen Mother*:

> Nor would she be caught by possible German Parachutists without a fight. While King George was being trained to use a tommy-gun on home ranges at Windsor and Buckingham Palace, Queen Elizabeth was adding to her skills by learning to fire a revolver. Harold Nicholson expressed amazement. "Yes," she said to him resolutely, "I shall not go down like the others."
>
> The King cherished a secret determination to lead a British "Resistance Movement," if it ever came to that. And no doubt his wife would have taken the role of a tiny but irrepressible Queen Boadicea. . . .
>
> Meanwhile the range of Buckingham Palace was alive with pops and bangs. Lord Halifax, who had been given permission to use the Palace garden as a short cut to his office, was puzzled the first time he heard the shots and enquired their cause. "Her Majesty's target practice," was the reply. As his path ran nearby, he decided it might prove a short cut to the next world and chose another route to work.[11]

The Queen became a credible shot, and ladies in the royal household also learned how to use both rifle and revolver. Churchill turned Britain "into an armed camp."

> People came to believe, so powerful was the Prime Minister's magnetism, that with probably no more than half a dozen rounds of ammunition apiece they could crush any invader on the beaches, the landing grounds, the fields and the streets, and the hills. His fiery spirit animated everyone, from the King and Queen down. Buckingham Palace became almost an extension of Churchill's war room beneath Downing Street. Every week he turned up for a buffet lunch with the King and Queen. Once when he arrived his hosts were both "out practicing." Target ranges had been set up in the palace gardens as well as at Windsor Castle. There the King became deadly with

tommy guns, rifles and pistols and saw that other members of the Royal family and all the equerries trained regularly. Elizabeth after a few weeks became a proficient sharp-shooter. . . .[12]

Churchill's encouragement of the royal couple's preparedness was such that he presented Her Majesty with a revolver.

Russian Women at Arms

Like the British, the Soviet Union also drafted women—unmarried women—later in the war, but most of them *did* serve in combat. More than 70 percent of the 800,000 Russian women who served in the Red Army fought at the front.[13] In the early years, thousands had volunteered. Training as all-female units, on completion they were posted with the regular army. They then served on the front along with the men.

Even before women were officially accepted into the Russian Army, Liza Ivanova led a guerrilla force of men and women against the Germans. She fought for more than a year, then was captured, tortured, and executed by the Nazis. Originally joining the medical corps, Vera Krylova commanded a guerrilla group when the Nazis marched on Moscow, for which she was awarded the Order of the Red Banner. She later fought with a battalion of ski troops. A scout in the Crimea, Maria Baide killed fifteen Germans and wounded several others, rescuing her unit, which had been pinned down by German machine-gun fire. Wounded herself, she was made a Hero of the Soviet Union, Russia's highest honor.

The 586th Women's Fighter Regiment, the 587th Women's Bomber Regiment, and the 588th Women's Night Bomber Regiment were staffed completely by women pilots, engineers, and mechanics, and a Russian all-female airborne regiment, commanded by Major Tamara Alexsandrovna, flew more than 400 sorties and 125 combat engagements, shooting down 38 enemy aircraft. Phyllis-Anne Duncan's *Russian Women Pilots* states that these regiments "were so successful and deadly the Germans feared them, calling them Nachthexen—night witches."

Many Russian women were trained as snipers, a task for which they seemed particularly well suited. Ludmilla Pavlychenko is credited with killing an astonishing 309 Germans, while Lance Corporal Maria Ivanova Morozova, who served as a sniper with the 62nd Rifle Battalion, won eleven combat decorations. Perhaps the most famous, though, was Tania Chernova, the sniper at the siege of Stalingrad, a prominent character in William Craig's *Enemy at the Gates: The Battle for Stalingrad,* and a heroine in the film of the same name.

Women serving in Russian and German combat units experienced some of the most devastating of wartime horrors. J. David Truby knew this as well as anyone: "One theme is present in all of the stories: for sheer cruel, emasculating brutality, the female Nazis and Communists were every bit as imaginatively violent as their fellow male troopers."

Truby reports the recollections of a German who was at the siege of Stalingrad: "There was absolutely nothing more frightening than to have to face Russian women lying on their stone doorsteps and firing until they were dead. These women did not know what giving ground meant. They killed, then died, in their place."

Collette Nirouet

Although the days of going to war disguised as a man were pretty well past, Collette Nirouet managed to do just that to join the French Army during World War II. She was posthumously awarded the Croix de Guerre.

A German who defied Hitler and became a heroine during the war.

World War II gave Marlene Dietrich, as a true American immigrant, the chance to use all her talents against the evil she knew the Nazis to be, singing on the front lines in Italy, North Africa, France and finally Germany. The troops treated her as a fully fledged GI because she often popped up (against Army rules) on the front to entertain and console the men. Because she refused *not* to live in field camps close to battle with "the boys," generals from Patton to Gavin (and a few troopers in between) threw up their hands and gave her personal arms to protect herself if they couldn't. She, on the other hand, kept them loaded in case she ever got a bead on the enemy. Here she waits in Holland, getting ready for a big push with the 82nd Airborne under General Gavin. The 82nd thought (and hoped) they might as well take Marlene with them. After the war she brought these guns home to remind her of the "brave boys who gave so much."

From the *top,* the internationally recognized profile of the No 1 MK III Lee-Enfield bolt-action SMLE (short magazine Lee-Enfield) in .303 British caliber, with the AK-47 assault rifle, in 7.62 × 39mm, their rugged reliability contrasting with the high-tech L1A1, the British equivalent of the Belgian FN FAL (*Fusil Automatique Legere*), in 7.62 × 51 NATO, and the space-age-appearing Steyr-Aug, in .556 (.223). Women are not infrequently pictured with AK-47s, and to a lesser extent with Enfields—both types are common internationally.

In the early years of the war, German leaders sneered at Russia's use of women soldiers, claiming it to be a sign of weakness and predicting a quick defeat. As the war ground on, however, increasing numbers of German women saw service, many as antiaircraft gunners. By 1944, almost a half million women were in uniform. One, Hanna Reitsch, became the only woman to be awarded the Iron Cross First and Second Class. She was a test pilot for military aircraft, including the experimental jet-powered planes, and piloted many of the German high command throughout the war. On many occasions she flew through skies exploding with antiaircraft fire and projectiles from hostile planes. In her long career, she set more than forty flying records, in both powered and motorless aircraft, and survived several crashes.

In 1945, Hitler reversed his original position and approved the formation of mixed-sex guerrilla units and all-female battalions in the army. A battalion of women was organized by Nazi leader Gertrude Scholz-Klink to wage the final defense of the Fatherland. And as Berlin itself was threatened, the girls of the Bund Deutscher Madel were ordered into battle along with the boys of the Hitler Youth, armed with only sticks and stones.

Erna Tietz said the Nazis hid from the public the fact that women were used in antiaircraft units. She herself manned such artillery, and served at the front. At twenty-two, Tietz learned to man a searchlight, lighting up Allied planes at night. She served in Berlin in a searchlight unit termed *Scheinwerfereinsatz*. The lights would work up to a distance of nine thousand meters. When the Allies realized this, they flew at ten thousand meters or higher.[14]

In 1944, Tietz was retrained, this time as a *Flakwaffenhelferin*, "flak weapons helper," or antiaircraft gunner. She was in command and operated the gun, an 88-caliber, with two other women in the battery. When asked if she knew if she had hit any airplanes, she replied that she didn't (three times), but then added that she "did not know, because several guns were in position everywhere around us and I don't know if *our* gun, that *we* had in position, shot down a plane." The fact is she and other women *did* operate these guns.

The Avengers—Abba Kovner, Vitka Kempner, and Ruzka Korczak

During World War II, Nazi propagandist Joseph Goebbels wrote in his diary about Hitler's targeted victims: "One sees what the Jews can do when they are armed." Three brave and resourceful Jews from the Polish ghetto, including two teenage girls and a young man in his mid-twenties—Abba Kovner, Vitka Kempner, and Ruzka Korczak—led a band of Jewish guerrillas from the Baltic forest to join the Russian Army in the attack on Vilna, Lithuania's capital (known to the Jews as the "Jerusalem of Lithuania").

The threesome's extraordinary adventures in fighting the Nazis are the subject of journalist Rich Cohen's *The Avengers: A Jewish War Story*. A photograph on the front of the dust jacket, taken in the streets of liberated Vilna, shows the girls—engaging and with alluring smiles—gingerly clutching their submachine guns. Their comrade, a gifted poet, appears distant and serious. Though he has the look of a Jewish intellectual, he too carries a submachine gun; his gaze reveals the agony of death and terror. Between them, the avengers are credited with killing thousands of Nazis, and of acts of sabotage worthy of a battalion of engineers.

Where did they get their guns? To quote Abba: "There are plenty of guns. We just have to take them from the Germans." The three collaborated to blow up trains, shot and poisoned Nazis, and caused endless mayhem as creative resistance fighters.

> At seventeen, Vitka and Ruzka were perhaps the most daring partisans in the East, the first to blow up a Nazi train in occupied Europe.... After the liquidation of the ghetto, the Avengers escaped through the city's sewage runnels to the forest, where they lived for more than a year in a dugout beside a swamp, fighting along-side other partisan groups, and ultimately bombing the city they loved, destroying Vilna's waterworks and its power plant in order to pave the way for its liberation.

On orders, Vitka blew up a train. She located the right place for the blast, on a trestle passing over a gorge about twelve miles from Vilna. She set the explosives at midnight, by herself, leaving her partisans in the woods. She then rejoined the others, each armed with a gun and grenades.

Later, the train ran over the detonator. As it ground to a halt, the engine lurched off the tracks, into a gorge. Vitka ran alongside the wreck, throwing grenades inside the cars. As the Germans scrambled out of the train, they fired their pistols. But they did not go into the woods after the partisans. According to Cohen, this was the "first such act of sabotage in all of Occupied Europe.... Over two hundred German soldiers had been killed. The SS then marched into the nearest Polish town and killed sixty peasants."

After innumerable daring escapades, and as the war neared its tragic end, the avengers left a ravaged Poland. Vitka and Abba proved instrumental in the Jewish exodus to Israel. Ruzka went to Palestine, "where she would be literally the first person to bring a firsthand account of the Holocaust to Jewish leaders."

As the book nears its end, the bond between Abba Kovner, Ruzka Korczak, and Vitka Kempner is symbolically cemented into eternity by their joint burial plot: the former two already at rest, with Kempner ready to join them when her time comes.

Elaine Mordeaux and Resistance Fighters

As important as the women were who served with the regular forces, they proved to be the very backbone of the resistance units. There are hundreds of stories about the heroism and resourcefulness of these women warriors. One account, related by J. David Truby, is of Elaine Mordeaux. Tall and slender, and in her late twenties, she was one of the top French Resistance agents. She was a crack shot, and fluent in German and English. She proved invaluable to the maquis, the OSS (Office of Strategic Services), and the SOE (Special Operations Executive), especially in the follow-up to D day.

With her unit, Mordeaux delayed the advance of the 101st Panzer, wrecking the road so thoroughly that the accompanying infantry never engaged in battle. Resistance members remembered her fighting fiercely to the end:

> "Yes, I remember that battle and Elaine. She was throwing dynamite down at the Germans from a cliff about forty feet above the roadway. Her Sten gun

A few of the numerous books dealing exclusively with women and the military, or including information on that subject. Such literature continues to grow at a rapid rate; books on this subject are among the fastest selling from shops like the Military Bookman, New York City, source of the majority of the titles pictured. Yael Dayan, daughter of Israeli military legend Moshe Dayan. For a period, Mr. Dayan's driver was Ahuva Gal, then wife of submachine-gun inventor-designer Uzi Gal.

Facing page: U.S. Marines on maneuvers; all these troops, undergoing training, are women (c. 2000).

Above: Virginia Ezell, lieutenant colonel, U.S. Army Reserves. *Lower left,* Edward C. Ezell, and at *top right,* with munitions magnate Samuel Cummings, of Monte Carlo and Alexandria, Virginia. *Center,* Mrs. Ezell with General Kalashnikov, inventor of the AK-47. *Lower right,* shooting at a Fabrique Nationale test-range facility, Herstal, Belgium.

was empty, as most of us had run out of ammunition. I was wounded and fortunately for me, left for dead later. But, before I passed out, I saw Elaine throwing more explosives and trying to get more ammunition from the bodies piled around her. She was shot by a sniper, I remember that." Within less than an hour, the 200 men and women had inflicted 3,000 casualties on the Germans, wrecking nearly three dozen tanks and roughly fifty trucks. That had to help the allies, and it was a woman, Elaine Mordeaux, who led the way.

One of the most formidable resistance efforts was in Yugoslavia, where some 2 million women served with Tito and his partisans. When the first all-woman unit was formed in 1942, seven hundred women volunteered for the 110 positions available. More female units were formed, but were later merged with the men's units.

Women warriors were not unique to Europe. In the Pacific theater, Chinese women received training from the Soviets, the British SOE, and the American OSS before going into battle against the Japanese. Women served with the resistance fighters in the Philippines. An all-women regiment called the RANI of Jhansi was formed in the Indian National Army and saw combat in Burma.

America's Competitive Rifle Shooters and the Imperial Forces of Japan

In 1960, Robert Menard, a commander on the USS *Constellation,* attended at meeting between U.S. Navy personnel and members of the Japanese defense forces. Coming only fifteen years after Japan's surrender and the end of World War II, most of those at the meeting were veterans. Men who were once adversaries were now battle-christened comrades who could confide in one another.

One of the Americans asked a Japanese admiral why—with the Pacific fleet soundly defeated at Pearl Harbor and the U.S. mainland in a pathetic state of unreadiness—Japan had not invaded the West Coast. Commander Menard recalled his frank answer:

> You are right. We did indeed know much about your preparedness. We knew that probably every second home in your country contained firearms. We knew that your country actually had state championships for private citizens shooting military rifles. We were not fools to set foot in such quicksand.

In wartime conditions, with millions of men away in service, those home-based firearms would have likely been fired by women.

The Owl and the Pussycat—The Duke and Duchess of Valderano

The Duke of Valderano's *The Owl and the Pussycat,* a tribute to his late wife, Honor, is described as "a remarkable record of their extraordinary life together . . . the kind of life about which most of us can only dream . . . a whirlwind trip around Europe, Africa and the Americas . . . experiences during the Second World War to their time spent combating international terrorism and organized crime . . . an audience with Hitler . . . civil war in Angola. . . ."

Honor's father was a highly decorated Royal Air Force officer, who rose to the rank of air marshal. She was descended from Edward the Black Prince on her father's side, and from the Plantagenet kings on her mother's. She spoke six languages, could converse in another four, and read Latin and Greek. The duke (descended from Italian nobility) and his duchess were both born into wealthy families.

Further, Honor was "a splendid shot both with a rifle and a pistol . . . and was totally fearless." At the end of the war, the duke and duchess rented a property in Rome belonging to the Princess Pio di Savoia. Once while driving from Venice to Florence on a deserted mountain road during a moonlit night, they were set upon by bandits.

We emerged at the top of the pass and below us, we could see the lights of Florence. I had just said to Honor, "Thank God, we have made it all right," when a man jumped out into the road, some twenty or thirty yards in front of the car, and fired a burst from a sub-machine gun which went just over the top of the windscreen. In an instant, Honor, who was sitting in the front beside me with the window open, leaned out and with a single shot from my long barreled Browning pistol, which she had been carrying on her lap during the whole journey, knocked the bandit head-over-heels into the ditch. We were traveling at about thirty-five or forty miles per hour, and I had no chance of stopping, even if we had wanted to. There were some scattered shots from further up the hill, and then we were round the next bend. Shortly afterwards we came safely into Florence. It was probably the best shot I have ever seen—but then she was an expert pistol shot.

Array of revolvers, each type with documented use by women in service circumstances. From *top,* Colt Single Action Army Frontier (e.g., by revolutionaries in Mexico, Central, and South America), .44-40; at *right,* Colt New Navy swingout cylinder double action, .38 Long Colt. *Second row left,* French Modelle d'Ordonnance 1892 in 8mm (caliber commonly, though erroneously, termed Lebel). *Right,* Russian Nagant Model 1895, dated 1937 on frame. *Third row left,* Webley No. 2 MK I in .38 S & W; at *right,* Colt U.S. Model 1917 of the New Service, in .45 caliber (can also fire .45ACP). *Bottom left,* S & W U.S. Model 1917 in .45 caliber (similar to Model 1917 Colt). *Right,* S & W Model 38 Airweight "Bodyguard" in .38 Special with 2-inch barrel.

an in-your-face movement that never seemed relevant to us because we were already free.... [We were] taught to believe that rewards come from hard work and perseverance":

Events have proven this true, through no fault of society generally but due to the path taken.

In my case that path led to Dr. Edward C. Ezell, curator/supervisor of the Armed Forces History Division, National Museum of American History, Smithsonian Institution, who was having lunch with his staff one sunny St. Patrick's Day at the Crown Pub, across the street from the FBI building, in Washington, D.C. My sister Elizabeth, an old friend of Ed's, decided we would be a good match, so she drove her skeptical sister to Washington.

I think everyone looks at certain events as turning points in their lives. Mine surely was on that day. By the time we met, Ed was already an internationally recognized expert in his field. In addition to his work at the Smithsonian, he was a contributing editor to several defense publications, and had written a number of books including various editions of *Small Arms of the World* and *The Great Rifle Controversy*, the latter about the development of the M16 assault rifle. He would soon publish *The AK47 Story*, a history of Russian small-arms design and the development of the Kalashnikov assault rifle.

Self-loading pistols with known service associations in the hands of women, including *top left,* Colt Model 1908 in .380, Colt Model 1908 .25ACP, *above* Colt Model 1911A1 in .45ACP. *Top center,* British Model 1913 Webley .455; *top right,* Beretta Model 1934 in .380, *above* Tokarev Model TT33 in 7.62mm. *Center right,* Walther Model 5 in 6.35mm (.25ACP), *above* German Walther P-38 in 9mm. *Center,* famed German Luger, Model PO8 in 9mm. *Bottom left,* German Model 1896 "Broomhandle" Mauser in .30 caliber. *Bottom center,* Beretta Model 92FS, most high-tech of all; U.S. service pistol known as M9, with Bianchi-made Model M-12 holster. The Imperial War Museum collections include Violette Szabo's .32 Harrington & Richardson, Christine Skarbek Granville's Radom, and Flora Sandes's Ecceveria handguns.

Thoughts on a Path Less Traveled

Virginia Hart Ezell is the president of the Institute for Research on Small Arms in International Security, and a lieutenant colonel of the ordnance branch, U.S. Army Reserve. Her recollections cover over twenty-five years of experience in the firearms field, oriented toward military small arms. She came from a small town in Pennsylvania, "the runt of a pack of four girls in a matriarchal family." She attended an all-girls boarding school in Virginia's Shenandoah Valley. "Women's liberation of the 1960s was

Facing page: *Center left,* Elizabeth "Libbie" Custer, who devoted the remainder of her life to perpetuating the memory of her deceased husband, killed at Little Big Horn. Jones's book is filled with admiring references to women who were respected members of Tito's partisans. *Left center,* Amy Katherine Ross, markswoman and police sergeant, taught shooting skills by her father before she was a teenager (see page 193). American army auxiliaries stand for inspection, with Krag-Jorgensen rifles, c. 1918. *Top right,* Kim Bowen Coburn, holding bazooka, and with camouflaged face; at one time employed as a telephone lineperson, she is now with the *Newport News Star* newspaper.

Cabinet Portrait
O. W. WAGNER
NEW ORLEANS, LA.

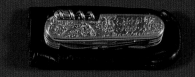

TWELVE MONTHS WITH TITO'S PARTISANS

MAJOR WILLIAM JONES

ATIONAL FRIDAY, AUGUST 11, 2000

Lamenting Destruction of the Temples

Israeli Army women read from the Book of Lamentations at the Western Wall in Jerusalem yesterday, the holy day of Tisha b'Av, as Jews marked the destruction of the First and Second Temples. The wall is the last remnant of the temple compound, on a hill that is also the site of Muslim shrines.

Rina Castelnuovo for The New York Times

FLASHPOINT: MIDEAST

TEMPLE MOUNT FUROR

Arabs rip today's ultra-right march

By LIBI DAN

Subject more than age determines the value of a postcard. This card from modern Israel is especially interesting because of the active role women have played in the military in that country.

Diplos to fight U.N. 'racism'

WASHINGTON — The United States will send a delegation to Geneva tomorrow to try to strip the anti-Semitic tone from an upcoming U.N. conference on racism. White House officials say the United States will boycott the conference in South Africa unless U.N. planners drop the anti-Israel rhetoric — drafts for the talks refer to "racist practices of Zionism," evoking the notorious 1975 resolution that Zionism equals racism. The Americans and Europeans also oppose language calling on them to pay reparations for slavery.

Brian Blomquist

HELLO MUDDER, HELLO FATAH: A Palestinian assembles a rifle yesterday during graduation ceremonies at a Fatah summer camp in the West Bank. *Reuters*

WORLD REPORT

Iran's culture war

Vigilante thugs 'command virtue and prohibit vice'

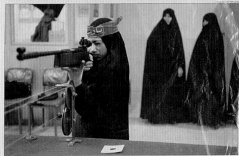

MORAL GUARDIAN. A member of the *basij*, the volunteer corps devoted to enforcing Islamic morality, takes target practice in Tehran.

Ezell's passion for his subject was contagious:

He opened up the world of the small arms community to me. Through Ed, I learned to appreciate small arms as the machines that they are, to be constantly curious about their manufacture and uses, and about the people who make and use them. He afforded me the awesome privilege of meeting and writing about the greatest engineers, designers and students of small arms of our time. It may seem an odd place for a woman, to work in a world some view as male-dominated and a bit rabid around the edges, but in reality it is an inclusive community no different than any other group of enthusiasts dedicated to their chosen area of study.[15]

In 1989 Ezell and his colleagues established the IRSAIS, a nonprofit organization with the goal of having small arms accepted as a serious academic subject. Virginia Ezell was selected as its head, while her husband would answer technical queries.

For a woman from a small town in Pennsylvania, born into a matriarchy where feminism had no part to play, working in the open and accepting world of small arms seems to be part of the natural course of things. It continues to be my privilege to attempt to record and disseminate information about the evolution of this most interesting of man-made machines.

The Vietnam War

During the U.S. war in Vietnam, women were used to deadly effect as combatants, infiltrators, and saboteurs by the Viet Cong and the regulars in the north. At her "Women Warriors" website (www.gendergap.com/military/Warriors.htm), Marilyn Brown notes that some three thousand women were serving in the South Vietnamese Women's Army in 1966, with many others fighting as guerrillas.

J. David Truby cites an incident that took place during the Tet Offensive in 1968. Fred Rexer, Jr., was a door gunner in a Razorback armed helicopter platoon. They were on a countersniper mission against a Viet Cong commando, firing a Chinese RPD light machine gun from the roof of a Cosen PX:

I was hand-holding my M60, and as the chopper swooped around the roof, I traded shots with the sniper. Finally I managed to catch the soldier in the open, moving from one ventilation duct to another, and wounded the quarry. The RVN's moved in and made the capture, taking the wounded sniper into a guarded hospital. Imagine my surprise when I learned that this vicious, wily terrorist who had pinned down forty U.S. and RVN soldiers and caused our gunship to scramble was a ninety-pound teenaged girl from the Red River Delta area. . . .

Women fought with the South Vietnamese government troops, the ARVN, as well. One, the mother of seven children, was known as "the Tiger Lady of the Delta" and served as an adjutant to the 44th Rangers. Portrayed as a devil by the Viet Cong, she was killed in battle in 1965.

A Miscellany of Other Twentieth-Century Conflicts

The proliferation of dependable firearms from the eighteenth century onward proved to be even more of a boon to women than to men. These "equalizers" did not depend on strength or reach or weight to be effective, or deadly, and women have learned to use them fully as well as men. Armed women have featured prominently in the scores of conflicts that have raged around the globe throughout the twentieth century and into the twenty-first. In Ireland, Israel, the emerging nations of Africa, and a host of other locales, these female freedom fighters (or rebels, depending on which side one is on) have definitely made their mark.

A rare photograph from the Boer War (1899–1902) shows a Mrs. Otto Krantz holding her horse's bridle, rifle under her arm and ammunition bandolier over her shoulder. She fought by her husband's side at Elandslaagte and on the Tugela River.

Women fought with ferocity beside their men in Cuba and the Philippines, and served with the revolutionary forces of Pancho Villa and Emiliano Zapata in Mexico between 1910 and 1920. J. David Truby, in his book *Women at War: A Deadly Species*, states that "one of Zapata's best snipers was a large, middle-aged woman who could handle a 7mm Mauser better than most males." In 1916, in recognition of her services, Zapata himself presented her with a scoped 1903 Springfield rifle that had been smuggled across the border. Truby goes on to say that another of Zapata's legendary *soldaderas*, "Adelita," was commemorated in a popular Mexican song, which the Zapatistas adopted. She was armed with a Colt Single Action Army revolver, in .44 caliber—and was known as a "fabled and savage fighter."[16]

During the conflicts that led to an independent Irish Republic, Constance Markievicz (known as the "Red Countess" for her leftist views) founded a paramilitary order called the Fianna Eireann in 1909. A captain in the Irish Citizen Army (with 120 men under her command) during the Easter Uprising of 1916, she was captured by the British and sentenced to death. Her sentence was commuted to life in prison just a few hours before her execution was scheduled to take place. Her Colt Thuer deringer pistol is pictured in *The Colt Engraving Book*, richly damascened on its barrel and hammer in gold. A rare photograph shows her holding a Colt New Service revolver. When she surrendered, she kissed her revolver before handing it over. She was proud of the number of men she had killed.

In the more recent "troubles" in Northern Ireland, the Irish Republican Army has used women warriors extensively. An all-female combat unit called Cummann nam Bann was formed in 1973. It was composed of women from age sixteen to twenty who were trained in weapons, explosives, and sabotage.

Although the Israeli armed forces do not currently use women in combat roles (though women are subject to the draft), female warriors were a major part of the nation's battles for independence. Zionist underground movements like the Haganah and the Lehi began training women for war in the 1920s, and they used the opportunity of World War II to wage guerrilla warfare against the British, whom they felt would never agree to a Jewish nation. Even after David Ben Gurion ordered that women could not continue in frontline combat, female commandos were active into the 1960s. One account states that General Moshe Dayan's daughter, Yael, a lieutenant in the Israeli Army, was fighting as a commando in 1966.

A shocking development of the ongoing strife between Israel and the Yasser Arafat–led Palestinians and their wave of terrorists was the attack by a female suicide bomber, on January 27, 2002, in Jerusalem. One Israeli died with the bomber, and 113 were injured. Responsibility for the tragedy was attributed by the terror group Hezbollah to a female student from Al Najah University, in Nablus, a city on the West Bank. In a few rare instances other female suicide bombers have since followed her example— each hailed as a heroine to the Palestinian cause.

According to the "Women Warriors" website,

Bracha Fuld trained Jewish women soldiers, led her own platoons, captained military detachments, and fought at the Battle of Sarona in Palestine during WW II. She was fatally wounded in 1946 during a battle with a British tank corps. A street in Tel Aviv is named in her honor.

Hanna Armoni was one of the Lehi's leaders and women were fully integrated as fighters in the organization's ranks. In 1946 both the Haganah and its combat arm, the Palmach, which grew out of the all-Jewish units who fought with the British in WW II, went "underground."

Israel's War of Independence, fought against the Arab nations of Egypt, Jordan, Lebanon, Iraq, and Syria as the British mandate ended, initially saw some twelve thousand women serving in combat roles, in mixed units on the front lines. Later, when pressure from Orthodox Jews was brought to bear, many (though not all) were moved to all-women units assigned primarily to support functions.

At *lower left,* exhausted female defenders of the new (and doomed) Spanish Republic. *Above,* Nationalist Rebel troops (Spanish Foreign Legion), relaxing on entering Drun, accompanied by a sole Red Cross nurse. Photographs, 1936, from the National Portrait Gallery, London (Herald Archive). Published in *Arms and the Artist,* Phaidon Press, London (1977). Remaining images from a Free China publication, *Pictorial Monthly,* No. 1, dated February 1939. Women are shown in uniform, at target practice, exercising, and in military assembly and review, depicted in cheaply printed magazine format.

Africa saw a huge upheaval during the twentieth century as independent nations emerged from European colonialism, and most of the wars for independence had women as leaders as well as combatants. A Rwandan woman led a revolt against the Belgian colonial government in 1926–27, and in 1929, the Nigerian Aba Riots, also known as the Women's War, saw tens of thousands of women take arms against the British, harassing government agents and attacking European-owned property.

Joyce Nhongo was commander of the Women's Detachment during Zimbabwe's war of liberation. She led her guerrilla forces in a number of battles including one which occurred [two] days before the birth of her daughter. When Zimbabwe won its independence she was appointed Minister of Community Development and Women's Affairs.[17]

Rani Gaidinliu was thirteen when she joined the fight for Indian independence in the 1920s; within three years she became one of the military and tactical leaders of the movement. Eventually she was betrayed, captured, and imprisoned for fourteen years.

Indian independence, the Greek Civil War, and the rise of the Chinese People's Republic—all called upon women to lead troops and fight on the front lines along with men, upholding a tradition of women warriors that has only lately begun to be appreciated.

Women in Law Enforcement

The first opportunity for women to serve in a law enforcement capacity in the United States came in 1845, when matrons were assigned to the New York City Police Department. They did not carry weapons, did not have arrest power, and were not considered real "policemen."

It wasn't until 1893 that Mrs. Marie Owens, a police officer's widow, was appointed to the

Chicago Police Department by the mayor, becoming the first woman police officer with arrest powers.

But it was Mrs. Alice Stebbins Wells, a graduate theological student and social worker living in Los Angeles, who became the first true policewoman, in 1910. Her principal area was youth problems, and her beat places of recreation like dance halls, skating rinks, and movie theaters frequented by women and children. Present-day juvenile bureaus and crime-prevention units reflect her pioneering work.

Women were beginning to perform police duties in other parts of the country as well. In 1915 the International Policewomen's Association was formed, and its charter was adopted a year later in Washington, D.C. The organization disappeared during the Great Depression.

Police and military handguns by Smith & Wesson and some of its competition. *Upper left,* S & W .38 Military and Police pre–Model 10 revolver, with S & W at *top right.* Nickel-plated handcuffs, also by S & W. At *left center,* Glock Model 17, and at *right center,* S & W Sigma Model SW 99. At *bottom,* S & W Model 639, and Ruger P94. Related badges represent a small number of the mix of personnel using specimens from this group, and more, of handguns—a relatively small percentage of which—though steadily increasing—being women.

62

Then, in 1956, at a San Diego meeting of Women Peace Officers of California, the International Policewomen's Association was reorganized as the International Association of Police Women, and, ultimately, as the International Association of Women Police (IAWP), which continues to the present with fourteen regional chapters worldwide. Its goal is to have a chapter in every country in the world.

According to the National Center for Women & Policing, a division of the Feminist Majority Foundation, which monitors the status of women in police work through annual surveys, in 2000, women comprised 13 percent of sworn law-enforcement personnel nationwide. That figure is up from 9 percent in 1990 and a low of 2 percent in 1972. Women of color in police work represent only 4.9 percent of personnel. In top-command law-enforcement positions, 10.3 percent of supervisory positions and 13.7 percent of line operations positions are filled by women, although more than half of the agencies polled had no women at all in their top positions.

Some of the early barriers to hiring women officers, such as unfair and unreasonable physical requirements, have been eliminated, and gradually the "men's club" attitude is changing as older officers are retiring. Where women do serve, they have been found to be far more effective than male officers in handling domestic disputes and rape and sexual-assault crimes against women.

Recruiting continues to be a problem, because many women see law enforcement, the most recent National Center for Women & Policing study states, as having an "aggressive and authoritarian image, an image based on the outdated paramilitary model of law enforcement that is still in widespread use." The report adds, "Once on the job, women often face discrimination, harassment, intimidation, and are maliciously thwarted, especially as they move up the ranks."

Women in Military Service for America Memorial—Arlington National Cemetery

On October 18, 1997, after eleven years of development, the Women in Military Service for America Memorial was dedicated at the Ceremonial Gates, Arlington National Cemetery. The memorial individually and collectively honors women who have served in the U.S. armed forces. Also honored are women who have assisted in direct support of the services, particularly during times of war or conflict.

The exhibits, visited by some 200,000 people annually, and as reported in the Memorial Foundation's website, www.womensmemorial.org, include:

- An interactive, computerized register that places the names, records of service, photographs, and memorable military experiences of individual servicewomen at the public's fingertips.

- A showcase of artifacts, text, and memorable images depicting the various roles women have played. Among the permanent exhibits are World War II and the Korean War. Temporary exhibits rotate throughout the year and have included "The Making of a Memorial."

- The fiftieth anniversary of the Women's Armed Services Integration Act, the Women's Memorial dedication, and the twenty-fifth anniversary of women in the Chaplain Corps.

- A Hall of Honor, which provides recognition to those women who have served with particular sacrifice, distinction, and achievement, and specifically those women who died in service, were prisoners of war, or were recipients of the nation's highest awards for service and bravery. This majestic room contains the sister blocks of marble used for the Tomb of the Unknowns, appropriately located with flags of the states, territories, and services.

- Film presentations depicting the roles women have played in America's military history in the memorial's 196-seat state-of-the-art theater.

- A panoramic view of monumental Washington.

- Voices of women throughout the ages captured in an arc of quotations etched into glass tablets, accompanied by the peaceful sound and movement of water in the Memorial Fountain and Reflecting Pool.

63

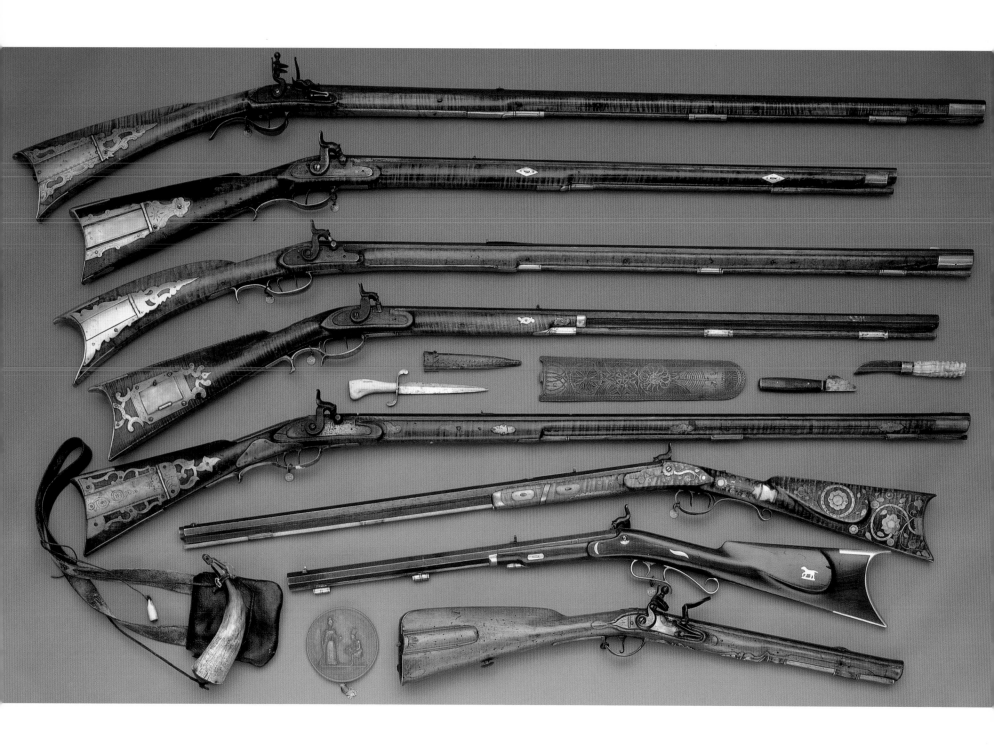

CHAPTER III

America's Unique Firearms Experience

It is only a question of time when to be a skilled markswoman will be numbered among the latest achievements. And not only will it be a recreative sport, but a step toward woman's independence.

—Mrs. E. B. Belknap, Wyoming, New York, quoted in *The American Shooter*, 1916, "Oh! How Those Women Could Shoot"

Firearms played a vital role in America's settlement and expansion, and American women were no strangers to their use—and even their manufacture and repair. Both the necessity to hunt and the need for protection from the sometimes hostile native culture made firearms a crucial component in the American experience.

An early example is the raid on the Dr. John Woodson home in Jamestown, Virginia. The Woodsons had come to the New World in 1619 on the *George*, with Governor Sir George Yeardly. In 1644, Sarah Woodson was at home with her two young sons and a neighbor, Ligon.

Facing page: Select group from Diane Ulbrich collection; composed primarily of Kentucky and plains rifles believed to have been made for women. From *top*, Kentucky rifle made in Allentown, Pennsylvania, with 39-inch barrel, the lock marked C. BAKER; converted to percussion, believed from Reading, Pennsylvania, school; lock inscribed THOS. TYRER RICHMOND; Virginia rifle, by O. & Z. Sheetz, converted to percussion; left side of half-stock rifle (*third from bottom*) made by Koppikus, Lexington, Kentucky, profusely inlaid with silver; New York state rifle with C.H.L. on patchbox lid; *bottom*, flintlock of German make, with fruitwood stock, an import to U.S. market, c. 1720. Although some of these and guns that follow could have been owned by a boy, the author regards the presence of striking decorations more likely to suggest a lady's ownership.

Charming image of girl with her Stevens single-shot .22-caliber rifle, c. 1900.

Her husband, returning home after attending to a patient, was attacked and killed by Indian marauders within sight of his family. Sarah quickly barricaded the house and handed Ligon a musket. She hid her son Robert under the washtub, and her other son, John, in the potato hole. When two Indians came down the chimney, Sarah scalded one with a pot of boiling water, and brained the other with an iron roasting spit. Ligon is said to have killed a total of eleven of the attackers with the musket before the Indians retreated. Descendents of the Woodson boys identified themselves as the Washtub Woodsons and the Potato Hole Woodsons. Among them were the notorious frontier outlaws from Missouri, Jesse and Frank James.

Guns and Women in Pioneer America

Although in some ways an inconsistent source, probate records occasionally reveal that the use of firearms was not limited to men in pre–Civil War days. The estate of Connecticut citizen Thomas Scott

was divided into two sections: one listing goods "delivered to the Wydow Scott for her use," and another listing "Goods of Tho: Scots sett aparte for his 3 daughters." Mrs. Scott received a fowling piece, a matchlock musket, a sword, and a pair of bandalers. The three daughters received a snaphance flintlock and "1 cok mach musket," apparently a matchlock.[1]

Historian Clayton Cramer has compiled an immense amount of data on the subject of pre–Civil War arms, and analysis of the information is helping to construct a picture of women and firearms from this obscure period.

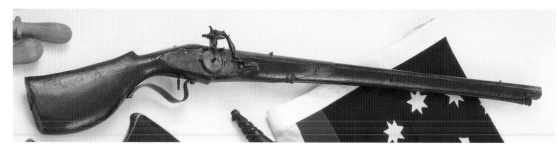

One striking discovery was the Reverend William C. Smith's frontier account, *Indiana Miscellany*. In it Smith observes that, despite a shortage of provisions during the War of 1812,

> usually they had plenty of meat. All the men were excellent hunters—some of them real experts. . . . Some of [the women] could handle the rifle with great skill, and bring down the game in the absence of their husband. . . .[2]

The 1818–19 journal of Henry Rowe Schoolcraft noted that Ozark children, on reaching the age of fourteen, "have completely learned the use of the rifle, the arts of dressing skins and making [moccasins] and leather clothes." His observation likely included girls as well as boys, because he also states that he failed at making small talk with his hostess and her daughters: "They could only talk of bears, hunting, and the like. The rude pursuits, and the coarse enjoyments of the hunter state, were all they knew."[3]

Cramer reports that

> at one isolated cabin, the lady of the house was home alone, and instructed Schoolcraft and his companion not only about "errors in our dress, equipments, and mode of travelling," but also "that our [shotguns] were not well adapted to our journey; that we should have rifles. . . ." Schoolcraft and his companion were astonished "to hear a woman direct us in matters which we had before thought the peculiar and exclusive province of men." It is very clear that Ozark women as hunters surprised a New Englander like Schoolcraft, but his comments also imply that what was surprising was the sex of his instructor, not widespread knowledge of hunting and firearms.[4]

Top left: Wheel-lock carbine that came to the New World on the *Mayflower*. Found in a restoration of the home of Pilgrim John Alden, Duxbury, Massachusetts, 1924. .50-caliber, restocked in American walnut. A gun of this type was likely used by Sarah Woodson in fighting off Indian attack. From the National Firearms Museum, Fairfax, Virginia.

Left: Rifle by Adolph Koppikus, of Lexington, Kentucky, and signed on the lockplate; richly decorated with silver, emphasizing floral designs—including seldom-observed flower pot and pearl inlay; overall length 42¾ inches; maker later moved to Sacramento (1849), then San Francisco.

Right: Hunting bag and horn of Jerusha Post; note oval brass plaque inscribed in script with her name. Horn 13¾ inches in length, along the outside curve. Post was born in Old Saybrook, Connecticut, in 1766; she married Peter Spencer, 1785, in Westbrook.

Measuring overall 59⁹⁄₁₆ inches, the rare early Kentucky rifle is smoothbore, .62 caliber. A piece of undoubted service in the Revolutionary War, the inscription LIBERTY OR DETH on the brass patchbox could have invited execution if the person carrying it had been captured by the British. Barrel made with lug to accommodate bayonet. Likely Lehigh Valley, Pennsylvania, manufacture, c. 1770.

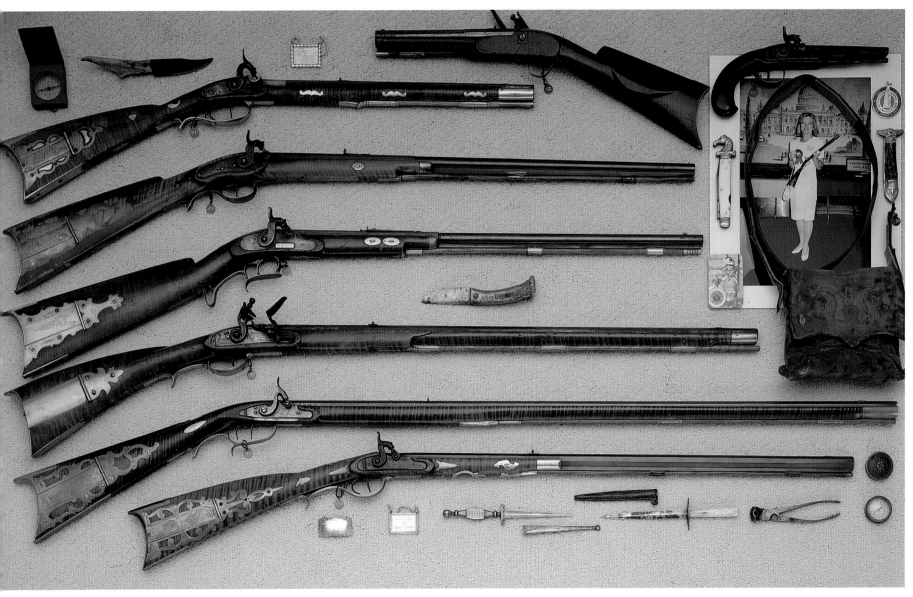

67

Top right, Kentucky pistol by Dreppert, also pictured *bottom left* of image on page 69. *From top,* rifle marked by A. Armstrong, Philadelphia; overall length 19 inches; c. 1800. John Setel (Cashtown, Pennsylvania) rifle with MARY LOU inscribed on the patchbox—accompanied by heart-pierced-with-arrow motif; it was believed to have been made for the gunmaker's wife; 29¾ inches overall. *Third from top,* Kentucky rifle with STEELE & WARREN—

ALBANY on lock, and ROBINSON on barrel; 34¾ inches overall. Maine-made rifle with A. SPALDING engraved on silver-inlaid lock panel; 40¾ inches overall. Kentucky rifle with lock marked TRYON PHILADA; probably made for a boy; attributed to Moll, Allentown, Pennsylvania; 43¼ inches overall. *Second from bottom,* Kentucky rifle by Elias Crissey, Hooversville, Somerset County, Pennsylvania; Bedford County styling, made in 1875—

prizewinner at the State Fair and Centennial Exposition of 1876; overall 51 inches. *Bottom,* rifle by Valentine Schuler (Shuyler), New Philadelphia, Ohio; 14 silver inlays; 42 inches overall. *Top right* shows collector Diane Ulbrich, winner of "Best Inlaid Rifle" at 1991 Kentucky Rifle Association convention, with Schuler rifle.

Women Depicted on Firearms, Swords, and Accessories, Seventeenth to Twenty-first Centuries

Carving on powder horns for Kentucky and New England rifles, though often rustic folk art, occasionally includes a female figure. After the Declaration of Independence in 1776, a horn might be carved with the liberty cap, or the Goddess of Liberty wearing the cap. These are quite rare, and only a few examples are recorded.

Motifs of women on the rifles themselves are also extremely rare, and have only been recorded as engraved, not carved. When women are depicted on elaborate swords or other edged weapons, the motifs are generally classically or patriotically inspired.

The dawn of the Industrial Revolution saw the expansion of the colonial trade in elephant ivory and mother-of-pearl, as well as the introduction of machine-made repeating handguns and longarms. Handgun grips became a medium for carved motifs in numerous themes. Some of those depicting women were in the form of patriotic themes, such as the Goddess of Liberty, the Liberty head, and the Goddess of Justice; only a few were nude figures. The majority of grips are in ivory, with pearl a distant second. Colt firearms are more likely to display these carvings, although some appear on other makes, including Smith & Wesson and Remington, with a limited few on Manhattan and Sharps pepperboxes. One of the finest carved-ivory grips is a New Model Army double-action Colt, deluxe engraved, with Hiram Powers's sculpture "The Greek Slave" carved on the right panel.

Women also appeared in firearms engravings, including a few on the Winchester Model 1866 lever action. Among the Winchester motifs were the Goddess of Liberty, Canova's "The Three Graces," and "The Greek Slave." A spectacular specimen of the Moore single-action revolver portrays the inventor's daughter. During Victorian times, the presence of women as engraved motifs was subject to the limitations of the day's conventions. These engravings are therefore inclined to be chaste.

In modern times, convention has been thrown to the wind and erotic motifs occasionally have been engraved, although nude women are generally depicted as classical figures. A few guns have been made as gifts for wives and girlfriends, in which portraits are engraved or inlaid. Twentieth-century artisan Alvin White was proud of the carved ivory grips he had created for single-action Colt revolvers, which were charming tributes to his wife, Violet.

Nancy Hart confronts British troops. Only known print; from the Hargrett Rare Book and Manuscript Library, University of Georgia Libraries.

Facing page: From Diane Ulbrich collection; most with striped maple stocks; from the *top:* Kentucky rifle by Jacob Stoudenour; Bedford County style; relief carved and with 20 silver inlays; 37⅛ inches overall length. Kentucky by Jacob Demuth; smoothbore; lock marked DAVIDSON AND CO.; probably made in Easton, Pennsylvania; 38½ inches overall. *Third from top,* English-made lock marked ROBBINS; extensive inlays including silver and abalone shell; rifle made in Lehigh Valley, Pennsylvania, c. 1825; 53¾ inches overall length. Rare lady's-scale Kentucky by master gunmaker John Armstrong; JA on lockplate; 57 inches overall. Elegant Lehigh County, Kentucky, signed JOHN RUP on barrel; HJ on wrist escutcheon; first quarter nineteenth century; attributed to Jacob Kunz and John Rup; overall 55½ inches. Elaborate half-stock Kentucky of Philadelphia make, marked TRYON; 1840s. *Second from bottom,* flintlock fowling piece with bird's-eye maple stock; overall 55 inches. *Bottom right,* a German Jaeger, likely a boy's or coach gun, of c. 1720; stock of fruitwood, with wood patchbox; 28¾ inches overall. Kentucky pistol converted from flintlock; likely made for a boy; the lock marked DREPPERT, early nineteenth century, Lancaster, Pennsylvania, area; 9 inches overall.

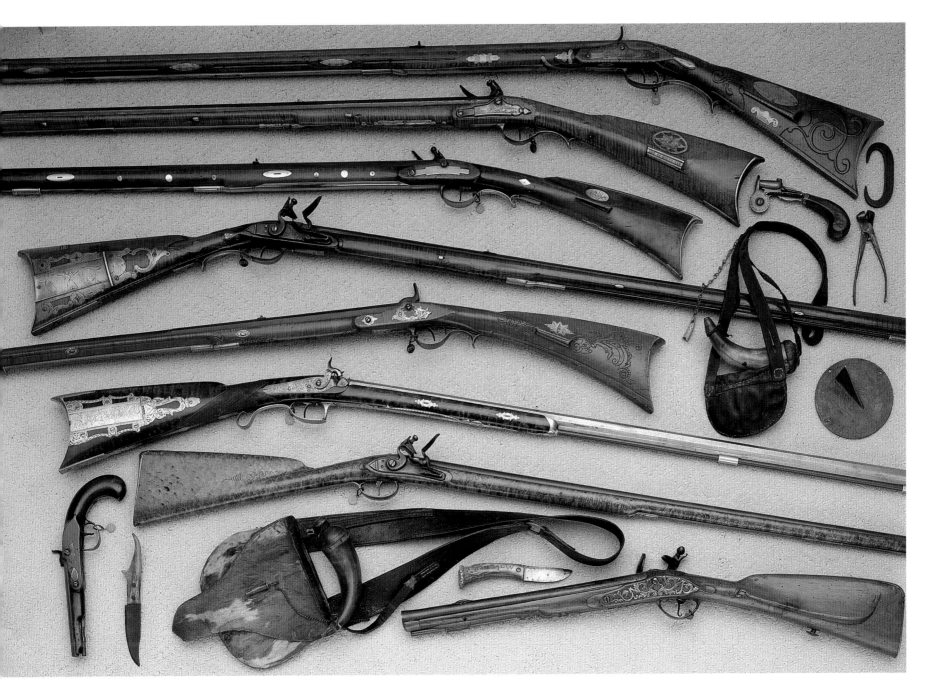

Comic Almanacs, c. 1835–50s, and Rough-hewn Frontier Figures

An expression of American pioneer spirit, and symbolizing the bold and hardy ways attributed to American frontier women, comic almanacs proved to be highly popular in the mid–nineteenth century not only in America but also in England. Illustrated with cartoon drawings, the tales presented women in heroic roles.

Despite their unadulterated imagination, the almanacs mirrored American women and the times in which they lived. Popular and widely distributed, they celebrated the freedom of life in America and helped attract hordes of immigrants to the New World. The tall tales gave readers, especially in the more "cultivated" East and in Great Britain, a general perception of America's frontier folk as rough and ready, prepared to take on all hazards. Including women in this picture was quite novel. These brave, bold, and independent women were a breed apart from any previously encountered in literature.

Even as late as the 1820s, frontier America could reflect on some two hundred years of hardship, and was destined to encounter yet another century of the same, producing a unique culture of self-reliance, independence, and hardiness that remains cherished to this day by millions of American women.

The Untimely Fate of a Huntress

Young Lottie Merrill, of Wayne County, Pennsylvania, had a reputation as an accomplished huntress—the *New York Sun* had published an account of her killing two black bears. When she was subsequently killed by her prey, *The Chicago Field* related the grisly details on April 9, 1881.

The Untimely Fate of a Huntress. . . . Miss Merrill has met a most tragic death, having been attacked in her hut by six bears, killed and eaten by them, and her remains, with the carcasses of her assailants, having been consumed by the burning of her cabin after the termination of the fatal combat. It appears she had, on the day of her death, killed a fine buck, which she had dragged home on the snow. Six hungry bears, attracted by the smell of the blood, had followed the trail to Miss Merrill's cabin, and, it is presumed, attacked her after devouring the carcass of the deer. The brave girl had undoubtedly made a heroic defense, as she had evidently killed two of the bears before being overpowered. The carcass of one bear had fallen against the cabin door, on the inside, imprisoning them all, when the cabin took fire and destroyed both the girl and her assailants. Within the cabin was found one of her hunting boots, her foot still remaining in it, her bent hunting knife, and the antlers of her last deer. Over three hundred persons attended her funeral. She was buried near her burned cabin, and upon her grave were placed a pair of antlers and a hemlock slab, bearing the following rude epitaph: "Lottie Merrill lays here. She didn't know what it was to be afeerd, but she had her last tussel with the bars, and they have scooped her. She was a good girl, and she is now in heaven. It took six bars to get away with her. She was only 18 years old."

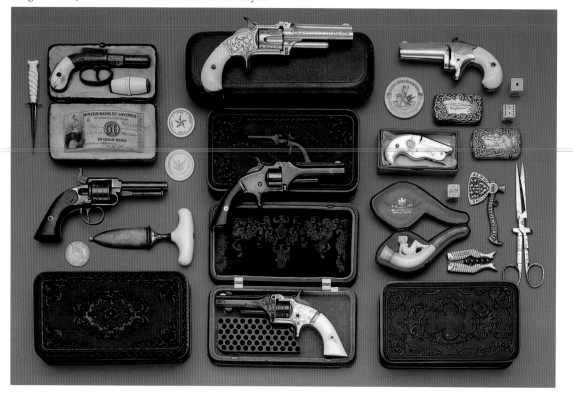

Protectors available to women in the mid–nineteenth century. *Top row, from left,* all three guns with ivory grips, Allen & Wheelock single-shot in .30 caliber, of pepperbox style; S & W New Model 1½ in .32 rimfire, nickel-plated, on top of its leather and wooden case; Colt 2nd Model deringer, .41 rimfire, nickel-plated; *center row,* Warner revolver in .30 rimfire caliber, above its gutta percha case and accompanied by walrus ivory-handled push dagger by Michael Price, San Francisco; S & W 1st Model, 2nd Issue revolver, .22 short rimfire with rosewood grips, silver-plated frame, on top of its gutta percha case; Hopkins & Allen deringer, .22 rimfire, nickel-plated and with pearl grips; *bottom center,* S & W 1st Model, 2nd issue revolver, engraved and with gold-plated frame, ivory grips, within its gutta percha case; at *bottom right,* in floral-motif gutta percha case, a Forehand & Wadsworth .22-caliber revolver.

Ida Wells-Barnett—Pioneer Crusader for Civil Rights—Carried a Pistol

In Georgia, in 1899, Sam Hose was thought to have murdered a white man, and was lynched by a mob of two thousand whites. Ida Wells-Barnett, of Memphis, Tennessee, researched the charges and proved that Hose was innocent. When she wrote editorials in her newspaper denouncing the lynchings of blacks by white mobs, the paper was raided, the presses wrecked, and the building torched.

Wells-Barnett traveled to many Southern towns investigating lynchings, and her campaign helped to lay the groundwork for the American civil rights movement. Armed with a handgun for self-defense, Wells-Barnett was quoted as boldly stating: "I felt if I could take one lyncher with me, this would even up the score a little bit."[5] She also maintained that "a Winchester rifle should have a place of honor in every black house."

Above, left: Model 1861 Navy pair; the relief-carved Goddess of Liberty ivory grips are considered the finest known. Etched decoration attributed to Tiffany & Co. Recipient of these revolvers was the original Buffalo Bill, William Mathewson (founder of Topeka, Kansas), to whom the cased pair was presented, in appreciation of his saving an entire wagon train. See *Steel Canvas* for image from Waterman Lilly Ormsby's *Bank Note Engraving* with female motifs, including Goddess of Liberty. Such scenes were an important source for engravers like Gustave Young in executing panels on firearms.

Women and Arms in the Old West
Martha Maxwell, "the Colorado Huntress"

Sturdy, independent, daring, and adventurous were the women who made the trek to the American West. From 1841 to 1866, approximately 350,000 emigrants traveled the 2,400 miles by wagon from the Missouri River all the way to California and Oregon. Knowing how to use a gun was as necessary as knowing how to deal with all the other chores of pioneer life.

Symbolic of the bold way in which many women embraced the West was the experience of Martha Maxwell, "the Colorado Huntress." Credited by many authorities as the founder of modern taxidermy, she was America's premier female naturalist. She caused a sensation at the Philadelphia Centennial Exhibition of 1876 with her extraordinary wildlife displays, which featured animals in natural poses within their habitats. The Kansas and Colorado Building featured "Woman's Work," a breathtaking presentation of her trophies, hunted and col-

Presentation Model 1862 Police from Colonel Samuel Colt to Mrs. Howell Cobb, whose husband was a powerful Georgian in national politics. One of about a half dozen known presentations from Samuel Colt to women. At the same time as the Cobb gift,

Colt presented bookcased Model 1862 Police revolvers to Mrs. John B. Floyd and Mrs. Jacob Thompson. All three women were wives of government officials destined to play important roles in the Confederacy during the Civil War.

71

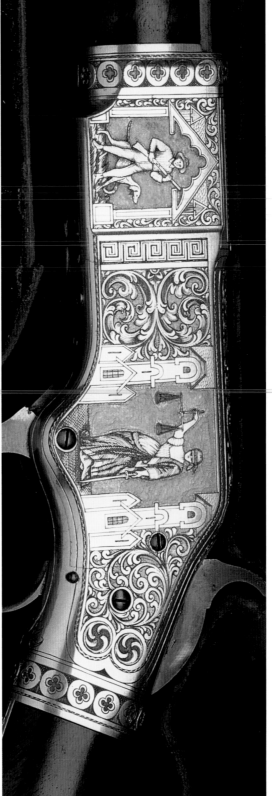

Extremely rare photograph from c. 1865 of Anna Elizabeth Dickinson (1842–1932), an orator, actress, and playwright. She was known as an eccentric egoist, but was considered a heroine by the abolitionists. She advocated harsh treatment of the South. The revolver is a Colt Model 1855 Sidehammer, engraved, and with ivory grips, the casing of velvet-lined rosewood— undoubtedly a presentation to her. Connecticut's Ann Sophia Stephens (1813–86) received a similar presentation, inscribed from Colonel Colt. She was editor of *The Ladies Companion*, founded *The Ladies World* (1843), and wrote the novel *Fashion and Famine*.

Center: Cased Winchester Model 1866 rifle engraved by John Ulrich, with Goddess of Justice motif. Serial number 79863. Displayed for many years at the Winchester Gun Museum, New Haven.

Presentation cavalry saber and scabbard, by Schuyler, Hartley & Graham, and inscribed to Captain F. X. Ebner, by the Sacramento Hussars, a historic California unit, April 26, 1872. Gilt bronze and silver-plated nickel-silver hilt, and nickel-plated steel scabbard. Seated Goddess of Liberty within elaborate design of the hilt. Damascus steel blade, etched and gilt, with silver overlay.

Facing page: S & W revolvers ideal for use by ladies. From the *top left*, No. 1 First Issue, engraved and with ivory grips, silver-plated and blued. At *center*, No. 1 Second Issue, with woman's head finely carved on ivory grip. At *right*, No. 1 2nd issue, silver and blue finish, also with ivory grips. At *right* in case lid Model 1½ Old Model, and to its *left*, on lid of its leather case, Model 1½ New Model. At *bottom*, two from the series of what is believed to have been five .32 single-action revolvers, presentations from wealthy New York commodities dealer William Ingraham Russell, 1891. Each was cased, engraved, and with inscribed pearl grips and case-lid plaques. Russell and his wife, with eight friends, termed themselves "the Immortal Ten." Three of the women were identified by grip inscriptions: Jill, Anna, and Ella (wife of Russell himself).

FREEDOM'S WREATH.

Freedom's wreath depicts Goddess of Liberty with tributes to heroes of free thought and action. Patriotic images of this ilk have inspired decorations on firearms throughout American history since the Revolutionary War.

Below: Moore deringer pistol, serial number 7, of Mary Doubleday; mate to similarly embellished pistol made for her husband, Abner, serial 15. Gold-plated, with blued barrel. In the popular mind of today, a pistol of this type would be associated with women of ill repute.

Facing page, top left: One of a series of books and articles by Elizabeth Custer, widow of Civil War and Plains Indian adventurer George Armstrong Custer. Having accompanied her husband on some of his expeditions in the West, and therefore aware of a soldier's hardships firsthand, she devoted the remainder of her life following his death at the Little Big Horn to perpetuating his memory as a frontier hero. She resided mainly in New York City thereafter, and died in 1933. By her own statement, a Remington deringer was her constant companion while traveling in the West.

Facing page, bottom left: Metropolitan Navy Model revolver, presented to Pauline Orr, daughter of a colonel in the army of the Confederate States of America, and niece of the governor of South Carolina. Although the identities of the presenters of this Civil War–period revolver remain unknown, Miss Orr distinguished herself as a founder of the Mississippi State College for Women, and as chairman of the English Department from 1885 to 1913. Upon retirement, she devoted six years to traveling the United States as a vocal advocate of the cause of women's suffrage. The Pauline V. Orr Building, at the college, was dedicated in her honor in November 1954.

Facing page, right: An unidentified Idaho huntress, with powder flask, shot sack, capper, and double-barrel percussion shotgun.

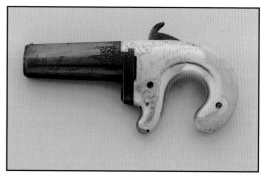

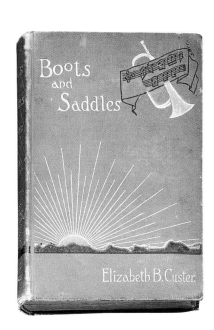

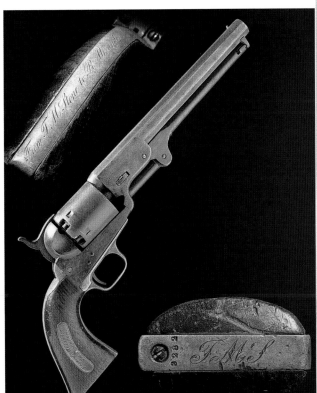

lected by herself. Mounted in a Western setting were elk, deer, mountain lions, mountain sheep, and an array of other North American game.

Her skills had been inspired by a combination of a love of wild animals, a keen instinct as a huntress, and a sculptor's eye at immortalizing her prey. At the age of ten, in her Wisconsin home, she grabbed a gun and shot a rattlesnake ready to strike her four-year-old sister. As a young woman she married lumberman James Maxwell, and in 1860 they immigrated to Colorado. As a hunting companion to her husband, she became a dedicated outdoorswoman. The work of a local taxidermist gave impetus to Mrs. Maxwell's determination to excel in this difficult field—dominated, of course, by men.

Her home in Boulder served as a site for exhibiting these masterful creations. In 1873, the city offered her an exhibition hall, which became the Rocky Mountain Museum. In 1875 the museum moved to Denver, and soon thereafter she was invited to put on the Centennial Exhibition presentation. Yet another accolade was the naming of the Rocky Mountain screech owl as *Scops maxwelae* in her honor—since she was credited with its discovery as a distinct species.

At the time of the exhibition in Philadelphia, the Evans Rifle Manufacturing Company of Mechanics Falls, Maine, presented Mrs. Maxwell with a rifle. On accepting the rifle, she stated: "The use of this rare gift shall be directed by a love of science and in pursuit of objects for the study of natural history; it shall be my trusted companion and assistant."[6] Her sentiments were in stark contrast to those of Texas Jack, who claimed, in a promotional statement about *his* Evans, "I can clean out a whole band of Indians . . . with it."

77

Ella Bird-Dumont: A Deadly Shot with Her Winchester Model 1873 Rifle[7]

J. T. Bird was a celebrated Texas Ranger, one of ten recipients of a presentation-inscribed Winchester Model 1873 rifle from the Texas legislature. He little knew that it would become the treasured possession of his bride to be.

Resigning from the Rangers around 1876, he pursued a wintertime whirlwind courtship of Ella Elger, of Young County. Of their first meeting she would remember fondly:

> There I beheld mounted on the most beautiful large black horse . . . a man in full western costume, that of a Texas ranger. . . . He had with him a fine Winchester rifle of the latest model which was awarded him by the legislature in 1873 for an Indian fight. It had a silver shield on it with his name engraved. . . .[8]

In 1877 they married. Bird rejoined the Rangers that March, and the following December they headed to the buffalo-hunting range. Now using

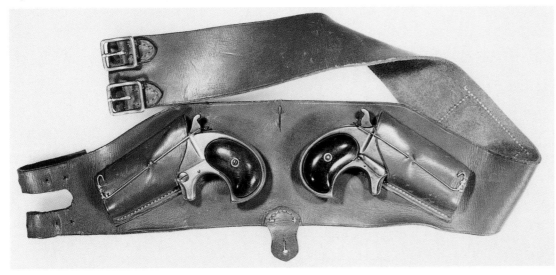

Facing page: Martha Maxwell, master taxidermist and gifted huntress, proudly displaying her presentation Evans repeating rifle, and attending to two of her popular mounts, as well as in hunting garb, ready to do some Colorado bird shooting with her side-by-side hammer shotgun. Naturalistic exhibit from the Colorado and Kansas pavilions at the Philadelphia Centennial Exhibition of 1876. Evans repeating rifle at *top,* the early model (.44 Evans 1-inch-long center-fire cartridge at *left*); at *bottom,* the more common New Model, with its .44 c.f. cartridge (1½ inch) at *right.*

Above: 24-inch holsters for a pair of Remington double deringers, of c. 1900. With its small waist size, this leather rig could well have served a woman. Note picture of Elinor Church Haight, of Indian Lake, New York (c. 1904–05), holding her Remington double deringer. Judging from the fishing tackle kit and the animal skins, as well as the white-tailed-deer catch-all and rifle rack, Miss Haight likely enjoyed the Adirondack outdoors.

In sizes ideal for use by ladies, this group of single- and double-action revolvers ranges from the Model 1 Second Issue at *top right,* to the .32 Single Action at *upper left,* to the .38 Single Action 2nd Model at *left center,* to the .38 Single Action 1st Model at *right center.* At *bottom left,* the No. 1 Third Model presented to opera singer Nilssen, and at *bottom right* the .38 D.A. with embellishments by Tiffany & Co. The yachting scene is from the back cover of the seldom-observed 1884 S & W catalog.

a Sharps heavy-barrel rifle, Bird presented the Winchester 1873 to his wife. She later recalled:

[He] was anxious that I should learn to use a gun. . . . Most every afternoon when [he] came in off the hunt Mr. Bird would give me training with my rifle shooting at targets. . . . I never neglected practicing [and] was about ready to banter my husband for a shooting match.

She soon became one of West Texas's best shots, and could shoot off the heads of prairie dogs. She claimed to have killed three wild turkeys with a single shot, and twice she killed a buffalo with a single shot.

Once while her husband was off dealing with his buffalo-hunting operation, she was con-

Third Model Colt deringer pistol, made expressly for Edith Kermit Roosevelt, second wife of Theodore Roosevelt. Gold inlaid and blued monogram attributed to engraver Cuno A. Helfricht. Grips of mother-of-pearl. Late 1880s–early 1890s; serial number 19959. Stanley Bullock recalled how the pistol came to him:

[President Roosevelt had invited] cattlemen and cowpunchers to ride in the inaugural parade [January 20, 1905]. . . . We were quite an atraction [sic] and had a hell of a time. Rode in the parade, roped a policeman and acted like the Easterners expected us to. Teddy had all of us up to the White House for a reception immediately after the parade. A few days later I was a luncheon guest of the Roosevelt family and Mrs. Roosevelt gave me that little gun as a memento of that occasion. The initials E.K.R. on the gun are hers. . . .

fronted with a situation that was potentially deadly. Comanche Indians had made a call to the Bird home:

Now imagine our plight. This house was about twelve feet square, two beds, five children, three women and seven Indians in it. . . . The object of their visit seemed mainly to trade clothing for groceries. . . . They kept on prowling and behold they found my [Winchester]. They set up the awfulest plavering and talking, every one had to look at it. The Chief took quite a fancy to it [and] began laying off his clothes, one by one. . . . It was useless for us to offer any protest as to our right in the way of etiquette. Our language was dead to him but finally the truth dawned on Mrs. Jones [one of the women] just before it was everlastingly too late. . . . She tried to explain to him why I would not part with the gun, that it was a present to my husband by the state. I wanted to add that it was given for killing Indians but thought it might be good policy to leave off that part of it.

Soon her husband and his fellow hunters returned, and the Indians departed—without the treasured rifle.

Yet another incident occurred, also with deadly possibilities, while camping on a buffalo hunt. Comanches were apparently sneaking up to the camp:

Behind the wagon sheet there was some fast work going on. I grabbed my gun, filled it with cartridges,

filled up my cartridge belt, buckled it around me . . . [and] ran with all my might. I felt sure they would follow in pursuit of me. . . . Pretty soon the form of a man appeared in the direction of camp. Of course, I knew it was an Indian in search of me. I could see him in the sky light and he looked large and savage. I thought at first I would kill him which would have been an easy matter. I drew a fine bead on him once, twice, and the third time came near pulling the trigger.[9]

She did not fire, fearing it would attract the other Indians. Soon she learned that caution had saved her from accidentally shooting her husband.

When her husband died in a blizzard, in 1888, she kept meat on the table with that Winchester. She also made gauntlets and vests for cattlemen of the area from skins of deer and antelope she had shot. Wildcats and lobo wolves fell to her sharpshooting in the 1890s.

An attractive and still youthful widow, Ella Bird found that her prowess as a shot stood her in good stead in chasing off unwanted suitors. On one occasion she walked out to meet a cowboy, holding her rifle at her shoulder. Her warning was "Keep riding," which he did—already knowing of her reputation as a crack shot. As stated by another: "Sure, I would rather any man in Cottle County would shoot at me than Mrs. Bird."

79

Ella Bird's Winchester Model 1873, the stock with its presentation plaque from the thirteenth legislature to her future husband, and the silver inscription that he added, symbolizing his name. Serial number 3518; a first variation, with special-order set trigger. The presentation plaque was attributed by curator Richard Rattenbury to custom gunmaker J. C. Petmecky.

Women of the West, ranging from cowgirls, ranchers, huntresses, and exhibition shooters to adventurers and outlaws. Of the latter two categories, Martha Jane "Calamity Jane" Canary at *upper left* (with Sharps rifle) and at *bottom center* (seated, with Stevens pocket rifle), "Rose of the Cimarron" (with large revolver, seated, *upper right*) and Pearl Hart (*right*, standing, foot on bucket, holding Winchester). Not pictured: the notorious Belle Starr, Cattle Annie and Little Britches, and Laura Bullion (a sidekick of Ben Kilpatrick of the Wild Bunch). *Top center,* believed to be Eagle Eye and his wife, Neola, contemporaries of Oakley and Butler. *Center,* Mamie Francis, performer and exhibition shooter. *Center right,* a strikingly beautiful member of Buffalo Bill's Wild West, with Colt Six-Shooter. Colorado huntress Martha Maxwell, at *bottom right. Top right,* revolver carried in apron by Margaret Mary Wilvers. *Bottom right,* Wyoming huntress proudly poses with coyotes shot by her, in protecting sheep or for bounty.

In 1897 Ella Bird remarried and settled in Paducah, Texas, where the rifle continued to serve her well. In 1934 Mrs. Ella Bird-Dumont presented the Winchester to the Panhandle Plains Historical Museum, where it symbolizes the valiant women, all too often forgotten, whose courage helped to tame the wild frontier.

.32-caliber Iver Johnson in the Apron of Margaret Mary Wilvers

Born in Belgium in 1866, Margaret "Maggie" Mary Wilvers and her family moved to the United States shortly thereafter. Eventually finding her way to Saline County in north-central Kansas, she married George Snyder in 1885. The couple kept a small farm not far from Salina.

Outlaws and hobos were a concern to both men and women alone on the prairie. Maggie carried a .32-caliber Iver Johnson top-break revolver in her apron pocket at all times to protect herself and her two children on the farm. One day the infamous Dalton Gang stopped and commandeered the farm while they rested and watered their horses. Although they did not threaten them, Maggie was prepared to defend her family.

Some years later Maggie gave the revolver to her son Henry, who eventually presented it to his daughter, Vera. Over the generations the gun has been passed down through the family, and today is owned by Maggie's great-great-grandson, Jeffrey K. Reh, general counsel and vice-general manager for Beretta U.S.A. Corporation. The revolver is displayed in Reh's office, a reminder of his plucky ancestor.

Smith & Wesson Model 1½ revolver number 112812, in .32 rimfire, inscribed on bottom of frame in Old English AUGUSTINE/TOMBSTONE/A.T. Accompanied by license issued by the city to a prostitute February 1, 1898, for the business of "ill fame." Owners Stephen and Marge Elliott, of the Tombstone Western Heritage Museum, are now searching for a photograph of the Augustine.

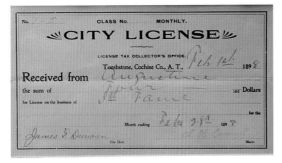

Although numerous references can be found in literature to black American women owning or using firearms, only one image has been found to date that depicts such an instance. Taken during the late 1880s, this studio photograph shows Mary Fields of Cascade, Montana, holding a Winchester Model 1876 Carbine (page 84).

Born a slave in 1832, Fields moved to Toledo, Ohio, after the Civil War. There, she found employment at the Ursuline Convent where she formed a close friendship with a nun named Sister Amadeus (believed by some to have been the daughter of her former owner). When Sister Amadeus was sent to Montana in the late 1870s to establish a school for Native American girls, Fields initially remained in Toledo. However, when she learned that her friend had become seriously ill, Fields went west.

Standing some six feet tall and weighing more than two hundred pounds, Mary Fields was an imposing figure. She was also an accomplished horsewoman who could manage a wagon and team with ease. In common with many who ventured west, Fields was quite familiar with firearms. Indeed, her contemporaries noted she never went out of doors without a Smith & Wesson revolver tucked safely underneath her apron.

While her distinctly unladylike behavior was tolerated by the nuns at St. Peter's Mission, it was not appreciated by the presiding bishop. Consequently, about ten years after she arrived, she was forced to leave. Fields then moved to nearby Cascade, Montana, where she set up a restaurant. Her generosity, however, soon caused that business and another similar one to fail. Through the efforts of Sister Amadeus, Fields was subsequently awarded a government contract to deliver mail in Cascade County, thus becoming the second woman and first black American woman to work for the United States Post Office.

For all her boisterousness, Stagecoach Mary, as she was popularly known, was also a gentle woman. She was held in great affection by the entire town of Cascade and her birthdays (she had two due to an uncertainty of exactly when she was born) were official school holidays for a number of years prior to her death in 1914.

—Herbert G. Houze

81

American Women Deer Hunters
Mary Augusta Wallihan

In America, women hunted deer with considerably greater freedom than their European sisters. Although Annie Oakley, Calamity Jane, and other superstars set the example, a number of lesser-known huntresses had successfully broken the gender barrier by the end of the nineteenth century.

The husband-and-wife team of Allen Grant Wallihan and Mary Augusta Wallihan studied and photographed deer on the frontier in the 1890s. The pair used rifles as well as cameras, as venison was their principal food. Mary, an excellent shot, often provided the food while Allen took the pictures. The final plate in their book *Hoofs, Claws, and Antlers* shows Mary posing with her thirtieth deer.

The majority of these images are advertising from the firearms industry from as early as the late nineteenth century to the end of the twentieth. A quite striking young woman at *bottom right* is dressed for the field and holds what appears to be a Model 1889 Remington double-barrel shotgun. Color poster at *center*—also used on the front cover of the Hansen & Co. catalog—depicts father Jay Hansen, son John, and daughter Kelsey, in a painting by Jim Kritz.

Right: At *left*, bronze sculpture from the Woolaroc Museum, portraying frontier women. These were among a dozen entrants in a national competition held at the auspices of Oklahoma governor Marland, in 1927, to honor the pioneer mother. The winning bronze showed a woman with her young son, clutching the Bible. Period advertising from UMC and Peters, and, at *right*, part of a frontier-women series by artist Mary M. Mazziotti (represented by O. K. Harris Gallery, New York); the acrylic on panel work (60 × 48 inches) is entitled "Hera" (1997). The inspiration for this piece is a photograph of Pawnee Bill's wife, May Manning.

Below: Collection of photographs from the Adirondack Museum, documenting dedication to white-tailed-deer and bear hunting by Adirondack huntresses. The most celebrated and accomplished of these was Paulina Brandreth, seated at *center* with lever-action Winchester Model 1873 rifle across her lap. To *left,* her sister, with Colt Lightning slide-action rifle. At *bottom right,* one of the Whitney family.

Above: Selections from the private collections of Teresa Shaver (at *right*) and Jennifer Hunter (at *left*), ranging from cowgirls and rodeo stars, to firearms-industry and cigarette advertising, to period photography and pulp-magazine illustrations. Hardy and self-reliant women of the West were fertile soil for innumerable visual interpretations.

Women lined up with an array of rifles, believed photographed in Wyoming, in the late nineteenth century. Stagecoach Mary, celebrated figure from Montana history, cradles Winchester Model 1876 carbine. Courtesy of Sister Mary Rose Krupp, Ursuline Convent offices, Toledo, Ohio.

Paulina Brandreth

Another remarkable woman, Paulina Brandreth, was not only a deer hunter and naturalist of considerable skill, but also a gifted writer, who began publishing articles on the subject when she was only nine years old. She grew up in the Adirondacks of upper New York state, and wrote under the name of "Paul" Brandreth in order to avoid the prejudice shown by many outdoors publishers toward women in the field. Paulina authored *Trails of Enchantment,* one of only seven books on deer hunting by women (out of more than two thousand total). It is still considered one of the finest of them all.

On one hunting trip, Paulina shot a huge, thirteen-point buck. Examining it as a possible addition to the American Museum of Natural History, famed naturalist Roy Chapman Andrews stated that it had the largest and heaviest antlers of any white-tailed deer he had ever seen.

Encouraging Women Shooters

If some publishers discriminated against women, many others went out of their way to encourage their participation in hunting. The editors of such publications as *The Rifle, Shooting and Fishing,* and *The American Field* bemoaned the fact that not enough women were given the opportunity to enjoy target shooting, hunting, and other firearms-related hobbies. *Shooting and Fishing* ran an editorial on December 5, 1889, titled "Women and Their Guns."

> We have always entertained the belief that there were many sports which have hitherto been recognized almost wholly as men's sports, that could be properly indulged in by ladies with great benefit to their health and happiness. With such impressions it is not strange that we were attracted to an article in the December number of "Outing," under the above title, by Margaret Bisland, who essays to teach her sisters as to the proper outfit to select by those aspiring to taste the delights of the chase.

The National Rifle Association and its magazine *American Rifleman* have always encouraged women to take up shooting and hunting. Women appear in the magazine frequently, and are depicted on a number of its covers.

Covers and contents of *The American Rifleman* document the National Rifle Association's support for the involvement of girls and women in the shooting sports. At this writing twelve members of the NRA board are women. Sue King, one of the twelve, has predicted that it will not be too many years before half the board will be composed of women.

85

bridge ——— vollen torrent which noisily tumbled in its stony ——— or more feet below us, the bark peeled off fr——— and the usually sure-footed porters were hurled ——— down into the rushing waters, whereas they at ——— ll were dashed headlong into the dubious channel, ——— pelled to struggle for their lives. For a hazardou——— nt, only a moment, although time and space a——— longated into eternities during like ——— tected from injury by my Palan——— y head d——— and completely submerged in thi——— in jeopardy of drowning. Several addi——— l ——— aren poor fellows, had all they could do ——— precipi ously descended the bank and plun——— im wate——— and extricated me with great difficult——— anquin in which I was helplessly buried beneath a——— ss of cushions, besides being under water.

Poor, ——— llows, in their wild efforts to carry me out of the——— the steep rugged bank, hopelessly slipped and ——— a second time, with serious injury to my spine, ——— struck the rocks. A second rescue, and I was ——— and helpless, as I thought per-manently disab——— bank. When I had somewhat recovered from t——— realized that my life depended upon reaching the ——— earliest possible moment.

Meeting the Ge——— at Massindi, where he had preceded me, I did ——— he fact of the disaster to him, although my helple——— ot possible to conceal.

THE COURT DRESS.

86

In its sheath, May French-Sheldon's dagger (a theatrical design) measures 11 inches in a straight line from one end to the other. It is of bronze, with paste jewels and steel blade. Without the scabbard, the dagger measures 8¹¹/₁₆ inches. The blade is not sharp, but the tip certainly is. The script inscription on the bronze throat reads BEBE BWANA/NOVEMBER 22./1893. On the back of the bronze grip is inscribed: POISONED DAGGER WORN BY/M.FRENCH-SHELDON/THROUGH HER EAST AFRICAN EXPEDITION/PRESENTED TO/WILLIAM Y.CHUTE/AS A TOKEN OF HEARTFELT AFFECTION.

Dagger pictured in *Sultan to Sultan,* including the above image, within the bodice of Bebe Bwana's dress. Evidently she had more than one on safari, since she speaks of trading to Sultan Mireali a "music box, and a jewelled belt and dagger" for his personal spear.

American Women in Africa

The African bush has captivated the imagination of Western civilization since reports began to appear in the press and in literature in the eighteenth and early nineteenth centuries. The ivory trade was but one means by which stories of the Dark Continent spread in Europe and the United States. Often the more daring of American women who risked death there were wives of explorers or taxidermists, such as Mickie Akeley and Sally Clark. But the first American woman to brave the dangers of Africa was a wealthy daughter of New England, married to an Englishman. She was May French-Sheldon, popularly known as "Bebe Bwana."

Bebe Bwana

Born in 1848 into a prominent American family, May French-Sheldon was an adventurer and traveler who braved the African bush, leading safaris where few white men, let alone women, had gone. A fascination for ethnology and anthropology resulted in her first African expedition in 1891, which was recorded in her book *Sultan to Sultan,* published a year later in Boston.

Preparing to set out from London's Charing Cross Station, she describes a "myriad of boxes and a bewilderment of non-descript packages— my tent, gun, table, chairs, pistols, photographic aparatus [sic] and personal affects. . . . I was without doubt actually bound for East Africa. . . . Gruesome remarks were intermingled with inspiring words of faith in my success. . . . 'Do be reasonable, and abandon this mad, useless scheme.'"

In Zanzibar, the sultan, much taken with her, ordered that her caravan be organized. To ensure the staff's loyalty, her headman had decreed that any deserter would serve "a year in the chain gang." But, she writes, "the Sultan . . . promised . . . far worse punishment,— to cut their throats if black-listed."

The expedition numbered 154 persons, plus forty volunteers, guides, and porters' slaves, all listed by name in *Sultan to Sultan.* The book also includes photographs and drawings of wildlife, native handicraft, pots and utensils, jewelry, weapons, habitat, members of tribes visited en route, and articles from Bebe Bwana's equipage. Her pistols were a pair of Colt New Model Army or Navy revolvers (with matching double holsters and cartridge belt), and her rifle a Model 1886 Winchester, for which the natives made a special decorated leather case.

Her weapons were with her constantly. Once she frightened off an attacking mad dog by firing one of her Colts over its head. When camped at night "my gun and pistols were my close companions. . . . I felt I should have at least thirty-one chances before reloading if attacked. . . ."

It wasn't long before her authority was tested by threats of mutiny.

> Then or never I realized I must demonstrate to these mutinous, half-savage men that I would be obeyed, and that discipline should be enforced at any cost. Only for one instant in perplexity I paused, a vulture flew overhead, I drew my pistols and sent a bullet whizzing after it, and brought it surely down at my feet, to the astonishment of the revolting men.
>
> With both pistols cocked, suddenly I became eloquent in the smattering of the Swahili which I knew, without interpreter, inspired with fearlessness and strength I started through the center of the rebellious throng, pointing first one, then the other pistol in quick succession at the heads of the men, threatening, and fully prepared, determined, and justified to shoot the first dissenter. . . . I turned upon them and said, "Every man who is not on his feet with his load on his head, when I have counted three, I will shoot!" They knew I would, and knew I had been empowered to do so by the Sultan of Zanzibar. . . .

Her shooting skills were impressive. She records bringing down a gazelle at 240 yards with her Winchester, and in less than an hour shooting nineteen partridges for the cooking pot with her revolver. At Lake Chala (near Kilimanjaro), Bebe Bwana was rowed out on a makeshift craft into waters teaming with crocodile. She shot ducks, as well as a monkey of an unknown species.

May French-Sheldon's contributions to the study of African culture have been termed unprecedented. She added to the appreciation of African geography and ethnography, and was a popular figure on the lecture circuit. In 1892, she was one of twenty-two women invited to join the Royal Geographic Society. Unfortunately, the invitation was withdrawn when conservative members refused to consider the presence of a woman in the society.

But Bebe Bwana had proven that a woman was capable of doing what men could do. Of four subsequent expeditions, one was to the Belgian Congo in 1894. She eventually retired in England, where she died on February 10, 1939, in London.

Mickie Akeley

Delia Reiss Akeley, called "Mickie" or "Bibi," was a woman of grit and courage whose skill as a huntress saw her taking the largest trophy elephant from Mount Kenya and a record-breaking Cape buffalo from the Tana River. She was the first wife of Carl Ethan Akeley, creator of the African Hall at the American Museum of Natural History, and a pioneer in modern taxidermy and museum exhibits. Akeley traveled extensively in Africa, was an inventor and filmmaker, an artist and author, a keen hunter, and a conservationist. For years Mickie was his daring and resourceful companion, without whom he would have perished in Africa on more than one occasion.

The Akeleys were married in 1902, and made their first safari together to Africa in 1905. Mickie went as Carl's assistant on an expedition to study and collect specimens of wildlife in British East Africa before the onslaught of settlers could diminish the animal population. The couple's professional hunter was R. J. Cuninghame, later to distinguish himself accompanying Theodore and Kermit Roosevelt on their grand safari of 1909–10.

On the 1905 expedition, Mickie had already taken one elephant as a specimen for the Field Museum, and was with Carl and Cuninghame on Mount Kenya seeking additional full mounts for display. Since Carl had used up his licenses, Mickie was called on to take over, and succeeded in bringing down a record bull. She was the first white woman ever seen on Mount Kenya.

In August 1909, the couple again sailed from New York, traveling via London, Paris, and Naples to East Africa. Arriving in Mombassa in mid-September, they rode the "lunatic express" railroad up to Nairobi, finalized their expedition, and purchased hunting licenses specifying a total of more than 380 animals plus unlimited lion and leopard—then considered vermin.

With 118 men on staff, the party set out from Nairobi on September 23, toward the Tana River region. The Akeley and Roosevelt parties would meet near the Nzpia River of western Kenya. Yet another American the Akeleys would meet on safari was James L. Clark—whose wife, Sally, was cut from the same cloth as Mickie.

The expedition continued into Uganda, in search of an ideal specimen of bull elephant. Finally, while leaving Uganda, the party happened upon an elephant—which quickly charged them. This one proved particularly fearsome, attacking the Akeleys three times. Carl related

how, in the second charge, the angry bull "had winded us and in an instant he started, ears spreading and closing, trunk thrashing the bush right and left, screaming with rage":

> Twenty yards away I fired a .475 and he stopped, then I threw more of the same as quickly as possible at the vulnerable spot which I should know so well and all the time M. sending in those little swift ones of hers as fast as she could work her gun and the result! He took them as a sand bank might—just a little spurt of dust and that was all.

Akeley wanted to quit, saying that the elephant had more than enough shot in it, but Mickie insisted that he finish the job. Akeley reloaded. In the third and final charge, the elephant finally went down. Akeley wrote that Mickie "sat down and drew a long breath before she spoke. 'I want to go home,' she said at last, 'and keep house for the rest of my life.'"

On another occasion, Carl was badly injured by a charging elephant. Mickie, at camp ten hours' walk away, took control as soon as she

Facing page: With a huge tusked elephant taken by her in Kenya, 1905, on an expedition for the American Museum of Natural History, Mickie Akeley demurely stands by her conquest. In another photograph she stands in front of the downed beast, with R. J. Cuninghame lying on one of the substantial tusks. At *right*, R. J. Tarleton and his wife, posed within their compound in Nairobi.

Above: Impressive array of books on hunting and shooting, all authored by women. Among the collection is the best book ever done on white-tailed-deer hunting: *Trails of Enchantment*. Paul Landreth was the pseudonym of distinguished huntress Paulina Landreth. Next to the front jacket cover for that title is a photograph of antiquarian bookseller Carol Lueder, seated with a stack of these captivating books.

got the news. While rain poured on her tent, she prepared medicine, bandages, and supplies for the rescue. When some of the men refused to accompany her, she waved her Mannlicher rifle and taunted them as "mommy's boys." When one of the natives grabbed her coat, trying to stop her, Mickie "struck out wildly with the stock of my gun. As he released me and fell, I ran back to the waiting men. To my dying day I shall feel the shock of that blow and hear, above the roar of rain and wind, the awful thud of a body striking the sodden earth."

At night, well into the bush but lost, she fired her rifle into the air and heard a responding shot. Carl was only a half-hour's walk away. Her bravery and determination saved her husband from death.

Carl also suffered numerous health problems on the trip, and it was Mickie who hunted for food and was in charge of the camp. Carl wrote in one of his journals that "once more Mickie pulled me back just as I was slipping over to the other side."[10]

It was while on this expedition that Carl Akeley had the vision of creating the African Hall of the American Museum of Natural History—to be his greatest work. Returning to New York in 1911, he set out to build it. In the four-elephant group displayed there, the last bull, called the "rear guard," was one of those taken by Mickie.

But the arduous times in the bush had strained the marriage. When the African Hall group was nearing completion, Mickie left for France to serve as a volunteer with the American Expeditionary Force in World War I. She returned a year later to an enraged husband, who resented her leaving him. It would be four years before their divorce, but their life together was over.

In August 1924, Mickie directed her own expedition to East and Central Africa, funded by the Brooklyn Museum of Arts and Sciences. She led

yet another expedition to Africa in 1929. Her book *Jungle Portraits* is a colorful record of both adventures. She later remarried, outlived her new husband, Warren Howe, and spent the remainder of her years living comfortably in a Daytona Beach, Florida, hotel. She died on May 22, 1970.

Carl also remarried, but although his new bride, Mary Jobe Akeley, joined him on some of his expeditions, she was never the brave huntress that Mickie had been.[11]

Osa Johnson—Explorer, Filmmaker, Huntress

In 1921, at New York's Explorer's Club, Carl Akeley met a husband-and-wife team of film-maker-explorers named Martin and Osa Johnson. He had an idea that documentary films about Africa could underwrite the building of the African Hall. Akeley persuaded the Johnsons to film in East Africa for the American Museum, and the ensuing production, *Trailing African Wild Animals*, proved a huge success.

The Johnsons flew "his and hers" airplanes, rubbed elbows with cannibals and headhunters as well as the rich and famous, survived numerous scrapes with wild animals, circled the globe six times—and through their films and writings became one of the most famous couples of the twentieth century.

Kansas-born Osa Johnson had never ventured more than thirty miles from her hometown before her marriage. Martin, on the other hand, had years of world travel under his belt—including trips with the writer Jack London. Their courtship lasted but a few days, and they married when Osa was still a teenager.

91

Several of the female authors featured in Kenneth Czech's *With Rifle and Petticoat: Women as Big Game Hunters, 1880–1940*—as well as the front of the dust jacket for that volume. All too often examples of these titles that have survived lack dust jackets. To the dedicated collector, a book without a jacket is anathema, though it should be noted that jackets did not become a standard feature until the early twentieth century. Interesting evolution of jacket design, over the next one hundred years.

At *center left,* Osa Johnson with Mickie and Carl Akeley, during an East African expedition funded by Kodak founder George Eastman. At *upper right,* Osa squares off against a mighty Cape buffalo, wielding her favorite Model 1895 Winchester, in .405 caliber—a viciously recoiling cartridge that the diminutive woman handled without complaint. Note this rare picture of the Johnson gun rack—only a portion of their imposing arsenal, many of them *her* arms.

Osa quickly demonstrated a natural affinity for adventure and an instinctive skill as a rifle shot. Martin dedicated his book *Lion: African Adventure with the King of Beasts,* "To Osa, my wife, who holds the gun." He says of her shooting, "I call it a talent because she had never done any shooting as a girl. Yet with a few days practice she began to bring in pigeons, wild goat, and fish as a result of her marksmanship."

One of the most dramatic moments of the Johnsons' film footage shows Osa being charged by an angry black rhinoceros in Africa. With one cool and deliberately placed shot she dispatches the creature as it is coming straight for her. While this sequence may have been dramatized through the magic of editing, the fact that she did shoot charging animals is well documented.

In fact, it was Osa who protected her husband from dangerous game: "In the serious work she also took a very serious part. She handled the gun while I cranked the camera." In *Safari,* Martin's 1928 thriller about their earliest trips to the Dark Continent, he says,

> Twice she has dropped elephants at my feet.
> Once a lion came charging for me in the open with swift powerful springs. I dared crank because Osa

held the gun. At fifteen feet she fired. The enraged beast stumbled but came on. She fired again. This time she dropped him so close I could touch his mane with my toe.

The feeling that Osa is so accurate a shot means a lot in my camera work. I am usually intent on the focusing and speed of film, and often do not even realize the danger facing us. Osa stands there coolly, gun in hand. If the game is too quiet she wanders forward cautiously and stirs it up. She seems to have no nerves.

On December 1, 1923, the Johnsons began a four-year expedition to Lake Paradise in Kenya, under the sponsorship of the Museum of Natural History, New York. One of their important patrons, Kodak founder George Eastman, would later join the expedition—an opportunity that the millionaire industrialist, a keen shot and huntsman, could not pass up. Also joining Eastman and the Johnsons was Philip Percival, who had accompanied Theodore and Kermit Roosevelt on their celebrated safari of 1909–10.

Early during Eastman's visit, Osa spotted a cobra on its way toward her guest. She quickly and quietly signaled one of her aides to kill the poisonous snake. Eastman wryly remarked: "A fine hostess you are. Snakes for dinner."

In 1925, the Duke of York—later King George VI—and the Duchess of York helped pull Osa out of Kenya's Eauso Nyiro River, where her safari car had become mired. They were joined by professional hunter Pat Ayer (who was guiding the royal couple on a shooting safari), and Mar-

93

ASTRID BERGMAN SUCKSDORFF

Tiger in Sight

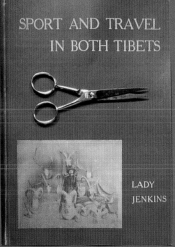

SPORT AND TRAVEL
IN BOTH TIBETS

LADY JENKINS

A
SPORTSWOMAN
IN
INDIA

ISABEL SAVORY

LIPPINCOTT

Peril
is My
Companion

HELEN
FISCHER

HOW I SHOT MY BEARS

MRS. R. H. TYACKE

I Married
A Hunter

MARJORIE MICHAEL

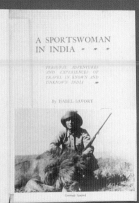

A SPORTSWOMAN
IN INDIA

PERSONAL ADVENTURES
AND EXPERIENCES OF
TRAVEL IN KNOWN AND
UNKNOWN INDIA

By ISABEL SAVORY

SHOT WITH "INFALLIBLE"

SHOT WITH "INFALLIBLE"

SHOT WITH "INFALLIBLE"

SHOT WITH "INFALLIBLE"

Hunting
Big Game
in Africa

CASUALS
IN THE
CAUCASUS

AGNES HERBERT

CASUALS IN
THE CAUCASUS

THE BODLEY HEAD

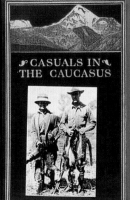

THE TIME
OF MY LIFE

Gertrude Sanford Legendre

ADVENTURES BEYOND
THE ZAMBESI

OF THE O'FLAHERTY
THE INSULAR MISS
THE SOLDIER MAN
AND
THE REBEL WOMAN

BY MRS. FRED MATURIN
(EDITH CECIL-PORCH)

HELEN FISCHER

tin—who managed to avoid getting stuck in the river, even though crossing at the same place. Martin gave the future king some lessons in motion-picture cameras and film. His Royal Highness commented that "Kenya is the gem of the Empire." And Osa's *I Married Adventure* noted that "the Duke was an excellent shot and altogether a perfect sportsman, as I have found most Britishers to be. . . ."

Over the years of their travels, the couple amassed an impressive array of firearms, which is described in an inventory published in *Safari*. There were three English Bland double rifles (.470 caliber); five bolt-actions—a Bland .275 Mannlicher, a Springfield sporter, a Rigby (.505), and two Jeffries (.404); three Winchester Model 1895s (.405) and a Model 1894 (.32); a Winchester shotgun (12 gauge); two Ithaca shotguns (20 gauge, one with sawed-off barrels); a Parker (12 gauge); and two Colt revolvers, one in .38 caliber, the other in .45.

Sportsman and collector Joseph Larkin has devoted years to a search for the guns used by the Johnsons, most of which were gifts, according to a letter from Martin, now at the Martin and Osa Johnson Safari Museum in Osa's hometown of Chanute, Kansas. "With our guns we had on the last trip we will have *twenty-five,* and most of them beauties made to our measure."

Facing page: British and American lady authors of hunting books, from the collection of Carol Lueder, accompanied by photographs of Irene Morden, on expeditions for the American Museum of Natural History (*lower left* and *lower right,* with husband Colonel William J. Morden); Yvette Andrews and husband Roy Chapman Andrews in Tibet (*bottom center*); Helen Fischer with black rhinoceros (*bottom right*), and Gertrude Sanford with trophy lion (*left center,* on Isabel Savory title page). Four drawings at *center* depict huntresses in the four seasons, used by Lueder on covers of her quarterly catalogs for Fair Chase, Inc. Note the impressive array of trophies taken by Lady Jenkins, on the cover of *Sport and Travel in Both Tibets.*

On January 13, 1937, the Johnsons were on a Western Air flight to Burbank, California, that crashed, killing Martin and badly injuring Osa. World War II made expeditions impossible for several years, but Osa was hoping to mount another safari to Africa in 1953. Then, in January of that year, she suffered a heart attack and died. The magic of the Johnsons' expeditions would live on in their writings and thousands of feet of movie film.

The finest tribute to Osa was by Martin:

For bravery and steadiness and endurance, Osa is the equal of any man I ever saw. She is a woman through and through. There is nothing "mannish" about her. Yet as a comrade in the wilderness she is better than any man I ever saw.

Sally Clark—Huntress and Sculptress

Sally Clark liked to call the photograph on page 93 "Two Lions, Two Shots, Two Minutes." The lions were taken by her in Kenya in 1928. Her husband, taxidermist, artist, and naturalist James L. Clark, wrote of the hunt in his autobiography, *Good Hunting.* Clark was on an expedition with his old friend Al Klein, hunting the Serengeti plains to collect specimens for the American Museum of Natural History's African Hall lion group. Unfortunately, Sally Clark and the only other woman on the expedition did not get along. As a result,

Mrs. Clark agreed to withdraw from the safari [and return to Nairobi]. Here she was to have stayed . . . to await my return from the field.

But what I did not know or suspect was that Mrs. Clark, not to be idle, had telegraphed her sister in New York to wire her five thousand dollars and to ask no questions. Then one day when Raddatz [one of the safari party with James Clark] came back from another trip to Nairobi [for supplies], he told me that he had run into Mrs. Clark and that she was encamped some twenty-five miles to the west of us with a white guide and a woman companion. She had al-

ready shot for herself, besides much other game, four lions, two of which were huge black-maned fellows that she had seen at a distance with her glasses and had stalked with her hunter. At eight yards she shot them both, within a two-minute period, killing each lion with one shot. A record for a woman![12]

Early in her career, Sally had been a buyer of fine lace for a New York department store, traveling frequently to Belgium and other countries in Europe. After her marriage to Clark, she took a strong interest in his work and accompanied him on many expeditions for the American Museum of Natural History.

Sally taught herself sculpture and produced some excellent pieces, including a life-sized bust of a Masai warrior and a reclining lioness. A competitive target shooter, she was equally skilled with rifle, shotgun, and pistol, particularly the Colt .45, with which she took delight in besting male opponents. A shooting competition at the Camp Fire Club of America is named for her.

Mrs. Roy Chapman Andrews—Duck and Woodcock Shooter

Thought by some to be the model for Indiana Jones, hero of *Raiders of the Lost Ark,* Roy Chapman Andrews's adventures captivated two generations of Americans as he explored the Gobi Desert. He was a star at the American Museum of Natural History, and credited his love of shooting as leading naturally to his love of taxidermy.

In his autobiography, *Born Under a Lucky Star,* Andrews pays homage to his wife, Billie. Discussing their country life in Connecticut, he notes that she could "kill a woodcock or cast a fly as well as I and she loves it, too. The other wives are not so keen as she but all of them look with an indulgent, if somewhat superior, eye on the childlike enthusiasm of their husbands. . . ."

She was "a fine shot. She didn't know one end

of a gun from the other until she married me, but practice and perfect natural co-ordination have made her shoot as well as the average man." At the end of a challenging morning afield:

> We haven't done so badly, either on the ducks or woodcock.... After lunch, an hour's sleep is indicated for we've been up since before dawn. Then the afternoon shoot. Last year at six o'clock in the afternoon of the first day I came into our bedroom. There on the bed lay Billie with one arm extended, pillowing Queen's black and white head [one of their two hunting dogs] which was half covered by Billie's blonde curls. Both sound asleep. The end of a perfect day![13]

Although Andrews does not mention her in his book, his first wife, Yvette, had also been introduced to shooting, and accompanied him on some of his adventures and expeditions.

Safari Some Fun! SOME FUN! Seventeen Letters Written to Her Mother, January to March 1935—a book by Lucille Parsons Vanderbilt

One of the most sought-after safari books among collectors is a 118-page memoir by Lucille Parsons Vanderbilt, a record of an adventure she treasured throughout her life. Only fifty copies were published, of which five were bound in Turkey morocco leather. Like the book, Lucille's safari was first cabin all the way. Her professional white hunters were two of Africa's best: Philip Percival and Baron Bror Blixen.

This charming volume, liberally illustrated with photographs, describes Lucille's journey by steamer to Naples, then on to Port Said, and all the stops along the way to East Africa, and back to her life of luxury in America. Aboard ship, she enjoyed clay pigeon shooting "every day . . . and yesterday I hit 9 out of ten! It is really very good and better than most of the men did! Hope I'll be a good shot in Africa."

From Assuan in Egypt, she flew by chartered plane to Khartoum, then to Nairobi, where she met cousin George Vanderbilt. There the party was fitted up with safari clothes—no attempts have been made to correct her quirky grammar or spelling:

> This morning the taylor arrived and measured us all for pants and shirts to wear in the bush. Lovely things with places for cartridges.... They were expensive but everyone else ordered them so I couldn't be outdone....
> My gun arrived and three hundred cartridges and I am going out for some target practice this afternoon.... I can't wait to shoot off my new gun. It's a 275 rifle what ever that is.[14]

She was pleased with the accommodations: "It's about the ritziest safari that ever set forth. Some fun! Some fun!"

On the first day of hunting, from their camp near the Serengeti plains, on February 15:

> George and I went straight off, to see what I could shoot at to get some practice with my new gun. We took a gun bearer and the second hunter. There is a white hunter for each of us to protect us in case we miss, and set off into the bush.

Her first kill was a topi antelope, prepared for dinner that evening. "It was sort of grim eating the poor little thing I had seen running around not long before, but we were hungry."

Baron Blixen had spotted a huge lion on the plain, which, after some stalking, they were able to take successfully—even though it charged and threw a scare into the party:

> Boy, let me tell you it was a thrilling moment and I had such a thrill as you will never know....
> I am so thrilled because George and all the hunters tell me I am an excellent shot....
> George gave me the rifle I use as a birthday present, and I couldn't be more charmed. It's such a sweet little gun, a Mauser 256 and a carbine, if you [know] what that is. I am just crazy about it....

Writing on March 3, from Arusha (Tanganyika), Lucille announced they were "just leaving now on our foot safari after rhino and buffalo!" She proudly wrote that "Philip Perciful [Percival] . . . told Blix that I was the swellest and bravest girl he'd ever been on safari with. It's quite a complement coming from him, because he is the most famous white hunter in all Africa...." Writing soon thereafter from the Rift Wall, in northern Tanganyika, she noted, "Our foot safari has begun at last, after all manner of delays and change of plans, but we are now off after rhino and buffalo, the most dangerous and exciting hunting in all Africa.... We always sleep with our guns beside the bed."

In a few days, Lucille had yet another thrill. Coming upon some rhino tracks, they set out on its trail.

> You just can't imagine the feeling of knowing at any moment you may come upon a rhino, who will 9 times out of ten charge at you. After about half an hour, I suddenly heard the bush breaking in front of me, and then George grabbed me and pulled me back and there I saw about 30 yards away, a tremendous rhino, and God but maybe it wasn't a nervous moment. George whispered for me to shoot, and by this time the rhino had seen us and had started for us. He was coming straight at us, not ten yards away by now, and I aimed the gun and fired. I was in such a state of excitement that I don't even remember taking time to aim, because when you see a great beast like that coming for you, you really get a scare.... Gosh, but you can't imagine how charged I was to think I hit the thing in my excited state, and shooting with a gun I'd never fired before, a 350 mauser, a much larger gun than mine, and it kicks like hell, but I was too excited to know it....

Lucille Parsons Vanderbilt having "some fun" on safari, Kenya, in 1934. Her privately printed book is considered one of the rarest ever published on big game hunting, with only fifty copies in print.

"We stopped for a picnic lunch"

Ready for anything

HEMINGWAY
ON HUNTING

ERNEST HEMINGWAY

EDITED BY SEAN HEMINGWAY
WITH AN INTRODUCTION BY PATRICK HEMINGWAY

Having heard of Cape buffalo nearby, the party set out to find a big one. After following three big bulls for over two miles, they heard a tremendous crash, and out came a huge bull—which she hit with a brilliant shot from 150 yards. It quickly disappeared into cover. Suddenly *three* bulls came charging out of the brush, and

ran right at us, then turned and ran completely around us, with us all firing away at them. It sounded like a war, but if you could see those three tremendous animals tearing along first right for us, and then rushing by us. Some thrill!! Well, the first one I shot fell with a crash after a bit. . . . George and I each got a buffalo and they are both beauties. . . . I haven't half shown you the thrill that comes when you see the animals . . . , but believe me it's something. . . .

The last adventure on the trip was a near plane crash, when the engine stopped. Miraculously, they glided down to a safe landing.

Hunting with Ernest Hemingway: Mary's Love of Shooting

"Miss Mary: the author's wife, new to big game hunting, too short for the task at hand, but tall enough to be the dedicated foe of a great rogue lion"—thus did Ernest Hemingway start his three-part short story, "Miss Mary's Lion," published in a weekly, *African Journal.*[15] An avid hunter and shooter, Hemingway introduced at least two of his wives to the sport, as well as several lady friends and the actress Jane Russell. A collection of twenty-three photographs in the archives of the John Fitzgerald Kennedy Library,

Facing page: Women who were close to Ernest Hemingway were expected to share his passion for hunting and fishing. At *upper left,* with his first wife, Pauline Pfeiffer, and a grizzly bear she shot in the Rockies. At *center* and *center left,* his fourth wife, Mary, not only enjoyed shooting, she wrote about it. At *bottom,* with actress Jane Russell. Martha Gellhorn, at *right center,* not only loved hunting, she proved to be a deadly shot. Among others who hunted with Hemingway were crack shot Rocky Cooper and her husband, Gary. Photographs from the Hemingway collections of Ellen Enzler-Herring and the John Fitzgerald Kennedy Library.

Boston, depict Hemingway, two of his wives, and some lady friends enjoying hunting.

Mary Hemingway particularly loved duck hunting:

I reflect that I consistently make donations to conservation societies and am, indeed, a devout conservationist. So why am I out here getting colder by the minute in the south wind, hoping to murder some ducks? Need of food cannot excuse me (as it does the locals). If I want the amusement of hitting something with a shotgun shell, I can shoot clay targets. I do not enjoy killing birds. But how else can one see 15 or 20 miles of lake and marsh in changing light and wind, and 180 degrees of sky, enlivened every few minutes by a flight of any one of 13 different species of ducks, not to forget grebe, coots and Canada geese? . . . 200,000 waterfowl crossed the Delta in one morning's migration in October 1951. . . . In 1966 and other years some of us out in the skiffs have seen at least 5,000 ducks at one time in our neighborhood skies. Which may, or may not, alleviate a sense of guilt at shooting a half dozen of them. Jimmy Robinson put it best in a letter to me: "For those who have seen canvasbacks and bluebills winging into the decoys, there is no other game," he wrote. But I wonder if we would go through the fuss and bother to get out there just to see them. . . .

We both [she is hunting with friend and guide Leonard Lavallee] light up and I have taken two puffs when I hear above the grass behind us the whirr of wings. Safety off quick, and there are four mallards flying right over us. I pick the lead bird and down he tumbles, rump over lovely head, into the reeds. Leonard jumps out of the skiff to retrieve, and brings back the drake, neatly dead, but not as beautiful as he was flying above us, busy with his life, ten minutes earlier.

Great country. Great day.[16]

Mrs. Katherine Perkins—Mother of Leigh Perkins, Orvis Entrepreneur

When Leigh Perkins bought the Orvis Company in 1965, he took the sleepy Vermont mail-order firm from a $500,000-a-year operation to $200 million in annual sales (1996). He tells this high-profile success story in *A Sportsman's Life: How I Built Orvis by Mixing Business and Sport.* Due

credit for Perkins's success in the world of hunting and fishing is given to his mother:

Fishing and hunting and the outdoor life are in my blood the way they are for so many American men—and, these days, many women as well. I had grown up caring passionately and intensely about those things, the way other boys cared about cars or sports. I just couldn't get enough.

While that made me a pretty typical American boy, there was one way in which I was unusual if not downright unique. Most boys learn about fishing and hunting from their fathers. The great influence in my sporting life was my mother. She taught me to fish and hunt, and she was my principal sporting companion for the first eighteen years of my life. It was an unusual situation, but it had a lot of advantages, especially in the disciplinary department. As my brothers and sisters often pointed out, I could get away with just about anything.

My mother was an attractive woman and a fine, competitive athlete. She was evidently born with a love for fishing and hunting in spite of the fact that neither her father nor her mother hunted or fished. She was, fortunately, born in Thomasville, Georgia, which is the capital of quail hunting in America. She was one of the finest wing shots I have ever known, easily better than I ever became.

I was riding along in the shooting buggy with her from the time I was one year old and not long after that went along in the punt boat while she hunted alligators. One of my early memories is sharing a boat with a twelve-foot gator that she had just shot. Gators do not stop moving for several hours after they have been killed, and the experience left quite an impression on a three-year-old boy

My father was the disciplinarian in the family—the only thing my mother could think of to punish me was to keep me from going on fishing trips with her, but that meant denying herself a companion.[17]

Schuetzenbunds and Schuetzenfests

Although artisans of Germanic origin dominated Kentucky riflemaking from the earliest days of the American colonies, the distinctive, formal shooting matches that originated in Germany, *Schuetzenfests,* were not established in the United

KOENIGIN
NEW YORK
SCHUETZEN
CORPS
LADIES
AUXILIARY
2000

HARTFORD
Schuetzen-Verein
38th ANNUAL
·R·E·C·E·P·T·I·O·N·
TO BE HELD AT SAENGERBUND HALL
APRIL 28th, 1902.
GENTLEMAN AND LADIES 50c.

G. H. FRIEDRICH
JEWELER
21 WARD ST.
ROCKVILLE, CONN.

Gruss aus

Mei Büchserl is gricht, so klein und so fein,
Mein Buab sel Ladstock der paßt grad hinein!

DRUCK U. VERLAG A. ZILBERG't CH MÜNCHEN

States until the mid–nineteenth century. A million German immigrants had come to America, some of them destined to work in factories like Colt's of Hartford—and not a few brought their German customs to the New World. Among the oldest forms of established shooting events held in America, the *Schuetzen* matches were set up first in the Midwest, then, later, in the East, the South, and the West—including San Francisco, which had a strong contingent for decades.

The oldest organization of its kind in America, the North American Schuetzen Bund was founded in 1865. It conducted an annual *Schuetzenfest*, which shooters attended from all over the country. By the end of the nineteenth century, such clubs were in virtually every community that had populations of Germanic ancestry. The *Schuetzenfests* offered target-shooting competitions, accompanied by Bavarian-style picnics. Even though these events were primarily supported by Germans, non-Teutonic participation was generally welcomed. Women played no small role in these festive occasions.

Preceding pages: Finely decorated *Schuetzen* rifles, with shooting vest of Virginia Scheller, who competes at *Schuetzenfests* with her husband, Max. The vest is the uniform for the New York Schuetzen Corps Ladies Auxiliary. Her crown as *königen* (queen) rests on the sash; worn at a fall outing by the lady winner of the shooting competition of the New York Schuetzen Club in the Catskills; it can also be worn at monthly meetings and special occasions.

Shooting medals on vest, and *königen*'s medal in box by sash. From the *top,* a parlor rifle, in .17 caliber. *Middle,* rifle by Buchel, in 8.15 × 46R caliber. At *bottom,* System Jung rifle built in Mannheim, Germany; caliber 8.15 × 46R. Two beer steins depicting women, c. 1910. From the extensive *Schuetzen* collection of Max and Virginia Scheller.

ON THE SIDELINES AT SWEET BRIAR FARM
Miss Kathrine Haskell and Miss Ann Bissell snapped while watching an event for men; otherwise Miss Haskell would have been in it.

At *far right*, Katherine Haskell in elegant fur-trimmed coat at Sweet Briar Farm; the caption notes that she and her friend were watching "an event for men; otherwise Miss Haskell would have been in it." Shot of Katherine Haskell Perkins, with two Florida swamp alligators and three-year-old son Leigh, reminds the latter of a quip that he was the decoy. He recalls that "as a teenage girl she got an older cousin to take her quail hunting and her minister to take her duck hunting in south Georgia." Her favorite alligator rifle was a Winchester .25-20.

Eleanor Roosevelt—Deadly from the Hip with a Revolver

First lady Eleanor Roosevelt was taught to shoot by her bodyguard, Earl Miller, a former navy boxing champion, a member of the U.S. Olympic boxing team, and a gymnast, swimmer, and target shooter. Her skill with a firearm was the subject of a brief note in Blanche Wiesen Cook's *Eleanor Roosevelt*.

> [Earl Miller] presented her with a growling but well-trained police dog for protection, and taught her to shoot so successfully that she actually came to enjoy target practice, especially in the country, on an open range, where she wore a holster and shot from the hip.

The pictures do not show the first lady shooting from the hip, but they do reveal her holster. The revolver appears to be a Smith & Wesson Military and Police.

As the daughter of the dedicated sportsman and hunter Elliott Roosevelt, and the niece of Theodore, one might expect Eleanor Roosevelt would have shooting interests—but it was Earl Miller who made her into a sharpshooter, and one who not only enjoyed target shooting, but who believed in carrying a handgun for the express purpose of self-defense.

Franklin Delano Roosevelt also had a Smith & Wesson—a .32 Safety Hammerless, now in a private collection. (The revolver was accompanied by FDR's New York City pistol license, issued some years prior to his election as president of the United States.) Mrs. Roosevelt's revolver was bigger, and she was unquestionably the better shot.

103

With a perfect shooting stance, and definitely wholly comfortable with a handgun, Eleanor Roosevelt looks like a shooting champion in these snapshots taken at Chazy Lake, New York, in 1934 and 1935. The prints were from Earl R. Miller, of Loudonville, New York, her bodyguard and shooting coach. Mrs. Roosevelt proudly shows her target, with friend Nancy Cook—most of the shots are in the black. Once when threatened by the Ku Klux Klan against making an appearance on behalf of civil rights in the South, Mrs. Roosevelt and a female companion fulfilled her announced mission—but in the drive to and from their destination, a loaded revolver was between them on the front seat.

Some of the best images collected over two decades by Wesley Powers, who specializes in BB guns, and photos of their users. Dating from the 1880s to the 1930s, these pictures hark back to a simpler time, with old-fashioned, small-town values and amusements. At *left,* the Metropolitan Navy revolver presented to suffragette Pauline Orr.

Air guns, with a single-shot .22 rimfire rifle, an early cast-iron cap pistol, and boxed Fox double-barrel play gun. From the *top*, a Daisy Model 27, King Model No. 5533, a Hamilton No. 15 (.22 rimfire), an Upton Model G, a Daisy pump No. 25, the cast-iron pistol (with decoration and patent date of December 27, 1887), and Daisy pump No. 16 with bayonet fixture, a rare Fox play gun with its original cardboard box. Factories making some of the BBs, .22 ammo, or .22 guns pictured in popular postcards at *top*.

Note charming advertising paper for air rifle maker, catering to women and intended also for the shooting pleasure of children

Youthful target champion Arlayne Brown, with one of at least two Officer's Model Target revolvers shipped to her as gifts from the Colt factory. Number 563717 is of .38 caliber, with 6-inch barrel, engraved by Wilbur Glahn, and recorded in the factory records as in Grade C, and sent to Miss Brown early in 1930. The other revolver, also an Officer's Model Target, of like caliber, was inscribed with her name, and had been presented a year earlier. Innumerable articles on Miss Brown appeared in St. Louis, Missouri, newspapers, celebrating her marksmanship. She was famous in the community by the time she was twelve years old.

Years later Miss Brown joined Ringling Brothers, Barnum & Bailey Circus, performing as an exhibition shooter. She was an expert with rifle, revolver, and handgun.

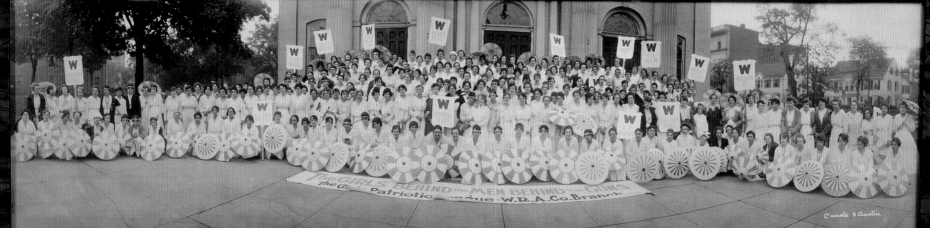

CHAPTER IV

Lady Gunmakers and Engravers, Collectors, and Antiquarians

This is the firm . . . whose Managing Director is a woman, Mmle. Therese Ducat. Miss Ducat conducted [us] through her factory and talked about the several versions of the Ducat over-under shotgun, which is the sole type manufactured. It was obvious that Miss Ducat knew her stuff, that she was highly knowledgeable about shotgun design and construction. We learned also that she is a first class claybirder and an ardent hunter—as, in fact, so many European women are.

—John T. Amber, editor, *The Gun Digest,* 1976

The origins of the gun trade in England and Continental Europe were generally in cities such as London, Liège (Belgium), Saint-Etienne (France), Munich, Tula (Russia), Eibar (Spain), and Stockholm. But major gunmaking centers also developed in smaller communities, among them Gardone (Val Trompia, Italy) and Ferlach (Austria). Women worked in the gun industry at each of these sites. The massive gunmaker reference work originally compiled by J. F. Støckel, later updated and expanded by Eugene Herr, *Der Neue Støckel,* lists hundreds of women. A

Facing page: Employment of women in the manufacture of ammunition dates back centuries. Their joining the ranks of gunmakers at major factories—here represented primarily by Winchester and Remington—was largely a result of wartime need, commencing with World War I. Note the tremendous number of women at Winchester, New Haven (*bottom*), each group with a sign identifying the section of the giant complex in which they were employed; c. 1917–18.

number of other sources also present listings—but at present this important story remains far from complete. Much additional research is required, as evidence indicates there remains a great deal undiscovered.

Twenty years of study by historian and collector John Banta has proven that the numbers of women involved in the gun trade are far greater than could be determined purely from gun markings or from the existing literature on firearms. A partial indication comes from the role of women in the military, including combat, and their work in factories, particularly where ammunition and powder were manufactured (women being more careful workers, and far less likely to light up a smoke and blow up the works). Other sources of information are city directories and government records, along with commercial data, such as the ledgers of the Hudson's Bay Company and other trading operations.

Banta's research has produced hundreds of photographs showing women with firearms, the gun factories where they worked, and relevant drawings, prints, and paintings. Although some women are listed as gunmakers because they carried on a business begun by their deceased husbands, noteworthy numbers were trained gunmakers in their own right, having completed the rigorous apprentice system and having worked on the bench actually building firearms, or making or refining parts.

Christie's arms and armor expert Peter Hawkins provided evidence that in France there were even more women who had trained as gunmakers than in Great Britain, and listed examples of Continental and British guns built by women. Standard sources of gunmakers' lists, such as Howard L. Blackmore's *Gunmakers of London, 1350–1850,* Jean-Jacques Buigne and Pierre Jarlier's *Le "Qui est qui" de l'arme en France de 1350 à 1970,* and Frank Sellers's *American Gunsmiths* yielded so many women that the author's original intent to list them all in *Silk and Steel* could not be accommodated.[1]

This chapter presents an array of firearms known to have been made by women, and cites some of the more important lady gunmakers, engravers, and stockmakers. It also provides an anthology of data and illustrations on women who made gunpowder and ammunition, as well as cannon, and on women who have been distinguished in arms collecting. Two women in particular are noted as major manufacturers, whose ownership of companies has been absolute: Mrs. Samuel Colt and Mrs. Oliver F. Winchester. And three of the foremost collections of arms assembled in the twentieth century were heavily influenced by the collaboration of the wives of the collectors: W. Keith Neal of England, and William M. Locke and Russell Barnett Aitken of the United States.

The study of firearms has drawn a vast army of

students and collectors, a group often thought of as gray-haired (and sometimes bald) old men, not a few with substantial paunches. Such is not the case. Although the number of women present at arms collectors' trade shows remains less than 20 percent, the ratio of women is gradually on the upswing.

Continental European Gunmakers and Artisans
Belgian Gunmakers

One of the most prolific of all gunmaking centers over the centuries, Liège has suffered in recent decades due to intense international competition, particularly from Italian, Japanese, and American gunmakers, and the emerging manufacturing skills evident in China and Eastern Europe. An analysis of its gender makeup is similar to what one finds in a study of any of Europe's gunmaking centers. Observations in Claude Gaier's *Four Centuries of Liège Gunmaking* are therefore generally pertinent to other countries:

> As early as the XVIIth. century . . . training consisted of apprenticeship to an established gun maker for a period of two or three years. The workshops were operated on a family basis, with a limited use of outside labour. Sons, daughters and wives worked side by side with the head of the family. . . . Although female labour is used, the women are only auxiliaries to the husbands and fathers. They are rarely found in business on their own account, unless they are carrying on the work of a dead husband.

In common with other countries, women have become much more of a presence since the early twentieth century, not only on the shop floor, operating machinery, but in checkering gunstocks, and in engraving.

Facing page: Pistols made for Thomas Jefferson, c. 1784; at the Monticello historic site. Gunmaker Mary Dealtry is listed as the widow of sword cutler and gunsmith Thomas Dealtry, of 85 Cornhill Street, London, 1784–86.

Anne-Marie Moermans, Master Gunmaker

Anne-Marie Moermans is owner and hands-on manager of Lebeau-Courally, founded in Liège in 1865, and makers of guns of the same quality as Holland & Holland, Ltd., and Purdey's. One of the firm's famous clients was Czar Nicholas II of Russia, whose picture holding one of his pair of side-by-side shotguns graces the catalogs of recent years. The firm produces shotguns with the Anson or Holland systems, in all gauges, including 16. Also in the line are over-and-unders, in 12 and 20 gauge, and express double rifles in big-game calibers. A double rifle of the firm's finest quality, a .375 H & H Magnum, with an extra set of .458 barrels, was featured in the documentary film *In the Blood.*

Mrs. Moermans is the niece of Joseph Verrees, who owned Lebeau-Courally for many years. She was raised by Verrees and his wife, and, as with the rest of the family, is well versed in the shooting sports and in the art of making fine guns. When Verrees died in 1982 (he had run the company from 1956), Mrs. Moermans assumed directorship of the company and has operated it ever since.

Thoroughly prepared to manage the firm, Mrs. Moermans notes "our clientele is not surprised at all to see me running Lebeau-Courally: they have known me for many years."[2] Describing the firm's products, she comments that "the Boss-Verrees type over-and-under shotgun represents the top of our production and, as far as I'm concerned, [is] the world's most beautiful gun sold today. With regard to the Chambord, another of our over-and-unders, I believe that it is also just as beautiful, but with an action that is totally different from what is mounted on the Boss-Verrees. . . ."[3] She plans to expand the range of Lebeau products, maintaining the high quality and prestige.

Under the Verrees company umbrella (which owns Lebeau-Courally), her operation works with Belgian stores and gun dealers, and for the last thirty years has handled Winchester's distribution in Belgium, among other brands of guns and accessories.

French Gunmakers

The listing of French gunmakers in *Le "Qui est qui" de l'arme en France de 1350 à 1970* records more than 170 artisans and their wives and/or family members in the gun trade. An example of relationships and dynasties is evident in the marriage of the distinguished gunmaker-artist Nicholas Noel Boutet. He inherited from his father-in-law, gunmaker Pierre DeSainte, the title of "Arquebusier de la Majeste." The gunmaking son of this marriage, Pierre-Nicholas, became a partner with his father, but was unable to carry on the dynasty due to his untimely death in 1816.

Typical of the more recent listings within the firearms trade is Miss Therese Ducat, maker of the Ducat over-and-under shotgun, in Saint-Etienne. A visit to her factory was the subject of John T. Amber's article in the 1976 edition of *The Gun Digest*, in which he lauded her extraordinary abilities in the shop and afield, and her in-depth knowledge of gun manufacture.

German Gunmakers—Bertha Krupp and Others

Judging from the numbers of Germanic names in the Frank Sellers sourcebook *American Gunsmiths*, it was not unusual for women in German gunmaking families to assist the family in building firearms, repairing them, and, sometimes, in selling them. But the most renowned figure in the history of German gunmaking is Bertha Krupp (1886–1957), whose family business was the foremost armaments operation in the world.

The eldest daughter of Friedrich Alfred Krupp

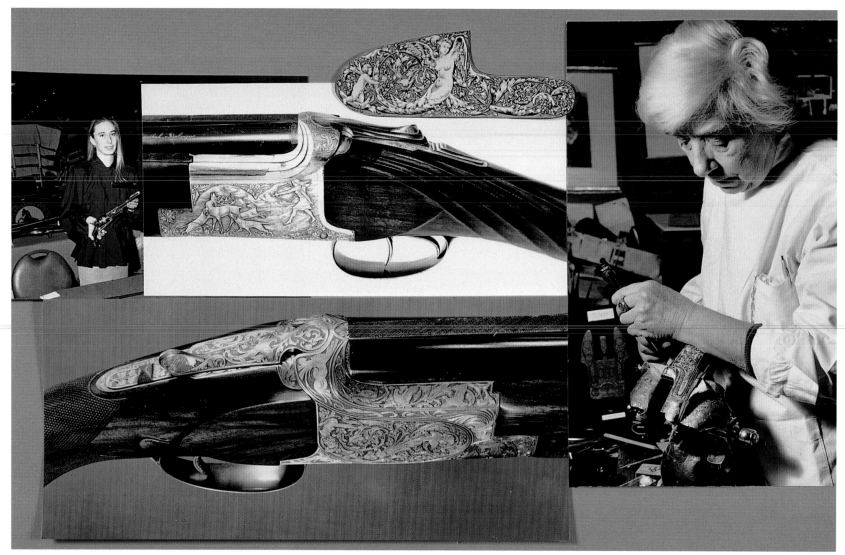

Belgian engraver Lyson Corombelle (1894–1971) at her bench in the later years of her career. One of the best known of female master arms engravers, she was taught the art by her talented father. The Browning shotgun at *bottom* was engraved by her; Diana graces this deluxe over-and-under, relief decorated by Corombelle—c. 1960. At *center*, Art Deco–style, Diana-themed Browning—from the Fabrique Nationale engraving shop, created specifically for the 1937 Paris World's Fair by Felix Funken (founder of the F.N. in-house engraving department, 1926; his work influenced generations of Belgian engravers).

At *top,* dummy lockplate by Fernand Vetcour, of c. early 1930s, with an elegant female motif figuring into the scroll décor. The artist later turned from arms engraving, taking up fine arts and still-life painting. He also taught at the Liège Academy of Fine Arts; several of his students were young ladies, some of whom took up arms engraving.

At *left,* Maria Laura Uberti, holding a Walker Colt made by her father, Aldo.

Facing page: Anne-Marie Moermans, master gunmaker, and owner of Lebeau-Courally. At *center,* she discusses fine points of gunmaking with King Juan Carlos of Spain. At *bottom left,* with staff of master gunmakers at Liège shop. Female motifs engraved on spectacular examples of the firm's gunmaking artistry.

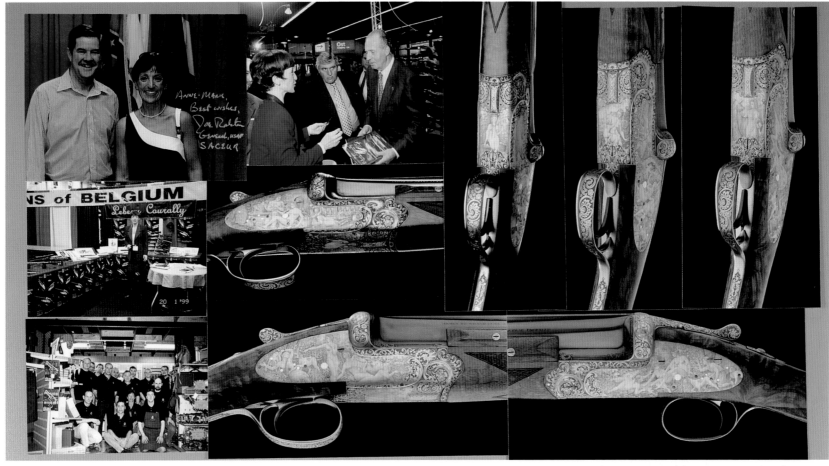

(who had no sons), Bertha suddenly inherited the extensive family holdings when her father, embroiled in a widely publicized scandal, committed suicide in 1902. Though still a teenager, she had been trained from her youth for an executive position. She had an inherent mastery of business, and was equally skilled in comprehending all facets of engineering and manufacture. She was also strikingly beautiful, possessed of a sharp wit, and was a prized marital catch—with an annual income of approximately $4.5 million.

Despite her abilities, it was unthinkable at the time that a woman should run the operation. No less a personage than the Kaiser himself selected a suitable husband for her. In October 1906, Bertha married an impoverished Prussian nobleman from the diplomatic corps, Gustav von Bohlen und Halbach. Although she did not neglect management matters, Bertha thereafter concerned herself primarily with the company's social-welfare agenda.

In her honor, Krupp employees named their 42-cm howitzers "Dicke Bertha." Thanks to Allied journalists, "Big Bertha" came to be the name applied to any German long-range railway-mounted gun. Among new plants built by Krupp for use in World War II was the Bertha Werk, in Upper Silesia.

Italian Gunmakers and the Fausti Sisters—Shotguns and Lipstick

One of the world's oldest gunmaking centers, the Gardone-Brescia area of northern Italy, has maintained its supreme industrial and marketing stature for over five centuries. Rivalries between

gunmaking families sometimes led to feuds, and even women carried firearms in the event of altercations. The involvement of women in the trade has continued unabated throughout that time. Today, more women have roles in the Italian gun industry than ever.

In the Italian weekly *Specchio La Stampa,* an international phenomenon was featured in an article titled "Shotguns and Lipstick: Fashion? Public Relations? No. Against any prejudice, the Fausti sisters deal with firearms. They produce

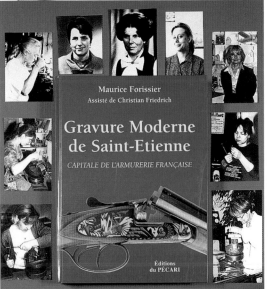

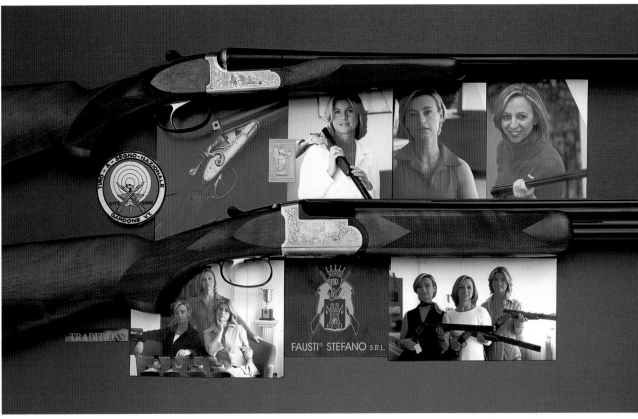

Above: The Fausti sisters, gunmakers of Gardone, Val Trompia. The shotgun at *top,* a Model Elite ST, in .410, 3-inch chambers, and 26-inch barrels; walnut stock, with fixed choke. At *bottom,* an over-and-under 12 gauge, with 26-inch barrels, and 3-inch chambers.

Left: Sterling silver belt buckle by Denise Thirion, for Suzette Rattenbury. Thirion mastered scroll engraving at Fabrique Nationale, Herstal, Belgium, and came to the United States in 1967 to work for A. A. White Engravers, Inc. Since the 1980s she has been a contract engraver for Colt's Manufacturing Co., Inc., known particularly for her exquisite scrolls, executed in several traditional styles.

Of the twenty-six engravers featured in *Gravure Moderne de Sainte-Etienne,* nine are women. *Clockwise,* from *lower left,* Myriam Granger, Veronique Lefranc, Christiane Freycon, Josette Malliere, Helyette Chamaret, Laure Guillet-Bonneton, Louise Bernard, Helene Gontel, and Ginette Neithoffer. As with virtually all aspects of gunmaking, excepting in forge shops, the percentage of women involved continues to increase.

Facing page: Engraving and gold inlaying of guns, spurs, drinking flasks, and accessories by master engraver Diane Scalese.

12,000 a year. Hereafter the story of a success by 'shots' of smile."[4] In a patriarchal culture, the sisters produce objects sold primarily to men—and the customers are clamoring for more. They are also among the most beautiful gunmakers in the world, along with rivals from Famars—two lovely women, second-generation gunmakers, with their own inimitable Italian style.

Fabio Poletti wrote in *Specchio La Stampa:*

Forget John Wayne. And also Calamity Jane. Even if they produce shotguns exported all over the world, the Fausti sisters don't have grim faces, and wear the pants in the office only to feel more comfortable. Their names are Elena, Giovanna and Barbara Fausti, daughters of Cavalier Fausti, gunmaker from Marcheno (Brescia), who spent fifty years in manufacturing guns with only one worry: not having a son as heir to whom to leave the company.

Giovanna, the second daughter, marketing manageress and responsible for the newest lines, smiles: "After all, our father is happy all the same...." Of course, he is. The company has a yearly 7-billion-lira turnover, manufactures 12,000 shotguns a year, 90 percent of which are sold abroad; anyone would be delighted with these three gunpowder sisters. And so are their 40 employees, mostly men, who have got used to bosses wearing skirts, pardon trousers!

Or they almost have, as explains Elena, the eldest daughter, who began working in the company right after earning her secondary-school diploma. "Our colleagues are not always on close terms with us, as they would be with a man. On Mondays, no one asks us how the football match was . . . or if we enjoyed the hunt. . . ." Not too bad! These are niceties the Fausti sisters have grown used to for a long time. After years and years of work, they have learned how to face every possible challenge. . . . Barbara has been able to combine their public and private clientele through one of the most successful corporate strategies. After years of commercial competition with Emilio Rizzini Company, Fausti Stefano & Figlie has taken over the trademark of that competitor. What's more, Barbara married its owner. . . . Well, they may be three ladies, but thanks to their *verve* they knock the spots off many men in a field where women have always been kept on the fringes. . . .

The Fausti sisters export their shotgun line to the U.S. market through Traditions, of Old Saybrook, Connecticut. Traditions also imports some of the Uberti line, a company in which two of the four principals are women: Mrs. Aldo Uberti, and her daughter Maria Laura. A protégée of scholar and author Umberto Eco, Maria Laura Uberti earned her Ph.D. from the University of Bologna, and—in addition to achievements as a gunmaker and marketer of Uberti firearms—she is an accomplished filmmaker.

American Gunmakers and Artisans

The most significant of the firearms craftsmen immigrating to America during the early and mid-eighteenth century were the Germanic gunsmiths, who established the manufacture of a distinctively American rifle. This new style of firearm evolved from the German and Austrian Jaeger rifles, which had been designed for target shooting and hunting. German-, Austrian-, and some Swiss-born gunsmiths responded to a demand from pioneer Americans for a rifle that would shoot farther, was lighter, and was of a smaller caliber. In the first decades of the eighteenth century, the Kentucky rifle was born.

While many pioneer women were trained to use these arms, a few are known to have played vital roles in their production. Among these were Alice Powell Ferree, of Allegheny County, Pennsylvania, whose husband, Jacob, was a distinguished riflemaker who had also established a powder mill. Recognized as the best shot in the county, she tested her husband's rifles and powder. Demonstrations of accuracy and performance were important to their gunmaking trade.[5]

Although over a hundred female gunmakers are listed in Frank Sellers's *American Gunsmiths*, John Banta has determined the total to be much higher. That women played a greater role in early American gunmaking is gradually becoming documented, though the research is laborious and challenging.

Even African-American slave labor was employed in the early production of American guns. In at least one case, the slaves worked under the supervision of a widow, one Martha Goosley, who ran her husband's shop for several years after his death.[6]

In one extraordinary instance, knowledge of the skills of gunsmithing saved the life of a tradesman's wife. Jane Fraser was married to an immigrant Scottish Highlander who was a licensed Indian trader. In 1755, while living near Cumberland, Maryland, she and two "Dutchmen" (probably Germans) were kidnapped by a marauding band of Indians and taken to Ohio. Her husband, thinking her dead or permanently captive, remarried. But Jane Fraser hadn't given up. Stealing a broken musket, she repaired it herself and made her escape. She managed to get back to Maryland, where she forced John Fraser to choose between her and his new bride. He chose her. She died on April 14, 1814, in Juniata Township, Bedford County, Pennsylvania.

Lancaster, Pennsylvania, gunmaker John Henry had a wife named Eliza who was a better gunmaker than he. On his death the shop was willed to her. Yet another maker of Kentucky rifles, Abner Klase of Ringtown, Pennsylvania, relied on his wife to make the gunstocks.

Facing page: *Across top*, Tracy Nelson (Geschickter), at sites around the world, in her capacity as vice president, Replica Firearms; *top left*, with Michael, Erin, and Patrick Wayne. *Far right*, as a baby, held by her father, Thomas B. Nelson. Metropolitan Museum arms and armor expert Anita Reinhardt, at *center left*. *Lower left*, Katja Kaiser, in the Metropolitan Museum's arms and armor gallery, at Butterfield's, and with friends at an antique gun show. At *center*, women making ammunition at Remington factory. *Bottom center*, from *left*, William B. Ruger's granddaughters, Adrienne and Amy, with Bob Lee, and Sotheby's Roberta Lucs; Anne Brockinton with Random House vice president and executive editor Robert D. Loomis, and executives with House of Collectibles; Ruger's daughter Molly, with cousin Cameron Wesselhoft Brauns. Colt historian Kathy Hoyt, at *right*, with Hank Williams, Jr., and predecessors Ronald H. Wagner and Martin J. Huber. *Above*, Ray and Pat Carvell, of New Zealand, with treasured gold-inlaid Colt 1851 Navy. *Above*, Michael and Carol Kokin, in their Santa Fe gallery, Sherwood's Spirit of America. To *left*, Linda Jones, president, Collectors Arms International, Inc. *Below*, Carolyn and William Chaney, chairman of Tiffany & Co., with author; *above*, Aldo and Giuseppina Moretti Uberti, gunmakers. Winchester Model 1866 at *far right*, with motifs suggesting ownership by a lady; held by owner Jan Quick. *Left*, Tatiana Rohde and Robin Duncan, instrumental in author's *The Paterson Colt Book*. *Below*, Rose Aziz and daughter Gail Aziz Firkser, Rutgers Book Center.

116

Boring Gun Barrels for the American Revolution—the Widow Catherine Smith

A Pennsylvania widow, Catherine Smith, made extreme sacrifices in the war effort against the British. In 1775, she built grist- and sawmills at the mouth of White Deer Creek. When war broke out, she added a mill for boring gun barrels to be used by American forces. These mills, as well as a hemp mill on the site, were apparently used as frontier outposts, and in 1779 Indian allies of the British attacked the complex and, in Catherine's words, "The Indians burned the whole works." In 1785 she petitioned the General Assembly at Philadelphia for the recovery of her property.[7]

Supplying Powder, Shot, Flints, and More—Boston, 1775

An advertisement by one Mary Jackson of Boston in 1775 offered an intriguing assortment of wares:

Imported from LONDON,
And Sold by MARY JACKSON,
At the Brazen Head in Cornhill.

POWDER, Shot, Flints, Brass-Kettles, Skillets, Warming-Pans, Frying-Pans, Nails, Brads, Tacks, Pewter Dishes, Plates and Basons, Sadler's Wares, Desk and Book-case Furniture; With a Variety of other *London, Birmingham and Sheffield* Cutlary Ware, too tedius to mention.

N.B. A Parcel of choice *Connecticut* Pork, cheap for the Cash, or exchange for Rum, Sugar or Mollasses.[8]

Apprentices and Immigrant Gunsmiths

That girls served apprenticeships to the American gunsmithing trade is proven by an advertisement run in the *Alexandria Daily Gazette*, August 14, 1809:

ONE CENT REWARD. Ran away from the Subscriber on Saturday last, the 7th instant, an appren-

tice girl named Winny Fielding. She is about 14 years old and slender made—she took with her sundry wearing apparel. The above reward will be paid for delivering her to me. All persons are warned against harboring or employing her. ROBERT NASH [gunsmith].

A more likely source of gunsmiths in the American trade was from the immigrant labor pool. Listed in *Passenger Arrivals at the Port of Baltimore, 1820–34* is an assortment of female gunsmiths entering the United States.[9] All of the following arrived in either August or September 1834: Elizabeth Boyes (born in Ireland); Angelina Burger (born in Germany); and Agathe Olnhousen, married to gunsmith Jacob Olnhousen (the family arrived from Germany, and moved to Ohio with their three children, all of them gunsmiths—including daughter Catherine). Also from Ireland was Anne Nugent, age seventeen, accompanied by a woman likely to have been her mother, Jane, age sixty, also gunsmiths.

A remarkable object of Americana from the Civil War, the deluxe Daniel Moore .32 rimfire Belt Model revolver, serial number 18. A portrait of the inventor's daughter is engraved on the lug of the 6-inch barrel, accompanied by numerous other decorative motifs. Engraver Jacob Glahn made pulls from the completed engraving, and examples appear in the scrapbook of L. D. Nimschke (page 95). The blued barrel is also gold inlaid, and the recoil shield is engraved with a globe motif. On the right side of the gold-plated frame is a cowboy throwing a lasso in pursuit of cattle. The cylinder is engraved with scrollwork and a Civil War encampment of Zouaves and the ironclad *Monitor*. On the top flat of the 6-inch barrel is an engraved oval panel, within which is the marking: D. MOORE/PATENT/SEP. 18, 1860. An arrow motif and panel scenes of bear, lion, hound, and game birds are on the barrel. This masterpiece of American gunmaking is remarkable also because it includes a tribute to the inventor's daughter, as attested to by granddaughter Mary J. Warren:

Daniel Moore, my grandfather, inscribed & patented this gun—called the Frontier Model . . . his daughter's picture is on the barrel. This model was made to show to President Lincoln. My grandfather and his daughter went to Washington with this gun, met & talked with Mr. Lincoln on the White House grounds. . . . The President gave my grandfather the "green light" and he was ready to start manufacturing the gun in Charleston when the Civil War broke.

At left, glimpses into the domain of Mrs. Samuel Colt. The "Armorer's Door" of the Church of the Good Shepherd, at *lower left,* was designed by Edward Tuckerman Potter; according to scholar William Hosley, "the kinship of religion, industry, and empire has rarely been so boldly proclaimed." From *top left,* the Colt estate and factory complex, a watercolor of Armsmear, and the memorial parish house of the Colt church. *At right,* views of the Winchester Mystery House of Mrs. William Wirt Winchester, and of her in carriage.

A Plains Riflemaker and a Gun-lock Maker

Author and researcher Dr. James Whisker discovered a rifle by William Defibaugh, presented to his wife and dated December 26, 1855. The rifle, of fine quality, and mounted extensively with silver, is believed to have been a Christmas present. This Bedford County, Pennsylvania, rifle was also decorated with relief carving. According to local legend, Mrs. Defibaugh did the sighting-in for her husband while testing his rifles.

Yet another discovery by Dr. Whisker was Fredericka Worner. The widow of a gunsmith, she is listed as a gun-lock manufacturer in the Lancaster (Pennsylvania) City Directory beginning in 1899, and from 1909 until 1917–18 she was the only one so listed. Born in Germany in 1833, she came to America in 1861 and died in Lancaster County in 1918 at eighty-five.

American Factory Workers in the Firearms Trade

Although Samuel Colt did not employ women in his Hartford factory to make guns, he did use them to manufacture skin cartridges for percussion revolving handguns and longarms. The cartridge works was in operation from the mid-1850s through the late 1860s, possibly into the early 1870s. Original factory records list the women from that operation, which was situated away from the main factory complex because of the risk of an explosion.[10] At his London factory, in operation c. 1852–57, Colt also employed female workers. These were the subject of a Charles Dickens article in *Household Words* in 1855.[11]

Deborah J. Warner, in her book *Perfect in Her Place: Women at Work in Industrial America*, describes the work flow at the Watertown Arsenal, in Massachusetts, where women were employed to insert bullets into the cartridges, which men had first filled with gunpowder. When the task became mechanized in the 1870s, it was the women who loaded the powder, and soon they were running the machines themselves. Illustrations in the monograph show cartridge making at the U.S. Arsenal in Watertown, in 1861, and at the Union Metallic Cartridge Company, Bridgeport, Connecticut, in 1877—both from *Harper's Weekly*. An engraving from *Scientific American* in 1881 shows female workers "wedging and grooving bullets at Remington & Sons, Ilion, New York."

During World Wars I and II, women played a critical role in the manufacture of both ammunition and heavy ordnance. Today, virtually every gun factory in the world relies heavily on women in production jobs, as well as, increasingly, in management positions.

Mrs. Elizabeth Hart Jarvis Colt

One of history's intriguing ironies is that the widows of Samuel Colt and Oliver F. Winchester—two of the world's most famous arms manufacturers—were majority owners and managed their respective companies for longer periods of time than their husbands had. And they were contemporaries.

Samuel Colt met his wife-to-be, Elizabeth Hart Jarvis, in the early 1850s while on holiday in Newport, Rhode Island. The daughter of an Episcopal minister from Middletown, Connecticut, she was immediately smitten by the flamboyant and colorful colonel. At that time only in his late thirties, Colt was already an international celebrity, founder of the world's foremost privately owned gun-manufacturing firm, and America's first industrial tycoon.

Married in 1856, the couple went on a six-month honeymoon to Europe, including a visit to Russia to attend the coronation of Czar Alexander II. The trip forged a close bond between them, though their life together would be of only a few years' duration.

Elizabeth bore the colonel four children, and a fifth that was stillborn. Tragically, only Caldwell Hart Colt grew to adulthood, though he, too, would die before his mother.

The colonel's health failed him early in the Civil War era, and he died on January 10, 1862. Elizabeth inherited the bulk of the estate, and from then until the company was sold to New York investors in 1901, she was majority owner—in effect, the boss. During her decades of ownership, Colt's dominated the handgun market, and brought out such renowned models as the Single Action Army, or six-shooter, a broad range of self-cocking revolvers, a variety of rifles and shotguns, and several models of Gatling guns.

From 1865 through 1901, Colt's president was Elizabeth's brother, Richard W. H. Jarvis. With gifted managers, and a factory so advanced and formidable that it was a training ground and destination for inventors and mechanics, the company maintained its dominant position and increased its significance until well into the twentieth century.

Blessed with good health and the spirit and largesse of a kindly patron, Elizabeth was the archetype of a community philanthropist, doting on her employees, supportive of the company, and a generous donor to the city of Hartford. When a major part of the factory burned on February 4, 1864, she ordered that it be rebuilt at once. In economic hard times, her wealth ensured that the company would continue and that payrolls would be met.

Elizabeth's cultural interests were many, and she became one of America's first art collectors. Widely traveled, well-read, and with a diversity of interests, she was deeply concerned about public welfare and education, and held views that were progressive for her time.

To honor the memory of her late husband, Elizabeth commissioned the first Colt book, *Armsmear,* a history of the man, his firearms, and the company. The first of two five-hundred-copy printings appeared in 1866, and the book was instrumental in launching what would become the Colt "cult." The books were intended as gifts from Elizabeth to friends, libraries, and acquaintances, and most copies known are inscribed to the recipients from her.

Noted in *Armsmear* was the Cabinet of Memorials, exhibits at the couple's palatial Hartford mansion, Armsmear, honoring the colonel. An arms collection that he had kept at the mansion was expanded, at his widow's direction, to include models and variations of arms in production at the time of his death. To

121

Some self-defense S & W revolvers, and a pistol, accompanied by period advertising—each was suited for use by women, and so they were catered to in advertising. From the *top left,* .32 Double Action Fourth Model, number 133038. *Top right,* .38 Double Action Fourth Model, number 373594. At *center left,* .38 Single

Action Third Model, number 0, and to its *right,* .32 Double Action Fourth Model, number 221133. At *lower left,* gold-plated .32 Safety Hammerless Second Model, number 117574, with rich engraving by one of the Young brothers, and mother-of-pearl grips, with purse holster. Also in similar holster, at *lower right,* .32

Safety Hammerless Third Model, serial 179726, likewise finely engraved by one of the highly talented brothers, in gold and with pearl grips. At *bottom,* nickel-plated .35 automatic, Model of 1913, number 1576.

showcase the displays, Elizabeth commissioned architect Edward Tuckerman Potter to design richly carved cases and appropriate quarters. These cabinets survive both in the Wadsworth Atheneum Museum of Art and in Armsmear itself. Mrs. Colt was one of the first in the United States to have an arms collection displayed in her home—which happened also to be the first Colt collection in a private residence.

On her death in 1905, the arms collection and a broad range of art, decorative art, and memorabilia were bequeathed to the Atheneum. Her collection of sixty paintings, many by distinguished Hudson River Valley artists, remains today the largest art collection extant that was assembled by a woman from that period. Her adviser in assembling the collection was Frederick W. Church, an American painter of considerable stature.

No firearms are known to have been made for Mrs. Colt, but she played a direct role in some of the company's presentation pieces, continuing a practice that was a signature in her husband's modus operandi. Among these gifts were revolvers for the New York Sanitary Fair—a Civil War charity equivalent to today's Red Cross. Among other gifts of guns presented at her direction was a police model to the author of the technical section of *Armsmear*, Professor J. D. Butler. Although the inscription on the backstrap says it is from "Colt's P.F.A. Mfg. Co.," the impetus for the gift was Elizabeth Hart Jarvis Colt.

That her son Caldwell loved shooting and revered his father's memory was a source of pride and satisfaction to Elizabeth, who understandably doted on her only child. Caldwell became something of a playboy, but that does not diminish his own role in the firm's success. His premature death in 1894 was a vital factor in his mother's decision to allow the company to be sold.

Elizabeth's public memorials to the colonel, and to Caldwell and the infants, were the Church of the Good Shepherd, completed in 1869, and the accompanying parish house, dedicated in 1896. Numerous references to the colonel are evident in the church, among them coats of arms and inscriptions, as well as the stained-glass windows. In the largest of these, the figure of Saint Joseph bears a striking resemblance to Colonel Colt. The main entrance has revolver parts reproduced as architectural elements, and is known as the Armorer's Door. Both church and parish house remain in active use today, as does Armsmear, endowed as a retirement home for the widows of Episcopal ministers.

Elizabeth also bequeathed to the Atheneum funds to erect a Colt memorial wing, and to place the arms and other artifacts on exhibition, as well as leaving thousands of her husband's papers to the Connecticut Historical Society. Still further, her will gave Hartford most of the grounds of Armsmear, establishing the Colt Memorial Park, and funds to erect a tableaux of marble and bronze honoring the colonel. To date no woman has more generously endowed Hartford, and her largesse has been excelled by few men.

Mrs. Oliver F. Winchester

In contrast to Elizabeth Hart Jarvis Colt, far less is known of Jane Ellen Hope Winchester. Born in Portland, Maine, in 1807, she married O. F. Winchester in February 1834. Coming to New Haven in 1847, the Winchesters expanded their fortune through a business partnership with John M. Davies of New York in a shirt-manufacturing business. Winchester's investments in the Volcanic Repeating Arms Company, succeeded by the New Haven Arms Company, later the Henry Repeating Rifle Company, and still later (as of 1866) the Winchester Repeating Arms Company, resulted in a substantial fortune.

Among Winchester's philanthropies was a thirty-six-acre gift of land to Yale College (for establishment of an astronomical observatory), and gifts to the Scientific School and other departments at Yale. At his death on December 10, 1880, majority ownership of the Winchester company passed to Mrs. Winchester, making her one of New England's wealthiest women. She was also one of the most generous. Winchester Hall at Yale was one of her gifts. Erected in memory of her husband, the cost was in excess of $150,000. Among her other grants was $15,000 to establish the William Wirt Winchester Fund at the Yale Art School.

As of early March 1881, control of Winchester was in the hands of Mrs. O. F. Winchester (4,400 shares), her daughter-in-law, Mrs. William Wirt Winchester (777 shares), and her daughter, Mrs. Thomas G. Bennett (400 shares) (there was a total of 10,000 shares). As in the case of the Colt company, operations were in the hands of competent managers, among them William W. Converse, the husband of Mrs. W. W. Winchester's sister, and T. G. Bennett. Interestingly, as of 1881, the company's employees were approximately 20 to 25 percent women—primarily employed in the manufacture of ammunition, comprising about one-half of that workforce. A relatively limited number of women were employed in the firearms factory.

T. G. Bennett became president in 1889, and remained in that position until 1911. Following the death of Mrs. O. F. Winchester in 1897, 2,475 shares went to Mrs. T. G. Bennett and 2,000 to Mrs. William Wirt Winchester. For more than two decades, until the company reorganized in 1919, the family retained majority ownership of the company's 10,000 shares, with the women firmly in control. Mrs. William Wirt Winchester died in 1922, and Mrs. T. G. Bennett in 1926.

Mrs. William Wirt Winchester and the Winchester Mystery House

A fantasy heralded as "the world's strangest monument to a woman's fears," the Winchester Mystery House was built by Sarah Winchester following the deaths of her husband and their only child.

On the advice of her doctor, Sarah had moved to the gentler climate of California early in the 1890s, settling in San Jose. The saddened widow was then advised by a mystic that so long as work on her new house on Winchester Avenue continued, Mrs. Winchester would not be haunted by the spirits of the victims of Winchester firearms. For some thirty-eight years, until her death at age eighty-two, teams of carpenters were kept at work on the house around the clock. Though partially destroyed in the earthquake of 1906, the home boasts 160 rooms on six acres of land, most of that space actually occupied by the mammoth structure. The mansion features doors and staircases leading nowhere, some columns positioned upside down, a window built into the floor, and combinations of thirteen, including thirteen steps leading nowhere, and, allegedly, a will of thirteen parts, signed thirteen times.

Recently, however, evidence has been advanced that suggests that the structure was simply a hobby, a diversion, and that Mrs. Winchester derived great pleasure from building, remodeling, and rebuilding. She certainly had more than enough cash to finance what seemed to be an outrageous eccentricity. Harold Williamson's *Winchester: The Gun That Won the West*, estimates that the grieving widow spent between $3 million and $5 million dollars on the mansion. Williamson also notes that Mrs. Winchester made shrewd investments in California real estate, and was generous to New Haven charities. She established a memorial to her husband, who died from tuberculosis, with a total donation to the William Wirt Winchester Sanatorium of $1.2 million. The structure was formally opened in 1916. Yet another of her charities was the New Haven Hospital.

Women in the Gun Trade—1904

In May 1904, *The Sporting Goods Dealer* queried its readers about women in the gun-making trade in the United States.

Women Gunsmiths.

One of our English contemporaries is responsible for the statement that the census of 1901 gives England and Wales credit for 188 female gunsmiths. It would be interesting to learn how well versed in the art of making or repairing guns these women really are, since this is a trade in which the male sex is generally supposed to have a monopoly.

We would be glad to receive information concerning women in this country, if there are any, competent to do work entitling them to be called gunsmiths.[12]

Responses to the notice, if any, have not been found to date.

The Parker Brothers

Mrs. Mike Hanson began working at the Parker Brothers gun company, one of America's leading shotgun manufacturers, in 1908, at age sixteen. She was "one of the few women who stayed on the job as an actual gun craftsman. [She did] checkering of stocks and fore-ends."[13] Two other women employed in the Parker factory were the wife of the foreman of the checkering staff, Robert Rebstock, and his sister-in-law. Both were checkerers.

Antiquarian Siro Toffolon learned from Walter L. King, grandson of Parker designer Charles King, that his mother was an exceptional shot, so good that she put on shooting demonstrations for the company. "My mother and father used to take me to shooting matches and shows, and she was an expert shot."

Alice Roosevelt Longworth and William B. Ruger, Sr.

One of the most colorful figures from the realm of American politics, Alice Roosevelt was the first child of Theodore Roosevelt. Her father used to say that he could run the country, or he could control Alice, but he couldn't do both. Alice married Speaker of the House Nicholas Longworth, and their only child, Paulina, grew up to become the wife of Alexander McCormick Sturm. When Sturm, Ruger & Company, Inc., was founded in 1949, both Alex and Paulina helped in the office. Alex designed the company logo, and was involved in developing the style and format of the early advertising.

Alex died in 1951, followed by Paulina in 1953, leaving their daughter, Joanna, to inherit their holdings in the company. Joanna was raised by her grandmother in Washington, D.C., and for decades was the largest stockholder in Sturm, Ruger & Company, Inc. In an intriguing example of history repeating itself, the company, which would overtake Colt, Remington, Smith & Wesson, and Winchester to become America's leading gunmaker, had a woman as its largest single shareholder.

From time to time Mrs. Longworth would be driven to Southport, Connecticut, then the site of the firm's main factory, where she would have a tour and see how things were going.

Diana Keith Neal at Bishopstrow House, 1972, with photo in field
of her father, and his gunroom at Guernsey, in the 1980s.

Two special guns from the Keith Neal collection, with lady's features. The four-barrel flintlock duck's-foot pistol in .56 caliber, by Goodwin and Co., London, c. 1810, 8¾ inches overall length. The Russian (Tula) flintlock rifle, made for Empress Elizabeth of Russia, by John and Peter Lintz, dated 1756; the escutcheon with her arms, a double-headed eagle surmounted by three coronets, and the top of the barrel with the interlaced initials EP for Elizabeth Petrovna; 41 inches overall length. From a garniture of pistols and shotgun from the Hermitage Museum, St. Petersburg. Christie's sales of the Neal collection, in 2000, 2001, and 2002, were landmarks in the history of arms collecting.

On occasion, when she wished to have a gun, the company would make arrangements for her purchase. Climbing into her limousine, she would motor back to Washington, happy to know that her granddaughter's investment was doing well.

Tracy Nelson Geschickter—Replica Gunmaker

Tracy Nelson's father, Thomas B. Nelson, is this country's foremost maker of replica firearms and an authority on submachine guns. Continuing the tradition of family ties as a factor in women becoming part of the world of gunmaking, Tracy grew up in a world of arms and munitions. Her life in that universe would be the envy of many:

I grew up around the gun industry. . . . Let's just say I was the only girl on the block with a full-sized shooting range in the basement. On many evenings my father and I used to shoot a .22 rifle at tin cans in the range after dinner. I still enjoy trap shooting very much today.

My father's friends were frequent visitors at our home. . . . Among them were the international munitions dealer Henk Visser, writer Tom Swearengen, militaria collector Alan Cors, and Interarms vice president Richard Winter. The Ingrams and the Stoners[14] are very close family friends. The Ingrams' daughter, Michelle, and I became friends at the Great Western Show [once the greatest gun show in the world, at Pomona, California] in 1986; we immediately connected, comparing stories about what it was like being daughters of well-known men in the firearms business. . . .

Even though we had this fascinating entourage of people through our home, I did not totally understand my father's work until I was in high school. I knew my father had written several books and articles about firearms. I didn't realize the impact of his work or his reputation in the industry until he took me to the Las Vegas Antique Gun Show in 1978. People were asking him to autograph books, and introducing themselves, commenting on what an honor it was to meet him and asking him technical questions.

I thought they had the wrong guy—"Dad, who do these people think you are?"

My father started selling replica firearms in the United States in 1968. When he began the business, I don't believe he truly comprehended the full potential of the product line. Movies, television, police and government training centers, live theater, veterans groups, old-time photo studios, all had a need for realistic replica firearms. We have sold more than 2.5 million replicas to date.

I began working full-time in the business in 1985, and initially planned to work for a short term, while I searched for a full-time position in broadcasting. . . . I have been working for Collector's Armoury for fifteen years, and began as a file clerk, working my way up to vice-president of product development as well as controlling all purchases.

Through our business, I have been fortunate to meet and work with some fascinating people, like Bob Brown, publisher of *Soldier of Fortune* magazine, General Kalashnikov, designer of the AK-47, Arvo Ojala, fast-draw coach, and Bill Adams, former owner of Atlanta Cutlery and Museum Replicas.

I have found being a woman in the firearms industry anything but boring. In the search for new products, I have been around the United States, and around the world. Being a woman and traveling alone to some of these locations has been a challenge and provided some interesting opportunities. At the invitation of Vista University, Johannesburg, I lectured on "Direct Marketing in America" (1991). During apartheid, in 1988, two friends on the South African police force "smuggled" me into some of the more dangerous areas of Soweto, where I took some intriguing photographs—even of the Mandelas' yard! I have witnessed coups in Bangkok and Zimbabwe, been stranded in Zambia, and experienced a memorable earthquake in Tokyo. It is ironic that through all the unusual places I have been, the only time I was ever robbed was in New York City, where I have been mugged twice.

Sometimes it has been difficult to be taken seriously in a "man's world":

At one trade show, some people were taking pictures of me holding our replica Uzi. A short man in a tall cowboy hat approached me and said, "Hey darlin', any idea when your boss will be returnin'? I had some

technical questions about your Uzi." It took a while to convince him that I was "the boss." He was surprised to find out that I knew both the model, and the designer himself, very well.

The entertainment industry has been a source of both business and pleasure: Among the films I've served as a consultant to on arms are *The Untouchables* and *The Bodyguard*, and I have enjoyed getting to know John Wayne's family, from some limited edition projects we developed for the Franklin Mint.

I have thoroughly enjoyed working in this business, and in the last few years more and more women are becoming involved. Many are daughters, sisters, or wives who end up taking over the family enterprise.[15]

Sharon Dressel—Master Stockmaker

Other than as machine operators, assemblers, or polishers in factories, women gunsmiths remain a rarity in the hands-on making of firearms in the United States. One of the best of the current crop of gunsmiths is the stockmaker Sharon Dressel. When a five-year-old girl, her grandmother said, "Child, if you can't do something right, don't waste your time with it." That credo has guided Dressel all her life, and has established her as one of the premier gun artisans in America.

She was the first female to enroll in a two-year gunsmithing program at a junior college, and her twenty-seven-hour week at the bench "covered everything from welding to woodworking to machining to metallurgy." On at least two occasions she considered quitting. But her teachers, especially Russ Holmes, convinced her to stay. "He backed me in any project and any approach I wanted to take in the class." Later she was influenced by master stockmaker Joe Balickie, who "really encouraged me to follow my dream and go into gunsmithing." After examining two of Balickie's creations, she "knew from that point on that [she] wanted to build custom guns. . . ."

At *lower left,* Diana Keith Neal as a little girl with her own special flintlock shooting kit. And as a grown-up firing a flintlock pistol, as well as in mod outfit at family's Bishopstrow House. At *top left,* fellow Liveryman of the Worshipful Company of gunmakers, London, Wendy Dyson. Remaining images at *top,* of Jim and Lesia Blanchard, while on safari in Africa, accompanied by Roman and Veronica Bubniw; among sites are (from *left*) Tsavo, Tanzania,

Murchison Falls (Uganda), Tanzania, and Mountains of the Moon (Uganda); Blanchard, the foremost collector of Manhattan firearms, died in 1999; his widow, Lesia, underwrote a book on Manhattans, a work in progress for publication in 2003. At *center,* Dennis and Karen LeVett, with daughters Amanda and Kate, 2001, with the LeVett collection of Paterson Colts. *Lower right,* Petra Martin on safari in Tanzania, 1985, with her fringe-eared oryx trophy, and local Masai. At *right,* the Parady sisters, whose innovations streamlined the works at Connecticut gunmaker

Traditions in the 1980s. To their *left,* Beverly Rhodes Haynes, from the Colt Historical Department. To her *right,* Bob and Margie Petersen, collectors of firearms and automobiles who have achieved legendary status.

The Dressel trademark is "tasteful, understated elegance." She thinks of firearms as "not really dainty, but sort of chic looking." Her skills resulted, in 1988, in her acceptance as a member by the American Custom Gunmakers Guild, the only other female member of which was an engraver. A fine shotgun she stocked for the North Carolina chapter of the Wild Turkey Federation, a customized Browning Citori 12 gauge, was one of the organization's most successful fund-raising projects.

Cartridge making at Colt's and at a government arsenal (*upper left* and *lower left*); with images representing the German cartridge firm of Brenneke, *above,* founded in 1895, and at times in its past managed by women family members. Winchester engraver Pauline Muerrle at her bench, *top center;* to *right* of Daniela Fanzoj, sales manager of Johanna Fanzoj, gunmakers in Ferlach, Austria, since 1790. Catherine Williams, Beretta USA, at *bottom center,* with Jeffrey K. Reh, Ugo Gussalli Beretta, and General Norman Schwarzkopf. At *center* and *far right,* women of America Remembers, Ashland, Virginia, makers of firearms honoring historic figures, including Annie Oakley. In *right* image, from *left,* Donna Wall, Karen Moore, Kirstin Puccinelli, Sage McMichael, Michelle Godsey, President Paul Warden, and Melissa Whitley, and Joseph Cusumano.

At *top right,* holding Bowie knife and Tiffany Colt, author's associate, Judi Glover. *Bottom right,* big game and bird hunter Julie Lombardo, with friend, visiting Connecticut c. 1990. Trophy mule deer taken in late '30s to early '40s by Ruth Leupold, in Oregon. Early on in her marriage to Marcus Leopold, her hunting enthusiasm was instrumental in inspiring Marcus to design a better sighting instrument—after an unpleasant hunt with a fogged rifle scope. Thus was founded what is today Leupold-Stevens, ranked among the leading scope makers.

One of her aims is "to specialize in building small guns for small people. I don't think the manufacturers realize how much demand there is for such a product. There are a lot of junior-size people, including women, who hunt."

Though she takes her greatest pleasure from stockmaking, she applies that same sense of perfectionism to metalwork: "You have to put in as much time as it takes and believe that what you're doing is worthwhile."[16]

Antiquarians and Collectors

The universe of antiquarians and collectors of arms has traditionally been populated by men. Few curators or directors of arms and armor collections have been women. Seldom has a woman written a book, or even an article, on antique or collectible arms. There are, however, four women who have each had a distinct impact on the appreciation and understanding of arms.

Anita Reinhard, Metropolitan Museum of Art

The career of Anita Reinhard spanned more than seventy years, and paralleled a gradual increase in the study of traditional arms and armor by European and American scholars. Her expertise has been matched by only a few in the history of the field.

Anita was born in Chester, Pennsylvania, in 1887, the daughter of Swiss immigrants. Her schooling was in Italy and in Switzerland, where she studied languages. She began museum work at the Commercial Museum in Philadelphia, then went to the Pennsylvania Museum (now the Philadelphia Museum of Art). In November 1919, she became secretary to Dr. Bashford Dean, curator of arms and armor at the Metropolitan Museum of Art, New York.

She did extensive bibliographical research as part of her work in what was then a new department at the museum, and her abilities led, in 1927, to her appointment as assistant curator—making her the first woman to hold a curatorial position in an American museum. That same year she went to Spain to negotiate the purchase of an important collection for the museum and for Chicago collector George F. Harding. A year later she was in Paris, supervising publication of two important museum catalogs written by Dr. Dean, the *Catalogue of European Court Swords and Hunting Swords* and the *Catalogue of European Daggers*. Stuart W. Pyhrr, the Metropolitan Museum's Arthur Ochs Sulzberger curator of arms and armor, notes that "the quality of their production was due in large part to her exacting standards."

World War II saw Reinhard assisting the department in projects on behalf of the war effort. She was a member of a government commission identifying major historic monuments in Europe, in order to spare them from destruction by Allied bombs.

Retiring from the Metropolitan Museum in 1947, at the age of sixty she traveled extensively in Europe, continuing her research. In the mid-1950s, she became the assistant to C. O. von Kienbusch, whose wonderful collection of arms and armor was bequeathed to the Philadelphia Museum of Art in 1976, and advised the museum on the collection's installation. In her nineties she was still studying and writing about arms and armor and the literature on the subject. She died on December 15, 1985, at the age of 98.[17]

Elsa Locke and the Locke Collection of Firearms

When William M. Locke began collecting firearms before World War I, little did he know that his companion for most of his life in this dedicated quest would be his wife, Elsa. The couple were married in 1915, settling at first in the Locke family home in Stanton, Nebraska.

The arms collection developed quickly after the war, and through the 1920s and '30s the Lockes traveled as much as possible, maintaining a steady correspondence with collectors, dealers, and private owners all over the United States.

Elsa Locke was crucial to the couple's unrelenting search for new specimens. She kept copious notebooks on their travels, and while her husband met with a collector, she often visited with the collector's wife. It was not unusual for her to learn things about a collection that her husband would not. Locke told the author of a visit made to Stephen Van Renssalaer, an early collector from a distinguished old New York family. He had hidden a cache of guns from Locke, but Elsa was shown these by the collector's wife. It was only because of Elsa's wisdom and sagacity that Locke was able to buy some of those pieces.

On retirement late in the 1950s, the Lockes were able to extend their travels in search of more pieces for their collection of American firearms—already recognized as the best ever put together—in public or private hands. Beginning in 1959, the couple visited England and Europe on several occasions. On a 1969 trip to Russia, they were able to see the Colts presented to Czars Nicholas I and Alexander II and their court. The Locke collection contained the mate to one of these famous revolvers.

The treasure of the Locke collection, the Sultan of Turkey Colt Dragoon, was acquired by yet another American couple keen on arms collecting, George and Butonne Repaire, after William Locke's death in 1972. It was their treasured possession until the mid-1990s, at which time they decided the cased revolver was too important to be held privately. They chose to donate it to the Metropolitan Museum of Art's Arms and Armor Galleries. The decision to make that gift was as much Butonne's as it was of her husband's.

Cathy Tolbert

COLT

FIREARMS

QUALITY MAKES IT A COLT

HELLWEG LTD

Team Bianchi

BIANCHI INTERNATIONAL

BIANCHI

Leslie Easterbrook

Famars

The Bianchi Cup

BEGINNER'S GUIDE TO THE SHOTGUN SPORTS

TO ORDER CALL TOLL FREE 888-GO SHOOT

Above: Petra Martin, with daughter Greta, in the wine cellar of their Napa Valley Martin Estates. Array of firearms, accessories, and memorabilia from husband and father Greg's collection, including a painting commissioned by Samuel Colt depicting a ship blown up in demonstration of his submarine mine, 1842. For Petra Martin hunting in Africa, see page 127. At age nine, Greta earned a lifetime hunting license in California.

Diana Keith Neal, Daughter of William Keith Neal, Antique Arms Collector Nonpareil

In Great Britain, another famous collecting couple was W. Keith Neal and his wife, Jane. For decades Neal was the world's premier collector of antique firearms. The Neals' daughter, Diana, remembers their collection of beautiful yet functional guns, which she was able to shoot from time to time.

My first recollection of shooting was when I was five or six years old. I balanced a small flintlock pocket pistol on the back of a kitchen chair.... Some twenty feet away was a rusty iron panel with a piece of white card in front of it. I don't remember any practice run with a black powder "blank"—this pistol contained a lead ball all right, and had been carefully loaded by my father, while my mother hovered nervously nearby, the whole business watched with amusement by our cook Gladys.

I do remember the impact on my hand—I don't remember whether or not I hit the target, but the initiation test had been passed, and it was the beginning of many hours of shooting antique guns and pistols with my father.

For a start, I was a useful slave in the workshop. A proper Victorian one, the workshop was top-lit and faced north like an artist's studio, with a decorative cast iron grate for a coal fire. This was where the bullets were made. The correct size of bullet mould having been selected, grey roof leading was cut up with a giant pair of scissors and heated in an antique crucible over the fire. I held the bullet mould closed tight, the handles wrapped in a duster, while my father poured in the molten lead. When cool, out rolled a bright silver ball with a small "sprue" of lead which I helped file down to round off the ball. It had to be a perfect fit; an iota too large and it could jam, a major task to dislodge from a barrel. . . .[18]

As new guns and pistols were added to the collection, "often in exciting great crates delivered by truck from exotic places," some needed to be stripped and cleaned. Neal preferred to do this himself, with only the occasional item sent to his restorer, Richard Chapman. Neal's favorites were the "plain but elegant English sporting guns from the mid-eighteenth to the early nineteenth century or cases of the best English pistols, made for gentlemen who imagined they might duel. . . ." Each gun was put to his shoulder "to see how it would shoot—did it fit? On many occasions he looked at me and said, 'Shall we try and fire this, Monx?'"

Sometimes, this presented a serious risk—such as the long-running experiment with a series of eighteenth-century German wheel-lock air rifles, trying to make the air reservoir valve in the stock airtight with a piece of leather.

Perhaps the funniest occasion, conducted with me in secret, was firing a "duck's foot" pistol. Romantically thought to have been made to dispel mutinies on board ship, genuine examples are extremely rare. We loaded up each of the four barrels, which splay out from the action and discharge simultaneously, but at an ever-widening angle, so one has no control of aim. There was a thunderous explosion, the lead balls fanning out and disappearing through various doors around the stable courtyard. The recoil nearly broke my father's wrist, and cracked the butt right through. He did admit afterwards that he had been somewhat overgenerous with the charge.

The more decorous firing sessions of these antique pieces took place on the lawn at Bishopstrow, the Regency house in Wiltshire where I grew up. These occasions became a kind of celebratory ritual to honour special guests. To qualify, my father had to detect in the guest a genuine fascination for the subject. Time was not wasted on those with simply an idle interest; the guns and pistols took time to prepare, and pieces had to be cleaned with cold, then boiling water and rubbed down afterwards. However, collectors from overseas—of which there was a steady stream, especially from the United States—tended to qualify for a cased set of Manton or Purdey dueling pistols—and retrieved from the grass an unusual souvenir of their visit, a completely flattened piece of lead, the very origin of a "SPLAT" from Dan Dare.

A cannon firing would honor state occasions, such as the coronation of Elizabeth II or her Silver Jubilee. For the former, watched eagerly by the entire village:

My father managed to co-ordinate detonation with the moment Prince Philip knelt to pay allegiance to the Queen. For my coming-out dance a cannon firing contributed to the cabaret. These were spectacular performances. A tractor dragged a three-pounder up to the top of the tumulus in front of the house and the cannon was aimed towards Boreham Fields, an ugly garrison sprawl near the neighbouring School of Infantry, on the edge of Salisbury Plain. A blank charge was fired of course, but the "whoomph" and flash was impressive, as a row of overexcited children waited for the bang, their hands over their ears.

Additional drama was added to these occasions by the presence of my father's current gun dog. "Far too cruel to keep Frisk/Boza/Ruskus shut up and miss the shooting," he would insist. Boza, a Newfoundland, would bark frenetically until the cannon was fired, and then tear off to retrieve the burning wadding in her mouth. Something about the smell of smouldering sulphur was as tempting to a retriever as a fallen bird.

Keith Neal's hero was famed sportsman Colonel Peter Hawker (1786–1853). A number of Hawker's guns were in the Neal Collection including the remains of "Big Joe," his duck gun, as well as "Old Joe," his double game gun, both "characters" from his Diaries. Hawker had lived not so far from Bishopstrow, at Longparish in Hampshire, near the famous trout stream, the Test.

Our homemade shooting range at Bishopstrow, which had originally been a grass tennis court, was formalised by the arrival of Colonel Peter Hawker's own target—a hefty cast iron disc, black-painted with a white centre, swinging from a six-foot-high tubular frame to allow for recoil. Much to his joy, my father had managed to acquire this from one of Hawker's descendants, the flying ace, Tyrrell Hawker. From now on, a bullet made a satisfactory clang as it hit the target, and enthusiasts had the additional pleasure of knowing they were aiming where once the great sportsman had fired.

Diana's mother was also a good shot, and "although she deferred to my father, when I was small, she was no mean expert on his collection." Since Neal was often away traveling, "in-evitably, some passionate arms collector turned up at home wanting a tour."

Normally [my mother] refused, but the Chief of the Imperial General Staff, Field-Marshal Sir Francis Festing, with his aide-de-camp, the Duke of Kent, was a tricky one. Could the field-marshal have a fifteen-minute visit on his way to the School of Infantry, the aide asked? It could not be longer than that; he would arrive at 6:00 P.M., and depart at 6:15, when he needed to attend the official unveiling of his portrait. It was more of an order. My mother agreed.

Bang on time a cavalcade of vehicles and outriders drew up, pennants flying from the car bonnets, and in full mess kit, the head of the British army stepped out of his car. I was about ten years old, awestruck by this giant in ceremonial splendour, carrying a stick. My mother nervously began her tour of the gun-rooms, starting in the bow-fronted Dining Room, where the walls were lined with guns, some along the mirrored alcove, others spread out on the table, before proceeding upstairs to the Arch Room and Yellow Gun Room (these were originally the spare bedrooms, which, as the collection grew, doubled as gun rooms, fitted with display racks, the wardrobes and drawers filled with pistols, to the confusion of non-gun-collecting guests).

At 7:30 P.M., the field marshal was still there, despite frustrated telephone calls from the Officers' Mess, where the reception was standing waiting. My mother had made a convert. Previously a collector of Japanese swords, Frankie Festing returned soon after to meet my father, and so began a long-lasting gun-collecting friendship between the two men. . . .

In 1976 Neal decided to move the collection to Guernsey, in the Channel Islands, buying a smaller house, the arms displayed securely in a converted adjacent barn:

After my parents' death, I found myself confronted with this enormous and spectacular collection which posed many questions for me and my two children. My son Erskine was aged eleven when my father died, and had luckily been old enough to be taught to shoot a flintlock pistol by his grandfather. Indeed their favourite sport together was firing a small flint-lock air rifle from his bedroom window. I knew my father had meant us to get some fun out of the collec-tion, beyond wrestling with questions of security and insurance. And it gave me time to think about its fu-ture, with the support of our ally, Peter Hawkins, a long-standing family friend.

Peter picked out a pair of English cased flintlock dueling pistols by Grierson, dating from about 1795, for Erskine. It did not take Erskine long to master his new toys and once more lead bullets were cast. I got the Hawker target out of store and we cleared the land at the top of the property, which revealed the re-mains of another old lawn tennis court. We had a new firing range.

Our first official guests to shoot were the new gov-ernor of Guernsey and his entourage who came for a tour of the collection. This brought back memories of the field-marshal's visit; I think I was as apprehensive as my mother had been. Plenty can go wrong with old weaponry, and hitting the centre of the target con-vincingly at fifteen paces can be more difficult than it appears. I did not want a misfire—and I certainly could not afford to miss. But all went according to plan; the governor, an admiral and veteran of the Falklands War, made an impressive figure shooting, standing sideways, straight as a ramrod, like an en-graving from a book of military exercises. And thankfully I managed a bull's-eye.

In recent times our fun with black powder has been curtailed, and the Guernsey property, which gave us secure and windless conditions, has been sold. Except for one memorable crisp December day, that is, my birthday, on a friend's farm in Dorset. Other guests included the actor and gun collector Michael Gam-bon, as well as my son and daughter. The owner of a Russian T-54 tank, our host fired it up and roared up the hill, the Red Flag fluttering behind in a cloud of diesel smoke, to the accompaniment of the flashbangs of the faithful Griersons. How W. Keith Neal would have approved.[19]

Kathleen Hoyt, Historian, Colt's Manufacturing Company, Inc.

The only woman to have been appointed histo-rian at any of the world's gunmakers, Kathleen Hoyt assumed her position with Colt's Manu-facturing Company in 1988, selected "by a very brave vice president of sales and marketing, Robert Morrison." The reason for Hoyt's reference to "brave" is evident in her statement of employment at the company in 1965:

I accepted a position in the Repair Department, known today as the Product Service Department. My supervisor was Al De John, one of the company's most experienced and knowledgeable employees, who first worked at the company prior to his serving in the European theater of World War II. De John and I responded to most of the phone and mail inquiries received from customers, a great learning experience for me, [which exposed] me to all aspects of the business, technical, historical, legal, public relations, and so forth—a perfect base to build on.

In 1965, as is still the case today, the majority of our customers were male, and most of my work associates were also male. At the time it was very difficult for a woman to be accepted by this male-dominated clientele. On many occasions I would be told by callers that they did not want to talk to a woman and to put a man on the phone! As time progressed and especially with repeat customers they began to recognize that I would not make a promise I could not keep and they began to trust me, and eventually to seek me out.

It was good fortune to work under Al De John, who was very progressive and willing to promote on merit, whether male or female. I also worked with master gunsmith Don Tedford who was willing to teach me anything I wanted to know. Both these men were my early mentors, and provided me with an astute education in firearms.[20]

Since her father and grandfather had both worked at Colt's for over thirty years, Kathleen was familiar with firearms when she joined the company. Gradually she acquired expertise, and advanced with the firm. By 1976 the custom engraving business had grown to the point that a formal custom shop was established, separated from product service. Soon she became custom shop coordinator, and as business grew, she became the shop's administrative supervisor—with ten employees reporting to her.

When the custom shop was downsized in 1983, I moved into the position of assistant supervisor for the customer service department, dealing daily with retail customers, dealers, distributors, and warranty stations—including customer complaints. Further, any firearms involved in legal issues were processed through my office, and I was the contact and coordinator between our legal department, product service, and the customer. At this point in time, the resistance to speaking with a female was beginning to subside, as long as you were able to hold your own in conversation and it was determined that you had some gun knowledge. There would be the occasional person who would insist upon speaking to my boss, and for a few years that gave me some joy, as my immediate boss was also a female (Diane Calvo).

Unfortunately there was a person then in charge of the product service department "who was quite chauvinistic and made no effort to disguise it." He and Kathleen "went head to head on more than one occasion, but through perseverance and a little of [my] Irish temper" he quickly learned "he was not going to get the better of me." On a few occasions, the department manager, Tom Uznanski, "would have to deftly referee."

In 1988 the company began the search for an individual to train under the current historian, Martin Huber, then aging and nearing normal retirement, and having to deal with some health issues. It appeared that I was the qualified candidate, but the issue did rise as to whether the 99 percent exclusive male clientele would accept a female. Uznanski, De John, and Morrison were all in favor of my appointment to the position.

But my reception as historian was somewhat negative: although I don't recall hearing any antifemale sentiment it was disguised behind comments that I would never be able to replace Ron Wagner, or Marty Huber. Being good friends with both previous historians, I did not feel that I wanted to replace them, but I did want to stand beside them. They had served the company well and deserved the level of respect they had within the company and with customers. From day one as historian I decided that I would have to work very hard to establish my place in Colt history. . . . I learned a great deal from my predecessors, who shared over 110 years of experience between them. Often Beverly (Rhodes) Haynes would join us, as she worked with Marty in the department since 1984, and I felt it important for her to participate, since she would be next in line for the historian's position. . . .

Kathleen Hoyt has finished her first book, coauthored with the late Don Wilkerson, entitled *The Official Record of the Colt Single Action Army Revolver—1873 Through 1895.* Further, she has assisted numerous authors and researchers over the years, and has, by far, the most comprehensive understanding and knowledge of the Colt factory archives. She has appeared in the History Channel series *Tales of the Gun,* and coordinates Colt's contacts with the several arms collectors associations, both around the country and worldwide. She has assisted in research work for the National Firearms Museum, and served on the Committee for the Preservation of the Rampant Colt Statue, now housed at the Raymond Baldwin Museum of Connecticut History. Her husband, David Hoyt, is a computer wizard, and is employed at Colt's as a senior systems analyst.

The Art of the Gun

The use of original designs to decorate firearms is rare. Most embellished arms carry on traditional motifs of scrolls, borders, and panel scenes, established years previously by other engravers, some centuries old. For an artist to create something fresh and original requires imagination and inspiration. Among the most accomplished of designers of firearms embellishments today is Tiffany & Company's April Flory.

Sandi Strichman's Colt Diamondback Revolver—by April Flory

When George A. Strichman, chairman of the board, Colt Industries, decided to create a special present for his wife, he—like so many other loving husbands—chose Tiffany & Co. as the source. This gift, however, marked only the second in Tiffany's post–World War I history of a firearm given to a spouse. How all this came about is revealing of one of the most exclusive domains in the atelier of America's greatest name in decorative arts.

In 1982 the author approached Strichman with the suggestion that he commission both Cartier and Tiffany to design deluxe firearms for his private collection of decorated Colts. Within a week, the chairman had a favorable response from Tiffany—and shortly thereafter we met with Paul Epifanio, manager of the company's corporate design staff. Within a year, designs had been completed for a deluxe pair of Single Action Army revolvers for the chairman's collection.

That commission complete, the chairman decided to order a revolver as a present for his wife, Sandi. The design staff traveled to the Strichman home at Premium Point, New Rochelle, under the guise of seeing the Strichman arms collection. April Flory, the designer of Mrs. Strichman's revolver, toured the residence with Paul Epifanio and made special note of Mrs. Strichman's own collections—where orchids were a favorite passion. It was the orchid that the designers suggested as the Diamondback's theme.

134

April Flory at her desk in the Tiffany & Co. design department, with drawings of designs created for Sandi Strichman and other clientele.

When the chairman approved, Flory created the elegant revolver pictured here. It was her first firearms design. The second was a Colt Third Model Dragoon revolver, for the author, inspired by the Battle of the Little Big Horn. Ms. Flory's third design was another Diamondback, also for the author, based on the Sandi Strichman orchid revolver. And her fourth was for the U.S. Historical Society, a Model 1860 Army Colt, an interpretation of the American-eagle motif, central to the society's logo.

These four revolvers comprise some of the most inspired and original firearms embellishments in the history of gunmaking.

THE TIFFANY & CO
COLT DIAMONDBACK
CUSTOM MADE FOR
SANDRA J. STRICHMAN
FOR THE
STRICHMAN COLLECTION

FEATURED IN
PATRIOTISM AND DECORATIVE ART
THE ARMS OF TIFFANY & CO.
LOAN EXHIBITION AND BOOK
1 9 8 8

The Sandi Strichman gold inlaid and *vermeil* presentation Colt Diamondback revolver.

CHAPTER V

Annie Oakley—Shooting's Heroine:
"A Little Lady Made of Steel Wires"

If women and girls would learn to shoot, they would add to their happiness by falling in love with one of the finest outdoor sports.

—Annie Oakley

Still a legend decades after her death, Annie Oakley remains not only the most famous lady shot of all times, but the most famous sharpshooter of either gender. The product of a humble background and a victim of child abuse, she not only mastered the shooting sports but became an accomplished horsewoman and athlete—and an authentic superstar. Miss Oakley's extraordinary achievements made her an international role model, led to her portrayal in films and on Broadway, and established her reputation as an American heroine who made her mark in a field thought by men to be their domain.

Facing page: Career of Annie Oakley, as well documented visually as that of any woman in America up to the early twentieth century. Press articles, often based on firsthand interviews, appeared on a regular basis. Endorsing the guns of selected makers, she was pictured using these arms—among them the Remington Model 12 slide-action rifle, Stevens tip-up Pocket Rifle, and even the Spencer slide-action shotgun, examples of which are pictured here, from the Ken Waite collection. In recognition of Oakley's tremendous impact on the popularity of the shooting sports, the Remington Arms Company gave her famous nickname to a line of cartridges. The "Sure Shot" brand appeared in the 1890s, and continues to this day—based on "Little Sure Shot," the nickname bestowed on her by Sitting Bull in 1884.

Center: Detail from 1901 poster capturing one of many remarkable feats in Miss Oakley's outdoor performances.

SHOOTING DOUBLES FROM A WHEEL

Known the world over as Annie Oakley, the girl who became the "Peerless Wing Shot" and "Little Sure Shot" was born Phoebe Ann Moses, on August 13, 1860, in Woodland, Darke County, Ohio. She had an early fascination with shooting, and "an inherent love for fire-arms and hunting." When her father died suddenly and tragically, her large family, Quakers from Pennsylvania, were nearly destitute. By age twelve, she had become the breadwinner, shooting game as a market hunter and mastering the skills of a trapper.

Annie's career as an exhibition shooter was triggered in 1881, when she met Frank E. Butler, a traveling marksman. His act specialized in challenging the local best shot to a match, for money. Visiting near Cincinnati, his well-chosen competition happened to be the teenage Annie— all of five feet tall and one hundred pounds. Of

course, she won the match—shooting at fast-flying live birds. After a year's courtship, the two married, and soon devised a traveling act, as the team of Butler & Oakley.

Their big break came when they were hired to appear in Buffalo Bill's Wild West, in 1885. A major star of Cody's troupe for a total of seventeen years, Miss Oakley also headlined with other Wild West shows, appeared on stage (as both shooter and actress), on film (she was the first woman captured on celluloid by Thomas Edison), as well as shooting challenge matches (often for money), competing in trap events, and coaching thousands of women on shooting. The esteem in which she was held was especially remarkable because show business people at that time were generally regarded as of questionable character and morals. Through all her experiences—indeed, adventures—in what was then a man's world (though beginning to change in ways that she heavily influenced), Annie Oakley forever remained a lady.

In the author's *Buffalo Bill's Wild West*, the chapter "Annie Oakley: Superstar, Athlete, and Modern Lady" presents a thoroughly illustrated, detailed biography of the amazing Miss Oakley. The reader is encouraged to review that material, and to fuse it with the present chapter, which presents new text and illustrations, and quotations from writings of the star herself, such as "Why Ladies Should Learn to Shoot" and other

inspiring works in which Miss Oakley encouraged women to take up the shooting sports, enjoy the outdoors, and be self-reliant. Previously unpublished photographs of firearms from her collection are also presented, as well as portraits and candid photographs from various periods throughout her career.*

Royal Admiration for the "Peerless Wing Shot"

As Oakley and Butler toured the United States and Europe, they collected press clippings and saved correspondence, and she maintained an autograph book, collecting signatures of the mighty and famous. The Oakley-Butler scrapbooks are at the Buffalo Bill Historical Center, Cody, Wyoming. Unfortunately, the couple often failed to cite sources and dates for these clips. As a consequence, establishing the date and place of an article is often problematic. The piece that follows—unusual in that it frequently quotes Oakley, rather than paraphrasing her, or simply writing about her—is from a U.S. newspaper dating from around 1918. The memoir was written after an interview with Miss Oakley in Pinehurst, North Carolina.

*See Appendix B.

Facing page: Reverse side of shooting mirror used by Miss Oakley, and its velvet case, the former covered in leather and bearing Miss Oakley's signature. Note the stamp of the markswoman's name on the coin, indicating it was she who shot it. Envelope *above* signed by Miss Oakley and probably donated to a charity fund-raiser. Envelope *above* and coin to *right* were purchased by an admirer, and subsequently traded for a container of beer at a Lancaster *Schuetzen Verein;* believed contributed by Miss Oakley. Note her signature on the envelope; likely a fund-raising opportunity for charity. Medals on her bodice are among those melted down by Miss Oakley, the proceeds given to charity.

Following page: Four of the best cabinet card Oakley portraits, with a coin shot by her during an English tour, and the coin used at a *Schuetzenfest.* Note the medals, as well as the array of guns, neat attire, hat with star, and her poise.

Memories of Annie Oakley: The Royal Box at the Queen's Jubilee and a Rifle Contest with the Prince of Wales

It was during the big trap shooting week at Pinehurst [North Carolina] . . . that we fell to discussing famous matches in times gone by. The old hands had many extraordinary things to relate, but Annie Oakley took the first prize. She said that she had herself shot many memorable contests in her time, but none that had gained the publicity and been favored with the unique interest and subsequent history of a challenge she accepted at the London Gun Club during the Queen's jubilee [1887].

"Queen Victoria herself had a box at the Wild West, and gave a party for the assembled flower of the Royal line of Europe, which started the adventure. I had a special program that day, and the novelty of the whole performance and particularly the unusual spectacle of a girl shooting took their interest to such an extent that I was sent for and presented to the company. It was almost too much—there were four kings and five queens, and a body guard of dukes and field marshals—Denmark, Belgium, Sweden and Italy. The Crown Prince of Germany and the Prince and Princess of Wales, and the Grand Duke Michael were in the party."

VICTORIA'S "CLEVER LITTLE GIRL"

"What was my impression? Well! the Prince of Wales was the popular idol of the people at the time, and created the most impression upon my fancy—particularly since we became fast friends, and had many a shooting match afterwards. The present Kaiser's father was a vigorous and kindly man, who received me with the greatest courtesy, and left the idea which has never been eradicated that he was of an altogether different temperament from the Kaiser. Queen Victoria was gracious, and said I was a very clever little girl. I was not so very little, and I was a married woman, but I suppose the costume gave the impression that I was shooting from the high school.

"Well! to go on with the story. The Prince of Wales and the Grand Duke Michael both took more than a curious interest in the shooting. The Duke was reputed to be one of the best shots in Russia, and Edward was no slouch with a gun. They wanted me to try it out under their accustomed conditions, and had a regular exhibition staged at the London Gun Club.

They were pleased all right. The Prince had a gold medal struck—I have it now some place—with the crest of the club on one side, and an inscription on the other, which read:

'You are the Greatest Shot I have ever seen. EDWARD.'"

THE WIMBLEDON RIFLE CLUB

"I don't suppose I really was, but they took a fancy to the idea of a country girl from the West outshooting their professionals. I don't believe however that it was there that the Grand Duke got the idea of tackling me himself. For a little while later the Prince asked me down to Wimbledon where they had the ranges and the military camp, and we took a crack at the running deer. It wasn't a real deer. They shoot with rifles at 100 yards at a target made like a deer that is drawn across the country, up and down hill, and behind rocks and obstacles on the dead run. The target is just on the front quarter—and it is considered a disgrace and cause of a penalty to hit the hind quarter. Idea of course is that such a shot would wound the animal and still let him escape to misery.

"Earl [de Grey], who was probably the best shot in Europe at the time, gave me some confidential and careful advice before I took the stand, and I succeeded in hitting the bull's-eye on the four-quarter five times running. The Prince was a very fair shot too; he hit it three times, and the other two were very close, perfectly safe to have killed the animal if he had been more [vulnerable] than pig iron. This gave the Duke an idea. . . ."

THE GRAND DUKE CHALLENGES

"The Duke sent me a friendly challenge to shoot against him at the Club, clay pigeons at unknown angles. I accepted promptly for the next morning. And then there was a pow wow. [Nate] Salisbury, the manager [of Buffalo Bill's Wild West], said if it was a possible thing I should shoot him off his feet. But Cody and Major Burke said it wasn't done, and that I must let him win. Now that was all very well, but if his reputation was correct, I wouldn't have to bother about the last view. It would take all I could do to hold up my end. We decided that whatever anyone thought of it I should make a real match of it, and

win if there was any way. From the traps and some things we had heard my husband, Frank Butler, and I decided that a good many of his fine records were made with the targets thrown only 40 feet. We decided to make a hard trial of it, and screw the traps down to throw a 65-yard bird. And then we all assembled, and the shoot was on. I will say that he was game, and a very good shooter too. He was at a little disadvantage, because his gun was too light for fast work. I beat him by a small margin, after a real contest."

THE AMAZING CONSEQUENCE

"And then you ought to have heard the howl. I hadn't suspected anything of the sort. Whether he did I can't tell. But anyway shooting was his long suit, and when it was reported that he had been beaten the papers . . . were pink with sarcastic accounts of this cavalier who was outdone at his own game by a little girl from Kokamo—of this Lockinvar who was no match for short dresses, and whose warlike career faded before the onset of the Indiana kindergarten. It was the most amazing and unexpected publicity I ever experienced. . . ."

Annie Oakley Guns on Display

The Oakley collection of firearms was publicly recognized as among the finest in America. From time to time pieces would be placed on public display, an element of the ongoing promotion of the celebrated sharpshooter. A piece in *The Commercial Gazette,* believed to be a New York City newspaper, tells of an exhibition of a new pair of 20-gauge shotguns. The set was likely by Charles Lancaster, built to Oakley's specifications in London. The clipping was saved by Oakley and Butler, and was found in their scrapbooks, at the Buffalo Bill Historical Center.

Wednesday, June 6, 1888

Miss Annie Oakley, the celebrated lady pigeon, pistol and rifle shooter, after an absence of almost two years with the Wild West show in England, France, Germany, Russia and Holland, returned to this city yesterday. . . . Her two twenty-gauge guns, with which she did such phenomenal shooting in the foreign gun club sweepstake shooting, will be on exhibition for the next three weeks at Bandle's gun store. The little lady is looking well, and from her talk is highly pleased with her trip.

Charles Lancaster Improves Annie Oakley's Shooting

The level of expertise among British gunmakers and shooting coaches on game shooting was superior to that in the U.S. firearms trade. From the moment Annie Oakley first performed in England, with Buffalo Bill's Wild West in 1887, experts appeared who were keen to improve her shooting. Most successful of these was renowned gunmaker Charles Lancaster. The British press followed the evolution of Oakley's improved marksmanship with intense interest. The fact that this natural shot was improving her performances thanks to British advice and guns was a point of national pride.

Among those who were keen to help was "Purple Heather," whose letter to the *Field* (December 10, 1887) had some revealing comments about Annie Oakley and her coach:

I may mention one fact, which will, I think, show that Mr. Lancaster can assist in the art of shooting. I met Miss Annie Oakley the first day she shot at his private grounds, and I was also present when she first came to our club ground (the Gun Club). At this period Miss Oakley could kill about one blue rock [pigeon] out of five. After Mr. Lancaster had finished his course of instruction she killed forty-one rocks out of fifty, and for this performance she selected her Lancaster 20-bores—a pair of beautiful guns built for exhibition shooting—in preference to her Lancaster 12's. Miss A. Oakley had previously told me that "her ambition was to kill thirty-five blue rocks out of fifty before she left England."[1]

Lancaster published the following letter from Miss Oakley in *An Illustrated Treatise on the Art of Shooting*:

New York, 8th Dec., 1888.

Dear Sir,—The four breech-loading hammerless guns you built for me are, in my opinion, as near perfection as it is possible to get them. The pair of 20-bores (weight 5 lbs. 2 ozs.), I have been using now nearly two years. I find them just as tight and sound as when new; I have never had any repairs except having the locks cleaned. The pair of 12-bores (6 lbs.) are as good as the 20's.

Since using your guns, and receiving a few lessons from you at your splendid private shooting grounds, my shooting in the field has so much improved that now I always make a good score, even at fast and difficult birds. With many thanks for the pains you have taken in making me such perfect fitting and fine shooting guns.

I am, gratefully yours,
(Signed) Annie Oakley,
"(Little Sure Shot)."[2]

The exceptional Stevens single-shot rifle custom-made for Miss Oakley by the company in the 1890s; .25-20 caliber, gold-plated frame; balance blued. Other side of frame is inscribed NUTLEY/N.J.

The table cover was probably made by her for her husband; the show belt was designed and made by her.

Could Have Killed the Kaiser

One of the best-known episodes in the career of Oakley and Butler was her opportunity to shoot Kaiser Wilhelm of Germany, during a command performance some years prior to World War I. As good as any known source for this episode is the following article in an as yet unidentified or dated American newspaper, in the Oakley-Butler scrapbooks. The piece, from c. 1918, was headlined: AN AMERICAN WOMAN WHO COULD HAVE SHOT KAISER! SHE LEVELED HER RIFLE DIRECTLY AT HIS HEAD BUT HIT ONLY HIS CIGARETTE.

The author, Margaret C. Gethchell, spoke to Oakley and quoted her extensively:

She could have shot the kaiser as if by accident and escaped unpunished. But she didn't do it.

Fact is, it was in those days of long ago before the kaiser became hated of mankind. He was then crown prince and was much interested in watching the American woman shoot. Standing at a distance of thirty feet from a row of men, each with a cigarette in his mouth, she would shoot the ashes off each cigarette.

Prince William asked her to try it on him, but she hesitated. She never had missed, but it was taking risks with royalty, for a slight deviation might have meant the wounding of the crown prince. So she had him hold the cigarette in his hand, and then she shot the ashes off.

Day of Wild West Past

"What a chance I missed," she has thought many a time during the last four years, "for I could easily have shot the kaiser, apparently doing it by accident."

The American woman who had this unique chance was Annie Oakley, one of the world's champion shooters, whose name brings up memories of the Wild West Show to the many thousands of people in this country and abroad who saw her during the seventeen years when she was costar with Buffalo Bill himself in his great show. . . .

Quail Shooting in Virginia

Although millions saw Annie Oakley in action as an exhibition shooter, scarce few had the opportunity to be afield, watching her in action against wild game. Those who saw her taking field shots found her every bit as impressive, if not more so, than in the show ring, onstage, or in match competition. No two shots ever seemed to be the same. "A Quail Hunt in Virginia" was datelined Berryville, Virginia, and was published in *The American Field*. The piece, a letter from Professor J. C. Schuyler, was discovered in the Oakley-Butler scrapbooks, and although the clip is undated, it appears to be from c. 1890.

EDITOR AMERICAN FIELD:—I noticed some time ago where one of your correspondents said that a good trap shot is not necessarily a good shot in the field. In this I fully agree with the gentleman, but it is by no means true of the rifle queen, Miss Annie Oakley, for I had the pleasure last November to hunt quail with her and her husband, Mr. Butler. They spent eight days with myself and family and during that time we had some pleasant shooting, wherein Miss Oakley demonstrated the fact that she is nearly as good in the field as at the trap. It is unnecessary for me to give her record at the trap, as every reader of your excellent paper is familiar with it.

November 2, last, Mr. Butler, Miss Oakley and myself took an early start to spend the day quail shooting. Miss Oakley took her 20-gauge Lancaster, Mr. B. his 12-gauge of the same make and I my 12-bore Parker.

Miss Oakley is a lover of the setter—the Gordon being her preference—and as luck would have it, I had a Gordon in my string of dogs. So I took the Gordon—Dash by name—one of my English setters and my pointer bitch Tammany Bertie, and away we went at a rattling pace. I did not make the drive a long one, but soon arrived at a favorite hunting ground of mine. We left the colored boy to look after the horse and were soon among the birds. The Gordon made game but was slow to locate, and the English setter got the first point. The Gordon and pointer backed in grand style, delighting Miss Oakley

and causing her to remark, "As perfect as a picture." "Very beautiful, indeed," replied Mr. Butler. "Well, here goes," says I to Miss Oakley. "I will flush them and then help thyself." "Thanks," said she. I moved forward a step or two and up went the birds. "Bang, bang, boom, boom," went the two guns. Two birds fell to the 20-gauge and one to Mr. Butler, while I had forgotten to shoot, my entire attention being centered on the accomplishments of the little lady and her husband.

"Professor," said Annie, "you must not let me rob you of your sport." "Thank you, Miss," he replied; "not at all; you are doing very nicely and I am enjoying myself very much. . . ."

We continued our hunting until dinner time and when we counted our birds we found that Miss Oakley had sixteen, Mr. Butler five, and I, eight, a total of twenty-nine. . . .

The next day the little lady and I killed thirty-two birds out of forty-two shots, she killing eighteen straight to my fourteen out of twenty-four. . . .

I never shot much at the trap and am only a fair field shot, while Miss Oakley is an expert at the trap, with the rifle or revolver, and is also a clinker in the field, which goes to convince me that there are some trap shots at least who are also experts in the field.

Annie Oakley's Shooting, and Insights on Feather-Weight Guns

For centuries gunmakers have been faced with the challenge of building guns for the field that are of the proper weight and balance. When Annie Oakley underwent a dramatic transformation in her shooting, as a result of British gunmakers and coaches, a significant facet of these improvements was lighter shotguns, and attaining the proper fit and balance. An undated piece of c. 1891 in *The Rod and the Gun and Country House Chronicle* reveals the impact of her British shooting experiences not only on her performance with shotguns but with rifles and handguns. The article was found in the Oakley-Butler scrapbooks.

At the Royal Hotel, Ashford, the other day, Miss Annie Oakley . . . once more exhibited her skill with

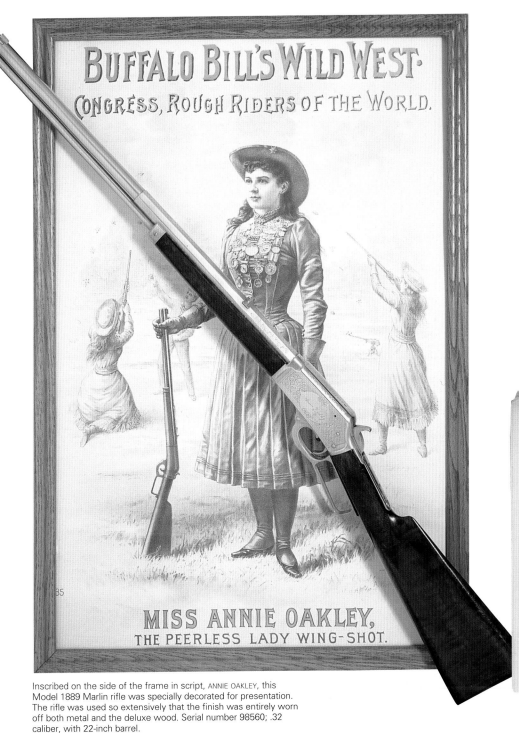

the shot gun, the rifle, and the pistol. . . . A visiting card held up edgeways was repeatedly struck upon its edge with a bullet from a pistol at a distance of twelve or fifteen yards. Miss Oakley then hit, with a 320-bore double rifle, two marbles thrown into the air, and afterwards, with a repeating rifle, she broke a piece of brick thrown up, and shattered a portion of it as it fell. Coins the size of sixpenny bits were struck with marvellous accuracy. Any man who "fancies" his shooting should see Miss Oakley perform; afterwards he will feel insignificant. . . .

Miss Annie Oakley fires away thousands of shots in her weekly performances; she uses several guns, and puts to a severe test their shooting qualities and lasting powers. "If you want to get a good gun," she remarked, "you must come to England. If I could obtain one in America, you may depend upon it that I should be glad to do so." We were pleased to hear her pay a just tribute of praise to Mr. Charles Lancaster. "Mr. Lancaster," she said, "made me a pair of guns when I first came to England. The fit is perfection; and, though I have fired thousands upon thousands of shots from them, they are as sound and shoot as well as on the first day on which they were built."

Inscribed on the side of the frame in script, ANNIE OAKLEY, this Model 1889 Marlin rifle was specially decorated for presentation. The rifle was used so extensively that the finish was entirely worn off both metal and the deluxe wood. Serial number 98560; .32 caliber, with 22-inch barrel.

Oakley "Ten Questions" brochure.

Speaking Directly with Miss Oakley

Of the more than forty years of press clippings in the Oakley-Butler scrapbooks, the number of articles that bear direct quotations from the couple is relatively limited. The more revealing of these pieces are from the British press. Because Oakley was so popular there, some of the articles were long and detailed. *The Rod and the Gun and Country House Chronicle*, of c. 1891, ran a piece by Basil Tozer (pseudonym: "20-Bore") entitled "An Interview with Miss Annie Oakley."

A day or two ago I called at the Horticultural Exhibition on Miss Annie Oakley, who is leaving in a short time for America. At the moment she was engaged, and, while waiting in the comfortably-furnished tent, I found occupation in admiring the artistic arrangement of everything there, from the guns in the corner to the portraits and knick-knacks on the table. Soon my attention was caught by a cheery voice without; and a moment later Miss Oakley was greeting me after the hearty manner of our Transatlantic cousins.

"So you have come at last?" said my hostess, with a charming smile and a frank look. "Pray sit down and make yourself at home. You have been into the Show? Yes? I hope you enjoyed it. Now we will have a cup of tea and a quiet talk, and you can ask me your questions. Interviewers are always full of questions!"

At first we talked of general subjects: of guns, shooting, riding, and sport; and some time passed, before we came to business. . . .

"Do you never feel tired after the performances?" I asked presently.

"I won't say 'never'; but—well—hardly ever. Shooting, you see, has become to me a second nature in a way. Sometimes—very seldom—my eyes ache a little. While shooting, I scarce realise that I have a gun in my hands. I look straight at the object to be fired at, and the moment the butt of the gun touches my shoulder I fire. A moment's hesitation invariably means a miss. I use guns and cartridges by many makers, and both black powder and nitro-compounds. One thing I am

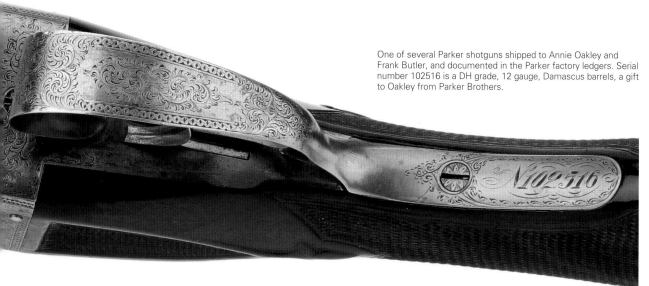

One of several Parker shotguns shipped to Annie Oakley and Frank Butler, and documented in the Parker factory ledgers. Serial number 102516 is a DH grade, 12 gauge, Damascus barrels, a gift to Oakley from Parker Brothers.

bound to admit: for a first-class gun I should always come to England. Our guns are well built, well finished, and shoot very hard; but their balance is not perfect. The handling of an American-made gun is undoubtedly different from the handling of a gun built over here."

"Now, would you think me rude if I were to ask your honest opinion of the shooting of English ladies?"

"Ah! an indiscreet question," she laughed back, as she refilled my cup. "But as you wish my opinion you shall have it. Candidly, I do not believe that English ladies will shoot well, or shoot with comfort, until they dress differently. It is impossible to shoot brilliantly in a tight-fitting bodice—absolutely impossible. Again, how can ladies expect to walk in comfort through fields of wet roots if they wear skirts down to the ground? Their dresses are soaked, then clogged with mud: and pleasure gives way to misery. No! What they ought to wear (that is, if they wish to shoot at ease) is a loose bodice of some soft material—tweed for choice—and a skirt about half-way up to the knee. Such a dress would look becoming; and surely, if ladies contemplate riding astride—to my mind a horrid idea—they cannot well object to dress for shooting in the way I have ventured to suggest."

I have heard ladies call Miss Oakley masculine. No one could be less so; and she is as fond of children as they are devoted to her. During my visit several little ones came into the tent, and their affection for its occupant—I mean its fair occupant—was proof of the kindliness of her nature.

There were some who suggested her brilliant shooting involved subterfuge:

"Do people ever insinuate," I asked, "that there is some trickery about your shooting?"

"Insinuate!" she cried. "On one occasion the audience became so persuaded that the targets contained some explosive which broke them as I fired that they appointed a committee to investigate the matter. That was not in London," she added.

"But," I interrupted, "did you not consider the insinuation a deliberate insult? Did you not ask the committee to apologise?"

"Oh, no," she replied good-humouredly: "you remember the Italian proverb: *Sospetto licenzia fede* ('Suspicion gives license to faith')? It is only natural that people should try to find fault. Perhaps, had I been among the audience, I might have done so myself."

Her modesty was admired by the reporter, and by the public:

Like many adepts, Miss Oakley is very modest. She refused to claim the title of Champion, to which she has every right; and, although she has won more prizes for shooting than anyone else ever did, she never mentions having won anything. Indeed, she seldom speaks about her hobby unless the subject be broached by someone else. . . .

"Are you as fond of shooting game as you are of shooting pigeons and targets?"

COW BOY PIANIST.   Miss. Mattie Babel.
COMPETISI.

"I love it. I should like to go into the country now, for a month's partridge-shooting. People often invite me to their houses to shoot, which I think very kind of them; but then I can't very well leave the Show. . . ."

I . . . asked if it were her intention to remain with the Show permanently.

She thought not. She was getting tired of moving about, and wanted to settle down. Of course she would be at the World's Fair next year. . . .

[Before taking the reporter out to shoot one of her rifles, Miss Oakley showed her some drawings by two young sisters, made for the *Sporting and Dramatic News*]. . . . When we had tried the rifle, she wished to show me over the stables. It was getting late, however; so, with a hearty hand-shake, she bade me farewell, laughingly enjoining me not to flatter her in *Rod & Gun*.

The Cashmore Shotguns of Annie Oakley

The Birmingham gunmaker William Cashmore had the honor of building shotguns for Annie Oakley. Yet another article from the Oakley-Butler scrapbooks is a letter from Cashmore, to a British journal in 1891, in which he reveals a wealth of detail on guns his firm built for the superstar. The reference to "Schultze" was to the favorite powder of Miss Oakley, since she and her husband were quite strict about their hand-loaded shotshells.

MISS ANNIE OAKLEY'S GUNS.

Miss Annie Oakley's guns are built on the Anson-Deeley patent, hammerless, without extension rib, 12-bore, 28-inch steel barrels, both choke, 6-lbs. Weight, bored to shoot 42 grains "Schultze" and 1 oz. No. 6 shot, average—right 208, left 212, in 30-in. circle at 40 yards. Miss Oakley speaks in the highest terms of the guns. I can make them a little lighter, if necessary, without running any risk. . . .

Cabinet card from Buffalo Bill's Wild West. Rare image showing cowboy pianist A. O. Babel with Miss Mattie Babel—both members of the Buffalo Bill's Wild West band. Colt Single Action Army revolver with each.

The Austrian Emperor Francis Joseph

In her day, few Americans traveling in Europe were accorded the opportunities frequently offered to Annie Oakley. She and Butler enjoyed innumerable privileges, not the least of which was being treated in a regal manner by European royalty. As part of a series of Oakley memories, a Pinehurst, North Carolina, newspaper ran "The Bullet Collection of Francis Joseph, Emperor of Austria." The undated article was subtitled "A Day's Hunt in the Imperial Preserve with Bronco Charlie and Kid Gabriel, and the Trophy She Brought Home."

. . . EXPRESSIONS OF AN EMPEROR

Among the numberless mementoes of her journeys—presents from princes and prizes for world's championships, orders and emblems and badges, souvenirs of the plains and the deserts, strange costumes and precious stones—she had forgotten about this curious collection of man's early murderous inventions until the death of Francis Joseph, the grand old man of Austria, was flashed over the world.

Of all the rulers of Europe her memory of him was the kindliest and the saddest. . . . Of a simple and friendly disposition, he had taken a genuine and kindly interest in the girl from America who could outshoot his expert riflemen. . . .

It came about in this way. The Baroness de Rothschild came to see her in the camp, and asked her to give an exhibition for the benefit of the orphans of Vienna. Of course she consented, and the largest fete garden in the city was filled to its capacity. . . .

The Baroness sent an envoy to the camp with an embroidered bag full of gold pieces. . . . But Annie considered that she was giving this party—such opportunities being the greatest pleasures she had in her unusual talent—and so she returned the golden shower to the children of the capitol.

The Baroness was of course delighted, and among the treasures that Annie did keep she has today an exquisite diamond brooch which that lady sent her in appreciation.

Her generosity inspired the Kaiser to invite the Butlers to Schonbrunn:

Oakley cabinet cards; another cover for "Powders I Have Used"; a trap that released live pigeons to fly for shooting contests; glass balls, which came to replace live pigeons; glass ball mold at *upper right;* and miscellaneous memorabilia of the period.

The Buffalo Bill's Wild West Winchester Model 1873s are a carbine, number 122973A, smoothbore in .44-40 caliber, and a rifle, number 633530, also in .44-40, sent to the warehouse February 12, and shipped July 11, 1908, to Johnny Baker, Bangor, Maine, c/o Buffalo Bill's Wild West; charged to the Wild West. Children with Miss Oakley are Baker's daughters Gladys and Della. At *center,* velvet mirror case, and a mirror used by Miss Oakley in shooting at targets behind her back.

This affair shortly afterwards reached the ears of the Emperor, and one day there appeared at the exhibition grounds a magnificent equipage bearing the royal arms and a highly decorated individual making inquiry for Mr. and Mrs. Frank Butler. He bore an invitation for them to wait upon his imperial majesty, and visit the great historic palace of Schonbrunn.

The Royal Paradox

It was there that Annie Oakley received the impression of the paradox of the old monarch's life. Himself thoughtful, simple, friendly and hospitable, but nevertheless receiving them in an ancient citadel, more like a fortress than a home, reeking with memories of intrigues and alarms. . . .

To her at that time his greatest interest seemed to be in the great Austrian arsenal. And he detailed an escort to show the Butlers over it. And as they went, Annie's last glimpse showed the ancient ruler poring over papers on his desk, heavy with the cares of a half century of contests and the burden of an imponderable world. . . .

The Butlers were awarded the rare privilege of hunting as a guest of the Kaiser:

This was not the only time she was the guest of the royal house. Shortly after this she had an opportunity of giving a practical demonstration with a shot gun. She went with as formidable an array of shooters as could be found on all the planet to shoot on the Emperor's game preserve. There was Buffalo Bill and Bronco Charlie, Frank Butler and Kid Gabriel—all of whose very existence was a tribute to their marksmanship under critical circumstances. Shooting pheasant during the morning they kept a small army of keepers busy with the bag. And then in the afternoon they were armed with double-barreled sporting rifles and sent to stalk the roe[buck].

Facing page: Oakley, Butler, and poodle George, in rare early *carte de visite*, c. 1883. Her Stevens-Gould No. 37 single-shot pistol, number 11143; from c. 1886. Gold-plated and blued, with pearl grips, .22 rimfire caliber; interchangeable 10-inch barrels, one of them smoothbore, for firing shot cartridges in exhibitions. One of the finest Oakley guns known. Accompanied by reduced-size reproduction of the best of all posters done in promotion of Oakley's career; by Enquirer Job Printing Company, Cincinnati, Ohio, c. 1901.

Rare photograph of Miss Oakley in full-length dress, with shotgun and stylish hat. Note 1907 date, and neatly written signature.

This was an old game in a new setting—but no great difficulty to those whose only dinner for weeks on end had been venison marketed with the Winchester. However it was about dusk before Annie came upon half a dozen peacefully feeding in a field of wheat. So innocent and trustful was the picture they made against the setting sun, and such a beautiful family group browsing and daintily treading the meadow, that she refused to shoot at all. And so brought back with her a memory of a delightful scene instead of a pair of antlers from the royal preserve of Francis Joseph, Emperor of Austria.

Photographs signed by Annie Oakley and Frank Butler were done for Cliff Baldwin. Image at *left* shows Annie Oakley, in August 1925, presenting (to quote from back of photograph): "the Women's Clay Target Championship trophy to Miss Gladys Reid of Portland, Org. at the 1925 Grand American Trap Shoot, Vandalia, Ohio. Annie broke 97 × 100 on this day. It was her one and only appearance at the firing line at the Grand American. She died fifteen months after this photo was taken."

Covers from two of the best books done to date on the life and times of Annie Oakley, with two of the most revealing photographs of her collection of shooting medals—most lovingly fabricated in silver and/or gold. At *upper left,* a tribute to Miss Oakley from *The Rifle,* at a time when she was rapidly becoming one of the most famous women in the world.

Regular *Annie Get Your Gun* revivals—on Broadway, in high school and college performances, and in regional theaters—are but one unflagging assurance of Miss Oakley's immortality. When Reba McEntire, herself a distinguished and enthusiastic shooter,

played Annie on Broadway, the show was given a fresh start. The Marlin Annie Oakley Model and the two America Remembers Model 1873 special issues reflect yet other ways of recognizing the legendary shot. The Annie Oakley Festival in Greenville, Ohio,

is an annual celebration of the city's favorite daughter, held on a late-July weekend. Souvenir at *right* depicts the bronze salute to Miss Oakley in Greenville's Annie Oakley Memorial Park.

Celebrating and promoting Betty Hutton and her starring role in *Annie Get Your Gun*, the MGM film made in 1950. The role of Frank Butler was played by Howard Keel.

Annie Oakley Volunteers to Organize Lady Sharpshooters

When the battleship *Maine* blew up in Havana harbor, Cuba, on February 15, 1898, many Americans called for a declaration of war against Spain. Annie Oakley, too, was quick to respond, offering to raise a volunteer corps of lady sharpshooters. Her letter to President William McKinley, from Nutley, New Jersey, on April 5, 1898, was brief and to the point:

Hon Wm McKinley President
Dear Sir I for one feel Confident that your good judgment will carry America safely through without war.

But in case of such an event I am ready to place a company of fifty Lady sharpshooters at your disposal. Every one of them will be an American and as they will furnish their own Arms and Ammunition will be little if any expense to the government.
Yours truly
Annie Oakley

No response came directly from the president. Instead, John Porter, McKinley's secretary, sent a polite but noncommittal acknowledgment.[3]

Exhibitions Before the Men at the Training Camps

Giving shooting exhibitions stateside before U.S. troops during World War I was a unique public service performed by Annie Oakley. In "Annie Oakley's Wonderful Work in Exhibitions Before the Men at Camps," Newton M. Romig wrote of the "Greatest Woman Shot" and how she was "Now Starting on Her Second Tour." Collected by Oakley and Butler in their scrapbook, the piece appeared in the Sunday edition of *The Philadelphia Press* on September 22, 1918.

As was the pride of Kipling after shaking the hand of Mark Twain, so it is with me today, for I have shaken the hand of Annie Oakley and have talked with her and her husband, Frank Butler, for more than an hour.

In the several announcements in these columns of the work these good people are doing for the service men of our country, I now find that I had a very slight conception of the really wonderful thing they are doing.

Nearly everybody has seen, admired and applauded the skilful marksmanship of Miss Oakley, but what an inspiration this skill must prove to the men who are told that good shooting is seventy per cent of the soldier.

Under the auspices of the Y.M.C.A., Annie Oakley has started on a second tour of all the training camps and cantonments, giving daily two and sometimes three exhibitions of an hour's duration before 7500 service men at each exhibition. . . .

Miss Oakley is the picture of health, proving that the clean, out-door life has paid dividends in full. . . .

A woman of medium height, slight and delicate of form and feature, I wondered that Annie Oakley has had the physical endurance for so strenuous a vocation, a clear eye, nerves of steel, and a wonderful power of concentration tell the tale.

Reluctant in talking about that which she and Mr. Butler are doing for their country, she grows eloquent in her praise of the manner in which the various units here are being prepared for the great welding process that is taking place somewhere in France. . . .

Showed Soldiers How

At one of the camps recently visited, an exhibition was given before an entire battalion of colored service men, and to vary the program with a bit of comedy a private was asked to place a block of wood on his head and at being tipped off to shake his head and run at the crack of the gun, thus dislodging the wood, he became very indignant and insisted at having the wood block really shot off. This little story was told me to prove the bravery of our soldier boys without distinction of color.

At the end of this tour Miss Oakley will go to Pinehurst, N.C., where she will again take up her duties with her shooting school. She has taught more than 9000 women how to shoot. Her wide experience in the handling of firearms makes her an excellent teacher, her method being mostly common sense mixed with one hundred per cent Safety first, patience and concentration. To instill confidence the first lesson consists entirely of the handling of the various guns without any actual shooting being done. A twelve-year-old girl from New York city has developed into a remarkable shot with rifle, revolver and shotgun under her tutelage. . . .[4]

"'Annie Oakleys' Increasing," in *The New York Times*

The impact of Annie Oakley on women carrying guns in self-defense was implied by a piece in an early-twentieth-century issue of *The New York Times*. The material in the article was picked up by *The Sporting Goods Dealer,* referring to these women as "Annie Oakleys," and it was saved in the Oakley and Butler scrapbooks. Headlined "'Annie Oakleys' Increasing," the article's subtitle was "Females Are Now Quite Generally Toting 'Shooting Irons' Along with Their Precious Powder Puff and Lip Stick."

There must be a number of amateur Annie Oakleys in the big cities these days, since womankind as well as mankind has taken to toting "shootin' irons." A writer in the New York Times, in commenting on the great increase in gun-carrying due to the crime wave, comments on the part woman is playing in this new development. Incidentally he gives the sporting goods dealer a merchandising thought—stock pistols for the ladies. . . .

The Sporting Goods Dealer went on to quote the *Times:*

"A considerable proportion of the customers in the pistol departments of New York stores are women. The dealers find it profitable to keep in stock a variety of small pistols more or less elaborately ornamented to cater to this custom. These purchasers usually insist on a small pistol which can conveniently be carried in a handbag or vanity box. The same receptacle will hold plenty of ammunition. It is startling to think that the attractive bags which we see swinging at arm's length along the street frequently carry deadly weapons. . . ."[5]

"A Little Lady Made of Steel Wires"

No tribute to Annie Oakley summed up her dedication and skill, her courage and sense of purpose, more than that from old friend Allene Crater Stone. In February 1926 she wrote a letter to the ailing superstar, then suffering from anemia. Miss Oakley would die on November 3, 1926.

The Stones—she an accomplished actress and he the famed comedian Fred Stone—had been close to Oakley and Butler since the 1890s. The shooting couple had introduced the show-business couple to trap and bird shooting. They forged a solid friendship. The Stones had seen their friends perform rifle, pistol, and shotgun miracles on a number of occasions, including on their farm in Amityville, New York. It was there that Oakley had set a shotgun record of 1,016 hits on brass disk targets—without a miss. The feat took three hours, and was a test of concentration, marksmanship, and endurance.

In writing to encourage her recuperation, Allene penned the most memorable of all accolades: "We are all sorry you have not been well. I know the 'stuff' you are made of 'Missie.' You will be well and strong again because you are just a little lady made of steel wires."

CHAPTER VI

Wild West Shows and Exhibition Shooters

Above: "Bonita, World's Champion Girl Rifle Shot"; note medals pinned to bodice of her fancy, fringed dress. She holds Winchester Model 1890 rifle, c. 1900. Possibly English, or from Durban, South Africa.

Facing page: Memorabilia, accompanied by four Winchesters and a Stevens, related to the career of Princess Wenona. From *top,* Model 1892 rifle, number 1200, the barrel stamped PROPERTY OF 101 RANCH WILD WEST SHOW INC. Two half-gold-plated Model 1890s with consecutive serial numbers 120374, 120375, special-ordered by Lillian Smith herself. Model 1890 with carved stock, similarly embellished on its other side with WORLD CHAMPION RIFLE SHOT and frame engraved CHAMPION RIFLE SHOT OF THE WORLD/PRINCESS WENONA. The Stevens stock similarly carved. See also pages 64–65 of *Buffalo Bill's Wild West* for other views of these guns, as well as page 157. All items from the extensive collection of Ruth and Jerry L. Murphey.

Editor American Field:—On March 20, 1884, I issued five challenges, open to the world, to shoot one or more matches with my daughter, Miss Lillian F. Smith, the California Girl, champion rifle shot of the world, twelve years of age. I have not received any reply from any one as yet.

I once more will say, I will match my daughter against Dr. Carver, Eugene Bogardus, E. E. Stubbs, or any other professional shot in the world, to shoot a bona fide match for speed and accuracy, using the rifle. I would like to hear from some of those parties. . . .

—Levi W. Smith, August 23, 1884

Though women the likes of Annie Oakley and Lillian Smith paved the way for others by presenting shooting as mass entertainment, the public—whether in Europe or America—had long been fascinated by talented shots. To be a sharpshooter in the New World, especially, was a badge of honor and of respect. Although this skill was generally associated with men, there are many examples of women being accorded accolades for their shooting prowess.

But it required a combination of improved firearms technology, a fascination with the West, and advancements in transportation and in entertainment facilities before stars like Oakley and Smith could shine. With the adoption of metallic cartridges and rapid developments in gunmaking, primarily during the Civil War period, firearms evolved that could be used effectively by exhibition shooters. The new .22 rimfire cartridge was a milestone for the Oakleys and Smiths, as were repeating rifles like the lever-action Winchester Model 1873, pump-actions like the Colt Lightning and the Winchester Model 1890, and the light, gallery loads in calibers such as .32, .38, and .44, which could be fired indoors.

Single-shot pistols, revolvers, rifles, and 12- and 16-gauge shotguns all became popular with these stars. When smokeless powders were introduced in the 1890s, performance and reliability improved, and the shows became much cleaner as well. Glass-ball targets gave way to clay pigeons; the evolution of the targets themselves were influenced by marksmen like Captain A. H. Bogardus.

Gunmakers' records prove a valuable resource in identifying the many exhibition shooters, though some remain obscure or unknown. While most of these performers were men, the number of women was significant, with the most celebrated of them all being Annie Oakley and Lillian (Princess Wenona) Smith. Their star status led directly to improvements in the acceptance of women as equal players in other sports as well; the gun was, actually and figuratively, the great equalizer. Women exhibition shooters led the way in raising both pay rates and respect for female performing artists. In contrast, actresses were still laboring under a popular misconception that associated their craft with dubious moral character.

Guns Bearing Women's Names—Lazy Kate and Lucretia Borgia

While, for some, calling a weapon simply "my Winchester" or "my Colt" is sufficient, using a woman's name for a favorite gun is a time-honored tradition. Brown Bess was the familiar name for the British military flintlock service musket, with Old Betsy its more common nickname, and one that is still used playfully for a firearm. Show business superstars such as Buffalo Bill and his partner Texas Jack Omohundro gave the practice maximum publicity.

Cody's favorite buffalo-hunting rifle was Lucretia Borgia, a .50-caliber Trapdoor Springfield. The favorite rifle of Texas Jack was Lazy Kate, a Remington rolling block, and the frontier hero waxed eloquent about her in a *Chicago Field* article from March 1881:

> She was of Remington patent, Egyptian model, caliber, .[50], and was presented to me by the Remington Gun Works, February, 1873. She was beautifully gold mounted, and at first I thought her too pretty to be of much real service, but I found my mistake in after years. I first used her on the stage; she made her debut at Niblo's Garden, New York, and for several months after received her equal share of banging and pounding around behind the scenes, such as all articles have to receive in that part of a theater. During the Summer I took her to Nebraska on a buffalo hunt, and Kate made her first appearance on the plains at Fort McPherson, Nebraska. There were several of us in the party, including Buffalo Bill, Dr. W. F. Carver, and some New York friends.

Jack chose the name because he couldn't work her quite so fast as some of the boys could their repeating rifles. He went on to describe some

risky hunts, including of buffalo, where the gun was badly battered. He brought her back to the States and put her in show business again—firing blanks every night.*

When Lazy Kate's stock was broken in an accident, Remington offered to restock her. Texas Jack refused.

> It was no use; Lazy Kate had seen her day (the same as we have all seen, or will have to see). I laid her quietly away in the property box, which served as her coffin at the Howard Athaeneum, Boston, until this Winter, when the box was set outside and the deep snow covered it. When I dug her up poor Kate was all rusted inside, and worse broke up than ever. I took her back to Remington's gun store, Broadway, New York, where I had gotten her six years ago, and there she will remain as a relic, perhaps, so long as the works may last.

*To Texas Jack, "the States" was civilization in the East Coast, e.g. New York City.

Rare cabinet card at *left* of Lillian Smith, with bodice prominently proclaiming her prowess as world-champion rifle shot. Young lady at *right* remains unidentified, perhaps an Annie Oakley or Lillian Smith "wannabe."

Lillian Smith: The California Girl and Princess Wenona

An authentic rival to the diminutive Annie Oakley, the "lady made of steel wires," Lillian Smith was rated by not a few observers as a better shot than her more famous contemporary. Their rivalry fuels arguments to this day among the cognoscenti. Suffice it to say, both were remarkably talented, and both had a take-no-prisoners intensity toward their artistry with guns and ammunition.[1]

Facing page: More from the Murphey Collection, unrivaled in 101 Ranch and Lillian Smith/Princess Wenona treasures. From *top,* Winchester Model 1873, with left sideplate inscribed PRINCESS WENONA, and top of barrel marked ONE OF ONE THOUSAND. Smith & Wesson handguns, at *top,* First Model Single Shot, .22, serial 19931; .38 Military and Police, number 6244; both custom-made for her in 1901. The Model 1892 Winchesters are both .44-40 carbines, with alterations allowing her to shoot from horseback.

Pawnee Bill and his wife, May, at *left. Center* image signed on the back with inscription: TO MAY LILLIE THE "PRAIRIE FLOWER" A HAPPY NEW YEAR TO YOU BOTH, KATE PARTINGTON DEC 30TH. 1890. Cabinet card at *right* shows Texas Ben and Texas Ann, from Dallas. Nothing is known by the author about this team of exhibition shooters, or about Kate Partington.

Lillian Smith was a California Indian, born February 3, 1871, at Coleville, Mono County, east of Sacramento, near the Nevada line.

Before her tenth year, she is reputed to have announced to her parents that she was tired of playing with dolls and wanted a rifle. A natural shot, she soon became the terror of the countryside, hitting birds on the wing, blasting bobcats out of trees, and taking top prize so often at turkey matches that the local organizers asked her to stop competing so that others (most, if not all, boys and men) could have a chance to win.

At the age of ten she was already giving exhibitions, showing off her comprehensive talents with shotgun, rifle, revolver, and pistol, and getting paid to do it. Her budding career was spurred on by her father, who was instrumental in organizing a demonstration in San Francisco at which the youthful sharpshooter garnered rave reviews. Word quickly spread of her prowess, and in 1885 she was billed as one of the shooting stars of Buffalo Bill's Wild West during their lengthy engagement at Erastina, Long Island, New York. In 1887 she was with the troupe on tour in England.

Both Lillian and her archrival, Annie Oakley, shot before Queen Victoria, and were hailed as shooting marvels by the British press, which was keenly interested in such crucial skills. As chronicled in *Buffalo Bill's Wild West*, the rivalry between the two gained momentum while they were both performing with Cody, and may have been part of the reason Oakley left the show to tour Continental Europe, leaving Lillian Smith to carry on.

Although Cody's standing offer of $10,000 to anyone who could best Lillian Smith was never successfully challenged, by 1889 Miss Smith, billed as "the California Girl" and "the California Huntress" and "Champion Girl Rifle Shot,"

Oakley friend Johnny Baker at *center*, clutching Winchester Model 1897 shotgun. At *left*, exhibition shooter J. W. Ware, in an image taken in London, 1903, when he was with Buffalo Bill's Wild West. At *right*, Mattie Biggs, Crack Shot (note medals on bodice), another exhibition shooter with Buffalo Bill's Wild West. At *top*, Plinky Topperwein with a rare card that she shot, dating from soon after she began her career with husband, Ad.

shooter, formerly with Cody and sometimes billed as C. F. "California Frank" Hafley, whom she married. For several years their act headlined as "Wenona and Frank, the World's Champion Rifle Shots." Their tours were cross-country, with performances at the Pan-American Exposition, in Buffalo, New York, in 1901, garnering enormous publicity. By 1909, Frank Smith left Lillian and remarried, ending their partnership. The shock of the separation was apparently of such magnitude that she was never quite the same again, although she could still shoot with magical skill.

Throughout her career, starting with her marriage to Jim Kidd, a reckless cowboy in Buffalo Bill's Wild West, Lillian had problems with gentlemen friends, lovers, and husbands. She also had the added baggage of an affinity for spirituous beverages, and a tendency to become unappealingly plump. It was the latter, as well as her poor use of the English language, which were targets of Annie Oakley's frequent barbs.

Finally retiring in the mid-1920s, Wenona took advantage of the generosity of the 101 Ranch by maintaining residence on property provided in recognition and appreciation of her loyalty to the massive Miller family enterprise, and in exchange for chores done around the estate.

Before too long she took up with a German artist, Emil William Landers, also residing on the 101. From 1922 Landers and Miss Smith shared twenty acres of land near Bliss, Oklahoma, having organized what they called Thunderbird Ranch, populated by a miscellaneous entourage of animals. By 1928 her health had deteriorated to the point that she moved into town (by then called Marland). She died in 1930, during a winter so cold that digging her grave proved nearly impossible. Most of the California Girl's personal effects were left to the Oklahoma Historical Society. Today, the leading collectors of

159

had left Buffalo Bill's troupe and Oakley had returned to the fold, enjoying top billing.

Subsequently, Smith toured first on her own, later with Pawnee Bill, and then with the Miller family's renowned 101 Ranch, which she joined c. 1906–07. Her most lasting partnership was with Frank C. Smith, an accomplished exhibition

Lillian Smith guns, accessories, and memorabilia are Ruth and Jerry Murphey, founders of the 101 Ranch Collectors Association.

Records set by Princess Wenona added to her legendary status. Yet to be broken, these are immortalized at the Ponca City, Oklahoma, gravestone memorial, erected in 1999 by the 101 Ranch Old-Timers:

Breaking Glass Balls
Thrown in the Air Using a .22 Rifle
323 Balls Without a Miss
495 of 500 Balls
100 Balls in 80 Sec[onds]

From the Back of a Running Horse,
She Broke 71 of 72 Balls
Thrown in the Air.

300 Swinging Balls in 14 Min. 33 Sec.
Using a Single Loading .22 Rifle

72,800 Swinging Balls in 6 Days
Using 4 Winchester Repeating
Rifles .22 Ca., 3 Hours Daily

Made 24 of 25 8" Bulls Eyes at 200 Yds.

Lillian Smith's Challenge to All Shooters—at the Age of Twelve

In its August 1884 issue, *The American Field* ran a challenge from Levi W. Smith, the father of Lillian Smith. She was a mere twelve years old at the time.

Editor American Field:—. . . I will match my daughter against Dr. Carver, Eugene Bogardus, E. E. Stubbs, or any other professional shot in the world, to shoot a bona fide match for speed and accuracy, using the rifle. I would like to hear from some of those parties. I will wager five hundred dollars that Miss Lillian can break one thousand glass balls in fifty minutes with the rifle. It took Captain Bogardus one hour to accomplish this same feat, using three shot guns. I will wager one thousand dollars that she can beat any one in the world as a gallery shot. I will also wager one hundred dollars that she can hit more common English pins, one inch long, stuck into a frame to be set in motion, to travel twelve feet in one and one quarter seconds, distance thirty feet (out of fifty shots), than any one else in the world, using a .22 caliber rifle.

It must be remembered that Miss Lillian is only twelve year old, and the first shot she made with the rifle was on April 2, 1880.

Lillian Smith: Endorsement of the Magazine Target Trap

In 1887, the newly famous Lillian Smith offered a magazine endorsement of a product pivotal to her public reputation:

BUFFALO BILL'S WILD WEST SHOW,
  MADISON SQUARE GARDEN, NEW YORK,
  February 15, 1887.

Mr. Joseph L. Raub, New London, Conn.:—

Dear Sir,—I take great pleasure in recommending your Magazine Target Trap. Having given it a thorough trial I pronounce it perfect in every way, and for rapid shooting it cannot be equalled. In a recent trial I broke 20 clay targets out of 22, thrown from your magazine-trap, using a .22 cal. Winchester Repeating rifle. I cheerfully recommend it to the shooting public. Wishing you success in future attempts,

I remain, respectfully yours,

LILLIAN F. SMITH.[2]

Dr. Ruth and Mrs. Ruth—Exceptional Shots

The May 21, 1881, issue of *The Chicago Field* and *The American Sportsman's Journal* carried a notice of the death of the gifted shot Dr. Ruth, and in the process identified his wife as a shooter of exceptional skill:

Death of Dr. Ruth:—Dr. John Ruth, the well known rifle shot, died May 3, at his residence in Oakland, Cal., from an attack of dropsy of the heart, a disease from which he had been suffering, at times, during the past year. He was born in Ohio and died in the prime of his life, being thirty-nine years of age. Dr. Ruth was a gentleman of quiet, modest demeanor, and during his visit to the East, accompanied by Mrs. Ruth, herself an expert pistol shot, made a great many warm personal friends, who will be pained to learn of his sudden death. His public exhibitions of his skill with the rifle entitled him to be ranked with the best shots of the day.

The Bartlett Family, the image at *left,* c. 1895. Nothing is known by the author about this exhibition shooting team.

Above: Cowgirls at *top,* ready for rodeo; virtually all of them were equally comfortable with horses and guns. At *center,* with banjo, Ella Bird Dumont, straight-shooting wife of Texas Ranger J. T. Bird. At *right,* May Manning Lillie, horsewoman, showwoman, and exhibition shooter. Actress, singer, and cowgirl Dale Evans, at *bottom center,* one of the most versatile of Western performers. Bonnie Parker and Clyde Barrow, the authentic dangerous Midwest characters, and convincingly playing the movie roles, Faye Dunaway and Warren Beatty.

Right: Jennie Cody and May Cody, from the Kemp Sisters' Wild West Indian Congress American Hippodrome Indian Museum and World's Best Rough Riders, which also included Colonel V. F. Cody. Note Winchester rifles held by each of the Cody girls, in vignettes to *left* and *right* of Cody. The Kemp Sisters claimed "Ministers Attend Everywhere and Pronounce It an Instructive Entertainment . . . [performing under] an Immense Canvas Enclosed Arena . . . [with] Comfortable Seats for 10,000 People." This kind of blatant copying of Buffalo Bill's Wild West must have been annoying to the originals—and was only one of more than 250 Wild West troupes from the period of the 1880s to the 1920s. Women played a role in virtually every one of these, primarily as performers.

The Chamberlins—Frank and Myrtle: Ropers and Shooters

Two of the more obscure American exhibition shooters from the late nineteenth and early twentieth centuries are Frank and Myrtle Chamberlin. The couple were billed as adept at novel rope juggling and lasso handling as well as for "Queer Tricks with Ropes and Whips," and skilled at "Shooting by Aid of a Mirror," and so forth.

Historian Lee Silva discovered a 1931 news clipping indicating that Frank was then sixty-five years of age, although a 1932 clip stated his age at near seventy. Frank claimed to have made five trail drives from Texas to Kansas by the time he was twenty-two, then settling down as a cowboy in Arizona, Wyoming, and on the Hash Knife ranch in Montana. He said he was with the Buffalo Bill's Wild West (for seven years) and with Cody rival Doc Carver (for several years), with whom he became proficient as a trick-shot artist.

Myrtle Chamberlin's clippings reveal her as Lottie Donaldson, born in Vasser, Michigan, on February 2, 1876. She met Frank when visiting her uncle's ranch in Montana, and he taught her all his rope tricks during their courtship. They married on June 1, 1897. An August 12, 1902, clipping said that "Mr. and Mrs. Chamberlain [sic] have appeared in all of the best vaudeville theaters in the United States as well as Europe, and perhaps there is not a couple before the public today that enjoys a wider acquaintance or a better reputation."

From a September 24, 1902, article: "The Chamberlins are likewise famous rifle shots and will give exhibitions at the range, shooting accurately from thirty different positions."

Cowgirls: Pioneer Professional Athletes

Nineteen hundred to 1940 was an exciting period for spectators of Wild West shows and rodeos, and an era when women were pioneering new territory. These women are recognized today as the first professional female athletes in America. They were daring souls, some of whom died riding dangerous horses. Due to these accidents, rodeo producers, especially after the death of Bonnie McCarroll in 1929, developed less dangerous events, and refused to permit women to compete at the same level of risk as the men. From World War I onward, Wild West shows, which became less dangerous to women performers, gradually diminished in their attraction and popularity as the rodeo evolved to replace them.

Photographers who specialized in capturing these adventurous and often attractive, colorful, and charismatic women played a role in helping to promote them to an ever-growing audience. In a career spanning forty years, one photographer, Ralph R. "Dub" Doubleday, is credited with taking some twenty thousand photographs, and publishing more than 30 million copies of these. His specialty was rodeos.

The collecting of postcard images is one of the most popular of hobbies, and cowgirls are in high demand. Among the most popular of these images are cowgirls with firearms. If for every twenty cowboy pictures there is one cowgirl, then the number of female images including a firearm is an even greater rarity. The presence of a gun places the sitter into yet another realm, of adventure, excitement, romance, and daring.

The National Cowgirl Museum and Hall of Fame

Firearms and images of armed cowgirls are among the displays at the National Cowgirl Museum and Hall of Fame. Consultant Elizabeth Clair Flood, herself a cowgirl, from San Francisco's celebrated Gold Rush family, finds the images of women with firearms captivating; several appear in her book, *Cowgirls:*

Often men left women alone on ranches when they went to retrieve stock. During these times women fended for themselves, with a gun if necessary. There's a gun in every corner of the cabin, said one Texas cowboy to his bride. Because ranches were so remote, women had to learn to confront hardship and to be independent and self-sufficient.

In a chapter of Judy Crandall's *Cowgirls: Early Images and Collectibles,* several armed women are depicted. Since her book includes a price guide, she notes that:

Firearms and ammunition were often sold by beautiful images of the American cowgirl. Items which feature these delightful yet alluring cowgirls are most desirable to the collector with rather high values due primarily to their scarcity. . . . Whenever a gun of any kind can be seen in the image, it increases the value of the photo. . . .

In the late twentieth and early twenty-first centuries, rodeo women have become more daring, and increasingly compete with men—just as they did in the pioneer days of c. 1900–40. At the same time, women are now competing with firearms in a variety of cowboy action-shooting events, a sport that is easily one of the fastest-growing shooting competitions.

Elizabeth "Plinky" Topperwein—Winchester Missionary

In 1903, one of the thousands of female Winchester factory employees was at her station fabricating ammunition when a handsome gentleman came through the factory, evidently familiar with the company's operations. The young lady, quite taken with the visitor, impulsively stated to a coworker, "Someday I'm going to marry that man." Her coworker was incredulous, but the determined lady's prediction came true.

Facing page: Plinky Topperwein and husband, Ad, in a collection of contemporary photographs, advertising, and targets. Typical size of a crowd on their exhibition tour in panoramic photograph at *bottom.* Overlapping with the career of Annie Oakley, Plinky came on the scene with shooting skills so versatile and remarkable that she set several records, which remain unbroken to this day.

That same year, Elizabeth Servaty married her champion, who was already a legend in the world of shooting. Adolph Topperwein traveled continuously as one of Winchester's missionaries—promoters of the company's guns and ammunition. Elizabeth joined him, but soon grew bored just watching him shoot, and asked that he teach her. Her natural aptitude was quickly evident, and she became so skilled that she ultimately joined his act, which he then billed as "Ad and Plinky Topperwein." (The nickname came from Elizabeth's enjoyment of shooting at cans, which she would ask for with her favorite line, "Throw up another one and I'll plink it.")

Plinky first earned national recognition at the St. Louis World's Fair of 1904, shattering 967 clay targets out of 1,000. This unprecedented achievement for a lady inspired the Winchester management to send her on the road with her husband. The couple traveled the United States from 1906 to 1940.

The Topperweins' act was a vital part of Winchester's marketing program. Adolph's achievements were heralded in the author's *Winchester: An American Legend* and in *Buffalo Bill's Wild West*. But hers were remarkable in their own right. Plinky's gift at the shooting game was so extraordinary that she dominated trapshooting

Champions in competition, and as exhibition shooters, Ethyl and Fred Etchen were ardent admirers of Annie Oakley and Frank Butler, whom they last saw at the Grand American, 1925. The Etchens won many shotgun events, and were instrumental in coaching son Rudy, destined to become among the most accomplished marksmen in shotgun history. His parents even arranged for Rudy to study under Ad and Plinky Topperwein. Fred was a Studebaker vice president, dealer, and distributor. The Etchens are posed in front of the latest-model car.

Promotional photographs and posters, with Dot Lind's S & W revolver number 522862 in .32 long caliber, with 2- and 4¼-inch barrels (it also had a 3¼-inch barrel), specially engraved with scrollwork and the image of her shooting on the right sideplate. Evidently both Betty Hutton and Howard Keel, shown here in their roles as Annie Oakley and Frank Butler, were among the many fans of Dot Lind.

for as long as she remained active in the sport, finally retiring from competition in the 1920s after the birth of their son.

In one of her greatest triumphs, Plinky hit 1,952 targets out of 2,000, setting a trapshooting record for both men and women. In that feat of endurance and marksmanship, she shot for five hours straight, using a Winchester pump shotgun. According to writer Ernie Pyle, a blister rose on her hand of such dimensions that in a few days she lost the skin from her entire palm.

Amateur Trap Shooting Museum director Dick Baldwin cites the shooting brilliance of the remarkable Plinky:

Ad began to teach her to shoot, and within three weeks of her first lesson, she was shooting chalk from between his fingers with a .22 rifle and splitting playing cards held edgewise at 25 feet. . . .

Six months after she pulled the trigger for the first time, she became a member of the famous Winchester trapshooting squad that toured the South in the fall of 1904. At Albany, Ga., the team broke the existing world's record by breaking 490×500. Plinky broke 96×100 that day. . . .

Shortly after winning the Sunny South handicap [a major shooting event, in 1909] Buffalo Bill presented her with an Indian-made beaded ammunition pouch that she wore continuously until her shooting days ended. . . .

She loved to quote the poem composed by her famous husband early in their marriage. . . .

Lincoln Was Right
You may hit some of your targets most of the time
And hit most of your targets some of the time
But you can't hit all of your targets every time all of the time.
No matter how great your skill and how hard you try,
Sooner or later you'll let one go by. . . .

Perhaps people may forget that she once broke 367 clay targets in a row, that she broke 200 straight 14 times, 100 straight on more than 200 occasions and

set an endurance record that still stands. But not a living soul who knew Plinky Topperwein will ever forget her great warm heart, which she wore openly on her sleeve in adoration of her accomplished husband and the man who made her famous. Nor will they forget her ready wit, her firm handshake, her cheerful voice and the way her eyes crinkled that ever-recurring smile. . . .

When the Trapshooting Hall of Fame selected its first inductees in 1969, Plinky was in this select group. Another woman shooter was also chosen in that initial year, and she was a great admirer of Mrs. Topperwein. . . . Annie Oakley. . . .

[Plinky] was once told by Annie Oakley that she was the greatest shooter of all times![3]

Plinky died at the age of sixty-three on January 27, 1945, and was survived by Ad, who lived to the age of ninety-three, and died in 1962.

The Shooting Linds—Successors to the Topperweins at Winchester

When fourteen-year-old Ernie Lind watched Ad Topperwein give a shooting demonstration in Springfield, Massachusetts, in 1930, the boy made a decision on the spot: "I'm going to be an exhibition shooter." Yet he couldn't possibly have envisioned that he and his future wife, Dot, would become the successors at Winchester to the legendary team of Ad and Plinky Topperwein.

At Springfield Tech High School young Ernie became a champion rifle shot, and was soon teaching others how to shoot during summers devoted to rifle coaching at New England camps. By the age of nineteen, he was on his way toward becoming a professional exhibition shooter.

Mirroring the career of the Topperweins, Ernie discovered Dorothy Westerberg, and taught her how to shoot. When Ad Topperwein decided to retire, Winchester-Western sought a successor, and found it in a new husband-and-wife team, the Linds. Ad Topperwein endorsed the couple

as his and Plinky's heirs. He took them to his Texas ranch and taught them the tricks he and Plinky had used. They added some of their own, and began touring the country as "the Shooting Linds."

According to an in-house article published by Olin Industries/Winchester-Western:

For their exhibition, the Linds use 10 rifles, 5 shotguns, and 5 pistols and revolvers, principally at aerial targets.

In addition to performing Topperwein's famous trick of drawing Uncle Sam with bullets fired from a Winchester 22, the Linds shoot such tiny targets as aspirin tablets, split playing cards, aim with mirrors, break four clay targets thrown simultaneously in the air before they reach the ground, shoot lying on their backs, shoot standing on their heads and give a dramatic exhibition of gun safety.

During a press interview, the Linds, with a mutual admiration reminiscent of Annie Oakley and her husband, Frank Butler, each claimed the other was the better shot. Dorothy went on to say, "It's to any woman's advantage to know how to handle a gun. . . . It takes them outdoors, which is good for their health. The exercise keeps them trim, youthful looking and attractive. It's a sport which they can share with their husbands or boy friends. They can pass on the knowledge to their children, which is important. And it's wonderful fun."

Appropriately, Dorothy Lind was called upon by MGM Studios to instruct Betty Hutton how to handle a gun for the forthcoming *Annie Get Your Gun*. Even though Betty did little actual shooting, thanks to Dorothy she looked the part on screen.[4]

A. Sonia Wright—Wild West Shooting Star

A shooting star about whom relatively little is known is A. Sonia Wright. In the private collection of Ethel Saign is a J. Stevens Arms Company

DOT AND ERNIE LIND

INDIANA GUN CLUB

SNAKE RIVER Trap & Skeet Club

NEW WESTMINSTER B.C.

Sunday, Nov. 23rd 1pm

FREE

Model 55 Lady Model, in .22 rimfire caliber, bearing the serial number 1. On the right side of the frame is engraved *Sonia Wright.* Stevens's records reveal that the rifle was built in 1898, in .22 short, later refitted with a .22 long rifle barrel in May 1933, as Miss Wright had shot out the bore of the short barrel.

In 1931 Miss Wright, using her married name, A. Sonia Goodman, wrote to Stevens regarding return of this rifle, following over thirty years of vaudeville use. Her letter noted she loved the little gun: "If it could talk, it could tell you some interesting tales." Stevens offered to return the rifle to her, so she could keep it as a memento of her vaudeville days. The company offered to "go over the rifle and fix it up in good shape and return it to you at our expense with our compliments."

Mrs. Goodman responded that "I am a wanderer on the face of the earth and am not figuring on many more years on this plane of existence. . . . The rifle I could not sell nor give as I always felt that it was not wholly mine. Though during my vaudeville days it was always a part of myself."

The company asked for a human-interest story from Mrs. Goodman, which Stevens could publish in a sporting magazine. Unfortunately, the letter was returned to the company, marked "Moved, left no address." No picture has been found to date showing this elusive shooting star.

Cowgirl Action Shooting

The subject of feature articles in *The Wall Street Journal* and numerous other mainstream publications, cowboy action shooting boasts a significant number of women competitors. In fact, women are such a vital part of the sport that one of its most active promoters and participants, Susan Laws, has authored a book on the subject, *Cowgirl Action Shooting.*

Except when competitions are performed in arenas, the ammunition used is live. The types of guns used vary from authentic-appearing Single Action revolvers, to lever-action rifles, and lever-action, pump, and double-barrel shotguns.

When the Colt company wanted to promote their Single Action Army line to the rodeo world, and to cowboy action shooters, they hired a woman competitor, Annie Bianco Ellett. In 1999, this former St. Mary's Notre Dame track star joined American Western Arms, whose president, Jack Sweeney, had directed Colt's program catering to this specialized market. In 2000 she won the world championship in mounted action shooting, one of several events in which she has gained distinction. In 2001 Bianco Ellett returned to Colt's, having swept three major prizes in that year: Overall World Champion in Single Action Shooting Society, Mounted Cowboy Shooting, World Champion of the Cowboy Mounted Shooting Association, and Women's Overall Champion. Annie Bianco Ellett even beat the men.

A popular figure at SHOT, the world's largest firearms-related trade show, and the NRA's annual meetings, Bianco Ellett is a stunningly beautiful model, who loves horses and loves to shoot—and is deadly accurate at it. Whether signing posters or sharing tips and experiences with fans, she is a persuasive, expert spokesperson for the sport, exuding the same appeal as Annie Oakley did years before.

Best known of the sanctioning groups is the Single Action Shooting Society (SASS), whose membership grows at a rate of approximately 20 percent yearly. Their newspaper, *The Cowboy Chronicle,* presents popular articles on all aspects of the sport, as well as extensive coverage of the numerous events, generally held on weekends all over the United States.

The other major sanctioning body is the Cowboy Mounted Shooting Association (CMSA), whose competitions are on horseback, and whose authentically styled firearms use specially loaded .45 Colt caliber blanks.

Although there are categories for women, junior and senior, ladies can compete in any of the following matches established by SASS:[5]

Pistol-Caliber Long-Range Repeating Rifle
Rifle-Caliber Long-Range Repeating Rifle
Single-Shot Long-Range Rifle
Deringer
Pocket Pistol
Original Double-Action Revolver
Plainsman

In CMSA events, where the targets are balloons, the riders follow a set course. Jim Rodgers, of Scottsdale, Arizona, introduced the mounted shooting event in 1992. His original intent was to provide an exhibition to entertain competitors and other spectators when the cowboy action shooting was otherwise at a lull. About 10 percent of the participants in the cowboy shooting competitions are involved in mounted events.

At all meets of SASS and CMSA, women are welcome as participants, exhibitors, spectators, and as employees and volunteers of the sponsoring groups.

Facing page: Annie Bianco Ellett's career began as a fashion model, and as an accomplished barrel-racing rodeo performer. In 1996 she entered into a contract with Colt to promote their firearms at trade shows and on the rodeo circuit, later doing similar promotions for the American Western Firearms Company. She was appointed the national spokeswoman of the Cowboy Mounted Shooting Association (CMSA). Her appearances at trade shows draw long lines of admiring fans, eager for signed posters and a word with an authentic star. In 2001 she renewed her association with Colt. She has her own clothing, holster, and boot line, and teaches mounted-shooting lessons at her Cave Creek, Arizona, "Mounted Shooting Boot Camp."

Above: Single Action Shooting Society star Susan Laws, aka Lawless Annie, wrote *Cowgirl Action Shooting* as a salute to the women of the sport. She and her husband, Jim (*left center, adjacent to Susan as mounted cowgirl*), are among the most active participants in the sport. Note colorful frontier costumes, and wide range of firearms, holsters, and accessories. Even collectors' trading cards are issued for some of the shootists. The holster and belt rig are by Wild Bill Cleaver, and reflect the rapidly increasing demand for outfitting this burgeoning market.

Arizonian Teal Rodgers-Henkel is among the authentic cowgirl participants in cowboy mounted shooting, an arena sport where specially loaded blanks are used, due to the live audience. A model, horse breeder, and trainer, Teal has ridden and shot since childhood, and has several television and movie appearances to her credit. On her horse Dusty, she won Top Woman Shooter in the Colt Celebrity Mounted Shooting Invitational (1998), held in Las Vegas—at the same time as the National Finals Rodeo. The award was presented by Annie Bianco Ellett. Teal's father, James T. Rodgers, founded the Cowboy Mounted Shooting Association and is chairman of the board.

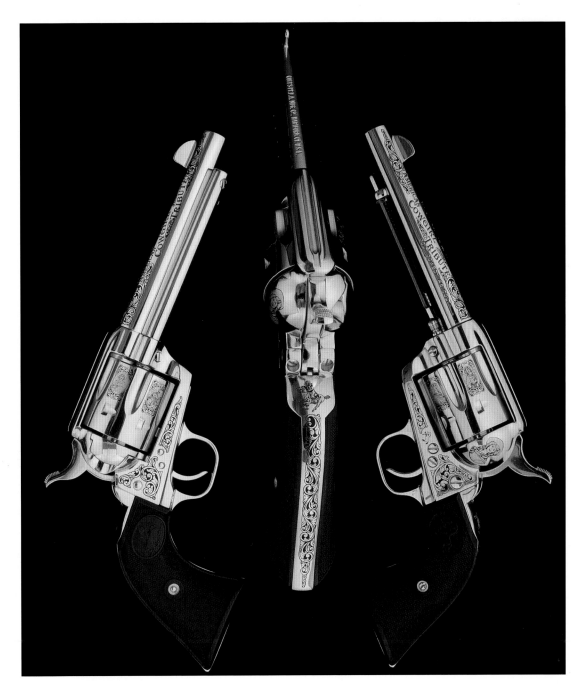

The End of the Trail and Winter Range

The Super Bowl of cowboy action shooting is the End of the Trail, regularly scheduled in January, right after SHOT. First held in 1992, the End of the Trail was actually in operation before SASS, which came to sponsor it, had been granted nonprofit incorporated status. Yet another competitive event, Winter Range, also began in 1992 and was organized to be more shooter-oriented, and to present more shooting opportunities, than the End of the Trail.

171

The America Remembers Cowgirl Tribute Colt Single Action Army revolver; .45 Colt caliber, with 5½-inch barrel; gold-plated and handsomely embellished with silver accents. This prototype bears serial number 001 of 300, as engraved on the butt. Grips of hard rubber. The first special issue saluting the cowgirl, built by a company that has specialized in creating firearms recognizing historical moments, organizations, and individuals in American history. The Cowgirl is tied in with the promotion of *Silk and Steel* and its issue coincides with the initial promotion of the book.

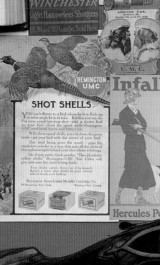

The Sporting Tradition

Being from a family line with generations of very strong and free women, I was privileged enough to grow up in an environment where who you are as a human being, is more important than who you are as a woman. I was left alone to do what I wanted. When I was tiny, I would one day go with my father hunting and fishing, another I would stay at home, playing with dolls.

It just so happened that my interest for dolls waned.

—Natasha Illum Berg, professional hunter, Tanzania, 2001

To the millions of men worldwide who are dedicated hunters must be added the ever-growing number of women who are taking up that time-honored sport. In her learned study "Hunting and Womankind" in *Argernis Jage?* Professor Monika F. Reiterer has pointed out that, in the

Facing page: Two Parker shotguns, and an A. H. Fox, with ammunition, advertising, periodicals, and memorabilia of the late nineteenth and early twentieth centuries. This proved to be a time of rapid advancements for women and girls, not only in the enjoyment of shooting sports in America, the United Kingdom, and Continental Europe, but in politics and social welfare. From the *top*, BHE grade in 28 gauge, BHE grade in 16 gauge, and the A. H. Fox in C.E. grade, also in 16 gauge.

Above: Purdey shotgun of Betty Lou Sheerin, a gift from her husband, Larry.

majority of European languages, the word *chase*—the German *die Jagd*, the French *la chasse*, Italian's *la caccia*, and the Spanish *la chaqueta*—is of the female gender.

Professor Reiterer goes on to observe that hunting is generally considered a "male dominion," despite the fact that many patron deities of hunting are female and that there have been "quite a few huntresses of historic importance, and even more females that have receded into historic oblivion, as history has always been written by men, for men and about men."

Though hunting deities are often female, acceptance of woman as a huntress has sometimes been limited. Reiterer asks, "How can those statements be reconciled?" She quotes a well-known author of hunting books, Fritz von Forell, who writes, "I do not deny that the sight of a lady clad in green, a feather in the hatband, with a shotgun and in leggings, always fills me with displeasure. I kiss her hand—I have no aversion against fair ladies, quite the contrary—but I abhor the ones in green clothes. . . ." Why does he hold those views, which are also common to a number of other males afield? Reiterer continues:

The apartheid of the genders is cherished as a sacred heritage by many hunters even today. Huntresses irritate. Good huntresses even arouse suspicion in some hunters because into that comfortable niche, the male reservation of hunting, those women introduce different attitudes, and challenge the traditional role playing. In order to understand this situation without prejudice it might be helpful to realize that male dominance has markedly developed under the influence of the Judaic, Christian and Islamic civilizations. Only where monotheism (the *one* god is always male!) replaced polytheism did an extremely patriarchal culture begin to develop.[1]

Professor Mary Zeiss Stange, Ph.D., on Women at Arms

The pathfinding spirit of pioneers like Bebe Bwana, Agnes Herbert, Sally Clark, Mickie Akeley, and the Maharanie of Jaipur has been passed to the current generation of women soldiers, police officers, hunters, and sharpshooters. In America, the most eloquent spokesperson on women and hunting is Skidmore College professor Mary Zeiss Stange.

Professor Stange's book credits include *Woman the Hunter* and (with Professor Carol K. Oyster) *Gun Women: Firearms and Feminism in Contemporary America*. Soon to be published is *Sister Predator*. According to Stange,

Today, two and a half million American women hunt. (Something like seventeen million more own guns for self-protection and sport.) They are college professors, cab drivers, waitresses, computer programmers, engineers and law enforcement officers; conservative full-time moms and radical lesbian activists. They challenge the ready identification of women with nature and nurture. It breaks down at precisely that point where any woman becomes armed and dangerous—a hunter (literal or figurative) who can both defend herself, and fend for herself. She neither needs nor wants a man to do it for her.[2]

Left: English sportswoman in poster by English ammunition manufacturer, c. early twentieth century; 18½ × 26 inches.

Below: Dating largely from the late nineteenth into the early twentieth centuries, these book covers and images reflect the fashionable nature of shooting among the well-to-do in Europe and America. The Honorable Mrs. Lancelot Lowther hunted extensively (and expensively) not only in Great Britain, but in the western United States. She and her husband, the fifth Earl of Lonsdale (known popularly as the Yellow Earl), wrote of their hunting adventures in books and in popular sporting journals. From late in the twentieth century, *Countrywomen* was both a popular book and a BBC-TV series.

Stange speaks from a feminist viewpoint, but acknowledges that many of her "sister gun women" do not identify with that movement, and an even larger number of avowed feminists, the majority, in fact, are decidedly against firearms. She and coauthor Carol Oyster note:

> Whether gun-owning women should identify with feminism is, in our view, ultimately a matter of choice for them. Far more to the point . . . we contend that feminists should pay serious, constructive attention to the fact that millions of women are not only armed, but also derive immense satisfaction and empowerment from owning and using guns.[3]

Looking at just one firearms-related activity, Stange notes that the number of women who hunt is actually *increasing,* doubling from 1 to 2

million in the United States in the last decade alone,[4] and that women are much more likely than men to take up the sport as adults, in spite of male chauvinism and the negative pressure they encounter from other women. As a result, women hunters approach the pursuit differently from men.

> Women . . . seem to approach gun use and safety with somewhat more maturity. . . . Firearms safety instructors universally affirm that women and girls make better pupils than males do. They are less inclined to see guns as symbolic extensions of themselves or to regard them as something they should "naturally" know how to use. They are more likely to ask questions not simply about how something should be done, but about why it should be done in a certain way. This concern for process, coupled with

One of the most articulate spokeswomen on hunting, Professor Mary Zeiss Stange was inspired, in her conversion to the shooting sports, by her marriage to Montana rancher Douglas Stange. *Woman the Hunter* is a thought-provoking book, and the follow-up to it, *Woman the Predator,* is sure to arouse widespread comment. As dedicated feminists, both Stange and coauthor Professor Carol K. Oyster, in *Gun Women,* challenge stereotypes from the antagonistic camps of certain opinionated men and stridently feminist women.

the fact that they are most often incorporating hunting into an already formed adult moral perspective, may carry over into women's approach to hunter ethics. It certainly helps to explain why game wardens generally report an improvement in overall hunter behavior when women hunters are present, and perhaps accounts for the fact that proportionally fewer women than men are cited for hunting violations.[5]

She goes on to say:

What we do know is that women hunt for approximately the same reasons as men, having chiefly to do with getting "away from it all," getting down to something primal and real, getting in touch with the sources of their sustenance—physically, with the animals that become their food, spiritually with the earth both they and these animals walk on. Women derive approximately the same levels of satisfaction from hunting as men do. They express these satisfactions in terms of the gratification of putting food on one's own table and knowing where it came from, the growth in self-esteem that comes from learning a difficult skill and doing it well, testing one's endurance and abilities, feeling more confident and more capable, more at one with nature. The reasons women hunt may be best summed up by Sandra Froman. "It makes me happy," she says, "to be alive."[6]

Refuting the conventional view of nature "that has developed in American civilization and, arguably, has reached its quintessential expression in such movements as animal liberation and radical ecofeminism," Stange points out that it

insists upon two assumptions: that humans are not really part of nature, and that our primary way of involving ourselves with the natural world is to destroy it. Yet perhaps the most destructive thing we have actually done is to idealize the natural world by projecting human laws and characteristics upon it, and expecting animals to behave accordingly.[7]

In an intriguing juxtaposition, she describes a woman returning home from field-dressing a slain deer, pausing to rock the cradle of her sleeping child.

It's an image as intricate as life itself. And it is so challenging to conventional ideas, or ideals, of femaleness that one needn't be an animal rights activist to find it unsettling. And yet, women who hunt will tell you it makes perfect sense to them. Disconcerting as the picture might look today, embedded in it is a primal intuition about human participation in the cycle of life and death. . . . Historically speaking, the idea that a woman must be as soft and as pink as her baby's nursery is a relatively recent invention.[8]

The progression of Mary Zeiss Stange's insights into women at arms culminates in her startling image of woman as predator. Being a predator, she says, is good.[9]

It means always being open to possibility, fully attuned to your surroundings, paying attention with all five senses. It means being keen-eyed and quick witted, stealthy and smart, confident and capable. It means knowing how to be patient and when to be impulsive. It means inhabiting the moment, trusting your own instinct, living with the consequences of your failures as well as your successes. When you are aware of yourself as a predator, you understand that the complexity of the stalk and the simple finality of the kill are two sides of the same reality—and it is that reality that keeps you alive. You are self-reliant, in the deepest of senses. You are capable of doing serious harm and of providing nurturance to others. You may fall prey to another stronger or savvier predator, but you will never be a victim.

Left: Collector Ken Waite not only has this splendid calendar art, but the original painting, by artist Frank Stick. 25 × 37 inches.

Top right: Clutching her Model 14 Remington rifle, this lady shooter is ready for the field, in a company advertisement from c. 1911–15.

Bottom right: The lovely lady in red is prepared to go both riding and shooting. Note the advertisement is by a bank, not a gun or ammunition company.

The woman predator

knows that life feeds on life; some of us live only because others die. She has heard the various arguments: that we have "evolved" beyond that view of nature; that we humans can rise above our instincts; that in the best of possible worlds, there would be no suffering or death. She knows these arguments are evasions, of the sort that arise from a dangerously death-denying culture, a culture at odds with its own human/animal nature. She understands that the best of possible worlds is, in fact, the one the hunter inhabits, the terrain she traverses as a predator, killing as cleanly as she can, for food and for pleasure. Here, nature is an intricate dance of life and death; and here nature is, necessarily, red in tooth and claw. There is a trace of blood under the woman hunter's fingernails, as she tenderly rocks her infant's cradle.

And in the final analysis, being a predator

is about female strength. It is about breaking down the stereotypes and barriers that keep us—women and men—alienated from ourselves, from one another, and from the natural world. It is about learning to live in that world responsibly, without pretense, and with an ethically developed sense of what it means and why we desperately need to let wildness back into our lives. It is about breaking the gender rules.[10]

Large-caliber revolvers for hunting. Jewelry designer and manufacturer Madeleine Kay was one of the first women to actively hunt with a handgun; her choice, the Freedom Arms single-action in .454 Kasull, with which she has taken dangerous game, as well as antelope (including hartebeest) and other animals. Clockwise, from *top*, the .44 Magnum S & W Model 29 with scope; the Ruger Super Blackhawk, in the same caliber; the Ruger GP100 in .357 magnum, made of stainless steel and with Magna-Ported extra-long barrel (6 inches); and the Colt Mark V Hunter with scope, in .357 magnum. Revolvers courtesy of Cubeta's.

The American Field ran advertisements in 1884 from the Worcester Excursion Car Company, which encouraged hunting parties to head west.

To Excursion and Hunting Parties

The Worcester Excursion Car Co.

is ready to lease their HOTEL CARS, fitted with Dining-room, Kitchen Sleeping Apartments, Electric Bells, and all modern improvements, especially for ladies and gentlemen, for a trip from one to twelve months to any parts of the United States, Canada and Mexico. The whole finish of these cars is in all respects unsurpassed. Diagrams, rates, and other information furnished by

JEROME MARBLE.
Pres. And Gen'l Manager,
Worcester, Mass.

Or by W. H. Shuey, Superintendent, Boreel Building, 115 Broadway, New York[11]

Woman's Part in Sportsmanship—from *The American Field* magazine

In a lengthy editorial on how the understanding and interest of women can be a source of pleasure and comfort to their husbands or brothers who enjoy hunting and shooting, *The American Field* was forthright in its wish that women would take up these pursuits:

Woman's part in sportsmanship does not necessitate her taking gun or rod in hand with her brothers or husband, although when she can do so it certainly adds to their pleasure, as has been repeatedly testified in these columns. The duties of life, or other causes, may prevent such active participation, and she can act well her part without it. What that part is has been partially indicated already, but it goes beyond this and extends to so influencing the man that his sports become elevating rather than depraving. . . .[12]

Gunmaker's advertisement contrasts with that of insurance company; elegantly attired huntress at *left,* and cowgirl with Remington percussion Army Model revolver at *right.*

Ken Czech's Study of Women Big Game Hunters

While researching his *Annotated Bibliography of African Big Game Hunting Books, 1785 to 1950,* Professor Kenneth P. Czech discovered enough titles by women to write yet another volume. *With Rifle and Petticoat—Women as Big Game Hunters, 1880–1940* pays homage to the rich literature by dozens of women hunters who wrote of their adventures afield. Some of them hunted during the new era of rights for women in the early twentieth century, recording their adventures in diaries, journals, or letters. Czech notes:

> Women suffered through the nuisances of insect infestations and climatic extremes. Indigenous peoples often viewed them with curiosity and excitement. Hefting powerful rifles, they bagged charging elephants, tigers and moose in a variety of hunting venues. They also battled the prejudices of men in their own time and space. Their legacy has spawned renewed interest among today's women in stalking big game throughout the world.[13]

Bottom right: Isabel de Quintanilla, wife of professional hunter Tony Sanchez-Arino, has more experience in Africa than most men, both as a photographer and huntress. *Upper right,* Helen Williamson enjoyed hunts, despite problems with her sight; her husband, Philip, a leading collector of books on hunting. Spread on Virginia Brooks from *Life* magazine, September 29, 1947. Photographs of India: Maharani Shivkumari of Kotah with tiger, and elephants used in hunting. She and the Maharani of Jaipur are good friends; both are experienced and skilled huntresses. The younger woman is the Maharani Shivkumari's daughter, Princess Bhuvaneshwari Kumari of Malesar, also an accomplished shot.

Betty Fitz in Utah

Above: Ellen Enzler-Herring, big game hunter and publisher (Trophy Room Books), at *top center* with husband, Jim, and at *right* with trophies taken on hunts around the world. Betty Fitz, the first female sport hunter to take *all* the North American game animals (total of twenty-six). Natalie Eckel, with trophy markhor ram taken in the Chitral Mountain area of Pakistan, was the first woman nominated for the distinguished Weatherby Award, the annual selection of the big game hunter of the year. *Lower left,* and with trophy bongo, Paquita Machris, who with husband, Maury, and friend Tom Knudsen hunted widely in the 1950s, supplying the Los Angeles County Natural History Museum with several of its African game specimens.

Left: Ken Levin, executive with Bismuth Cartridge Company, with daughter Sarah (at *left*) and friend Lili Sams, during a day in the Texas outdoors. *Top left,* Buffalo Bill Cody with a group of female members and visitors at Buffalo Bill's Wild West headquarters at the Chicago World's Fair, 1893. To *right,* Martha Maxwell, "the Colorado Huntress," holding shotgun and in field attire. *Lower left,* women on the American frontier, taking aim, and resting after a successful wildfowl hunt. Ruger poster lady Kelly Glenn-Kimbro on the cover of *Women & Guns* magazine. *Bottom right,* "The First Lady of Wildfowling," Sis Kelm.

Game cookbooks by women, or coauthored with men, accompanied by pictures of some of the authoresses. Some of these chefs are also huntresses. This collage was made possible through the initiative of chef Priscilla Martel (*center,* in red sweater), who recognizes the impressive presence of women in the world of game cooking. The rapidly increasing presence of women in the ranks of U.S. hunters has inspired an increased appreciation for game cooking, which in turn has attracted more women to the shooting sports. The number of restaurants serving naturally fed game is also on the upswing.

Game food and women; at *left,* Cynthia Keller, of Restaurant du Village, fine-tuning roasted wildfowl on a fireplace grill. At *lower left,* Cynthia and her husband, Michele, with friend, working dogs in the field. Quoting Priscilla Martel, partner with Charles Van Over in their company, "All About Food":

Participating in the hunt then thoughtfully preparing what is harvested rekindles my connection to the natural world. In our chaotic lives, we often forget how nature nurtures mankind and how our self-reliant forebears thrived on the bounty of the land. As

Henry David Thoreau wrote, "He may travel who can subsist on the wild fruits and game of the most cultivated country." Beyond the taste experience that makes cooking such a pleasure, cooking wild game is an enriching experience.

Czech's remarkable bibliography lists over 120 titles that were written either by sportswomen, or by men about women shooters. An impressive total of eighty-five of these books were written solely by women. Another ten were coauthored by women and men (generally husbands). A listing of secondary titles presents yet another thirty-nine works, ranging from W. H. Davenport's *Celebrated Women Travellers of the Nineteenth Century* to *Travellers in Africa: British Travelogues, 1850–1900* by Tim Youngs. A selection of dust jackets provided by Professor Czech is on pages 90 and 91.

Hunting from 1940 to Today

While it may be a revelation to most that women both hunted and wrote about their adventures prior to World War II, their presence afield after that time is far less surprising. Illustrations and memoirs in *Silk and Steel*, and in the accompanying museum exhibition and documentary film, reveal that women's participation has become a dominant feature of sport hunting in the past six decades.

No longer are we surprised to learn that someone's mother, daughter, sister, cousin, wife, girlfriend, or female acquaintance has taken up the sport—and is wholly dedicated to it. The myriad of sport-hunting periodicals, books, and frequent television and radio programs have given the public an increasing awareness of women hunters—a solid and rapidly expanding segment of the hunting world.

Today, attendance at the Safari Club International annual convention is about evenly balanced between women and men, whether attending as hunters and huntresses or as exhibitors. Although hunting is not the major thrust of the National Rifle Association annual meetings, women are no less in evidence, again as both attendees and exhibitors.

These dramatic trends are reflected in the careers of several women whose lifestyles are captured in pictures, and in their own words, in the pages that follow. Some operate their own hunting preserves; some have media associations; still others are professional writers or guides; while not a few are involved as activists in the promotion of hunting. Some are simply dedicated huntresses. Their experiences help us understand the rapid explosion of interest by women in the sport of hunting.

Virginia Mallon's Pheasant Ridge

After Pan American Airways closed its doors in December 1991, Pan Am executive Virginia Mallon turned down a lucrative offer from Delta Airlines, sold her Manhattan apartment, and moved to a hundred-acre farm she had purchased in upstate New York's Washington County. In the fall of 1975, she had enjoyed a Continental Pheasant Hunt on a preserve in Sag Harbor, Long Island. This was her introduction to hunting, and it had made a lasting impression.

On moving to her farm property, Pheasant Ridge, Mallon decided to organize her own shoot. "I knew I could organize a business and bring in people with the necessary expertise to breed the birds, groom the land, check the guns and ammo, handle the dogs, cater the functions, etc." By visiting shooting preserves in England and Ireland, she gained firsthand knowledge of their makeup, and about habitat development. Returning to the United States, she developed a dozen butts around a hillside ridge where the birds would be released, the design preventing shooters from seeing other positions. Although the season in New York lasts from September 1 to March 31, she has limited the preserve's hunting to three months "to encompass the inviting fall foliage season and to avoid the

threat of heavy snowfall beginning in December. The preserve is kept open during the summer months with special and regularly scheduled programs."

She has retained a nationally recognized shooting instructor to provide lessons, and has set up a practice range where upland-style pheasant hunts can be simulated using clay targets flung to imitate the angles of flight of the birds. This same course is used for warm-up flurries before the Continental Hunts.

During her time with Pan Am, Mallon had traveled throughout Africa, and had assembled a collection of African memorabilia. Converting a three-story barn, she added a gallery of wildlife and African art to the Pheasant Ridge complex. The gallery opened in the summer of 1997, and two years later, she took up hunting herself, enrolling in the Orvis Shooting School in Vermont. As mistress of the Continental Pheasant Hunt at Pheasant Ridge, she is not able to participate in the hunt, but "I am presently working with several of my clients to put together a two-week hunt in Zimbabwe and South Africa."

Recognition for her achievement has come from more than the success of Pheasant Ridge. In 1988 Mallon was presented with the New York State Enterprising Women of the Year Award, at the annual meeting of the Enterprising Women's Leadership Institute.

Donna "Didi" Hall-Foss

A native of Michigan, Donna Hall-Foss began her business career during World War II as a department head, responsible for leasing nineteen hundred units for the Federal Public Housing Authority. For the next several years, as a matter of necessity, she pursued a varied business career to support her two children and herself. During her tenure as co-manager of the Kiva

Women in the field, including several wielding Freedom Arms .454 Kasull revolvers. *Lower right,* Didi Hall-Foss, Cape buffalo trophy, and husband (and Congressional Medal of Honor winner), General Joe Foss. To *left,* Suzie Brewster, with husband, Bill, and friend. To *left,* Mossberg executive Dennis Kendall, with wife,

Bridget, on honeymoon in Africa. *Upper left* row of photos showing outdoor writer Kathy Elting with trophies taken in North America. *Upper right,* Judy Woods and husband, John. *Center,* Josephine Kagika, of Beretta Gallery, New York, taking aim in Peter Horn's office. *Lower left,* several photographs of journalist Brooke Chilvers, including with husband, professional hunter Rudy

Lubin, of Haut Chinko Safaris. *Center left,* three employees of Swarovski Optical, photographed soon after passing their tests for a German hunting license. *Upper right,* Helen Williamson, from some of her hunting expeditions, including with array of birds and in safari car.

184

From *top left,* Madonna taking shooting lessons at the West London Shooting School, firing a Beretta—every bit the English country lady. This image was taken from *The Daily Mail,* December 2000, just before her wedding to Guy Ritchie, which featured shotgun shooting and a duck hunt. Missourian Judy

Wood's charming blind for whitetail and wild turkey hunting, beneath Weatherby, at *top.* To *left,* Linda Carmichel in Vintagers outfit. *Far right,* by muzzle of Browning, huntress from the Moretti or Bernardelli family, photographed in the mountains near Gardone, Val Trompia. On cover of *Sports Illustrated,* Mr. and

Mrs. John Olin on a pheasant shoot. *Bottom* shotgun, a Sigarms TT45. Guns and most of ammunition and memorabilia courtesy of Cubeta's; the patches are from the private collection of owner Al Cubeta.

With trophy lion and accompanied by delighted trackers and skinners, professional hunter and philanthropist Rose L. Piroeff on safari in East Africa. On their honeymoon, in 1954, the Piroeffs went on a six-week safari in Kenya—the first of several. The Piroeffs were among the founders of the African Safari and Conservation Club of Philadelphia, along with Mrs. Hallock duPont and counsel from Kermit Roosevelt. At *center,* Danielle Reed, who began shooting at age nine and hunting at twenty, most of the latter in Alaska, though her first outing was in Alabama; she has also been afield in Connecticut. At *left,* Dayna Wenzel, who started hunting after winning a charity fund-raising bird shoot—which included having the chef prepare what had been shot. It was her first hunt: "The rest is history." Period postcard and advertising images collected by Mrs. Wenzel. At *right,* Anne Brockinton with black and brown bears, taken by her in Alaska, with the Rosenbruch family's Glacier Guides. Elephant and African trophies, with handsome elk, taken by Nancy Bollman, who has hunted extensively in Africa, North America, and the South Pacific, one of increasing numbers of women who have taken the "big five" of elephant, Cape buffalo, rhinoceros, lion, and leopard.

Club, a special events arm of the Phoenix Chamber of Commerce, she met the well-known World War II ace, Medal of Honor winner, and sportsman Joe Foss.

In 1966 they formed a film-production company, traveling to locations around the world for their weekly syndicated television show *The Outdoorsman—Joe Foss.* Donna worked in administration—negotiating contracts with sponsors, planning locations and formats—and took still photographs on location for sponsors to use in advertising.

In January 1967 they married, and continued to work as a team until her husband's death at age eighty-seven in late 2002. They had traveled

the world in their evangelical work as well, and hosted evangelical events in their home and on tour, in conjunction with hunts, business conventions, and air shows.

Hall-Foss has served on several boards, and is currently active in the Shepherds (a prayer group), serves on the Board of Generation Ministries (Family Matters), manages family-owned commercial properties, acted as her husband's business manager, was ghostwriter of two books and several articles, as well as several book forewords, and is the author of *A Proud American.* Now in progress is a history, *American Football League and the Story Behind the Super Bowl.* She also remains active in politics,

Photographs, publications, and publicity for the Women on Target program, which encourages female participation in the shooting sports.

Facing page: With rifles from Cubeta's, snapshots and memorabilia of women's hunts around the world. *Upper right,* Susan Campbell Reneau's career has included approximately a dozen books on hunting and wildlife. Denise Luke on safari, beneath fore end and barrel of Marlin lever-action at *top.* Carol Kokin at *right,* about to step into a safari car. *Lower right,* Linda Carmichel in Africa, sharpshooting wife of *Outdoor Life* shooting editor Jim Carmichel. Suzie Schaaf* in Zimbabwe, at *center,* beneath Winchester Model 70 with all-weather stock; to *right,* Sissy LaVigne, on safari in Botswana with her granddaughter. Several images provided by members of Sables, among them President Barbara Strawberry, Janet Nyce (both *upper left*), and, at *lower left,* more from Brooke Chilvers.

*Sarah Jane (Suzie) Schaaf spent a week in May 1997 near Bulawayo, Zimbabwe, taking 700 head of game; natives thought she was magic, making several different single-shot kills, some at more than one hundred yards. Three of her trophies qualified for Safari club International gold-medal status, two for silver and two for bronze. Schaaf was the first woman guided by professional hunter Cliff Walker, who was awarded Zimbabwe's Hunter of the Year Award for 1997.

Parker Gentry and Holland & Holland's Ken Davies contemplate a victory bottle of champagne during an event in England; duck shoot and large Cape buffalo represent two worlds of hunting. Lynn Wyatt accompanied her son on a risky bow-and-arrow hunt for polar bear in the Arctic; she generously hosted the launch of author's *Steel Canvas*, aided by H & H, benefiting the Houston Museum of Fine Arts. Among those present was huntress Wendi Phillips, former sporting arms specialist, Sotheby's, New York.

and in 1995 founded an investment group of twenty women.

Besides being a big game hunter, she is a fly-fisherwoman. In 1975 she was presented the Hunter of the Year award by the Conservation Hall of Fame, for the highest number of one-shot trophies in Africa in that year. She holds the record, at 639 yards, for the longest single-shot kill during the International One-Shot Antelope Hunt, held annually in Lander, Wyoming (1973). In 2000 she shot for the twenty-ninth year in the Joe Foss Dove Shoot, sponsored by Liberty Mutual Insurance Company.

She is the mother of two children, grandmother of two, and great-grandmother of three.

Women on Target—Opening Doors for Hunting and Shooting

Women on Target introduces women to target shooting and hunting, and is one of the most rapidly developing programs of the 4.5-million-member National Rifle Association. The concept was launched in 2000, and its stated goals are:

To generate positive local and national media coverage for the shooting sports through the use of women's recreational shooting and hunting events.
To promote our host clubs and sponsors of shooting sports for women in local and national media.
To involve new women in the shooting sports, and support and promote ongoing opportunities.
To present to currently participating women, recreational shooting and hunting events which provide opportunity, education, and continuing avenues of involvement.
To promote and support the goals and programs of the National Rifle Association.
To support those organizations which share our philosophies.

Women on Target is overseen by Mary Sue Faulkner, director of community service programs, and Stephanie L. G. Henson, manager, NRA Women's Programs Department, with full support of the officers and staff of the association.

In 2001, approximately thirty instructional shoots were sponsored by Women on Target, and some fourteen hunts were organized, as well as fourteen charity shoots. These events were held coast to coast, and promise to increase significantly as agendas evolve. Women

on Target's potential is revealed by the fact that women active in shotgun shooting from 1989 to 1997 grew 23 percent—from 958,000 to 1,170,000. The number of those participating in sporting clays, in about the same period, more than doubled.[14] Social acceptability of the shooting sports among women has also grown. Trying to exclude women from them is now regarded as a waste of time.

Research of the same period also reveals an increase of 15 percent in the number of women hunters—from 1.75 million to over 2 million. According to the National Rifle Association, 11 percent of the overall hunting population is composed of women.

Women are also recognized as quick studies in the shooting sports, helped along by the fact that, unlike in most sports, success is not dependent on strength; more important are such factors as eye-hand coordination and timing. As recently stated in the *Houston Chronicle*, "Without strength as an ally, men hold no edge over women. And one by one, women who can outshoot men are stepping to firing lines at shooting ranges around the nation. Get used to it, gentlemen."

For statistics as of 2000–01, developed by the National Shooting Sports Foundation, see Appendix D, page 286.

Susan Campbell Reneau—the Making of a Hunting Woman

Susan Campbell Reneau writes books about big game hunting, wildlife conservation, and Western history from her mountaintop home in Montana. She was the first woman editor for the Boone and Crockett Club, and produced ten books on big game hunting and wildlife conservation between 1992 and 1997. She also edited, compiled, and wrote the twenty-five-year history of the Foundation for North American Wild Sheep (FNAWS), *Putting Sheep on the*

Mountain. Her four-hundred-page book, *Colorado's Biggest Bucks and Bulls and Other Great Colorado Big Game,* was published in August 2001.

Hunting makes my heart beat faster and my eyes flash with adventurous memories, but it wasn't always that way. Throughout my life as a young girl growing up in suburban and urban surroundings, my mother hated the thought of killing any animal and

was a big fan of Bambi. I was indoctrinated that a good hunter was a dead hunter. Shooting a wild animal for sport was not in my mother's vocabulary. She had been raised in Chicago where guns were synonymous with gangsters and hunting was synonymous with macho men who were uneducated and crude.

My father didn't object to hunting but never did it. His passion was fishing and my job was to gut the catch. I loved the opportunity to hike with my dad, bait the hook, talk with him about everything on my

mind, and share in the experience of the catch. My father was a gruff Marine Corps officer who didn't quite know what to do with a daughter, so fishing was our way to communicate. That was my full experience with the great outdoors until I met Jack Reneau when I was eighteen years and seven months.

Although a huntress of considerable experience in Europe, Great Britain, and Africa, Anne Brent's specialty is white-tail hunting—at which she clearly excels. Her wins in white-tail competitions in Texas rank her among the most accomplished deer hunters in America. The collage reveals a broad array of sporting pursuits. With husband, John, holding pheasant take, at *upper left.*

A lifetime sportswoman, Betty Lou Sheerin of San Antonio, Texas, and Newport, Rhode Island, has hunted North America, Africa, the United Kingdom, and Europe. Her 28-gauge Purdey, a gift from her husband, Larry, ranks among the finest shotguns ever made. Gold and engraving were by K. C. Hunt, featuring floral scrolls, Western-art motifs, and cattle brands. Picture of couple at *center right* was taken in a lull during a bird shoot. Note exceptional white-tailed-deer trophy at *bottom right*. One of the Sheerins' several enthusiasms is the Buffalo Bill Historical Center, Cody, of which Larry is the longest-serving member of the board of trustees.

Former Monterey County District Attorney Julie Culver and chocolate Labrador Lucy, with quarter horse Nova and cattle on her Salinas ranch property; at the wheel of her Dodge Viper; with California governor Pete Wilson and Senator Bruce McPherson; clutching a bundle of confiscated marijuana; emerging from the courtroom and in media interview after winning a conviction in a triple-murder trial; pigeon and clay shooting; and on safari in Zimbabwe with sable and lion trophies.

Husband-to-be Jack was a keen hunter and hiker, but he never invited her to hunt, since she repeatedly told him that "hunting was cruel and heartless." Marrying shortly after college, the new Mrs. Reneau said she "would gladly cook the meat but not hunt it." Her philosophy was that hunting "was a difficult and athletic sport that [she] didn't choose to start."

The birth of three sons from 1977 to 1982 gave her husband hunting partners.

> Periodically, he'd ask me to join them but I felt this was a male bonding session and I relished weekends alone with our dogs, a strawberry bubble bath, and a good book. Now that my sons are young men I do not regret my decision because I see in their eyes and their body language a deep and abiding respect and adoration for their father. I see a communication level with Jack and his sons that would not have happened without their yearly treks up mountains, across iced streams and down scrub oak–covered draws in search of elusive big game.

Seventeen years before I began to hunt I wrote my first big-game hunting book, *Colorado's Biggest Bucks and Bulls*, with Jack, that recorded the hunting stories and photographs of the most beautiful of mule

Above: Penny Reneson shooting driven grouse in England, captured on film and in one of husband Chet's classic watercolors, "Grouse Hunting," as depicted in Robert K. Abbett's *The Watercolors of Chet Reneson*. An active sportswoman since childhood, Penny Reneson can stalk up to within yards of a white-tailed deer. Frequently joining her husband on hunting and fishing trips, she not only has extensive outdoors experience but is a masterful game chef.

Right: A "Becoming an Outdoorswoman" T-shirt and a "Women on Target" carryall bag are joined by an apron promoting Kate Feduccia's *Woods N Waters* TV series. Shotguns by, from the *top,* Browning, Beretta, and Benelli (the innovative Nova series) are all perfectly suited for use by most women—although relatively few models of shotguns or rifles are presently built specifically for the women's market. Guns courtesy of Cubeta's, Middletown, Connecticut.
Founder of the Becoming an Outdoorswoman program was Christine L. Thomas, who from her Wisconsin base has spread the organization's innovative programs to every state of the union.

deer, whitetail deer and elk in Colorado. The book was published in 1983 and became a bestseller in hunting circles. Through the writing of big-game hunting books I lived vicariously through the men and women who took trophy animals in North America and shared the love of hunting with my husband who often co-authored the books with me.

Seven years before I began hunting I allowed my husband to hang his trophies on the wall with glass eyes and all. My son's collection of an outstanding antelope on the plains of Jordan, Montana, prompted my change of mind in 1992. My husband never said a word but revealed after I began to hunt that he was stunned when I made the pronouncement after years of hearing me say in a shrill, wifely tone, "I'll cook the meat but I will never, NEVER allow those stuffed heads in my house."

As her sons became older, and two of them married, Susan Reneau decided to take up hunting. Her first season was in 1998, following completion of a hunter safety course, and a "Becoming an Outdoors Woman" workshop. Her sixteen-year-old son Rich had helped guide her in accuracy with a rifle. "It was a tender moment of mother-son communication, just as my father had shown me so many years before, but in a reversed role."

My first hunts with Jack and Rich were joyful experiences filled with lots of hiking, early morning breakfasts and cold sunrises. Rich helped me load my rifle and instructed me on the art of stalking antelope, elk and deer. This teenager who thought his mother was slightly weird suddenly became a thoughtful teacher who shared his three years of hunting experience with a novice mother. His concern and tenderness sincerely moved me although I dared not tell him when I was tired in the field, for fear he'd stop.

The interaction with Rich proved "an added bonus to hunting that most women never experience, because they choose not to join their husbands and sons in the field." After taking an antelope, her first, with a single shot, she harkened back to advice they had given her about breathing and trigger control.

Throughout my three-year journey my relationship with Jack has expanded and deepened. My communication with my teenage son has improved, and my confidence in my athletic abilities has increased. Before I downed my first buck and cow elk I began to doubt whether hunting was for me, but after I accomplished my goals and took those first animals, I realized that hunting is much more about joining nature and becoming a part of patterns in life and death. I still enjoy the stalk and the hunt more than the killing. Watching the sunrise above the horizon provides peace for my soul.

Yes, hunting is male-dominated but slowly this is changing as women like myself muster the courage to venture outside the comforts of their houses, get their feet muddy and their hands ice cold to come face to face with nature in its raw ferociousness and silence.[15]

Amy Katherine Ross—from BB Gun to Spokane Police Department

Daughter of Anchorage attorney Wayne Anthony Ross and his wife, Barbara, Amy Katherine Ross is from a family devoted to the shooting sports. The youngest of four children, she was not to be outdone by her three older brothers. By the age of three she had her own BB gun. When she had mastered safe gun-handling techniques, her reward was a Chipmunk bolt-action .22 rifle. With it she shot her first squirrel at age six.

Amy also started shooting a handgun while six years old. At seven, she got a revolver of her own, a nickel-plated Smith & Wesson Model 19. That didn't satisfy her—she saw her older brothers carrying .45s and said many times that she wanted a bigger gun like theirs. Her father remembers:

When Amy was nine, she called me down to the basement one day. She had a .45 pistol in her hand. "Watch this, Dad," she said. She then proceeded to field-strip that .45 down to all of its component parts. She then put it back together again. "When did you learn that?" I asked her. "My brothers taught me," she stated proudly, "and you told the boys when they

could field-strip a .45, you'd buy them one, so I want mine!" As a result, for her ninth Christmas, Amy got a nickel-plated Colt .45 semi-automatic pistol. She shoots it very well.

When she was eleven, Amy announced that she wanted to take her .45 to school. Her school was having a Science Fair and all students were expected to participate by preparing a science project. Amy said she wanted to do her project on her .45, and the history of its development.[16]

The principal, a woman, once assured this would be safe, agreed to the project. "Amy entered her .45 and won first prize. Anchorage mayor Tom Fink judged the exhibits." Now, at twenty-one, Amy has excelled as an equestrian, graduated from college with a degree in criminal justice, and completed the Spokane, Washington, Police Academy. Though her intent is to become a lawyer, she is currently serving with the Spokane police.

Unlike her brothers, Amy didn't get her first big game animal until she was seventeen, but not for lack of trying. From the time she was six, she accompanied the boys and me on our hunting trips, and she packed her share of moose. One week before she left for her first year in college, Amy took her first moose, and I had the joy of accompanying her on that hunt. I was glad to have that opportunity before another man comes along and replaces me as the important man in her life.

Alisha L. Rosenbruch, Registered Alaskan Guide, Master Taxidermist, and International Big Game Hunter

Daughter of Jim and MaryAnn Rosenbruch, both master Alaskan guides, Alisha, at age twenty-one, is already a superstar in the allied worlds of hunting and wildlife conservation. Since taking her first big game trophy—on safari in Africa at age ten—she has garnered more experience in the wilderness, in taxidermy studios, and in tutelage under big game authorities than anyone her age in the world. She has hunted on five continents, taken some twenty-seven species

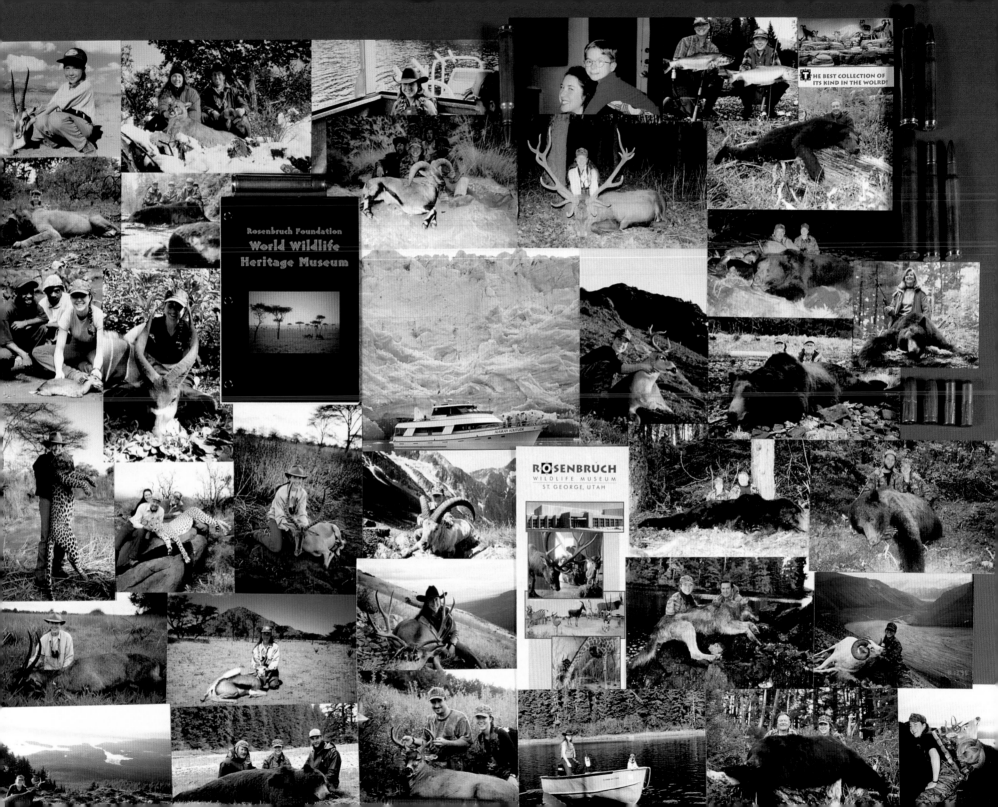

THE BEST COLLECTION OF
ITS KIND IN THE WORLD!

Rosenbruch Foundation
World Wildlife
Heritage Museum

ROSENBRUCH
WILDLIFE MUSEUM
ST. GEORGE, UTAH

Facing page: Alisha L. Rosenbruch, master taxidermist, huntress, and the youngest female registered Alaskan guide/outfitter (licensed at the age of sixteen). Represented are hunts on five continents. Her sum total of experience in the field equals or surpasses that of any male or female at her age level in the world. Several of the specimens displayed at the Rosenbruch Wildlife Heritage Museum were taken by her, and are consistently of record-book stature. At *top right,* Alisha with husband (as of 2001), Zach Decker.

Above: *Center* and *right,* Alisha Rosenbruch—scenes from Russia, Alaska, Africa, and western China; in Las Vegas with her family at Safari Club International. Family group photo, with Alisha holding a trophy awarded to her as Young Hunter of the Year, 1997; from *left,* Keith Wenzel, Mildred Rosenbruch, sister Michelle, mother MaryAnn, Alisha, Jim Rosenbruch, sister Andrea, sister Angie, brother Bud, and Dustin Hammer. Photographs at *left,* writer and editor Susan Campbell Reneau, hunting, target shooting, learning, coaching, and standing proudly with her three sons.

BALAVIL · INVERNESS-SHIRE

WHEN HOT
SHOTS BURN OUT

GLOUCESTERSHIRE

Purdey

HOLLAND & HOLLAND
IN THE FIELD

STAPLEFORD PARK

WATCH DOG.

GAME
CONSERVANCY
U·S·A

Conservation
Through Wise Use

SHADOWS
on the GRASS

ISAK DINESEN

Facing page: The sheer joy of a day in the field, U.K. and continental style: at top *left,* Czar Nicholas II with the Czarina, he armed with a matched pair of LeBeau-Courally shotguns (serials 31831, 31832), waiting for a drive, while Alexandra plays the more traditional role of taking it all in (likely just prior to World War I). Several of these images are from the rich advertising tradition of Holland & Holland, Ltd. Cartoon figure a tribute to Parker Gentry,

and her renowned skill afield at driven birds. At *bottom left,* the three Hawkins girls, Emma, Lucinda, and Penelope, daughters of John and Robyn Hawkins of Australia, October 1994; each of the young ladies had just killed a stag on the island of Jura, off the west coast of Scotland; it was the first for Lucinda—whose trophy was a royal. Their mother took her first stag in 1988, in Inveraray, with Dora, Duchess of Argyll, as the stalker.

Above: Model Deborah Langley Horn has extensive big game and bird-shooting experience in Africa and Europe, as well as equal success in hunting and in clay-pigeon shooting in the United States. She was an NCAA champion skeet shot and an accomplished shooter before meeting husband-to-be, Peter, later appointed vice president of Beretta USA, with years devoted to hunting expeditions. Their son Lee has the genes, and is rapidly developing as an accomplished shot and sportsman; he recently bested his mother at sporting clays.

My mother and rhinoceros shot to protect farm workers on coffee estate near Ngong.

My mother and a Blixen coffee estate manager out hunting for the cook's pot accompanied by farm employees. Note donkey and pack saddles used for retrieval of game meat.

My mother's buffalo was entered into the Rowland Ward record book. It was shot during the time that she owned a holiday fishing bungalow along the river passing through Nanyuki. It descended from the icy heights of Mount Kenya. The river then flowed through the thick forests inhabited by elephants, rhinoceros, buffalo, lion, leopard and many other forest species.

Karen Blixen with two lionesses, both cattle-killers, shot on her coffee estate. Lions in those days were considered as vermin and therefore not included on game licenses.

The versatility of the Indian Calvary camel saddle. Two can ride when necessary. Judy is mounted on the back seat where normally an army rider would carry his equipment, including food, water, bedding and ammunition.

Being held by my mother, seated on lioness cattle-killer. Note terrier dog, Pelle, and Ngong hills in the background.

This photo shows Frank Hibben's wife, Brownie, who had difficulties mounting a horse due to knee problems. This problem was overcome because she was able to mount a camel with ease. On command (To tap) the camel would lower itself onto its chest and drop on the ground so that she could straddle and sit in the saddle comfortably. The rider could also use the designated safety rope. Eventually Brownie took a liking to my personal favorite riding camel, Leruko.

Mrs. Dorotea Tham, owner of a large estate in southern Sweden, with her elephant.

Barbro Holmberg, my sister, with her second heavy tusker. These tusks are thick nearly to their tips.

Judy with her specially treasured evenly matched 100-pounder. Note the thickness of these tusks compared with the hands of the two men holding them.

Judy in the horse and camel block with a 100 pounds plus trophy taken at the foot of the Matthews Mountains.

Judy with her first 100-pounder.

Another shot of Rosemary Pancotto and her elephant.

John and Betty LaGarde with super impala — note the wide spread — trophy taken in the Isiolo area.

Mrs. Cramer from Switzerland with her Sudan elephant ivory (1975).

Barbro shown above with two different but equally impressive sets of tusks.

Myself in open country with a dream-sized trophy.

Author with client, Margareta Wolf, and his record Cape buffalo bull.

Bitten Clausen and myself with low country leopard.

of big game—several of them in the record books—and has a range of delighted clients with record-sized trophies. Her career is on course to rival that of any Alaskan guide in history, and she continues to rack up hunting adventures that may well eclipse even those of her father, a nominee for the Weatherby Award and considered one of America's most accomplished shooting sportsmen. Consider the following observations, made by Alisha at age twenty. They reveal dedication, expertise, and a respect for the outdoors world.

> For as long as I can remember, I have been around guns and the world of hunting. I was present on my first bear hunt at the age of ten days. All the years of my youth I was able to accompany my parents in our family guide operation in Alaska, Glacier Guides, Inc. Home schooling enabled the freedom to be "at sea" throughout the entire hunting season, and thus, I accompanied my dad in the field every day he hunted from age eight on, and have been part of the hunt for nearly every one of Dad's trophies in the last ten years. My sweet parents had the foresight to allow me the freedom to participate in the life they built with such love and care. It has become a passion closely shared between us.[17]

In 1963, after hunting in Alaska, Jim and MaryAnn Rosenbruch decided to pack up and leave their home in Reno, Nevada, and move north. Appointed to a position with the Bureau of Indian Affairs, Jim devoted the next two years to visiting all the Indian villages in Alaska. After a thorough look at the state, the family located in the southeast Alaska archipelago, in 1964.

Facing page: Many of these photographs include truly impressive trophies of African big game taken by women on safari. The majority of images come from Andrew Holmberg's *The Amazing Life of Andrew Holmberg*, published in 2000 by Trophy Room Books. Images at *upper left* are from Anthony Dyer's *Kenya Pioneers and Hunters*, from the same publisher; note Karen Blixen on her Kenya property, sighting rifle, and with a black rhino. At *upper right*, Blixen with *two* lions shot by her.

Thus was laid the foundation of my early introduction to hunting. All five of the children in our family had the same opportunities of growing up as I have. However, the two oldest sisters, Michelle and Andrea, married outside the "dream," and drifted from the life that has become my obsession. My brother, "Bud," has the same pursuits and guides with us still in Alaska. The sister between Bud and I, Angie, proves invaluable in the office and loves to get out on the hunt, although only as an active observer.

Hunting in Alaska for brown and black bear, despite all my other devotions, has most definitely become the most loved. Dad and I hunt together whenever possible and share an amazing tie in thought and action. Our parallel of thought is often surprising, even to us. I have apprenticed with the best bear hunter in the world! Over the last thirty-six years he has been hunting bear in Alaska every spring season, and every fall season. He has hunted in nearly every bay, cove, and inlet in the entire southeast panhandle. To draw on that wealth of knowledge has been rewarding to say the least.

The young female big game hunting guide draws mixed reactions from the clientele:

> It used to bother me when, upon initial introductions, clients arriving aboard the seventy-two-foot *Alaska Solitude* "base camp," would literally cringe as Dad indicated I would be one of the guides. Now, I just sit back and smile. We rotate clients each day, so no one gets "stuck" with anyone, so there lays a gleam of hope for them. However, upon return from the first evening of hunting I daresay it is exceptionally rare when they aren't singing praises. Just surprised, I guess.

Her arsenal has been developed through experience, and an awareness of changing technology:

> I shoot a .375 Remington Model 700 as backup with a Swarovski 1.5-6x56y Pro Hunter scope for maximum light-gathering capacity. Swarovski 10x42 binoculars provide amazing clarity and extended hunting time through light gathering. A .30-06 Remington has served me well for much of my North American hunting, but Dad's .300 Remington has been my weapon of choice on overseas hunts. I recently commissioned Match Grade Arms of Spring, Texas, to build me an ultra-light .300, also on a Rem-

ington action, and in tradition I am putting a Kahles 3-12x56 illuminated reticule scope on it. [This is] my ultimate dream rifle that will most likely serve for a very long time. I prefer to get comfortable with one rifle and shoot that *one* a lot. I load, for the most part, all my own bullets and prefer to use Sierra Boat-tail 180 grain. I don't change loads much, and have found that it is very predictable what that load will do in various circumstances.

Occasionally there are moments of truth in dealing with bears, who always present the possibility of danger. In the course of one month, the Rosenbruchs were charged by two brown bears:

> One time in particular was rather hairy. We were coming down the river [on which] Bud had just harvested his bear . . . having hunted late in the eve way up the river, then dealing with his bear once it was down. It was all but black dark with the customary "heavy mist" of southeast Alaska soaking up the remaining light. There had been a sow with a single yearling cub fishing at the mouth on the way in, and as we eased by her, she had winded us and ran. Well, here we were again, what with her trying to fish and she winded us again. Initially, she was probably seventy to eighty yards away. She "woofed" her cub off to safety (he headed for the woods), and here she came. Let me tell you, it is un*real* how quickly those yards were cut. At nine steps she stopped, blowing hard, popping and snapping teeth, and growling low. A short standoff, and she retreated. The *only* reason she didn't keep coming I think had to do with the fact that there were three of us (Dad, Bud, and I), that we were spread apart, and that we weren't going anywhere. If someone had broken to run, there is no doubt she would have had them. I will say she had about a millisecond left before the lead would've been flying, but it's a hard call to make—especially with her motherhood status, although the cub would most likely have survived.
>
> So much of a successful hunter lies in what Dad and I have coined the "3 I's": instinct, imagination, and, most of all, inspiration.

Most of her worldwide hunts are with her parents, and so much time together in the wilderness has cemented a bond of both family and

199

Featured are members of Safari Club International's Sables. Note historic Peter Beard collage, *right,* from *End of the Game.* Under "sharpshooter" shoulder patch, old photo showing younger members of the Cottar family, legendary dynasty of African safari hunters. At *right,* Natasha Illum Berg, professional hunter in Tanzania, with Cape buffalo. At *left* and *above,* several members of the New England Sables. In hunter orange, Victoria J. Gelling, a Ph.D. from Fargo, North Dakota, who began hunting at age six, and her mother (with moose). *Bottom left* and *bottom right,* Isabel de Quintanilla; latter including husband, son, and trophies. Sables president Barbara Strawberry with elk at *center.*

Selection of postcards from nineteenth- and early-twentieth-century France, depicting photographs and art of women in the field—some of them professionals in the hunting community; from *La Chasse au Debut du Siècle par les Cartes Postales* by Noel Dijoux. Remaining photographs from Jacques Vittier's *Big*

Game Hunting in Asia, Africa and Elsewhere. On several of his expeditions, Vettier was accompanied by his wife, Kandice (with warthog, at *bottom right,* and in several other photographs) and daughter Vanessa. At *bottom right,* Mrs. Elsa Talayero and her husband pose with two sets of elephant tusks, one of which

weighed in at some 163 pounds each side. They were nine feet, four inches long—the largest ever shot by a woman. In southern Sudan, 1979, Mrs. Talayero quite nonchalantly took this remarkable trophy.

MIN VÄN FJÄLL-PIPAREN
Bengt Berg

BENGT BERGS DJURBÖCKER · TIDEN

BENGT BERG

Farligt storvilt

BENGT BERGS DJURBÖCKER · TIDEN

friendship. Their extraordinary amalgam of experience afield inspired the Rosenbruchs to develop a 33,000-square-foot wildlife museum:

> The new facility features the largest indoor mountain in the world, with nearly one-quarter mile of pathway winding up through the plains and swamps of Africa, into North America, and on into Europe and Asia, then ending up back in the desert and forest of Africa. Approximately 250 life-mounted animals will be displayed in their natural habitats. Many of my personal animals will be included in the project. The balance are displayed in my own home. The project is widely supported by private, public and political entities. The grand opening was in March 2001, the fulfillment of a twelve-year process.

A two-hundred-seat auditorium and an up-to-date taxidermy facility are part of the museum complex. Alisha is a keen student of the taxidermist's art, and enjoys the field's artistic freedom. She is also a talented artist and photographer, primarily of wildlife. Her insights on the hunting life:

> Hunting is a very personal affair. Many people look at the same issues with very different views. For me, hunting has little to do with the killing, and everything to do with the experience. José Ortega y Gasset said something rather prophetic in his book *Meditations on Hunting:* "One does not hunt to have killed; one kills to have hunted." Being out in the great wild and undisturbed places of this planet seeking its fantastic wildlife is something so dear to me I know not how to explain my feelings. There is a spiritual connection that fully envelopes the true hunter and conservationist.
>
> I feel that "we do not inherit the earth from our parents, we borrow it from our children."

Of the 2,087 hunting guides in Alaska, only thirty-five are women.

Top right shows Inger Illum with huge Asian buffalo, taken with an express double rifle, in India. Wildlife photo books by her husband, naturalist and talented photographer Bengt Berg. Dead tiger; revealing relief brought to natives when this dreaded beast, perhaps a man-eater, met its reward, likely for killing domestic animals.

African Safaris and Indian Shikars

The magic of Africa has fired the imagination of both men and women for well over a century. Three women who have answered its magnetic attraction are representative of what it takes to fully enjoy the wildlife of that continent. Each has been a hunter, and one of them visited nearly every country with both rifle and camera. Their stories are among the most compelling in the world of women and arms.

Elizabeth Cross: From a Privileged Life in England to the Bush in Kenya

Elizabeth Cross was born into wealth in Victorian England. Her grandfather was Lord Privy Seal and winner of the Military Medal in World War I. Elizabeth arrived in Mombasa, British East Africa, on Christmas Day 1919, aboard the steamer *Garthe Castle*. Her service as a nurse on the front lines during the First World War left her suffering from shell shock and the effects of gassing. Nonetheless, she had earned a reputation as one who could get more wounded soldiers into an ambulance than anyone else. In Kenya she was seeking peace and solace as a farmer.

Cross, the only woman settler on the ship, carried a gift from her father—a 16-gauge shotgun designed to help prepare her for the bush. Her farm was fifty miles northeast of Nairobi, near the Tana River. She spent much of her time hunting, both for food and for sport. Writing to her father in England, she noted:

> Next time we go out there will be a moon and we are going for five or six days. So we will be able to sit up at nights for the beasts as they come to drink. I love seeing game just as much as trying to shoot it, so does Van Breda, who is lucky. [He was an elderly Boer neighbor, who taught her to hunt.]
>
> If Mr. Dashwood is fit and I can ask to get away, we've planned a heavenly trip for the end of next month, when the grass will have been burnt and the moon will be up. If we can raise a suitable chaperone

we are going to hunt buffalo in the Ithana Hills for a week which will be too wonderful and thrilling for words, only I must try and raise a rifle I can shoot with before then. Van Breda is trying to get an awfully pleasant couple called Collington to come. He is an A.D.C. at Fort Hall and was in Peter Carew's battalion of the K.A.R. [Kenya Army Regiment]. They are both as mad on game as I am. So if they can get leave to come too everything in the garden will be lovely.

Not long thereafter, Elizabeth sold her farm, invested in oxen and an ox wagon, and set up a transport business. Years later her son-in-law Anthony Dyer wrote, "This is a tough business for anyone to take on. I know she did it well for in the fullness of time . . . she taught me many things that I should have known about. . . . During her time in the transport business she was 'On Safari' the whole time. She hunted and wrote poems about her life. She was often very lonely and homesick."

In a poem about an evening in bush camp, Elizabeth captured the perils and fears, sights and sounds:

> . . . *Now bush-veldt music fills the dark*
> *A hyaena howls his misery;*
> *Staccato falls the jackal's bark:*
> *A Grevy calls his absent mare,*
> *A deep roar brings the echoes down*
> *And at this note I turn my eye*
> *To where beside my blankets brown*
> *The "Rigby"—primed—is standing by . . .*

Elizabeth Cross died in 1964, at sixty-seven. On her tombstone is inscribed: "Her children rise up and call her blessed, her husband also and he praiseth her.—*Proverbs.*"[18]

Irene Morden—Sharpshooting Grandmother

The obituary of Colonel William J. Morden, explorer and hunter, in an undated clipping from the *New York Herald Tribune*, contains a brief

note that hints at the role played by his widow, Irene, in their numerous expeditions around the world—most of them for the American Museum of Natural History:

> In 1947, he went to Central and East Africa to bring back information on disappearing tribes there. His wife, Mrs. Irene Hambright Morden, former personnel director for General Foods . . . accompanied him as co-leader on several expeditions—and after he damaged an eye during a trip to Alaska, she did the shooting for the team. They published a book on their 1947 expedition entitled, "Our African Adventure."

The *Catalogue of the American Museum of Natural History Film Archives* lists five expeditions conducted by Colonel Morden, in which Irene not only participated, but was coleader. These trips were in 1947 and in the 1950s. The catalog notes that on the 1956 trip

> Irene Morden's stated goal . . . was to bag a black-maned lion and a leopard. She succeeded with the lion. The hunt is recreated for the camera and she poses with the lion. The skinning is also photographed. Irene bags a rhinoceros and poses with that as well. The nearby Masai women, on hearing of Irene's success with the lion, pay her a visit, singing and dancing in her honor and Irene joins in the dance.

Researching the American Museum's collection of still pictures produced photographs of Irene, proudly posing with her lion.

Isabel de Quintanilla—the Professional Hunter's Wife

Isabel de Quintanilla, born in Valencia, Spain, married the well-known professional safari hunter, conservationist, and adventurer Tony Sanchez-Arino in 1963 and is the mother of their three sons. She has since been on nearly one hundred safaris all around Africa, as well as in Australia, Central Asia, Eastern Europe, and beyond. Over thirty-five years she has accumulated a wide experience in wildlife photography, exploration, hunting, conservation, and the study of primitive peoples and tribes. She has also traveled extensively around the world as a freelance journalist.

She has organized and conducted photographic safaris—in Zimbabwe, Tanzania, Botswana, Namibia, and Kenya, as well as in several other countries—for female clients, often the first of their kind in many of these locations. Well known among the sportswomen of Spain, she is often requested for lectures and personal appearances.

In connection with a uniquely multifaceted career, she has written numerous articles and has been the subject of several interviews. Her photographs have been widely shown in gallery and museum exhibitions, and she has made several television appearances. In recent years she has conducted a radio program on the social life of Valencia, the broadcast becoming one of the most popular in the city.

Accomplished in Spanish, French, English, and Swahili, she is active in the International Federation of Tourism Journalists and the Mediterranean Organization of Tourism Journalists. A keen animal lover, she has several pets at her Valencia home. Her hobbies are classical music and sailing, and she holds a license as a yacht captain.

Her book, *Many Trails Through Africa,* has been published in Spanish, and will soon appear in an English-language edition. The work recounts the fascinating life of this woman who has been able to mix motherhood with hunting and exploring in the world centers of wildlife adventure.

Inger Illum Berg, by Herself, Shoots Two Tigers—1934

Inger Illum Berg came from a long line of hunters and huntresses, and proved herself to be a deadly, calm, and cool shot under stressful conditions. Inger's husband, Bengt, introduced her to hunting, and their son, Lens, wrote a memoir of his mother in the form of a letter to his daughters, so they might better appreciate their grandmother's daring and steely nature. Her granddaughter Natasha Illum Berg is a professional big game hunter in Tanzania.

Inger Illum Berg proved herself in the field:

Her ability with a shotgun was fairly good but with a rifle she became very good. In the beginning they went roebuck stalking and moose hunting. Later in 1937 when they bought the estate of Eriksberg she did a lot of red deer, Fallow deer, Sika deer, Mouflon sheep and wild boar stalking. As my sister and I grew up we had, every fall, a competition with her about who would be the best shot. She was hard to beat. As a hunter she was very compassionate about the game. Once, when a very big and beautiful red deer stag became fifteen years of age, grandfather told her, "It is about time to take him out. He is an enormous trophy and yours alone. Stalk him whenever you like." In her eyes he was so beautiful, that every year when she saw him in the rut, she let him go. He died, a natural death, at the age of nineteen.

Berg was the only family member who successfully hunted elephant. This came about when she and her husband were in the Sudan filming and photographing wildlife. Their camp was not far north of the border with Uganda, between Juba and the river Bar El Ghazal.

One day while they were in camp a light aircraft landed not far away and out stepped their old friend Bror Blixen. He was in northern Uganda to find a very big elephant for an American client. He had heard, I suppose through some kind of jungle telegraph, that his Swedish friends and compatriots were in the area and dropped in. While there, he asked your grandfather if he would come with him on some control shooting of elephants in northern Uganda. . . . Bror then turned to your grandmother and gave her the same offer. She accepted and off they flew. Two days later they were back and she could tell everybody that she had taken a bull elephant with a perfect shot.

On a trip to the Himalayas in 1930, Grandfather Berg wanted to film and photograph the lammageyer, or bearded vulture. In order to catch the bird in its nest, a hoist had to be constructed. But only Inger could be lifted, due to her husband's size and weight. The assignment was dangerous. She agreed to do it, but only on the condition that she be allowed to try for a big male tiger when they returned to India.

When finished in the Himalayas, down to India they went. He to photograph the Indian rhino and she to try for a tiger. After several tries and misfortunes she shot a tigress. With this she was a little disappointed as she had been promised a big male. . . . A year later when your grandparents were in Oslo, Norway, he to make a speech and show pictures from India to the Norwegian Hunters Association, one of the pictures was of your grandmother with her tigress. The subtitle was: "Women's equality outside the kitchen." Afterward she was approached by a hunter and asked if somebody else was helping her hold the gun. That was like a shot straight into the heart of this proud lady.

Returning to India in the spring of 1934, Inger had her second chance for a big male tiger. She was in the Kalibit Range, above the Tapti River, a renowned tiger-hunting district. While the Bergs were busy filming, the divisional forest officer arrived in camp.

At the same time their old shikar Mattu came and reported that a big male tiger had killed a water buffalo in the Kekrinala Valley some kilometers away. [Inger] . . . decided that she was going to try to take this tiger. Earlier she had said that your grandfather had brought her bad luck when it came to tiger hunting, so she asked Mr. Vahid if he would go with her, on elephant back, to the place of the kill. To this he agreed. The buffalo lay beside a waterhole in a small area of open and naked forest. Before sunset a machān (platform) was built in the only stable tree close by, about fifty yards away from the kill. There she made herself comfortable with some blankets and two rifles: her own, calibre .360 cordite with open sights, and your grandfather's double .470 with a

4-power scope. She hung some branches, with leaves, around her for camouflage. Mr. Vahid then rode away, but outside a small village about one km. from the kill, he left three Indians and one elephant to be able to pick her up after she had signalled with a horn that the tiger was dead.

It was going to be a full moon during the night but it would not come up before one hour after dark. At 7:20 P.M. she heard a distinct "aooong" but far away. At 8:00 P.M. she heard the same but much closer. Shortly thereafter something came gliding through the denser forest out in the open and half-moonlit area. By its slender shape she concluded that it was a tigress. Somewhat annoyed, as she had been promised a big male, she lost all fear. . . . When the tigress came up to the kill she lined up the .470 scope behind the shoulder and pulled the trigger. The tiger . . . died by the waterhole. . . . Then she signalled the Indians to come with the elephant. This she did many times and as they had not come after half an hour she even fired a signal shot in the air. Expecting them to arrive any time she started to crawl down on some lower branches. Sitting there with her spotlight aimed at the tigress she heard, far away, another "aooong." This time much stronger. Quietly and quickly she climbed up onto the machãn again. Most of the camouflage branches had fallen down but she hid herself as well as possible and reloaded the .470. By then it was about 9:15 P.M. and the moon had properly come up so the waterhole and the kill were well lit. . . . Now her heartbeat was set racing as a mighty male tiger came walking out in the clearing. He ignored the tigress and went straight for the water buffalo. As he stood over his kill she slowly lifted the rifle and once again sighted the scope behind the shoulder. . . . For the next ten minutes she aimed at him but never shot again. This was on the 24th of April 1934.

Then, so as nobody ever could say to her, "Who was behind the gun," she went to Mr. Vahid and asked him to write a certificate.[19]

Inger Illum, the tigers, and the game warden's certificate are pictured on page 278.

Proud lady with Marlin takedown slide-action shotgun, with take in the field. From company advertisement of c. 1900.

CHAPTER VIII

Target Shooting—Precise Science and Demanding Sport

The highly popular Schützenliesel, with target on her hat, from a beer stein associated with *Schuetzenfests*.

Facing page: Ranked high among the greatest rifle shots of modern times, Patricia ("Piffa") L. M. Schroder has won virtually every coveted prize in British rifle shooting, and lends her elegance, insight, and wit to a world all too often misunderstood by outsiders. Her achievements as a marksperson have been an inspiration to numerous new generations of shooters in the United Kingdom and abroad. Through her regular columns in British magazines and in books, interviews, and seats on boards and committees, she has been highly effective in preventing target competitions and the shooting sports from being banned.

Women are finding trapshooting even more enjoyable than golf and tennis. In the shooting game a women is not classed as a woman. She meets men shooters on an equal footing, and there is nothing that pleases her more than to beat her lord and master at his own game. Shooting makes a woman agile and alert. I have shot at the traps with many women and never have I seen an ungraceful one who used a shotgun well.

—John Philip Sousa, orchestra leader and composer,
The American Shooter, September 15, 1916

One of the oldest sports, target shooting with firearms continues to evolve, grow, expand, and prosper. A business and sport of international scope has evolved from the simple, sometimes sublime and satisfying pleasure of hitting targets, employing an array of oftimes refined, high-tech arms. In all its sundry disciplines, the sport ranks among the most complex of the multibillion-dollar firearms industry.

Participation by women varies considerably in the many and diverse forms of competition. For example, benchrest shooting of muzzle-loading rifles attracts relatively few women, while trapshooting and sporting clays draw large and increasing numbers.

No matter what the event, however, more than at any other time in history, women and girls are stepping up to the firing line, competing with one another and with men and boys, and pushing the envelope of competitive shooting. Although this phenomenon is largely based in the United States, most of the forms of target shooting can be found throughout Europe. Even in the Middle and Far East, shooting facilities are increasing in popularity. According to the Department of Firearms Control of the National Police of Japan, as of December 1999, there were 221,282 licensed firearms owners in that country, of whom 3,908 were female (1.77 percent of gun owners).[1]

Military service has always been a source of marksmanship training, and as women are expanding their role in the armed forces, they are learning the mechanics of guns, and how to shoot them safely and precisely. As is often the case, those who never had the chance to shoot before are often quick to become enthusiasts. Although simply shooting at paper or military targets doesn't garner a great deal of audience interest, the rewards to the dedicated participant have always been substantial. One of the world's finest rifle shots, Olympic gold medal–winner Launi Meili, notes, "Everyone thinks about sport as exerting your body to the limit, but shooting is exerting your mind to the limit. It's at the level of a chess game. But instead of playing against an opponent you're playing against yourself."

Trapshooting's rapid ascent as one of the foremost shooting sports was in no small measure due to its acceptance as a sport akin to golf, with an appeal to the country-club set. A not-inexpensive pursuit, its participants are often moneyed, and shooting venues continue to be at luxury sites, such as Gleneagles in Scotland, and the Greenbriar and the Homestead in the United States. Annie Oakley was an early promoter of the sport, as were companies like Remington, Winchester, and Du Pont.

As is often the case, when one is good at something, that something becomes a passion. For vast numbers of women, target shooting has become exactly that.

Competitive Shooting in the United States and Great Britain

In the nineteenth century, although women did not often participate at the highest level of national competitive shooting, they were present in the throngs of people who attended these events. The crowds following rifle shooting were comparable to today's fans who flock to view professional sports like tennis or golf. At one time, target competitions were held in ranges, which were in the center of cities or otherwise easily accessible. It should be remembered that from the 1870s until World War I, champion shooters were given star status, and one of the best of these, Annie Oakley, still remains the most celebrated shot—of either sex—in American history. *Schuetzenfests* proved so popular in Germany, Austria, Switzerland, and the United States that events sometimes lasted for up to two weeks, with some competitions even organized as part of wedding celebrations.

Wimbledon and Bisley—Origins of a National Sport in Great Britain

Continuing the traditions established by aristocratic competitors from previous centuries, and as an outgrowth of the national Volunteer Rifle movement in the late 1850s, Britain's National Rifle Association was established in 1859. The

209

Remington-UMC promoted shooting clubs and assisted in their organization, as did some of the firm's competitors, particularly Winchester. Here, an interesting come-on: "Men and women are enthusiastically testing their skill with the Automatic Pistol . . . familiarity gives a certain sense of security—particularly to women." Note contact address in the historic Woolworth Building, New York City.

NRA was also a reflection of the vibrancy of the British gun trade, which boasted some of the most talented craftsmen in the world. The new organization's specific intent was "for the encouragement of Volunteer Rifle Corps and the promotion of rifle shooting throughout Great Britain."

Variety of old and contemporary books on female shooters, as well as videos, catalogs, the indispensable (for a shotgun shooter) Black's *Wing & Clay* guide, and the design for a new women's shooting-sports magazine. *Queen and Country* is a tribute in pictures and text to the keen interest in country sports of Queen Elizabeth II.

A competitive rifle range was established at Wimbledon Common, and the first meeting and national matches were held there in 1860—opened by Her Majesty Queen Victoria. Competitions were held annually, and winners were awarded cash prizes as well as elaborately embellished trophies—some of the most garish creations of the Victorian period. Although women were not involved in these events at the beginning, Queen Victoria was supportive of them,

and, upon firing that opening shot in 1860, was awarded a duplicate of the association's gold medal by Lord Elcho, council chairman.

A few women later competed at Wimbledon, and their numbers began to gradually increase when the range was moved to Bisley, Surrey, in 1889. The new range, approximately forty minutes by train from London's Waterloo station, was much more convenient for participants.

The first meeting and annual competition at

Top center: The Cambridge University Long Range Rifle Club Cup, won by Patricia L. M. Schroder in 1977, 1984, and 1986. The cup, an original of the Cambridge trophy, is of silver, and dates from the days when winners of the two-day match rifle competition were given a cup for four wins only; they were no longer eligible to be awarded a fifth, as four cups were deemed "sufficient for any gentleman's dining table." One side of the cup is embossed with the theme of war, the other side, with that of peace.

Below: Selection of striking awards to Patricia L. M. Schroder in her career spanning over two decades as British rifle-shooting champion, 1973–1996. Included are medals won and kept, and trophies and cups that are returned annually, known as "challenge" cups. The shoulder patch "ELCHO 1996" is worn on one's arm, with the "dangler" beneath, with year or date badges. Schroder shot for Ireland every year, as indicated, in the Annual Imperial Meeting (some nineteen times), and was then vice-captain of the Irish Elcho team; in 1996 she was team adjutant for the match. At *left center,* a homemade "wind gauge," used by some competitors for the long-range match rifle competitions, at 900, 1,000, 1,100, and 1,200 yards.

211

"Target Practice" by Tom Lovell (1986) captures the spirit of a young woman on a ranch, learning to shoot, with a Model 1866 Winchester. The artist wrote of this painting:

Leisure was a rare commodity on the plains in the 1870s, but there were moments. Now the sod house is finished, a shelter for the stock has been made, and maybe some corn has been sown. Dad thinks it is time for daughter to learn to use the Winchester. The prairie wind whips her apron but her sight picture is good. Some tin cans are at risk.

Oil on canvas; 34 × 24 inches.

From *top left*, Agnes Buckles's trapshooting career spanned thirty-eight years; she won awards in numerous competitions. To *left*, women shooting pistols in Gastinne Renette's shooting gallery, Paris. *Below right*, German painted targets. *Lower left*, charming group from Hartford *Schuetzen Verein*. Judi Stern, wife of arms-collector expert Bruce Stern. Bottom *center*, Tom Lovell's "Target Practice," superimposed picture of the NRA's

Holly Miller. *Above*, Suzette Rattenbury firing muzzle loaders. Rifle champion Eunice Berger on cover of *Shooter's* magazine; childhood picture of artist and singer Jillian Glover. *Lower right*, sporting clays champion Linda Joy, also an accomplished artist. *Above*, Gail Offringa, with daughters Abigail and Olivia, enjoying some plinking. *Bottom right*, Donna Bianchi examining holster business reports on computer screen. *Above*, Jo Hanley, about to dust some sporting clays.

Several pictures from March 1998 of peaceful march organized by the Countryside Alliance in London—300,000 turned out in protest of government policies on field sports. The march in 2000 numbered 500,000, said to be one of the largest demonstrations in British history. A number of other images representative of British shooting sports.

Bisley was in 1890, opened by a royal party that included the Prince and Princess of Wales, Princess Victoria and Princess Maud, the Duke of Connaught, and the Duke of Cambridge (then president of the NRA). It was the Princess of Wales who fired the first shot of the meeting at the new site, pulling the trigger by means of a red silk cord.

Despite the fact that the first official shot fired at both Wimbledon and at Bisley had been by women, it wasn't until after World War I that women became more active competitors. By 1927 the number of women competitors at Bisley had reached seventeen.

The first woman to win the coveted Queen's Prize was Marjorie Foster, in 1930, a feat that proved a national sensation. In 2000, Joanna Hossack was victorious. At age twenty-one, she was also the youngest winner since the first champion, Edward Ross, in 1860.

Creedmoor and Camp Perry—the American Experience

Inspired by a group of Union Army officers who were concerned about the poor quality of shooting by Civil War soldiers from urban environments, the National Rifle Association of America was established in 1871 with the specific intent to "promote and encourage rifle shooting on a scientific basis."[2] The organization's first president was New York City's Major General Ambrose E. Burnside, a hero of the Civil War, a dedicated marksman, and the inventor of a breech-loading carbine bearing his name.

Soon men, women, and children flocked to ranges like Creedmoor, on Long Island,[3] where events of international stature were held— among them matches pitting the American team against English and Irish teams—drawing crowds and attention comparable to World Series baseball today. Some of the marksmanship

awards were designed by distinguished jewelers such as Gorham and Tiffany & Co. The layout of the range was heavily influenced by that of Wimbledon. Creedmoor has long since been replaced as a shooting range, first by Sea Girt in New Jersey (1892), and then by Camp Perry, Ohio (as of 1907).

In those post–Civil War decades, with competitive rifle shooting more organized and shooting clubs becoming more common nationwide, editorialists made a point of encouraging women to take up marksmanship. *The Rifle* took pleasure in promoting shooting by ladies, and in recognizing that women were taking up the sport in noteworthy numbers.

> It is not strange that, with the amount of enthusiasm existing at the present time among gentlemen interested in rifle and pistol practice, their wives, sisters, and lady friends should partake of the interest in this pastime. . . . [It] is no uncommon sight to see ladies at the rifle range [and] many of them are becoming capital shots.
>
> Rifle and pistol shooting is recognized as one of the cleanest sports, and there are many reasons why a lady should learn to use a rifle and pistol. The skill of some of the ladies who occasionally visit the Walnut Hill and the Lynn (Mass.) rifle range is surprising; and it is a fact that they often surpass the efforts of some of the sterner sex. During the past month Miss Annie Oakley was kind enough to show a large number of ladies and gentlemen about Boston how proficient a lady could become in handling rifle and gun.
>
> Most of our readers know how the enthusiastic rifleman is inclined to decorate his sanctum with trophies of the chase and souvenirs of victories on the rifle range. The same mania has seized the markswomen of New England; and it is not uncommon to see, amid Kensington work, decorated pottery, and paintings, a handsome .22 or .32 caliber rifle, a Stevens pistol, or a Smith & Wesson revolver.
>
> Ladies are rapidly becoming interested in rifle and pistol shooting; and why should they not?[4]

For decades, women were involved in the NRA matches only as spectators or as presenters of awards, among them the Wimbledon Trophy,

presented by Princess Louise on behalf of Great Britain's NRA. The first woman to compete in an international rifle event was Mrs. C. C. Crossman, in the 1919 Dewar International Smallbore Match against the British team (the United States won). Symbolic of the acceptance of women in Camp Perry National Match competition was the establishment of "Squaw Camp" in 1920, welcoming couples (married), women competitors, and visiting ladies.

Schuetzenfests
Schuetzenfests, Schuetzenvereins, and Damenschuetzen

Schuetzenfests quickly gained popularity in Germanic communities and neighborhoods, including in such major cities as New York, Philadelphia, Baltimore, Cincinnati, Louisville, Chicago, Milwaukee, St. Louis, Charleston (South Carolina), and San Francisco. The numbers of participants were often substantial enough that spacious shooting grounds— known as *Schuetzenplatz*—were purchased and facilities built that allowed for shooting events on a grand scale. In New York, one of these sites, Jones's Wood, was the private shooting gallery of the Zettler Brothers, and catered to both men and women. It was the most popular club and emporium of its kind in the city. A *Schuetzenverein* was a club of marksmen, of which there were many in the United States.

Competitions were by no means limited to men: women and children were also encouraged to shoot. Surviving prints and photographs, rifles, memorabilia, and memoirs demonstrate that opportunities for enjoying these events were not gender exclusive. Traditional parades, costumes, foods, and *Schuetzen*-styled rifles lent a strong Germanic flavor to the competitions—which often lasted for days, and sometimes for as long as two weeks. Dancing, singing, eating, and drinking were punctuated, at least in daytime,

with gunfire. The events in which women competed were known as *Damenschiessen.*

Following the practice in Deutschland, a king was chosen based on his prowess as a marksman, and he chose his queen. The *Schuetzen konig* and *Schuetzen konigen* reigned throughout the event. Numerous prizes were displayed at the *Gaben-tempel*, sometimes including rifles. Traditional costumes remained de rigueur until the period prior to World War I, when anti-German pressure forced the participants to Americanize—even to give events English rather than German names.

American gunmakers like Frank Wesson developed rifles for these matches, and a style of buttplate, the Schuetzen, is found not only on rifles made for the traditional competitions, but on Winchesters, Sharps, Remingtons, and Stevens.

The *Schuetzenfest* tradition had virtually died out by the mid-twentieth century due to various cultural influences and the negative impact of World Wars I and II. But in the late twentieth century, the festivals and their style of shooting, and the collecting of *Schuetzenfest* memorabilia, made a remarkable comeback. And just as with the original events, women again became a significant part of the competitions and festivities.

At this writing there are over forty *Schuetzen* groups in the United States, partly spurred by the generous support of the Coors Brewing Company, of Golden, Colorado, whose vice

president for many years, Max Goodwin, was instrumental in promoting the revival of a sport that never had gender bias.

The Schützenliesl Beer Steins

Throughout Bavaria, and even in German communities in the United States, Schützenliesl was a wildly popular beer waitress whose fame was launched when she was twenty-one years old and employed at the Sterneckerbräu brewery restaurant in Munich. Besides being reproduced on steins (of which there are several, and in such materials as porcelain, glass, and stoneware), her image was published in advertising. Villeroy & Boch's one-liter number 2235 stein bore an image based on the "Die Schützenliesl" painting by Friedrich A. von Kaulbach. The company also used her image on steins numbers 2029 and ECS 448. Blatz of Milwaukee extensively employed the image of Schützenliesl in advertising, even in an embossed and painted metal sign

measuring 3 × 2 feet. A standard feature is her hat in the form of a target.

Referred to as the "Golden Age of Steins," the period from 1880 to 1910 saw innumerable variations, in decoration and in materials, of the image of the pretty waitress. Liselotte Lopez in "Schützenliesl Beer Steins" notes:

> Nearly every stein manufacturer ... produced his own version of Schützenliesl steins in any and all techniques, from plain gray-blue salt glaze relief stoneware to hand painted, decal decorated or etched variations. . . . In America she's often called the "Target Girl" because of the flat, disk-like target-shaped hat that sits rakishly on her flying braids.[5]

From the extensive stein collection of Max and Virginia Scheller, these selected examples all feature women. They are accompanied by a custom Winchester Model 1885 High Wall rifle. This elegant example, in .22 long rifle, with a heavyweight barrel, and *Schuetzen*-style accompaniments, was specially made for women of the Hartford *Schuetzen Verein*. It has Pope rifling, and is believed to have been put together by Harry Pope himself when he was a member of the Hartford group. In front, row of beer steins, second and fourth from *left*: Schützenliesl, with target on her hat. Second from *right* is the Venus Stein.

215

Facing page: Richly embellished *Schuetzen* rifles from the Scheller collection, most with decorations of women. Rifle at *top,* partially visible, showing bottom of Harry Pope heavy-barreled Hartford *Schuetzen Verein* .22; shows wear from rest, on bottom of barrel. Next rifle *from top,* by Buchel, caliber 8.15 × 46R. *Middle* rifle with breech System Jung, made in Mannheim, Germany; caliber 8.15 × 46R. *Bottom* rifle *Zimmerstutzen,* or parlor rifle; .17 caliber. At *left,* by Carl Stiegele, Munich, depicting exquisitely decorated barrel with a hunter and animals, and deluxe decorations of scroll, in gold. The goblet at *left* was a shooting prize. The young lady on an old shooting target (between bottom two rifles) known as *Schuetzen Scheiben.* Cartridges are the standard 8.15 × 46R.

Women and girls target shooting and plinking in the Adirondacks. Several such scenes are in the extensive collections of the Adirondack Museum. These date from the 1890s to the mid—twentieth century.

Miss Sunbeam Says Rifle Shooting Does for Women More Than a Beauty Doctor Can Do

In the March 15, 1916 *American Shooter*, champion rifle shooter June Haughton, known as "Miss Sunbeam," was quoted as saying of her favorite sport:

> Shooting . . . induces healthy appetite, restful sleep, perfect digestion, fine muscular condition that makes walking a pleasure—does all, in fact, that women are paying high-priced beauty doctors to try to do for them. I know of no healthier exercise than shooting, next to which I class dancing.

She was attracted to the sport "as a means of livelihood, when, broken in health, she was obliged to give up trained nursing."

Noma McCullough: Match Rifle Champion

At five feet tall, and weighing 112 pounds, Noma McCullough is a petite near-twin of Annie Oakley. But instead of shooting exhibitions, she specializes in match rifles—at ranges up to one thousand yards. Writer Gary Amo has categorized Mrs. McCullough as "not one of the best 'women' [highpower rifle] shooters [in the United States], but quite simply one of the best—certainly ranking among the top 20 or 30, perhaps even among the top 10." For six out of the previous nine years she has won the

Champion benchrest rifle shooter Faye Boyer, an active competitor since 1980. The only woman in the United States Benchrest Hall of Fame, she has competed on the U.S. team in the World Benchrest Championships in France, Finland, Australia, the United States, and Italy, and in October 2001 in New Zealand. She is the winner of numerous gold, silver, and bronze medals, and victor in the women's competition at the Super Shoot seven times. Firing a one-hundred-yard target with a spread of only .135 inches is not unusual for this talented sharpshooter. In 1991, at the World Benchrest Championship in France, she fired a .1973-inch group at two hundred yards—for which she received a standing ovation.

women's national high-powered championship. She was the only woman to win the Wimbledon Cup, a thousand-yard competition, shot at the Camp Perry national matches (1980). How does she do it?

I've worked to control my thoughts. When I shoot offhand, I think the shot into the X-ring. I direct my thoughts to the center of the target. I think about

what I want that shot to do. And when I lose a shot, I've let some negative thought come in. . . . You have to shoot in the subconscious. . . . I'm working now to control my visualization. When I put the rifle in my shoulder, that starts my mental program. I think about what an X looks like, I relax, I focus on the front sight, and the shot breaks automatically.

Another component of her training program is exercise: she runs three or four times a week,

Target double-action revolvers, by S & W, accompanied by appropriate medals and advertising, each ideally suited for use by women. From *top left*, Model K-22 Outdoorsman, and at *top right*, .38 Hand Ejector Target, Model of 1879. *Center left*, .38 Military & Police Target, inscribed to Frances R. Stone, from thirty shooters of the Revolver Division of the Westfield (Massachusetts) Rod and Gun Club. The recipient stated that it was "a wonderful gift! And to make it really special, Mr. Douglas Wesson personally selected it for me. . . . It is a super gun and I won many prizes with it." Miss Stone had been governor of the revolver division of the club. At *center right*, a .32 Regulation Police Target Model. *Lower left*, a .38 M & P Model 1946, and at *lower right*, a .32 Regulation Police Target.

several miles' distance. As the mother of two boys, she squeezes in practice and exercise as time permits. The mental aspect of shooting remains paramount: "When I'm shooting, I'm in another world. It's mentally fatiguing and mentally relaxing at the same time. I'm so totally involved with what I'm doing, with the moment, that it's actually like Zen."

How do male shooters accept her? "They treat me as an equal," she says. "That's the great thing about our sport. Everyone is the same on the firing line. We're all shooters together, trying to do our best in a very demanding sport."[6]

Competitive Shooting with Handguns
Judy Woolley—IPSC Champion and Professional Shooter with Team Smith & Wesson

In 1985, Massachusetts-born Judy Woolley became the first woman selected as a member of Smith & Wesson's professional shooting team. The competitive discipline of the six-member team is known as "action shooting," a highly refined sport that borrows aspects from a variety of other shooting events. Competition is against the clock, accuracy is paramount, and firing is from an array of body positions, using a mix of holds on the handgun. Targets vary from paper silhouettes to steel plates. The director of a freestyle match can design the course and makeup as he or she wishes. Various scenarios are set up, and the shooting may be required from standing, kneeling, or prone positions, using one hand (sometimes the weak hand) or both hands. The shooter may be in the open or firing from behind a variety of barricades. Every match is different, making it exciting for shooter and spectator alike.

Judy Woolley and her husband, Charlie, began shooting together when they were dating in Massachusetts. They subsequently moved west, settling in Montana, to avoid the restrictive gun

laws in their home state. They began action shooting in 1985, and both quickly became top competitors.

After winning a string of major competitions, Judy retired from competition in 1996. S & W historian Roy Jinks, himself a member of the factory team, states that Judy Woolley is hands down "the best female action pistol shot of our time."[7]

The World of Trapshooting and Skeet Shooting

Of a total of some 60,000 competitive trapshooters in the United States, about 15 percent are women. An additional 700,000 shoot non-

competitively, and about 70,000 of these are women. The championships, known as the Grand American, have been held in Vandalia, Ohio, since 1924. Men and women compete on an equal footing. If a woman's score is high enough, she keeps shooting against the men for the championships, but there are also separate prizes for women competitors.

The director of the Trapshooting Hall of Fame and Museum, Richard A. Baldwin, can point to fifty years of experience as a shooter and as an employee of the Remington Arms Company. His father was a Remington professional shooter and agent, and knew legendary sharp-

shooters Annie Oakley, Frank Butler, and John Philip Sousa. Baldwin, in addition to overseeing

the museum, actively researches competitors and their history. Sifting through thousands of photographs, reviewing shooting records, and recording the best of the champions, he has identified some who had been lost to posterity—the best of the best—not a few of whom were women.

One trap tyro, whose face appears in a number of photographs from competitions of some seventy years ago, looks as if she has stepped from the pages of *The Great Gatsby.* A beautiful young girl, stylishly dressed, she is often shown holding a richly engraved single-barrel Ithaca gun (a favorite of several top shots for decades). Baldwin's search for her identity finally struck pay dirt when he discovered the name "Marie Krautzky" written on the back of one of the images. Later, he found the name on another photo: "Marie Krautzky Grant, Ft. Dodge, Iowa."

THE SPORT ALLURING – SHOOTING OFF A TIE
THE WINNING SCORES IN TRAP SHOOTING ARE MADE WITH
DU PONT
Smokeless Shotgun Powders

Baldwin took a chance that the name might still be in the Fort Dodge phone book. Finding it, he dialed the number, and was soon speaking to ninety-eight-year-old Marie Grant, alert and delighted to reminisce about her decades of competitive shooting.

219

Marie's father had been a master gunsmith from Rokitnitz, Austria, who immigrated to America in 1893, settling four years later in Fort Dodge. It was he who, in 1910, developed a single-trigger mechanism for double-barrel shotguns. For the next four years he converted thousands of double-trigger guns to single triggers, and in 1914 sold his patents to the A. H. Fox Gun Company. Marie was raised in a family of shooters and, with her native talents, became a champion. Baldwin rates her as one of the top two American women trapshooters of her day, and she possessed such talent and achievements that she has subsequently been inducted into the Trapshooting Hall of Fame. The citation reads, in part:

On August 17, 2001, Marie Krautzky Grant was voted into the Trapshooting Hall of Fame, at Vandalia, Ohio. She is the 21st woman to be enshrined and joins the likes of Annie Oakley, Plinky Topperwein, and such male champions as Captain A. H. Bogardus and W. F. (Doc) Carver. At 98 years of age she is also the oldest ever elected to the Hall of Fame.

Now confined to a wheelchair, Marie had lived in her family home since childhood, finally entering a retirement home in 2000. She was ac-tive in trapshooting at a time when the sport was growing rapidly, and when women were becoming an increasing presence competitively.

The number of women who remain in the championship ranks is not yet significant, but one who has achieved such status is Ruth Keim Flayderman. In 1974, she beat two thousand entrants—both men and women—and won the Vandalia Handicap, a major event at the Grand American. At the 2001 Grand American, Jackie Smellenberger, the thirty-one-year-old daughter of a Trapshooting Hall of Fame enshrinee, won the same shoot. She broke 98 × 100 from the

Selection of trophies and other awards won by Marie Krautzky (Grant) in her distinguished trapshooting career. In most instances she placed first. The events cover the years c. 1908 to 1947, during which time she won at sites around the country, though much of her shooting was in and near Iowa.

NANCY HOLMES
1

NANCY HOLMES
2

NANCY HOLMES
3

maximum handicap of 27 yards to beat a field of 3,192.

Today's top lady—ranked by Richard Baldwin as the best female trapshooter of all time—is Nora Martin, of Carlisle, Kentucky: "Her gift at the game is in the Annie Oakley class."

222

The Women's Shooting Sports Foundation

A milestone in the annals of women's participation in the world of firearms was the establishment of the Women's Shooting Sports Foundation (WSSF) in 1988, by Doug Painter of the National Shooting Sports Foundation (NSSF) and Sue King, a competitive shotgunner who served as founding chairman. Additionally, quite a few active female shooters came on board as enthusiastic advocates.

King recalls how the idea was conceived one day by several women at J. Herters' Shooting Grounds in Houston.

We were all grousing that men were getting bigger trophies, and more prize money. It occurred that we didn't get big trophies and big money because there were not enough of us. There were serious women shooters, but we also realized we needed to draw more women into the game. I suggested that we hold an all-ladies shooting event. Sandy Brister—one of our best sporting clays shots—looked me in the eye and said, "Where are we going to find eight women who are going to do this?" All of us present pitched in, we approached our contacts in the firearms industry for prizes, and in 1988 we held the first lady's charity classic, known as the Mother's Shoot—held on Mother's Day weekend—and always benefiting a women's-issue charity.

The charity tie-in made for an outreach to non-shooting women, and those who would support a

Sue King's appointment as first executive director of the Women's Shooting Sports Foundation is easily understood given her lifelong career in the world of firearms. Active as a hunter with rifle and shotgun, a target shooter, and a competitor in shotgun events, she also has been instrumental in educating the public on firearms-related issues. Note Sybil Ludington Women's Freedom Award. Family portrait at *lower center*.

women's charity. One of our causes was a shelter for abused women. That first year, we had ninety-eight shooters—larger than that year's Texas State Sporting Clays event!

The 1980s were not good years politically for gun enthusiasts, and one of the goals of the event was positive exposure for the shooting sports. That inaugural shoot attracted a considerable amount of publicity, drawing all three major TV affiliates in Houston, plus the major papers, and a camera crew from ESPN.

Browning jumped on board, and stayed with us for the next ten years, which was how long I did the shoot before retiring as chairman. The company gave us a Browning Model 321 shotgun. That first year I won it—and then never competed again. Included in the entry fee was a full day of free lessons the weekend before, plus free ammunition, supplied by Winchester—more than they had ever previously donated for any event.

Sponsors Browning and Winchester were simply outstanding. The idea grew very quickly from a single event, to four events a year, and then to almost forty events, in different sites around the country. It was obvious that the shoot was very exportable and that the concept would work well anywhere—if you made the right selection of location.

Launched after that first competition, the WSSF developed a series of charity events, which also served as a forum for attracting women to the shooting sports. Sue King remembers:

Because men had felt a bit left out we created a game called the couples' cup, held the Sunday following the lady's event, for husband and wife teams. We didn't use the typical sporting clays target presentation, and the shoot was a little more trouble to put on for the clubs, since we designed multiple target presentations. This meant that all at once, both men and woman were on the shooting line at the same time. The couples had to develop a strategy to determine who would take which shots, coordinate on reloading, and so forth—timing was crucial. This made the event very exciting. If we had seventy women shooting the lady's event, we would have at least that many in the couples' contest the next day.

These shoots created mountains of favorable publicity, and we always used them as media vehicles. I judge success based on the numbers of participants, and how much media coverage we got. A lot of our work was handing out guns and other prizes, but also developing the publicity. By the time I retired we made it a practice to track our media. We were reaching 42 million readership and viewing public *per year*, and not once did we get a bad story!

I began to think the WSSF might survive. But eventually, in 1997–98, I had to retire from all this activity, due to my husband's poor health.[8]

Sue King—Hunter, Shooter, and WSSF Founder

Sue King is one of the most gifted shooters in America. As hunter, shotgun and handgun shooter, instructor of personal protection, and an NRA training counselor, she has a remarkably broad experience. A member of several shooting and hunting organizations, she was also on the Winchester Industry Team and captain of Browning's Women's Team.

Mrs. King was interviewed before appearing at the "Women Calling the Shots—Leadership Roles for Women in Shooting" session at the 2001 annual meeting of the NRA.

Growing up in the country, I didn't know that a world existed without guns; everybody in my family shot—my grandfathers, my grandmothers, my father, and both my mother and her mother rode, hunted, shot, and fished. . . . Our country place was known as the "camp," and that's where I spent every day that I was not in school. . . . [I] was the only child in the family for ten years; then a brother was born, and a couple of years later a sister. They too took up shooting.

My father gave me a Remington single shot, bolt-action .22 rifle, with a shortened stock, when I was three years old. That's when I started shooting, with his supervision. All my allowance money was spent on .22 shells. I also had a BB gun; when I ran out of .22s, then I would get out the BB gun, the traditional Red Ryder, by Daisy.

With that BB gun I learned a great deal about trajectory and windage, because if the sun is right, you can see that BB, it's slow enough. . . . I don't think I ever saw a telescopic sight on a gun until I was eighteen years old. Until then it was all iron sights.

King's skills as a coach for both men and women attracted a large following:

I spent a great deal of time teaching, though most of my students were men; most of the women I taught came because their husbands wanted them to go hunting with them, or to shoot recreationally. . . .

I stopped coaching in about 1990. In that day and age, the shooting sports for women concept had not been thoroughly embraced, either by industry, or by the American public. That was also when Paxton Quigley was leaping into mainstream America through her clinics and numerous media appearances, even on *60 Minutes*. We also had the NRA's "Refuse to Be a Victim" program, which highlighted the necessity for personal protection. This was a program by women for women. I didn't have to advertise, all we had to do was keep a schedule posted, on a counter at the gun club, and the women just signed up in droves.

King had become the first every-day-of-the-week woman advocating firearm sports and safety since Annie Oakley. She was also the first full-time woman instructor in America. Furthermore, she had so much credibility in the shooting community that she was asked to write on the subject. Though some of her articles dealt with handguns, most of her pieces were on shotgunning.

King has her own opinion on the skill level of women versus men in competitive shooting:

I'm probably one of the few women who will tell you that women cannot shoot equally with men in some of the shooting games. I know women don't like to hear that, and most men speaking in that area try to be "politically correct."

When considering reflexes, visual acuity, focus, and concentration, we can shoot equally. But when it comes to shooting at two hundred clay targets a day, swinging an eight-pound gun, time after time after time, over a course of several days, women will fatigue quicker than men . . . unless women go to extraordinary lengths to develop upper body strength.

Even though a woman's reflexes are certainly as fast as a man's, and even though she will begin her mount on the target at the same moment as a man—I think a man completes the move more quickly, and he will not fatigue as quickly. I always held my highest average in .410 and 28-gauge guns, which are lighter and produce less recoil and fatigue. There are more shot pellets with a 12 gauge, which makes it generally less difficult to hit the targets.

She is highly optimistic regarding the future role of women in promoting shooting sports.

There's no question but that women are going to become more and more influential in the shooting sports. I'm speaking not only in terms of the industry, but in the legislative arena. As an example, consider the NRA—more women are on the board now than ever.

When I joined the NRA board in 1992, you still weren't taken too seriously as someone who might know a bit about guns, ballistics, and shooting—it was still an old boy's club. One of the reasons that has changed quickly, and significantly, is we now have on the board some women who really know what they are doing. These are women who can hunt as well as any man, who can talk ballistics with any competitive shooter, who do their own hand-loading, are very successful competitively, and who make wonderful role models. . . .[9]

Shari LeGate and the Women's Shooting Sports Foundation

Sue King's successor as chairman of the Women's Shooting Sports Foundation is Shari LeGate, who had worked for King and has a broad range of experience. LeGate impresses one as not only a gifted administrator and leader, but a professional athlete much in the tradition of tennis star Chrissie Evert or golfer Nancy Lopez. LeGate's introduction to shooting was by chance. LeGate was born in Chicago

Target, clay, and live-pigeon competitions are represented in this selection of women shooters. Top shot Julia Armour, a consistent winner among live-pigeon shooters, at *center*, in blue, competing at the Campeonato del Mundo de Tiro de Pichon. Photographs supplied by Women's Shooting Sports Foundation, Safari Club International's Sables, and a Pennsylvania club developing women's shooting programs, with encouragement of owner Bill Bachenburg. The competition guns are, from *top*, Remington 11-87, Beretta 682 Gold, and Ithaca single-barrel trap, courtesy of Cubeta's.

to a family who had no experience with firearms. Shari's first spark of interest came while watching a televised skeet match between Robert Stack and Mike Ditka. "I've been shooting for twenty years, but did not start until relatively late in life," she recalls. "I find that to be true with quite a few of the women with whom I work. It's not that they are against guns, they simply have not been exposed to them. . . ."

Introducing women to shooting is her main objective with the WSSF. She finds that women who are unfamiliar with firearms are often afraid of them. The organization conducted more than seventy free or low-cost clinics in 2000 to provide a nonthreatening introduction.

> We teach safety, proper behavior, what opportunities there are for them—such as hunting—with rifle, shotgun, or handgun: sport shooting, competitive target shooting, and several other disciplines. We give them proper instruction, so they don't have to go through what I had to experience: at first my coaches were well meaning, but not professionals. However, I got very lucky after two years in the sport, and met a coach who taught me what I needed to know, and I eventually won, a lot. That coach, Richard Aitken, also became my husband.
>
> Our clinics also offer the shooting sports in a very friendly environment. We supply guns, targets, ammo, instructors, and we are mobile: we travel around, all over the country. In some cases we have high-profile events, where we bring in Olympians to teach. Here the class can learn from the best—you can't learn firsthand from Tiger Woods in golf, or from Michael Jordan in basketball, but in shooting we arrange sessions where women can walk out and shoot next to, or learn from, champions who are the shooting sports equivalent of Woods or Jordan. Olympic medal winners Kim Rhode and Launi Meili have both done sessions with us; we have contacts with all of the shooting stars.

The WSSF hosts a booth and runs clinics at most major hunting, sport-shoot, and outdoor events. They also exhibit in less traditional settings such as bridal fairs and cooking shows.

LeGate doesn't avoid a challenge; she even tried the Million Mom March: "I looked at their website, and their litany seemed to be about safety and education." She discovered, however, that "as their program progressed, the message clearly changed: it became licensing of gun owners and registration of firearms."

> I have had situations where perhaps I couldn't persuade a woman to become a passionate hunter or sport shooter—but I can *almost always* persuade them to open their mind and change their opinion. We try to listen, and look for common ground.
>
> We know that guns can be dangerous and we don't try to hide that. Our goal is to educate, not mislead.

LeGate's dedication is contagious, and she believes there is nothing more exciting than introducing another woman to the shooting sports. "I'm very lucky, because I have the opportunity to see the excitement and the energy when these women fire that first shot and hit that first target."

> You see a woman's confidence and self-esteem grow, and those are traits that transfer into a person's everyday life. These women may not become a passionate lifelong shooter like me, but they become part of the sport. I see this happening all the time.
>
> I know my sport, I know the issues, when I speak I do so with passion, and I speak from the heart—and that's what the sport means to me.[10]

The Ultimate Competition: Shotguns in the Olympics
Kim Rhode, Olympic Champion

Shooting her Perazzi MX-12, loaded with Federal cartridges, Kim Rhode took the 1996 Olympics by storm. Barely seventeen years old, she won the gold medal in one of shooting's toughest competitions: double Olympic trap, where two clay pigeons explode from the traps at such speed that only about one and a quarter seconds are available for the shooter to score hits.

Describing the highlights of her experience, Rhode recalls:

> [For the opening ceremonies we] got all dressed up in our red jackets, hats and skirts. Most of us about had heart failure when we found out the jacket was 100 percent wool! It was extremely hot and humid. When it was our turn to walk out into the stadium, all the female shooters decided we were going to hold hands. So when we walked out with all the other athletes, we all held hands and held them up high. It was really exciting when the whole stadium went absolutely nuts. I looked for my parents in the crowd [they have always been supportive of her career], but it was like trying to find a needle in a haystack. Every one got really quiet when the torch was lit; it was very moving. . . .

Rhode had a shaky start, with a bad first practice day, and had a case of nerves prior to the preliminary rounds:

> Once I got out there, I was really nervous the first round but I started to mellow out. The crowd really cheered when they introduced me. I could hear people shouting my name, and it was an awesome experience. Once we started the round of shooting I didn't hear anything, I was focused on each target. After I got through shooting the first round, I went back and sat down in the tent, grabbed some water, and talked a lot with my teammates. I was still really nervous. I knew my score was at the top of my squad, so I knew I had a chance to medal. I just repeated this after each round and Lloyd [Woodhouse, U.S. shotgun coach] kept coming up to me saying, "You're doing good, you're doing good." . . . I knew throughout the match exactly where I stood. After the three preliminary rounds I went out to the stands to say hi to

Facing page: Some highlights from the extraordinary career of Kimberly Rhode, who began shooting competitively at the age of eleven. At twelve she became the youngest girl to shoot one hundred straight in skeet. She is also the youngest ever to represent the United States on the Olympic shooting team—and the youngest to represent any country in the shooting sports. She presently holds or has tied dozens of world records, and regularly competes in American skeet, international skeet, international doubles trap, and bunker. Besides her 1996 gold medal in international doubles trap, she won the bronze medal at the 2000 Olympics in Sydney. *Time* magazine selected her as one of the top-ten athletes of 1996. Among her other interests: skiing, line dancing, scuba diving, surfing, fishing, and hunting.

everyone who had come to watch me shoot. I thought it would be better than sitting back and being really nervous and talking myself out of it. It helped to pass the time, although it was very hot. I went back a few minutes early to cool off and get a drink before the final round.

Walking out to the final round was really exciting. I was still very nervous—it *was* the Olympics. After I missed one of the first pair, everyone in the crowd did this rumble and I think that helped to make me realize that I had to get my act in gear and focus. I dropped four of the first eight targets, but I knew I hadn't lost it as everyone around me was also dropping targets. I told myself that I can't let it go this easy. I worked so hard for this and I wasn't going to give it up. After that I began running them. I kept telling myself one more pair, one bird at a time. As I got to the end of my round I didn't know if I was ahead or not. I never once looked at the scoreboard. The second I knew I had it was after my last pair when the crowd went wild. Even then I didn't believe I had actually won it. I thought maybe the crowd was cheering for someone else. It didn't clink in my head. I couldn't believe it. Lloyd hugged me so hard it hurt.

When I stood on the podium and saw the American flag going up as they played our national anthem, I realized what I had done. A lot of things ran through my head during this time. I thought about the good and hard times I had shooting. Everyone who helped me get here. All the long hours of practice, and it really hit me what I had actually accomplished. It was all I could do to keep from crying. I wasn't expecting the medal to be so heavy when they put it around my neck. It was just the greatest moment of my life.

Since her victory, Rhode remains intensely dedicated to shooting, and continues to rack up a record of successes that rivals that of any male *or* female shooter in American history. In assessing her Olympic achievement, it is important to note that she was not competing just with shooters her own age, but against seasoned athletes—many of them older, far more experienced, and far more practiced. Another thing that made the competition so intense was that the pool of skilled competitive shotgun shooters in America was far larger than the number of competitors faced by the figure skaters, gymnasts, and participants in many other Olympic sports.[11]

Pigeon Shooting: An Exclusive Sport
Laura Revitz—International Pigeon-Shooting Champion

Although she has tried most other forms of shotgunning, pigeon-shooting champion Laura Revitz believes her sport "is truly the most fascinating as well as the most difficult discipline." She first shot in Portugal in 1974, and two years later she entered her first World Championship in Madrid. She won first place—as she did later that year at the "Grand Premio" in Milan, and in several other shoots in Spain. Since then, she has won more events than she can remember, and in such glamorous locales as Morocco, Egypt, Italy, Andorra, Portugal, Argentina, Brazil, and Mexico. In 1996 she was elected to the United States Fliers Federation Hall of

A national heroine in Belgium, Anne Focan has won numerous competitions in a career whose highlights from 1993 to 2000 include gold, silver, and bronze medals, and championships throughout Europe and the world. She shares credit for her world-rank achievements with her coach and companion, Dr. Thierry Lobeau, coach of the Belgian shooting team.

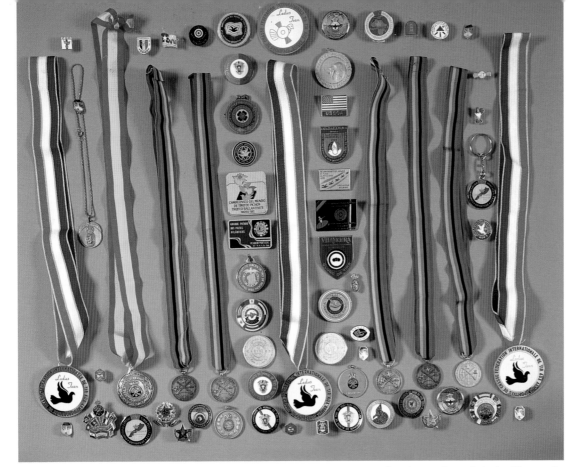

Among sponsors or patrons of the shoots are King Juan Carlos of Spain and King Mohammed VI of Morocco. Those who travel the pigeon-shooting circuit stay in luxurious hotels, like La Mamoonia in Casablanca or at the estates of competitors. Gambling has been a tradition since the days when Annie Oakley competed in the sport. And although there are fewer aristocrats on the circuit today than in the old days, there are some—as well as royalty, such as Morocco's Prince Moulay Rachid. There are also many professionals competing, representing such renowned gunmakers as Perazzi and Beretta.

Natural talent is important in pigeon shooting. On the subject of preparation, Revitz says:

> The only practice is bird hunting, or possibly zz-zz, a plastic target that has two little wings on it. The clay target fits inside the plastic. The ring for zz-zz is bigger than in pigeon events, and you are allowed two shots at the target. The clay target has to fall within the ring. It is thrown from a box that has a motor in it, running at 6,500 rpms. It floats, doesn't even take off and fly. In Europe this new sport is known as Helices, and has its own world championship.

Fame, and she remains active in numerous shooting and conservation groups.

In this style of competition, birds are released from a box and must be taken before they fly outside a fixed boundary measured from each of six boxes.[12] Revitz regards pigeon shooting as the true "sport of kings, right up there with polo."

> A lot of people don't participate because this is such an expensive and challenging sport. At the same time it is a very social competition; you meet the very nicest, upper echelon of any country you're in. You have the opportunity to learn all the customs, and on a one-on-one basis. I love to visit Europe, and am there about five months, beginning with the Spanish circuit, which starts in January. Once I discovered pigeon shooting, I never looked back.

Competitors often bring along their families, and the club sites usually offer golf, tennis, and other recreations. A Federation event might have as many as five hundred competitors. Further, whole families come to the outskirts of the shooting grounds—they hope to capture those pigeons that happen to fly away and for a chance to roast them on the spot, enjoying a special kind of festive barbeque. The birds that we shoot either go to market or are given to local hospitals and orphanages.

Clay pigeons are so-named because they replaced live pigeons in certain shooting competitions. The process broadened the scope and appeal of shotgun sports. The far less expensive artificial pigeon was first made of glass, later of clay. Laura Revitz ranks among the most active and successful of shooters in this genre, and regularly competes on the circuit, which is primarily in Europe.

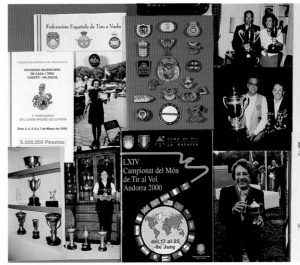

229

Revitz is the only American—man or woman—who has won all of the world's pigeon-shooting events. In recognition of her achievements, she was elected a member of the exclusive Club de Tiro Somontes, located on government grounds in Madrid near the king's summer palace. "As a member of the club, when I won the World Championship and the World Cup, they put my name on the wall, and after I won the European event, they put my name up again."[13]

Sporting Clays: The Hottest Game in Shotguns
Jo Hanley—Sporting Clays Level III Shooting Coach

At Level III, the highest rating bestowed by the National Sporting Clays Association sanctioning body, Jo Hanley is one of the top shooting coaches in America, a seasoned specialist in taking good shooters and forging them into top-level competitors. Only a handful of coaches in the Western Hemisphere have earned that status, and Hanley's students come to her from all over the country to pick up on her finely honed skills.

A top-level competitor in her own right, and an experienced bird and big game hunter (including on safari in Africa), Hanley bases her tips on keen observation, insights learned by experience, and on a great deal of dedicated shooting. She feels that instinct is crucial, and that "making shooting a shotgun too much of a science is the kiss of death, not broken targets." Hanley thinks that teaching sporting clays is often best done on a skeet field "which is wide

Triathlon athletes, in photographs by Robbie George, at a winter meet, Snow Mountain Ranch, Colorado, and a summer meet at Salt Lake City, Utah. Weatherly Stroh (number 37) and Clara Coleman (number 76), joined by several other competitors. Yet another sport advancing rapidly in popularity with women

American Rifleman covers from December 1928 to modern times document the dedication of girls and women to target-shooting competitions, as well as to hunting.

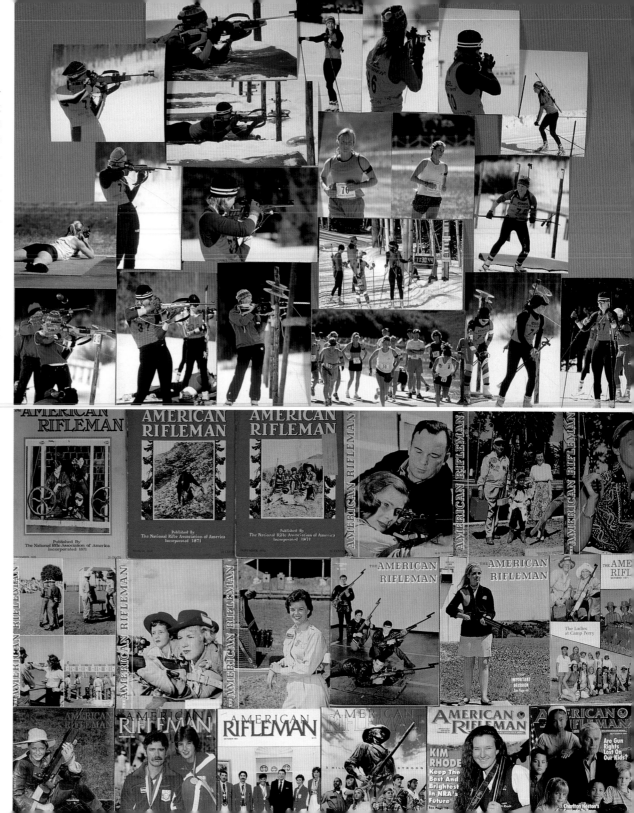

The precise science of target shooting with .22 long caliber rifles: a Mossberg Model 144 LSB at *top,* with 26-inch barrel, with a modern, laminated stock; Marlin 2000-L, with 22-inch barrel. Photographs include the *Schuetzenfest* group from New Braunsfeils, Texas, whose tradition of shooting extends back to the city's founding by German immigrants. Winchester promotional photographs show high school girls enjoying competitions. Magazine cover pictures British shooting champion Piffa Schroder, and is one of the most striking images of beauty on the shooting range. Rifles and accessories compliments of Cubeta's.

open—no trees, bushes, or short windows of opportunity to contend with. On the matter of gun fit she notes, "If you're going to run in a marathon race, your shoes better fit perfectly. If you're going to shoot a shotgun, same deal, the gun better fit perfectly. . . ."

She also feels that some shooters in sporting clays are becoming too serious. Her advice: "We're not out here to *fight* our shooting—keep it simple, keep it positive, and even when missing, remember to keep it *fun*."[14]

Air Rifles
Nancy Johnson—Olympic Champion in a High-tech Shooting Sport

Air-rifle shooting drew an extra boost in exposure in 2000, with the Olympic gold-medal performance of University of Kentucky graduate Nancy Johnson. Her victory in Sydney, Australia—under extreme pressure—was the first of many gold medals for the United States, and was a classic example of grit, determination, and concentration.

Shooting in the Women's 10-m Air Rifle competition, the twenty-six-year-old from Phenix City, Alabama, advanced to the final round, which pitted the eight highest-scoring women against one another. On the last shot of the ten-shot event, she took the gold, beating silver medalist Cho-Hyun Kang of Korea by one-fifth of one point—497.7 to 497.5.

A native of Downers Grove, Illinois, Nancy began shooting at the urging of her father, Ben Napolski, in 1989. He enrolled her in a marksmanship class at the local Junior Rifle Club. Consistently hitting bull's-eyes, she competed at the Camp Perry National Matches in 1990 in smallbore shooting. A year later, however, she was diagnosed with nerve damage, and it looked as if her shooting career was over. But back at Camp Perry in 1992, she was soon se-

lected for the U.S. women's randle team, and placed high in the intermediate junior category in the Smallbore Prone championships.

While at the University of Kentucky, Johnson's shooting coach switched her from .22 caliber to air rifle, and it wasn't long before she excelled at this discipline, competing on an athletic scholarship for two years. In 1996 she was selected as a member of the U.S. Olympic shooting team. Though she finished in thirty-eighth place in Atlanta that year, she had attracted the attention of the commander of the Fort Benning–based Army Marksmanship Unit (AMU) and was invited to train along with the Army Shooting Team.

In 1998 she married fellow AMU shooter Ken Johnson and the couple moved to Phenix City, across the river from Fort Benning. While there, the Illinois State Rifle Association, working through the NRA Foundation and Friends of the NRA, secured a grant that helped pay some of her traveling expenses while she trained and competed.

One of America's shooting stars, Johnson remains in the sport as a competitor, a coach, and one encouraging others to participate. "I know I want to stay involved in the sport . . . to give something back after everything it's done for me."

Heidi Forgett and daughter Susan set records in muzzle-loading shooting that were instrumental in promoting the sport on an international level. Together they assembled the finest collection of Morgan James target rifles, and then set about to use some of them in their match shooting. The highlight of their competitive careers was the 1986 World Muzzle Loading Rifle Championship match. Val Forgett's manufacturing enterprise, the Navy Arms Co., served as an extra impetus to develop this challenging arena of competitive shooting.

232

The Vintagers: A New Dimension to the Sport of Shooting

A new passion for high-end shooters, which incorporates elements of reenactments, marksmanship, fine and historic fowling pieces, and high fashion is the Vintagers. The group was created in 1994 by current president Ray Poudrier of Hawley, Massachusetts, and three other enthusiasts of side-by-side shotguns, rifles, and sporting clays. A favorite topic of periodicals on fine guns, but also featured in such mega-circulation publications as *The Wall Street Journal* and *New York* magazine, the Vintagers—despite the expense of participation—is rapidly growing.

New York showcased this newest of gun sports in an article called "Shooting Party."

> "Few people realize that when people talk about guns and shooting," vintage-arms dealer David Moore declares amid a jamboree of Edwardian hunting clothes and elegant handmade shotguns, "this is what they are thinking about." Forget red-necks in camouflage, lumberjack plaids, and safety-orange vests—there's not a pickup truck or gun rack in sight at the World Side-by-Side Championships in the Hudson Valley's Millbrook, where gun enthusiasts are sparing no expense to realize an idealized vision of the great era of game-hunting and bird-shooting that ended with the First World War.
>
> In the world of shooting, what separates the Land Rover gentry from the Dodge dudes is the choice of weapon. Here, it's a custom-made side-by-side shotgun, preferably created in the turn-of-the-century style with curved hammers reminiscent of a flintlock and detailed hand engraving. The best guns are British models—new or old—that cost anywhere in the five figures. This fall weekend, the elite British gun-maker Purdey casually takes an order at its booth for a pair of shotguns; a nice round $100,000 makes the deal worth the trip from London.
>
> Having eliminated the riffraff, the annual championships have become something of a bespoke ball for Anglophile hunters. . . .
>
> The "Vintagers" call themselves the Order of Edwardian Gunners, but aside from a few clay-target competitions, this is only vaguely a sporting event.[15]

Vintagers' founder and president Ray Poudrier is in several of these snapshots, including one in which he is holding a hammer shotgun to *left* of trademark serpentine hammer on scarf. The 2001 competition was held at Sandanona, the Orvis shooting property in Millbrook, New York. Sporting clays and Vintagers events are distinguished by the numbers of strikingly attired women, many of whom are dedicated shooters. *Bottom right,* Lauren Chase, with pet Jack Russell; *above,* Poudrier's wife, Melanie, an occasional shooter, and part of a staff that accounts for these events' ever-growing success.

CHAPTER IX

The World of Make-Believe

Thomas A. Edison visited Miss Annie Oakley's tent today, at Buffalo Bill's Wild West show, after seeing the performance, he examined her guns. Miss Oakley asked him if he could not invent an electric gun so she would not have to use the French powder. He replied, "I have not come to that yet, but it may come."

—*Wanderer*, Paris, France, Aug. 29, 1889[1]

The first female superstar of show business was not an actress, but rather a performer whose dazzling skill with props was the basis of her fame: the props were guns, and the star was Annie Oakley. Photographic images, contemporary programs, press clippings, and memoirs of the time have painted a glowing canvas of the adventures of pioneers like Oakley. Although the Wild West shows reached millions of fans in America and Europe, film reached an even bigger audience. How fitting that the first movie was also a Western—and that women played a role: *The Great Train Robbery* was shot by Edwin S. Porter for the Edison Company in 1903. Even before that ten-minute feature, the Edison Company had produced motion-picture entertainments based on the popularity of the West.

In Wild West shows, in film, in carnival and circus acts, and in traveling exhibitions before a variety of audiences, women with guns were active in the evolution of new show-business entertainments. Along with rodeo performers, these courageous and talented young women rank among the first stars in American show business, and a broad range of performances wherein firearms play a role have evolved into modern times.

A contemporary of Annie Oakley's, Sarah Bernhardt was an actress of extraordinary powers—and also a talented shot. Her shooting enthusiasms reflected the popularity of sport hunting and target shooting among the fashionable set in France in the nineteenth and early twentieth centuries. Miss Oakley's performances in Paris and throughout Europe were among the most popular entertainments of the time—as was also true of Miss Bernhardt's.

Women with guns proved a vital stage in the early evolution of women in show business. As the entertainment mediums of the twentieth century evolved, the use of guns by women was given a boost by the outdoor industry's catering to that segment of the market through extensive advertising, the proliferation of points of purchase, and the availability of places to shoot. A significant period of this evolution coincided with women's suffrage, and with most of the silent-film era. The past century has shown a clear and steady development of women's mastery of guns in all show business mediums.

As always, the world of entertainment has had an impact on the viewing public. In today's culture, not a few female shooters have been introduced to the sport through TV and film, and some female performers through their show business careers—among them, superstar, diva, musical marvel, and multifaceted actress Madonna.

Sarah Bernhardt—"the Greatest Actress of All Time"

Though born the illegitimate daughter of a courtesan, and of middle-class Dutch-Jewish lineage, Sarah Bernhardt became the most celebrated actress of her time. In rating the twentieth century's top one hundred stars, *Variety* called her "the first superstar-Diva." Her birth in Paris on October 23, 1844, placed her as a contemporary (though nearly a generation older) of yet another woman of humble birth who would rise to fame on a different stage: Annie Oakley—Little Sure Shot.

While Miss Oakley was never an actress with the skill and dramatic powers of the Divine Miss Sarah, and Bernhardt's flamboyant lifestyle contrasted sharply with the conservative, role-model behavior of Little Sure Shot, both ladies shared a keen respect for and enjoyment of guns and shooting.[2]

Miss Bernhardt displayed a collection of Oriental weapons in her luxurious and cluttered Parisian apartment, and had some exquisite rifles

Facing page: Peter Beard's collage featuring models Eva and Brook Walls dramatizes the make-believe world in which firearms rule in the fantasies of screenwriters and directors.

S & W Model I Third Issue (*top*) was a presentation from D. B. Wesson to world-renowned Swedish opera singer Christina Nilsson. Gustave Young embellished the steel parts on the revolver, and is also credited with the gold inlays on the grips.

At *bottom*, Tiffany & Co. S & W .38 Double Action revolver, stamped with a *T* and globe logo, identifying the piece as exhibited at the Paris Exposition, 1900. Serial number 268107.

Grip of heavy-gauge blued steel, overlaid with sterling silver; barrel and cylinder etched to match. Probably a design of the celebrated Paulding Farnham, considered Tiffany's greatest creator of the rare and the beautiful in decorative arts.

and handguns. The most deluxe of the latter was by the celebrated Parisian gunmaker Gastinne Renette. In addition she owned a target rifle, richly engraved and inscribed with her name.

Miss Bernhardt was also in possession of a handgun, for self-defense, throughout her thespian travels, and she knew how to use it. A close call with a gang of kidnappers, while touring the United States, took place near St. Louis, in January 1881. Attracted by the publicity stunt of a display of her jewelry in a local shop, the gang planned to ambush her private rail touring ensemble. As a convoy of her Palace car and three Pullmans, known as the "Sarah Bernhardt Special," was headed toward Cincinnati, the thugs planned to uncouple the cars, and carry out their scheme.

The plot was foiled when one of the would-be robbers was discovered strapped beneath her coach. His confession to Miss Bernhardt was reassuring, at least for her safety: "We would not have done you any harm in spite of your pretty little revolver." Eight detectives then laid a trap for the remaining members of the gang, and the train was sent ahead, without Miss Bernhardt on board. In the ensuing shootout, the members of the seven-man gang, led by Belgian Albert Witbyn, were killed or captured. Witbyn was hanged—though Miss Bernhardt appealed for clemency.

In 1977 Christie's of London sold Miss Bernhardt's favorite revolver, a six-shot of .30 caliber, spectacularly inlaid and engraved, by Gastinne Renette. She described this piece in her memoirs, *My Double Life*, as a "prettily chased revolver with cats-eyes," which was always with her "any time I go to a place where I think there is danger." She added that "I am not a bad shot for a woman." Among her shooting adventures was the opportunity to fire, in December 1880, by courtesy of a director of the Colt Firearms Com-

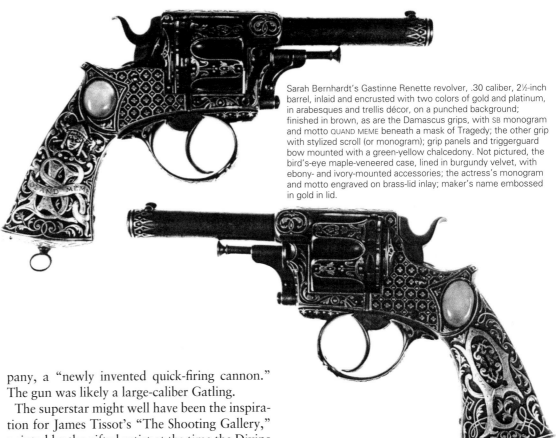

Sarah Bernhardt's Gastinne Renette revolver, .30 caliber, 2½-inch barrel, inlaid and encrusted with two colors of gold and platinum, in arabesques and trellis décor, on a punched background; finished in brown, as are the Damascus grips, with SB monogram and motto QUAND MEME beneath a mask of Tragedy; the other grip with stylized scroll (or monogram); grip panels and triggerguard bow mounted with a green-yellow chalcedony. Not pictured, the bird's-eye maple-veneered case, lined in burgundy velvet, with ebony- and ivory-mounted accessories; the actress's monogram and motto engraved on brass-lid inlay; maker's name embossed in gold in lid.

pany, a "newly invented quick-firing cannon." The gun was likely a large-caliber Gatling.

The superstar might well have been the inspiration for James Tissot's "The Shooting Gallery," painted by the gifted artist at the time the Divine Miss Sarah was the toast of the world's theatergoers. Photographs, paintings, drawings, and prints of fashionably attired lady shooters are not uncommon from La Belle Époque.

Among Miss Bernhardt's lovers were two keen hunters and marksmen, and owners of numerous firearms: H.R.H. Edward, Prince of Wales, and His Excellency, Emperor Franz Joseph. Annie Oakley also knew these monarchs, and was the subject of their unremitting admiration.

With their extensive touring schedules, one wonders if the two international performers ever met. If so, they could have communicated on many common subjects—both being independent women of means unburdened by the shackles of Victorian convention. Miss Oakley could have extended lessons in shooting, for

which Miss Bernhardt might have traded theatrical guidance, each being the greatest of their time in their respective areas of expertise.[3]

Advertising and Women—the 1890s to the Roaring Twenties

Coming from a predominantly frontier culture, American women were in perfect position to take up shooting interests. The heroic example of Annie Oakley and her contemporary markswomen, and advances in women's independence, meant that marketing firearms to this audience was a legitimate target for the firearms industry. Thus, in an era commonly thought to

Stills from some of the innumerable Westerns in which women wield firearms. *Bottom center,* in *True Grit* Kim Darby (playing Matty) fires her Walker Colt, which promptly knocks her to the ground. At *lower left,* Katharine Hepburn fires a Winchester lever-action, while John Wayne as Rooster Cogburn (in film of same name) cranks rounds through a Gatling gun. *Bottom right,* shooting coach Arvo Ojalla probably taught more women to shoot than anyone in Hollywood's history; he is in vaquero costume on the set of the Steve Martin, Martin Short, and Chevy Chase comedy, *The Three Amigos.*

be restrictive to women, the firearms industry, particularly in the United States, actively promoted the participation of women and girls in the shooting sports. A veritable avalanche of advertising and promotion established the period from the 1890s to the 1920s as the golden era of

firearms marketing to women;* in the late twentieth century, that phenomenon occurred yet again, but was subject to some negative reaction in the mainstream press.

*Documented in "A Gun in Her Hands: Women in Firearms Advertising, 1900–1920" by Maureen Christensen, and in the two-volume *American Sporting Advertising*, by Bob and Beverly Strauss.

Although a few of these ads appeared as early as the 1890s, in the main the spread was from 1900 through 1920, with the majority c. 1905–15. The earliest piece presently known to the author is an 1889 Union Metallic Cartridge Company calendar, in which a demure young lady is in the field, reloading her rather elegant hammerless sidelock shotgun. She bears a striking resemblance to a figure then becoming known around the world—Annie Oakley. A rather provocative image of a cowgirl with a handgun was the theme of a poster by Hopkins and Allen, date yet unknown, which also picked up on the Oakley–Lillian Smith syndrome.

The fact that women were becoming increasingly active in a rapidly growing number of Wild West shows, of which the 101 Ranch (established in 1893) and Pawnee Bill's were among the most successful, helped to make these bold and daring performers themes for firearms advertisements. Such shows rapidly became America's national entertainment, and were so termed in the press and advertising of the day. At the same time, the shows reflected a reality: women in the West had developed their own style through an often rugged existence—ranching, roping, shooting—and they sometimes owned their own spreads.

As noted by Maureen Christensen in "A Gun in Her Hands":

While women in the East were stepping up the campaign for the vote, rallying for the freedom to move beyond the confines of home and family, women in the West had been doing just that, breaking the bonds of conventionality, quietly in daily life on ranches and publicly in Wild West shows and rodeos. These women were often a different breed than the Eastern sportswoman who hunted or shot clay pigeons, but the gun industry recognized the appeal and romance of the Western myth and enthusiastically undertook the association of its products with that popularity.

Highly romanticized dime novels occasionally dealt with Wild West women themes, and in real life there were the Belle Starrs, Calamity Janes, and Cattle Annies of the frontier—though none of them was ever considered for industry advertisements.

Christensen's Eastern sportswoman was the other archetype to appear in the period's flurry of posters, calendars, catalogs, magazine ads, and other such advertising memorabilia, a development influenced by Theodore Roosevelt, a dominant figure in American politics and the foremost shooting sportsman and conservationist in U.S. history. An enthusiastic and effective advocate of the outdoor life, a hunter of wide experience in the West, and an endorser of sports activities, Roosevelt used his "bully pulpit" as president (1902–08) to promote a healthy and vigorous lifestyle. As bemoaned by some of his Republican contemporaries, he was also an advocate of women's rights, and in time came to favor the then controversial matter of suffrage—yet another factor in the targeting of women by contemporary firearms industry advertising. (In 1920, women were finally given the vote, though Western states—where women had proven their independence—had already voted in favor of suffrage. Wyoming led the way in 1890.)

The early twentieth century was a peaceful time, and a prosperous one, represented by a rapidly developing consumer mentality. As the firearms industry sought new markets, the Victorian standard of women confined to a quiet home life and protected from the vicissitudes of the dangerous world beyond was rapidly changing. (The introduction of the automobile played a role in this dramatic transformation.) The period from 1896 to 1916 is considered a second wave of feminism, and a reflection of that movement is the series of the firearms industry's pro-

motions to the women's sporting, or outdoors, market.

Among magazines that ran features about women and the outdoors, *Recreation* and *Outing* were two in the forefront. Advertising in these publications reflected the increasing sophistication of that art form, also revealing developments in technology and new products. Moreover, the advertisements and news features informed the public of women's sporting activities, and served to encourage those not already doing so to become participants. Other magazines of the time that were part of this phenomenon included *Harper's*, *The Pacific Monthly*, *McClure's*, and more sporting-oriented publications like *Shooting and Fishing* (1888–1906) and *Arms and the Man* (from 1906; it became *The American Rifleman* in 1923).

In World War I women assumed roles in industry, which was required by the lack of men on the home front. At Winchester, for example, production employees in 1900 were 25 percent women, primarily in the cartridge facility. By 1919 31 percent of the shop workers were women, with female workers in the ammunition

The Mandrell sisters, active supporters of charity events organized around shooting competitions, and dedicated shooters themselves.

Larry, my friend, wish you could been here. Arvo Ojala

plants at 50 percent—but the actual number vastly increased due to wartime demands.

Firearms sales had increased tremendously from the late nineteenth century into the World War I era, and the appeal of shooting sports to women was also helped considerably by the widespread adoption of smokeless powder in the 1890s—making the sport far cleaner than in the black-powder days. A rash of new cartridges and firearms was instrumental in developing lines of guns that focused on women and boys, among them the J. Stevens Ladies Long Rifle, Nos. 11, 12, and 13 (a .22 rimfire, from c. 1899) and Marlin's Model 25 (also in .22, from c. 1909). Professional exhibition shooters like Plinky Topperwein also helped to attract women to the shooting sports.

But after some thirty years of marketing, other factors brought about an abrupt decline in the firearms industry's outreach to women. Wild West shows had become passé after about 1918, with the originator himself, W. F. "Buffalo Bill" Cody, having died in 1917, and World War I bringing about the collapse of many of the troupes. The Wild West image, which had helped gunmakers in appealing to the women's market, was fading. Social changes after women's suffrage, and a decidedly weakened women's movement, seemed to have diminished the attraction of women to outdoor sports. World War I had sent shock waves through American culture, men had a revival of dominance, and there was a resurgence of Victorianism as domesticity made a comeback. The coming depression was also instrumental in diminishing the role of women in firearms-industry promotions.

However, despite being less visible in advertising, women remained active in shooting sports, though often only those actually participating in

The lucky Arvo Ojala coaching Marilyn Monroe on how to fire a Colt Single Action Army revolver.

them were aware of it. This phenomenon remained true until the close of the twentieth century, when new waves of feminism brought the firearm and women's use thereof back into public awareness. Part of the more recent promotion of firearms and the shooting sports has been through the popularity of television programming, particularly on ESPN, TNT, and the new OutdoorSports Channel. Further, women have been influenced by such factors as the popularity of charity events sponsored by such stars as the Mandrell Sisters and other high-profile film, television, and music-industry celebrities who are keen shooters.

Cliff and Dick Baldwin—Shooters and Shooting Coaches

Cliff Baldwin was contracted to coach Ethel Merman for her role as the original star of Broadway's *Annie Get Your Gun*. On and off for three weeks, Baldwin taught Merman shooting skills and safety, and trained her to handle guns as if she were a professional. Dick Baldwin remembers that "Miss Merman had never had a gun in her hands before Dad started to work with her, but by the time the show opened in New York City she looked like a shooter should."

In the 1959 hit film *Butterfield 8*, starring Elizabeth Taylor, Dina Merrill, and Laurence Harvey, the skeet-shooting sequence was filmed at the Remington Gun Club in Lordship, Connecticut. As Harvey and Merrill fired away, Baldwin remembers that he "was behind the skeet houses breaking the birds for them. The movie showed them shooting and it appeared they were hitting the targets, but it was actually me that hit them. All they did was swing the gun and shoot into the air." On camera, roles with firearms have, not infrequently, introduced film stars to the

Mae West on the range, 1934, accompanied by burly bodyguard Jack Criss, from the Gangster Bureau of the Los Angeles District Attorney's Office. Miss West clearly knows how to wield this fully automatic weapon, which is fitted with a 50-round drum. From the Margaret Herrick Library, Academy of Motion Picture Arts and Sciences.

sport of shotgun shooting—and several have become dedicated participants.

In later years, Merrill's daughter Nina became a shooting champion, a member of the Sturm, Ruger & Company all-ladies shooting team, and, for a period of years, was the communications director of Holland & Holland, Ltd., New York. Winner of several shooting awards, she has also hunted big game in Africa, and has participated in a number of bird shoots in the United States and abroad.

Women and Guns in the Movies and on TV

As women became more self-assured and assertive, this became increasingly reflected in the

entertainment media—particularly in the movies, and later in television. The register of movies in which women used firearms is a lengthy one: of the more than seven thousand Westerns made by Hollywood since *The Great Train Robbery*, several hundred had women in roles in which they carried, and most often used, a firearm.

Among the most high-profile of these is *High Noon*, in which Grace Kelly kills an outlaw with a Winchester rifle. Another is *Annie Get Your Gun*, starring Betty Hutton. In one of Hollywood's best Westerns, *True Grit*, the determined and courageous Kim Darby fires a Colt Dragoon revolver at a despicable outlaw—and the recoil promptly knocks her to the ground.

The BFI Companion to the Western, a salute to the genre by the British Film Institute, lists an array of actresses who have starred in film and television Westerns. Among them are Julie Adams (*The Dalton Gang* and several other films, plus TV performances, including *Yancy Derringer*), and Jean Arthur, who played Calamity Jane in Cecil B. DeMille's *The Plainsman;* in *Shane* she was fearful of her son's admiration of the mysterious gunfighter played by Alan Ladd. In *A Ticket to Tomahawk* Anne Baxter portrayed a sharpshooting young lady, one among several of her roles in Westerns. Peggie Castle starred in *Two Gun Lady* and on a number of TV Westerns, notably *The Virginian* and *Lawman.*

Among other actresses with shooting roles—most of them in Westerns—are Yvonne DeCarlo, Drew Barrymore, Kim Basinger, Annette Bening, Liz Hurley, Joanne Dru, Katy Jurado, Dorothy Malone, Vera Miles, Demi Moore, Maureen O'Hara, Ruth Roman, Katharine Ross, Barbara Stanwyck, Andy McDowell, Sandra Locke, Mary Stuart Masterson, Claire Trevor, Ali McGraw, and Raquel Welch.

Besides her suggestive remark about a pistol in a man's pocket, and whether or not he was happy to see her, Mae West was keen on shooting and was an enthusiastic target shooter. In Emily Wortis Leideer's *Becoming Mae West,* the buxom star is pictured with one of her bodyguards, at a rifle range, posing with a Thompson submachine gun—which she had evidently been firing. Leideer states that after a scare when robbed at gunpoint of cash and jewels, she "took to sleeping with a pistol next to her bed."[4] Shelley Winters starred as Ma Barker in

the film of the same name, and enjoyed the shooting sports off screen.

A real-life deadly accurate wing and rifle shot, Jane Fonda wielded space-age weaponry in *Barbarella,* a production of her then husband, Roger Vadim. In the science fiction thriller *Alien,* Sigourney Weaver proved capable of dealing with an unnatural and formidable monster. In the cult film *The Matrix,* Carrie Ann Moss was accurate with her guns, and cool under fire. In *Lara Croft: Tomb Raider,* Angelina Jolie struck a classic swagger with hip holsters and their contents: a pair of Desert Eagle automatic pistols, with which she blazes away with devastating effect. In real life she is a keen collector of knives. Juliette Lewis was extremely nasty in the quite violent *Natural Born Killers,* and her shooting skills were showcased in *The Way of the Gun.*

Mira Sorvino was deadly in *Replacement Killers* (her father, Paul, is an accomplished sport shooter). In *Desperado* with Antonio Banderas, the strikingly beautiful Selma Hayek joined in the virtually nonstop gunplay. Exotic and sensual Patricia Arquette proved deadly in *True Romance.* Linda Hamilton's roles in *Terminator* and *Terminator II* are classic screen portrayals of a self-reliant woman, equipped with some quite serious small-arms ordnance.

Enemy at the Gates celebrated Russian snipers—male and female—from World War II. The film was one of the most convincing portrayals of women as frontline combatants in the nerve-wracking and perilous duel to the death with the Nazis.

Two films that have earned special notoriety are *Thelma and Louise* and *Baise-Moi,* chronicling women who fall into lawless behavior. In the former, Geena Davis and Susan Sarandon portray two friends who become entangled in a crime spree and shooting rampage. This modern

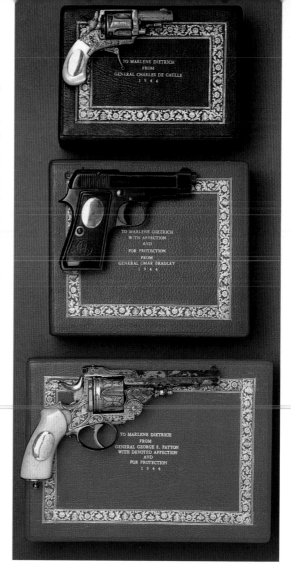

From the estate of Marlene Dietrich, and sold prior to her death, these handguns were gifts to her from generals with whom she had close friendships. Each is inscribed with gold plaques documenting the presentations, and cased in velvet-lined, jewelry-style boxes made by master craftsman and bookbinder, the late Arno Werner. *Top* and *bottom,* more collector's items than for practical use, but the Beretta Model 34, at *center,* from General Bradley, was a popular pistol before, during, and after World War II.

Facing page: Some stills from the over seven thousand Westerns made include Raquel Welch (*top left*) in *100 Rifles,* and (*bottom center*) Gary Cooper, with Grace Kelly, contemplating his Colt Single Action Army in the classic *High Noon. Bottom right,* Betty Hutton holds the deluxe Model 1892 Winchester of Annie Oakley (now in Cody Firearms Museum), in her role as Annie Oakley in *Annie Get Your Gun.* Holster and cartridge belt by Wild Bill Cleaver, the best of contemporary Western leathermakers.

242

Western demonstrates the acting and gun-wielding skills of both actresses, and captured the popular imagination during a period of feminist activism in the 1980s. The explicitly sexual and brutal *Baise-Moi* was termed by *Entertainment Weekly* as "graphic, hardcore, the most ungussied expression of female sexual rage ever thrown up on screen." In both films, guns were crucial props.

Among the more forceful, well-armed, and renowned TV policewomen, private detectives, or neovigilantes were Anne Francis in *Honey West*, Diana Rigg in *The Avengers*, Teresa Graves in *Get Christie Love*, Lindsay Wagner in *The Bionic Woman*, Holly Robinson Peete in *21 Jump Street*, and the dynamic trio of Farrah Fawcett, Jaclyn Smith, and Kate Jackson in *Charlie's Angels*. Turning to culture from the perspective of the New Jersey mob, *The Sopranos* showed Janice Soprano wasting a lover with salvos from her handgun. Tyne Daley played the role of a policewoman in one of the Dirty Harry series of Clint Eastwood films. Later, she became a policewoman in *Cagney and Lacey*, a TV adventure story of two female detectives. The beautiful Angie Dickinson starred in the long-running series *Police Woman*. The science fiction fantasy *Star Wars* showed women armed with make-believe weapons created for the screen. Another television program with an armed and knowledgeable heroic female star is Erin Gray in *Buck Rogers in the 25th Century*. Lucy Lawless in the nongun- but weapons-oriented program *Xena: Warrior Princess* is often cited as a take-charge, take-no-prisoners heroine. *China Beach*, a made-for-TV series broadcast on the History Channel, is based on the adventures of nurses in the Vietnam War. Star Dana Delaney, as well as women in other roles, occasionally shoulder and fire M16 rifles.

Whether or not they were keen sport shooters offscreen, a bevy of additional beautiful women have proven adept as on-screen shots. Among them: Susan Hayward, Myrna Loy, Marlene Dietrich, Katharine Hepburn, Marilyn Monroe, Shelley Winters, Stella Stevens, and Ursula Andress (her bra pistols in *What's New Pussycat* remain a classic). From more recent times are Candice Bergen, Gina Rowlands, Madeleine Stowe, and Pamela Anderson Lee.

Dale Evans, "Queen of the West"—Disciplining Unruly Sons

In her spirited foreword to Elizabeth Clair Flood's *Cowgirls*, Dale Evans, Western actress, singer, and wife of the King of the Cowboys, Roy Rogers, told of an out-of-the-ordinary means of disciplining her boys:

> One afternoon in my living room, the boys (Dusty and Sandy) were wrestling and rolling all over the floor and knocking things over. I was tired of hearing myself repeating: "Stop it. Stop it. You're going to knock something over that will set the house on fire"—but they just ignored me. So, I ran all the way down the hall toward the big closet where I kept my show pistol and gun belt, and grabbed a whole bunch of blanks, loaded my gun, and ran back in there shooting blanks off just as fast as I could. "Sorry boys," I said. "But I needed to get your attention."

Training Women in the Entertainment Media in the Use of Guns

No one had to train Annie Oakley in the use of firearms. On the other hand, both Mae Lillie and Plinky Topperwein were taught how to shoot by their husbands, both from scratch. The same was often true of other exhibition shooters, some of whom later became involved in film work.

As Western film and television entertainments blossomed in the 1950s and 1960s, one specialist, in particular, came to be recognized as *the* shooting coach: Arvo Ojala. A farmer from the Yakima Valley of Washington, Ojala loved to shoot, and had a local reputation as one who could—in a split second—draw his revolver and blast the head off a rattlesnake. The doomed creatures bred in a den on his apple ranch.

Critical of the way he saw actors using their guns, Ojala visited Hollywood. He quickly established a reputation as one who not only knew about guns, but could teach those who didn't. He had a standing challenge: pull the trigger of a cocked Colt Single Action revolver while pointing it at his midriff, *before* he could do the fast draw and fire! He was never beaten. For the movie *Return of Jack Slade*, Ojala trained star John Erickson, and thereafter, his position as Hollywood's shooting coach was secure. To quote *Guns* magazine's "The Man Who Teaches Hollywood Stars to Shoot": "Small wonder the name of Ojala has become a kind of legend among those who use guns professionally in films or just for sport."

His male students have included Frank Sinatra, Hugh O'Brian, Sammy Davis, Jr., Rory Calhoun, and Kevin Costner (*Silverado*). Among his female students: Marie Blanchard, Peggy Castle, Anne Francis, and Marilyn Monroe. About the latter, Ojala remembers: "Somehow I found it was taking me an awful long time [to coach her]. But she didn't seem to mind. And I certainly enjoyed it." All three of Ojala's daughters became expert shots in their own right.

Katharine Hepburn, Samuel Colt, John Wayne, John Huston, and Harry Jackson

In the June 1968 issue of *American Heritage*, Ellsworth S. Grant wrote the lead article, "Gunmaker to the World," a celebration of the life and legacy of Colonel Samuel Colt. In 1982, Grant followed up that piece with his book *The*

Colt Legacy. A native son of Connecticut, Grant was the brother-in-law of the celebrated actress, indeed icon of womanhood, Katharine Hepburn. Miss Hepburn's sister, Marion Hepburn Grant, was keenly interested in the Colt saga. She and her husband wrote extensively on Hartford and Connecticut historical matters. Ellsworth Grant also made films about the Connecticut River and Connecticut manufacturing, some of which were narrated by Katharine Hepburn.

Miss Hepburn was captivated by Samuel Colt, both his career in arms and as a Connecticut manufacturing pioneer. She was also an admirer of the gifted artist Harry Jackson, whose sculpture "The Marshal III" captured the spirit of one of Miss Hepburn's close friends and costars, screen icon John Wayne.

When making *The African Queen* Miss Hepburn learned of hunting from John Huston, who frequently went out in the African bush in the morning before the filming started. Documentary filmmaker John Hemingway tells a story of her having initially been critical of Huston for those shooting forays. One day, Huston invited her along. She was so impressed with the ritual and practice of hunting that in the future she requested that she be able to accompany him, even offering to carry his rifle.

Through her admiration of Wayne, Jackson,

Some of the strikingly attractive women competitors at the Hollywood Celebrity Shoot, August 2001, as photographed by journalist/actor James Swan. *Top,* from *left:* Lisa Laughlin, Shari LeGate (executive director, Women's Shooting Sports Foundation), Leslie Easterbrook, Lindy Teague, and Heather Lowe. Second row, from *left,* Sally Hampton, Erin Gray and Kelly Bovino, Erin Gray, Lee Benton, Sally Brown. Third row, from *left,* Desiree Kelly, Jennifer Savidge, Olympic medalist Kim Rhode, Lee Benton, and Kelly Bovino. Bottom row, from *left,* Anne Lockhart and daughter, and Heather Lowe.

THE AMERICAN COWGIRL
NEW POSTER

IMAGES of the OLD WEST
By JERRY CRANDALL

Okavango Delta, Botswana

CHRISTMAS GREETINGS
From
Phil & Linda
Spangenberger

MERRY CHRISTMAS
From PHIL & LINDA SPANGENBERGER & SIDEKICKS

and Huston, and her support of the film and literary projects of Ellsworth Grant, Miss Hepburn revealed an understanding and appreciation of the gun in history.

Elizabeth Taylor's Skeet-Shooting Lesson

For a three-year period in the 1950s Larry Sheerin, a San Antonio sportsman, polo player (with Laddy Sanford's championship Palm Beach and New York team), and oil and gas magnate, visited Hollywood with his friend film producer Merwyn LeRoy. Already LeRoy had seen his prediction of major stardom for a young actress come true, following quickly on her early, remarkably promising career: that of Elizabeth Taylor.

One day cowboy star Andy Devine and Sheerin were at a Los Angeles shooting range, in the company of Miss Taylor. Both gentlemen were expert shots—and they guided the soon-to-be starlet through a couple of rounds of skeet. She was, recalls Sheerin, "not only beautiful, but a very credible shot."

Elga Anderson Gimbel—Film Star, Adventurer, and Shooter

While staying as a guest at the Wildenstein family's Ol Jogi ranch, in Nanyuki, Kenya, the author met one of the world's most beautiful women: Elga Anderson Gimbel.

Elga was accomplished on many levels. German-born, she had lived in Europe, completed a successful modeling career, and entered the film

Facing page: "The American Cowgirl," Linda Spangenberger, and her husband, Phil. At *lower left*, with Gene Autry. In cowboy action shooting competition, the guns are loaded with live rounds. Their performances, coaching in the entertainment industry, and array of other activities have helped popularize reenactments of the Wild West.

world in her early twenties. She had starred in a string of films, among them *LeMans* with Steve McQueen, and had costarred with Sean Connery. While visiting in New York she had met Peter Gimbel, an heir to a department store fortune who eventually produced and directed the documentary film classic *Blue Water, White Death*. She was swept off her feet by his adventurous yet urbane nature. While at Yale, Peter was a boxer, and pursued a variety of sports interests. A friend of Peter's father was Alexander McCormick Sturm, Yale, Class of 1947, son of a keen fan of boxing and cofounder of Sturm, Ruger & Company, Inc. It was through Sturm, Sr., or from yet another boxing connection, heavyweight champion Gene Tunney, that Peter got serial number 203 of the Ruger Standard .22 self-loading pistol, out of the very first production batch.

When the author met Elga, she was in mourning over the tragic death of her husband, a victim of leukemia. She spoke of a storage locker full of guns that Peter had left, and wondered what to do with them. Elga, who lived mostly in New York, was also interested in learning how to deal with the crime-ridden metropolis as a single woman, though her residence was in a relatively safe Sixty-third Street town house.

Soon she was introduced to one of the best shooting coaches in the United States, Emanuel Kapelsan, of Philadelphia, and decided to have a security check on her New York residence. After attending private sessions with Kapelsan, Elga soon became an accomplished pistol shot and no longer feared for her safety. Her best target was posted on the master bedroom door of her town house—as a warning to any intruder.

Elga was a great admirer of Steve McQueen—himself an arms collector and dedicated shooter—and she had fond memories of Peter's love of guns. Despite her pleasure at shooting,

she never followed through on getting the almost-impossible-to-obtain New York City carry permit. In the mid-1990s her health took a disastrous turn, and she died shortly thereafter. But before her fatal illness, and in appreciation of my suggestions for her safety, Elga surprised me with the gift of Peter's Ruger pistol number 203.

Linda Spangenberger—Champion Cowgirl and Reenactor

Phil and Linda Spangenberger are a contemporary team combining Old West firearms and accessories expertise with riding and shooting skills. They perform in reenactments, commercials, film and television entertainments, and in trade shows, rodeos, and cowboy action shooting.

Phil Spangenberger taught shooting skills to a number of performers in film and TV. Among his women students have been Catherine O'Hara, who played Calamity Jane in *Tall Tale*, starring Patrick Swayze (a Disney production, 1994), and Krista Allen, for a guest-star appearance on the hit TV show *The X-Files*. He also taught gun handling to Shannen Doherty, a star of the television series *Charmed*, for a Western-theme sequence. Another of his students was Ali Carter in *American Outlaws*, a film about the James-Younger gang. Further, he worked with three actresses, including supermodel Frederica VanDerwall, who appeared as henchwomen to the villain in *Wild, Wild West*.

Phil has also taught other women about shooting, including employees of Petersen Publishing Company's firearms and hunting-and-shooting periodicals, such as *Guns & Ammo*. Some of these women had been deathly afraid of guns, but in the training process fell in love with the shooting sports. As one of the ladies remarked to Phil: "I can see why you guys like this—this is fun!"[5]

Women armed in films, for crime or adventure, took a new twist from the 1980s onward, as they often assumed traditional male roles. Symbolic of this trend were *Thelma and Louise, V.I. Warshawski,* and *Terminator 2,* in which Linda Hamilton proved capable of handling any firearm or destructive device. In

Angelina Jolie's *Lara Croft: Tomb Raider* and the 2001 French film *Baise-Moi* ("Rape Me"), women shooters revealed a new level of take-no-prisoners aggression. *Baise-Moi,* a kind of French *Thelma and Louise,* was reviewed by David White, i-Film, as the "Wham-bam-please-don't-kill-me-ma'am" movie of the

year. Far from politically correct, the production was banned in France.

Facing page: a turning point in American crime films—Faye Dunaway and Warren Beatty in *Bonnie and Clyde.*

Known as "the California Cowgirl," Canadian-born Linda Spangenberger learned how to ride, break, and train horses growing up on the outskirts of Los Angeles. She has appeared in a number of Wild West shows in the United States and Alaska, and performs with Phil in his trick-shooting and rough-riding acts. Her roles range from the gun-toting "Lawless Linda" the lady bandit to a modern-day Annie Oakley. Since the early 1990s, she has also participated in the Spirit of the West riders group in the Tournament of Roses parade, representing the John Wayne Cancer Institute.

As a horseback-riding coach, Linda prepared Rob Lowe for the starring role as Jesse James in the feature film *Frank and Jesse*. She also coached popular character actor Tom Bowers for his mounted scenes in the TNT film *Riders of the Purple Sage*, starring Ed Harris. Besides making an appearance on the *Guns of Remington* program, she was a horse wrangler for several action scenes in the History Channel's *Tales of the Gun* series. The Spangenbergers also appeared in a CBS promotional video for the TV miniseries *Lonesome Dove*. Linda served as a hand double for Pamela Anderson Lee on the TV series *VIP*, twirling a Model 92 Beretta—much trickier than performing with a Colt Single Action Army.

A pioneer member of the Cowboy Mounted Shooting Association (CMSA), Linda is the most decorated woman in that sport. As three-time world champion (1995, 1996, and 1997), she is one of the only two female contestants at this writing to win more than one world title. Linda has also won the SASS World Championship (1998), and several other national awards, as well as state championships in Arizona and California, and innumerable trophies in regional and local events.

The World of Reenactors

There may be as many as 1 million people involved in reenacting worldwide, which includes such competitive/entertainment activities as cowboy action shooting. The dedication of reenactors and their collaboration with the world of film and television—including the History Channel's *Tales of the Gun*—and with various other forms of entertainment (plays, parades, and anniversaries of historic battles)—have brought valuable knowledge of firearms to the public. Not a few women watch *Tales of the Gun*—a fifty-two-hour series of programs, most of which can be enjoyed without being indoctrinated in hardware and technical nomenclature. Women will not necessarily pick up a gun magazine, but they watch these television shows in significant numbers.

Today's army of reenactors in the United States covers all historical periods from the French and Indian War and Revolutionary War all the way up to the present. Even medieval and Renaissance history have become subjects for reenactors, though primarily in European countries and Great Britain. Women are a crucial part of reenactments; although it is not unusual to see a woman in a line of shooters, they mainly appear in support positions. Encampments, in which women are extremely active, often accompany events staged with reenactors, with commercial areas designated for sales of products to the public.

There is no question that film and television, through decades of adventure-oriented entertainment, have made the firearms used in these shows interesting, appealing, indeed captivating objects. Not a few collectors started the pursuit of firearms as a response to their enjoyment of these programs.

Lauren M. Cook and Civil War Combatants

Watching a reenactor at an Antietam battlefield event in 1989 emerge from the ladies' rest room, a National Park Service ranger discovered that the infrantryman, Lauren M. Cook, was a woman. Although women had served in Civil War battles, at that time they were forbidden to do so in reenactments. She was asked to leave the park. Cook's response to this hypocrisy was twofold. First, she instituted a suit challenging the all-male battlefield reenactment policy—and won. Simultaneously, she set out to document the role of women on the front lines, with both the North and the South.

As of 2002, Cook is among a growing number of women who are shooting participants in Civil War battlefield reenactments. The more complicated and time-consuming task of researching women as frontline soldiers has culminated in the publication of the book *They Fought Like Demons: Women Soldiers in the American Civil War*, coauthored with National Archives military archivist and historian DeAnne Blanton.

Pooling their scholarly efforts, and encouraged by the discovery of descendants of Sarah Rosetta Wakeman, Cook and Blanton carefully researched and recorded the wartime service of

Scattered throughout the collage, scenes from releases of *Annie Get Your Gun*, starring Barbara Stanwyck and, later, Betty Hutton. *Lower left* and *left center*, Gail Davis in her role as Annie Oakley, for the TV series. Marilyn Monroe in *River of No Return* at *top left* and *right*. Press advertisements promote *Annie Get Your Gun* in millennium-period revival on Broadway, as well as a mystery film starring Nicole Kidman, armed with shotgun. *Lower center*, action-Western *The Quick and the Dead*, starring Sharon Stone, with Leonardo DiCaprio, Gene Hackman, and Russell Crowe. *Lower right*, former national champion trapshooter Lily Sieu (with Bob Stack, *right*) and (*below*) singer Francine Sama, photographed at Hollywood Celebrity Shoot, 2001. *Upper right*, filmmaker Riva Freifeld at target practice with AR-15 rifle, and with Pardini air pistol and competition glasses. *Right center* and *below*, Jean Wallace Wilde, actress and wife of Cornell Wilde, and a keen huntress and accomplished shot—as well as the mother of sons who carried on a family tradition of hunting and fishing. Firing the Ruger Single Six is Lynn McGrath Tone, award-winning copywriter/creative director, savvy shooter, and keen sportswoman—and wife of Jean Wallace Wilde's son, Pascal.

"ANNIE GET YOUR GUN"
An M-G-M Release

R62/102

I'm a Girl

FRANK BUTLER

FB

Frank Butler

some 250 women from both sides in the conflict. Blanton's curiosity had initially been aroused when she discovered an obscure file in the National Archives, kept by a post–Civil War clerk in the office of the adjutant general. The theme of that file was women caught serving in uniform, in both the Northern and Southern armies.

In the *New York Times* feature article "When Janie Came Marching Home," Cook stated that she was particularly surprised by the fact that "these women did something so unacceptable to society at that time, but they were so accepted by the men they served in the ranks with. . . . It was war, and on the battlefield people couldn't afford to indulge in social conventions."[6] Particularly so in Confederate ranks: nearing war's end, women who served on the front lines tended to no longer conceal their sex.

Of immense satisfaction to Cook was the discovery that at least eight women fought at the original battle of Antietam; of that number, five died. That men in the ranks accepted these courageous women soldiers as comrades at arms has inspired women reenactment participants, particularly in Civil War events.

Sarah J. Rittgers, Smithsonian Institution, National Museum of American History, Behring Center—*The Patriot*

Sarah Rittgers joined the staff of the National Museum of American History as a summer intern. In time she became a secretary in the Department of Military History. She is now a curatorial associate, and a specialist in firearms, overseeing some ten thousand weapons at the Washington, D.C., site. In her spare time, she fires in muzzle-loading competitions, and took first in a two-hundred-yard match at the National Muzzle Loading Rifle Association annual shoot in Friendship, Indiana, in the summer of 2000. A protégée of Edward C. Ezell and Harry Hunter, she and Hunter were the subject of "Around the Mall and Beyond," in *Smithsonian* magazine. She also served as a consultant on the feature film *The Patriot,* starring Mel Gibson:

> Working on *The Patriot* was a fun project. Not only did I assist with firearms questions, but one of my tasks was to read the script, and the subsequent changes, and comment upon them. So my involvement ranged from firearms advice to any aspect of military history and life during the colonial era. When we first started working with Centropolis, the people dealing with costumes, props, and scripts came to the museum to view original objects and talk to us about their use. I pulled Revolutionary War firearms and accoutrements from the national collections so they could view them, take photographs, notes, and ask questions. I believe the object that most impressed them was George Washington's battle sword. They were also intrigued with the long-arms and engraved powder horns. I spent a lot of time describing the loading process and the military tactics of the day. I was going to have the opportunity to watch them film some battle scenes, but a few weeks before this was to happen, I went into premature labor and was forced to bed rest for the rest of my pregnancy. There went my chance to watch them film. It was great to work with them and then see the final product on the big screen.
>
> I have not met many other women firearms experts. I have met many that are good shots, however. When we go to Friendship we spend a lot of time with the Clark Frazier family, in which the mother, children, and grandchildren all shoot—and shoot well enough to win! Another fine shot is Marnie McClausland, who shoots for Thompson Center firearms.[7]

The Royal Armouries Museum and the Frazier Historical Arms Museum

Bringing history alive with actors and actresses, in a museum setting, has been perfected in modern times by the Royal Armouries Museum in Leeds, England. Their theatrical-educational programs were developed under the inspiration of Guy Wilson and interpreted by John Waller and his Armouries staff. The scripts have been written by Wilson himself, based on meticulous research and careful analysis. The Frazier Historical Arms Museum, in Kentucky, has picked up on the highly successful Royal Armouries Museum programs. The Frazier is developing a series inspired by the Armouries, and adding their own programs.

As of 2002, the interpretations by female performers at the Royal Armouries Museum are as follows:

The Adventures of Mother Ross—The true story of a woman who, in the eighteenth century, spent much of her life masquerading as a male soldier.

Oregon Trail, 1848—A settler heading west tells the story of what it was like to cross America in a covered wagon.

Cawnpore, 1857—A survivor of the Indian uprising against the British tells of the siege and its terrible aftermath (presentation billed as having "strong content").

Annie Oakley—The life of the famous sharpshooter in her own words.

The Shell Girl, 1914–18—A worker at the Barnbow munitions factory in Leeds talks about the great danger faced providing ammunition for the war effort.

Special Operations Executive, 1940–44—An SOE agent talks about the extreme courage and resourcefulness needed to work for British Intelligence in occupied France.

Introducing Actresses and Celebrities to Guns and Shooting

Many actresses have to handle guns, as dictated by the roles they are given. Many have also become keen shots, and enjoy guns and shooting in their private lives. Among these actresses and other high-profile women are Leslie Easterbrook (*Police Academy*), Lee Purcell (*Mr. Majestyk*), Erin Gray (*Buck Rogers*), Susan Howard (*Dallas*), Reba McEntire (*Buffalo Gals*), Elaine Giftos (*War of the Worlds*), Terry Moore (*Peyton Place*), Connie Stevens (*Hawaiian Eye*), Stella Stevens (*The Poseidon Adventure*), Ashley Judd (*Double Indemnity*), Sharon Stone (*The Quick and the Dead*), Anne Lockhart (daughter of actress June Lockhart, who starred in *Battle Star Galactica*), Leah Thompson (*Red Dawn*), Khrystine Haje (*Head of the Class*), Kim Delaney (*Tour of Duty*), Lisa Blount (*An Officer and a Gentleman*), and Madonna. Cybill Shepherd is a skilled shot, as are Whoopi Goldberg, Joan Rivers, Heather Locklear, Vicki Lawrence, and Suzanne Pleshette. Some of these women were introduced to firearms and shooting in preparation for on-screen roles. Others, like Sharon Stone and Susan Howard, already knew about firearms and were experienced shots.

Many of these entertainers have enjoyed the mystique, the romance, and the sheer fun of firing guns, and have gone on to become keen shooters. Some started off with attitudes against guns and the shooting sports. When Phil Spangenberger began coaching Trevor Morgan, one of the child actors in *The Patriot,* Morgan's mother stated: "I know you are very professional, but I have to tell you that I am nervous around all these guns." After the training period, however, she not only felt comfortable but was receptive to the interest of her son in acquiring a flintlock "Brown Bess" musket—just like the one he fired at British troops in the movie.

Sharon Stone learned to shoot from her father, and was quoted in *Vanity Fair* as saying that one of the most exciting things she ever did was shoot an AR-15 rifle. When, years later, she voluntarily surrendered her guns to the police, she explained in an interview that she did so because she felt it unfair that, living in a protected environment, she should have guns, when poor and disenfranchised women were denied them.

Other women associated with the entertainment industry known to be keen shooters are songwriter Caroll Connors, writer of "To Know Him Is to Love Him" and cowriter of the theme for *Rocky*; author and beauty expert Beverly Sassoon of the Vidal Sassoon family; and actress Kate Capshaw, whose husband, Steven Spielberg, is known as the foremost film director of modern times. A number of producers, directors, and other Hollywood luminaries enjoy firearms in their private lives, and often their wives and girlfriends are keenly interested in shooting.

Firearms are often glamorized in films, television, and other entertainments, but they are equally demonized—along with their users. Show business, while frequently treating firearms as icons, has also created a kind of monster object. Such an interpretation has instilled a fear of guns in some of the public, particularly in women and girls. All too often the entertainment industry fails to depict the safe handling of firearms, and is guilty of the most excessive violations of historical fact. At times there are screen errors in the basic operation and performance of firearms. The most common such shortcoming is the failure to portray the stunning impact from the noise and concussion of small arms as they are fired within an enclosed space.

The Autry Museum of Western Heritage—the Dynamic Duo of Jackie Autry and Joanne Hale

When Gene Autry decided to create the Autry Museum of Western Heritage, he had three gifted allies. One was his old pal and fellow star of Western films Monte Hale. The others were their wives, Jackie and Joanne.

The museum was a project the two couples had long discussed, and had been a bequest in the will of Gene's first wife, Ina. In the spring of 1980, Gene's personal arms collection numbered only about one hundred pieces, most of them Colts, with some Winchesters and miscellaneous other makes. The bulk of these had seen use in Western films and in the several television programs Gene had produced.

In 1982, George A. Strichman retired as chairman of the board of Colt Industries. Soon the Colt Industries Museum firearms group came on the market, followed within a year by the chairman's private collection. The Autry Museum bought both collections. Within the span of a few years, the museum quietly and judiciously put together the finest collection of historical Western firearms in the world.

253

Gene and Jackie Autry, with Monte and Joanne Hale. Their dedication, intuition, savvy, and energy, combined with the Ina Autry estate, and aggressive fund-raising and marketing, created a landmark institution: the Autry Museum of Western Heritage.

The two persons most responsible for building the arms collection were Jackie and Joanne, the penultimate "Dynamic Duo." When Gene wanted to acquire the Bianchi Frontier Museum, the ladies were sent to Temecula, California, to thrash out a deal. Two days later, they had successfully negotiated acquisition of the entire museum.

Jackie and Joanne realized that the museum's collection was a powerful draw for public attendance. When the Franklin Mint wished to issue replicas of such treasures from the museum as the Theodore Roosevelt Single Action Frontier revolver, the two women put together a contract, even garnering permission to market the pieces in the museum shop. And when the state of California wanted to pass a law to make replicas subject to the same restrictions as shooting guns, Jackie and Joanne testified against the concept at a hearing of the state legislature. The ladies won, of course.

One evening, at the Sportsmen's Lodge, Los Angeles, prior to the annual Golden Boot Awards—the "Oscars of the Westerns"—the Autrys and the Hales had the opportunity to purchase a treasure trove of Theodore Roosevelt guns and memorabilia, including the rancher-president's Colt six-shooter and its holster, and his Winchester Model 1876 carbine. On the spot, and without hesitation, they bought these treasures for the museum.

Opening night of the Autry Museum was a walk down memory lane, attended by dozens of cowboy and cowgirls stars, among them Dale Evans and Roy Rogers, Maureen O'Hara, and Chuck Connors. Jackie and Joanne could look back on the creation of the museum as a great challenge, which they met with boldness, determination, and insight. And Gene and Monte could almost burst with pride: they knew that without Jackie and Joanne, the entire museum

project, including the building complex, would have proven insurmountable.

After Gene's passing, Jackie assumed the position of chairman of the board. Having served as executive director for nearly ten years, Joanne retired, and is now president. The Autry Museum of Western Heritage draws approximately 500,000 visitors annually. The institution is a tribute to two fine couples, and especially to "the Dynamic Duo," whose vision has made it unrivaled in historic arms of the American West. Fittingly, four of the most outstanding pieces were custom-made for Annie Oakley.

"Are You Ready?" Riva Freifeld—Filmmaker and Competitive Shooter

Documentary filmmaker, producer, and editor Riva Freifeld is presently engaged in a ninety-minute production for television on the life and career of Annie Oakley. Freifeld's own sport of preference is competitive target shooting.

A red light is flashing somewhere in my peripheral vision. The match director, behind me on a podium, signals the start of the Rapid Fire Stage of the Women's Sport Pistol competition at the Empire State Games in Albany, New York. In my right hand, the Hammerli Model 280 Olympic .22 pistol is pointing at a forty-five-degree angle to the ground. I go into the zone.

I let out half my breath. I will my adrenaline to go down, down, down, and my heart rate to lower to about fifty-two beats per second. Concentration. Focus. Utter stillness.

The light turns green. I have three seconds to raise the pistol, acquire a sight picture, and put one round in the center of a bull's-eye target twenty-five meters away. I have practiced this move many times over the last three months. It is tricky. Seemingly endless practice has been necessary to find the best solution, to "feel" the exact position of the gun as it comes up, so that only a minor sight correction is necessary at the very end.

Only this isn't practice anymore. I'm in the middle of a gut-wrenching competition, with eleven other

women on my left and right. Seven seconds at the forty-five-degree angle, three seconds to fire one round, repeat five times. A short rest period, then another string of five shots, for a total of thirty shots.

What am I doing here? I am a documentary filmmaker, a resident of the Upper West Side of New York City, the epicenter of liberal Democratic heaven. I don't know anyone in my field who owns guns. I tend to work on projects about relevant social issues. Gun violence is one of those issues.

I had started my career back in the '70s with the early cinema-vérité pioneers. I was known as a film editor who could also structure and write, someone who could find the hidden story in hours of amorphous footage. But my career had taken an unusual turn. Two years earlier I had been hired by the production company of a prominent PBS talking head, as one of three editors on a series called *What Can We Do About Youth Violence?* The producers wanted me to edit a segment about a group of Los Angeles teenagers who were now disabled and in wheelchairs as a result of having been shot.

In my editing room at WNET, I screened the "dailies," the raw camera footage. The gunshot survivors were all inner city boys who seemed to have been involved in the drug trade. As I listened to their stories, I concluded that they alone were responsible for what happened to them, not the "proliferation of guns" or any other so-called epidemic.

Unfortunately, this was not the message the producers and funders wanted to convey. I could no longer work on the project. To learn more about guns, I took up target shooting as a hobby.

So here I am, willing myself into a Zen-like state of being and nothingness. Seven seconds and . . . the target starts to turn, I raise the Hammerli and fire one round into (hopefully) the ten ring. The match has begun. . . .[8]

Katja Kaiser—Auction House Arms-and-Armor Specialist

The world of auction houses, especially on the top level, is akin to the entertainment business. Combining fashion, marketing, scholarship, and pizzazz, companies like Christie's, Sotheby's, and Butterfield's have revolutionized what was once a rather staid, conservative, commercial operation.

For several years in the 1990s, Butterfield's had a high-profile woman in their arms-and-armor department: German-born Katja Kaiser grew up in Hanover, and later lived in West Berlin, around the time the Wall collapsed. Before she joined Butterfield's she was unfamiliar with firearms, and had no idea her homeland was a country where gunsmiths (some of them women) had produced some of the finest, most beautiful weapons the world has ever seen. Here she tells how she came to be an arms-and-armor auction specialist:

> "And by the way, the job opening is in our Arms and Armor Department," said the Butterfield's Auctioneers' human resource director upon my second interview for what had been advertised as a "manager position in one of our specialty departments." Her matter-of-fact statement caught me so much off guard that I don't even know how my short response, "Great," came across. I had envisioned working with antique objects—but guns?
>
> In any case, I was hired and shortly after assumed my duties as operations manager of the San Francisco–based Arms & Armor Department, which was then headed by Director Greg Martin. My new office was inside a windowless, secured warehouse; my desk surrounded each day by up to five thousand firearms and related objects—dating from the fifth century B.C. to the twentieth century.
>
> Quickly I learned that Butterfield's Auctioneers was then the world leader in the field of fine, collectible firearms and other weaponry, Western memorabilia, and militaria. What I didn't know was that the following four years (1996–2000) would change my perspective on many issues, establish opinions in thus far uncharted areas and open to me the doors to a world I never knew existed.

Growing up in Germany, Kaiser "was aware that the possession of firearms was strictly controlled" and she "never had seen anyone carrying or known anyone owning a gun":

> Through Butterfield's I met many collectors and dealers of fine arms and armor, men who are exceptionally successful in their businesses, collectors of impeccable taste, and (many of them) keen hunters. I learned that being a hunter and wildlife conservationist in one person is not an oxymoron but a sign of respect for life. As a result of many conversations I had with gun collectors, I came to believe that the freedom to own firearms, whether to strictly collect or to use them for sport, indeed reverentially, in hunting, is a very important citizen's right that should not be tampered with.

When offered the opportunity to learn how to shoot, she "was eager to try." In a few days she learned to use self-loading pistols, revolvers, shotguns, and rifles:

> To my amazement I found out that I was a very good shot. With some training, I became successful even at skeet shooting, although I tend to "shoot from the hip," thus disobeying all rules of the sport. I even went on a hunt and drew first blood on a ranch in Texas's Rio Grande Valley: a nicely sized fallow deer whose rack is now mounted on one of the walls at my home. Learning to shoot was a tremendously fulfilling, liberating experience. Myths I had heard before, such as about the forceful recoil of the Colt .45—supposedly making it difficult for a woman to hold—were dispelled literally shot by shot.
>
> I realize that my job experience at Butterfield's Auctioneers was unique. From what I have heard I was the only woman working as operations manager and then later on as assistant director of a major firearms auction house in the entire world. Looking back, I would not want to have missed this time for anything and I look forward to many more adventures with the friends I made during those exciting years.[9]

255

One of the most accomplished women in the history of the shooting sports, the NRA's first female president, Marion Hammer. A lifetime shooter, her mastery of the world of firearms also extends into the legislative arena. Her interview for *George* magazine, by John F. Kennedy, Jr., was one of numerous highlights in a career that continues unabated at this writing. Ms. Hammer's NRA service is a reflection of the organization's recognition of girls and women as vital participants in a sport where the genders are equalized by skill with firearms.

CHAPTER X

Women at Arms: Today and Tomorrow

When you're shooting, you are standing in the forest for really long periods of time, so you end up looking at the leaves and the sky and the trees and you have a lot of time to meditate. . . . I eat birds. You have more of a respect for the things you eat when you go through, or see, the process of killing them.

—Madonna, actress and entertainer, BBC Radio One interview

When dependable, affordable firearms came on the scene in the mid–nineteenth century, they were called "equalizers." No longer did the ability to hunt for food or to defend oneself require strength and special training. Ordinary people could resist tyranny, in all its guises, as never before.

Today, as the evolution of arms development continues, that equalizing effect is applying increasingly to women, who are finding that more manageable sizes and calibers are providing them with an entrée into hunting and self-defense that is truly empowering.

This is also borne out in military and police participation. Women are fulfilling roles hitherto prohibited to them—and succeeding admirably. As the final sexist barriers fall, it is interesting to note what the women at arms of today are heralding for the future.

There is a negative side, too. Great numbers of women and girls, living in urban areas, will

Kim Rhode acknowledging applause upon winning the gold medal in 1996 Olympics, Atlanta.

know of guns only from films and television, where fantasy becomes taken for fact. Guns in schools, guns in street gangs—these paint a pervasive and false picture of the role and potential of firearms in society.

The heated debate over firearms continues, but the dynamics are changing. And a key reason for the change is that more and more women are taking up shooting, as a sport or a hobby, for hunting or for self-defense.

The research for this book uncovered the stories of a significant number of women who had little or no knowledge of firearms whatever prior to their adult years. Yet once introduced to the world of firearms, having learned the basics of safety, of performance, of the traditions of target shooting and hunting—and sometimes even of gunmaking—they found an appreciation that involved art and craftsmanship, history, mechanics, and romance. What in many had been a baseless fear was replaced by knowledge and experience.

The women at arms of today and tomorrow are making their presence felt and their voices heard as advocates of constitutional rights, as heroines—known and unsung—of battle and police action, as guardians of important arms collections, and as huntresses and champions of conservation.

Women Firearms Advocates

Paxton Quigley—Former Antigun Activist Turned Gun Advocate

America's foremost proponent of self-defense training for women today, Paxton Quigley spent twenty years lobbying for restrictive gun laws. Her full-circle conversion occurred when,

258

Elizabeth Clair Flood's *Cowgirls* celebrates these daring women, a few of whom are represented here in a selection of postcards—the collecting of which has become a nostalgic passion. Some of the images are more sporting oriented (like Christmas card at *lower left* of book), but the majority are from the West and of the late nineteenth century up through post–World War I. Note Mrs. Sarah Winchester at *top center,* a card printed by the Winchester Mystery House, San Jose. The Huntington Library's booklet of Wild West women cards depicts one of the best-known images on its front cover.

after what happened to my friend, I said, 'This isn't going to happen to me. I'm going to learn how to shoot a gun.'"

Today, her landmark books on women and self-defense—*Armed and Female* and *Not an Easy Target*—have each sold well over 200,000 copies. Called an "icon of gun-toting feminism" and "a sort of contemporary Annie Oakley" by a London newspaper, she has made over three hundred television and radio appearances, including *Oprah* and *60 Minutes*. Quigley has worked as a bodyguard for celebrities and gives "personal protection" classes for business-women. She taught actress Geena Davis how to shoot for her role in *Thelma and Louise*. She has personally taught more than seven thousand women to shoot. "Even if you don't want to buy a gun, at least know how to shoot it, how to handle it," she advises. "You might be in a situation where there's a gun present and you don't even know how to unload it."

For many years a spokesperson for Smith & Wesson, Quigley hosts an informative website

259

Above: Books, monographs, magazines, photographs, memorabilia, and videos revealing the breadth and scope of shooting interests.

Foremost among the advocates of self-defense for women is Paxton Quigley, whose television appearances and radio interviews are legion. Following the September 11, 2001, atrocities, she has become even more in demand, with frequent speaking engagements on self-protection in the age of terror.

in 1986, a friend was attacked in her home. Even though she called 911, the police did not arrive in time. As she attempted to run out her door, her assailant caught her from behind and raped her. Visiting her friend in the hospital, Quigley asked, "If you had had a gun, would you have shot him?" The answer was "Yes." Quigley notes, "I always had this naïve belief that if I picked up the phone and called the police, they would arrive almost immediately. But,

(www.paxtonquigley.com) that also offers her books, several types of pepper spray (she believes that many approaches to defense are necessary), and her own invention, the SuperBra, which is designed to conceal either a .38 snubnose revolver or a canister of pepper spray.

Quigley has never had to use a gun in a life-threatening situation, but one of her clients has. When a man tried to break into the client's home, she grabbed her handgun and confronted him: "Don't move or I'll shoot!" He asked, "Is it loaded?" Her reply, "Just try me!" sent him running.[1]

Two other advocates are promoting their insights into female empowerment, in their own way, as leaders in the National Rifle Association, long a proponent of women in hunting and shooting. Marion Hammer, the association's first female president, came to the organization from many years of involvement in sport shooting. Sandra Froman, who is currently second vice president at the NRA and second in line for the presidency, did not become interested in firearms until her thirties, undergoing a conversion experience similar to Paxton Quigley's.

The Ladysmith series, and other self-defense handguns by S & W. From *top right,* First Model Ladysmith, with 4-inch barrel. *Top left,* Second Model Ladysmith. *Center right,* Third Model of the Ladysmith, with target sights. *Center left,* Third Model Ladysmith. Contrary to myth, the model was not discontinued by D. B. Wesson due to its popularity with ladies of ill repute, but rather because it was difficult to produce, and prone to breakage. At *left* of longtime Smith & Wesson representative Paxton Quigley, the Chief Special Target revolver, and with barrel pointing upward *below,* a Model 317 Airlight. At *bottom center,* a Model 3913 Ladysmith, and at *bottom right,* a Model 642 Ladysmith.

Right: At the Camp David skeet range, Jacqueline Kennedy firing a Model 23 Winchester side-by-side; her husband, the president, using an over-and-under Model 101 Winchester; both in 20 gauge. These pictures, taken c. 1962, reflect John F. Kennedy's interest in firearms. The Department of the Army gave him a flintlock musket as a birthday present. Colt presented him with an M-16 rifle, and he is also known to have received a Spencer repeating carbine of Civil War vintage. Mrs. Kennedy fires from the left shoulder, and, characteristically, does so with instinctive elegance.

Marion Hammer, First Female President of the NRA

Marion Hammer's election in 1996 as the first woman to preside over the venerable National Rifle Association resulted in huge media interest and coverage. No stranger to firearms and shooting sports, Hammer had served as executive director of the Unified Sportsmen of Florida for nineteen years, and was also director and secretary of the National Muzzle Loading Rifle Association. She is a hunter and a competitive shooter with both rifle and pistol. Her awards include the 1985 "Man of the Year" Roy Rogers award—she is the only woman ever to receive it—and the 1995 Sybil Ludington Freedom Award.

One of her major contributions has been her advocacy of the NRA's Eddie Eagle Gun Safety Program for children, which was recognized by the National Safety Council's award, in 1993, for Outstanding Community Service. Among her many media interviews, one of particular significance appeared in the April–May 1996 issue of *George* magazine. The session was conducted personally by the publisher, the late John F. Kennedy, Jr. This was only the fourth issue of *George,* and Hammer was the first woman Kennedy himself had interviewed for the magazine.

Kennedy, it turned out, hunted birds and shot skeet. Hammer recalls, "During breaks in the interview, he told me that he really enjoyed shooting, so I was surprised to learn that he was totally unaware that his father had owned guns. Nor did he know that his father had been an NRA Life Member."

When the interview was completed, Hammer presented Kennedy with two of the author's books, which contained information on the Colt Frontier revolver and AR-15 rifle presented to the president by Colt's, and a Revolutionary War–period flintlock musket given to him by the Department of the Army.

It was Hammer's observation that "this unas-

Sandra Froman at work and play. Her energy, broad experience, legal expertise, and knowledge of the world of firearms qualifies her, as well as anyone, for presidency of the National Rifle Association.

suming young man had little or no exposure to the real politics fueling the firearms debate. . . . Here was a young man whose father had been tragically assassinated, yet he didn't blame the gun—he was not a gun hater."[2]

Sandra S. Froman—NRA Vice President

Second vice president of the NRA, a past president of the NRA Foundation, graduate of Stanford University and Harvard Law School, Sandra Froman had no idea she would be an enthusiast of firearms until after her thirty-second birthday. "Where I grew up, in the San Francisco Bay area, we didn't have guns in the home. My dad didn't have a gun, I never went shooting, and I never went hunting. Guns were simply not a part of my life."

A criminal trying to break into her home late at night—twenty years ago—made the matter of self-defense immediate. "I chose to become responsible for my own personal safety, learned the law about guns, sought out advice about what kind of firearm would suit my needs—and bought my first handgun. . . . Buying that gun and learning how to use it represented real liberation—real freedom. Owning a handgun for the good purpose of self-defense made absolute common sense."

Today, she is one of the most convincing advocates of firearms ownership in America. A natural shot, "shooting quickly became a passion." When she told women in her California law office that she was going to the range, "they were stunned."

After being elected to the board of directors of the NRA, Froman met several female hunters, among them Sue King and gun industry executive Brenda Potterfield, who became her mentors.

> I managed to shoot pheasants and a chukhar on my first bird-hunting trip to Missouri. Sue King invited me to come to an NRA-sponsored Women on Target

hunt in Texas. After a day and a half of creeping around in the thorny brush and silently waiting, I experienced thirty seconds of heart-stopping excitement before firing my rifle. I couldn't believe that I had taken my first mammal, a feral hog. The following year, I went back to Missouri and, coached by Brenda's husband, Larry, shot my first turkey, which we cooked with morel mushrooms from the woods and fresh asparagus from the Potterfields' garden. The following fall, I shot dove in Arizona, which became a tasty treat marinated in prickly pear syrup and grilled on the barbecue. Now I am a walking, talking chamber of commerce for women who want to learn to hunt safely and responsibly.[3]

Froman feels that female gun advocates are successful because it is difficult for the press, politicians, and business to say no to women claiming the right of firearms ownership. She is confident that asking gun retailers for more shooting programs directed at women will bring results because "women are a fast-growing segment of the market." Going to the press and requesting balanced coverage of firearms issues relating to women will prove beneficial because "women and guns are newsworthy." Seeking funding for events like "Friends of NRA" will work because "women have buying power." Going to a school board or PTA to promote the Eddie Eagle™ Gunsafe program will be taken seriously because "the program has been proven beneficial in reducing firearms accidents among children."

Her talks support defending firearms freedoms, which she feels "could be lost or significantly diminished in our lifetimes." In memory of her late husband, career law enforcement officer Bruce Nelson, Froman sponsors the National Firearms Museum's "Long Arm of the Law" exhibit. She supports funding for the NRA Endowment, as well as educational programs on firearms matters: "We are stewards of a great legacy left us by America's founding fathers. They changed history when they gave us

the United States Constitution and the Bill of Rights," she says, and in closing invites her audience to join her "in following their footsteps by securing America's great firearms heritage for the millennium." She often adds: "If you can carry a man's groceries, and can carry a man's baby, you can certainly carry a man's gun."

Women at War

The face of war changed dramatically as the world moved into a new millennium. Limited internecine conflicts have thrust the larger powers into peacekeeping roles, while the threat of extremist acts has demanded home-defense strategies that echo the resistance movements of old. When the surprise attacks were launched against New York City and Washington, D.C., on September 11, 2001, a new war, the war on terrorism, was declared. It has prompted a combination of high-tech, surgically precise defense tactics and guerrilla-style, in-country confrontation. And an investigative function, which traces and seeks to freeze terrorist funding sources, has become increasingly important.

In all these areas, women are serving as never before.

Defying the Taliban

Risking their lives to confront the fundamentalist rule of the Taliban in Afghanistan, women took up arms. A headline in London's *Sunday Telegraph* heralded them as "veiled but deadly—female fighters who defy Taliban."

In 1998, when Taliban militia forces attacked the village of Qalai Khoja, Northern Alliance resistance fighters taught their wives to shoot, and armed them with AK-47s and machine guns, referring to their "secret weapons—their wives." Sharila, aged thirty-six and the mother of six children, was one of these women. When the Taliban again raided the village in 2000, while the men were away, she and eight other wives fought back, in a cornfield: "I fired five hundred bullets and we killed twenty-five Taliban." What would she do should the Taliban return? "I would shoot them. I wouldn't ask questions." Her husband, Hashim, states that all the women and children in their village know how to use weapons. "They can take a Kalashnikov to pieces, clean it and reassemble it. The men teach them. If we are to die, we want to die in our homes."[4]

Women in the U.S. Military: 2001

In the early 1990s, the war in the Persian Gulf, Operation Desert Storm, saw women in almost every area except explicit combat roles. Service since in the Balkans, the Middle East, and Afghanistan is resulting in the erasing of even that distinction. Women now pilot fighter aircraft and serve aboard naval combat vessels. And they have had their share of combat casualties: eleven women were killed during the Gulf War, and two died aboard the USS *Cole*.

Women now comprise 16 percent of U.S. armed forces, up from 12 percent during Desert Storm (15 percent of the army, 13 percent of the navy, 19 percent of the air force, and 6 percent of the marines). And while some areas are still off limits, such as the elite Special Forces teams, the army's infantry and artillery units, and the naval submarine service, women are eligible for 91 percent of jobs in the army and 99 percent of the jobs in the high-tech air force.

A *Newsweek* feature published in the wake of the September 2001 terrorist attacks interviewed some of the U.S. military's women at arms (noting that pilots in the navy and air force can only be identified by their first name or call sign). Lieutenant Ashley, an F-14 Tomcat pilot stationed aboard the USS *Carl Vinson*, was flying combat missions over northern Afghanistan.

263

One mission saw her at fifteen thousand feet looking for her targets, two antiaircraft batteries. She found and hit the first, then started receiving enemy fire.

"I was thinking, 'You don't want to hang around here,' but we had another target, so we came around and hit that, too," she says. Flying back to the carrier, Ashley . . . 26, couldn't stop grinning. "I was smiling at the fact that I had done my thing for the country."

An A-10 pilot at Davis-Monthan Air Force Base in Arizona, Captain "Charlie" notes, "We're starting to be just one of the guys. Now people talk about you and you're the fighter pilot—not the female fighter pilot, just the fighter pilot."

Gradually, the article notes, perceptions are changing and some of the most vociferous concerns are being proven wrong. Mixing men and women has resulted in performance that is as good, or better, than with all-male units, and

Jenny Matthews's "Women and Conflict" exhibition was the culmination of fifteen years spent documenting "the lives of women caught in conflict."* The brochure notes:

She has travelled across Europe, Central America, the Middle East, Africa and Asia. The result is an exhibition of photographs that is profoundly intense, both moving and passionate.

While photographs of women in conflict regions usually portray them either as tragic victims or as exotic fighters, this exhibition presents the women photographed as individuals, with stories to tell that bring into focus the invisible effects of war. . . . For many women, times of conflict are about trying to carry on as normal. For others, the climate of violence prevents any form of normal existence. Women can be both the victims of war, and take an active part as soldiers.

Press articles counterclockwise from *top left: The Sunday Telegraph* (October 28, 2001); *The Daily Telegraph,* November 2, 2001; *The Sunday Telegraph,* October 28, 2001; *The New York Times,* July 26, 2001; and *The Daily Telegraph,* November 2, 2001.

*For a piece on Phoolan Devi, India's "bandit queen," see *The New York Times,* July 26, 2001

while sexual harassment and pregnancies are still problems, the military is learning to deal with them more effectively. In addition, "many of the servicewomen *Newsweek* interviewed said they thought of their male squadmates as brothers."

Will women eventually become integrated in every area of military activity? Linda Grant DePaw of the Minerva Center, a military think tank, thinks so. She notes that intelligence and technology are the cornerstones of U.S. military superiority. It's not as if "we're still attacking with fixed bayonets."

Although the matter of equality in the services remains unresolved in many respects, "most American servicewomen wouldn't trade their experiences for anything."[5]

A Police Hero

Among the many heroes of the attack on New York's World Trade Center is Kathy Mazza, a captain in the Port Authority police. An unconfirmed report, cited in a letter to the editor of *The New York Times*, states that she fired shots from her sidearm to blast open a glass wall and allow hundreds of people trapped inside to escape. What *is* confirmed is that she and a male officer, Lieutenant Robert Cirri, were last seen entering the crumbling building to search for survivors, and she remains among the missing.

Mazza is representative of a new breed of female police officers. Entering the force from a career in nursing, she championed the use of automated defibrillators to allow first responders to treat sudden cardiac arrest. An article in *Newsday* noted, "In 1992, Kathy Mazza underwent open-heart surgery to correct a quarter-sized hole. Exactly one year later, she was credited with saving her mother, who was complaining of chest pains. Mazza recognized that her mother's arteries were blocked. . . . At least

14 New Yorkers can make the same claim. Mazza's 1997 initiative to train some 600 officers to use defibrillators in airports is credited with saving 14 to 16 lives, according to Port Authority estimates."[6]

"I Live in Deeds—Not Years"

That simple motto summed up the engaging life of Electra Havemeyer Webb, pioneer collector of American folk art, and the creator of the Shelbourne Museum, in Shelbourne, Vermont. Heiress to the Havemeyer sugar fortune, Electra's childhood was one of privilege and opportunity. Taking a cue from the collecting instincts of her parents—experts on European Impressionist paintings and generous benefactors of the Metropolitan Museum of Art—Electra headed in an opposite direction: the often simple, charming, but nonetheless artistic everyday artifacts made by early American craftsmen, artisans, and painters. The result of decades of intense collecting activity was the Shelbourne Museum, a village of treasures opened in southern Vermont, near Bennington, in 1952.

Though her schedule was seemingly full, and in her later years there were not only her five children, but several grandchildren, to round out her life, she had a great passion for hunting, both on horseback to the hounds and with rifle and shotgun. She and her husband, J. Watson Webb, Sr., enjoyed shooting expeditions far afield: quail, pheasant, and other game birds in the United States and Canada, grouse in Scotland, and bear and other big game in Alaska. The Webbs had a fifty-thousand-acre hunting camp in the Adirondack Mountains of New York called Nehasane.

Electra's pursuit of game was just as dogged as her hunt for American antiques and folk art. She was quoted as saying: "I'm afraid I'm a killer. I

like hunting. . . . I like big game trips and I like sport of all kinds." Her fighting spirit was tested on some of these hunts, as recalled by a friend: "Sometimes she waited until the animal was about ready to reach out and blow his breath on her before she would shoot. She found her guide running the other way while she was still waiting there to shoot."

At the relatively young age of seventy-two, Electra had a brain hemorrhage, and died shortly thereafter (1960). The Shelbourne Museum was her masterpiece, and her most extraordinary material legacy.

Women Conserving a Firearms Heritage
Mrs. Irene Roosevelt Aitken—Collector of Fine Guns

A member of the prestigious Visiting Committee of the Metropolitan Museum of Art's Arms and Armor Department, as well as that of the Department of European Sculpture and Decorative Arts, Irene Aitken not only has a finely tuned eye for fine arms and armor, but oversees the distinguished collection formed by her late husband, Russell Barnett Aitken. In recent years, she has refined and expanded the collection.

Her introduction to guns and shooting was a typical one. "John [Roosevelt, her first husband] gave me a 12-gauge shotgun to fire; it was my first gun, but the recoil was rather intimidating. That experience stifled any interest of mine in shooting. . . ." She nonetheless enjoyed attending shooting events, and notes that "his mother, Eleanor Roosevelt, loved to fire handguns, and was remarkably good at it."

Russell Aitken had studied art and was an artist himself, and was particularly interested in ceramics. He also loved French and English furniture, painting, and snuffboxes—and Irene Aitken shared all those enthusiasms, along with his love of shooting and the collecting of fine arms.

265

Harris's Angels is the name given to the executive women at Harris Publications, whose array of shooting periodicals is one of the broadest based in the firearms field. Owner Stanley Harris recognized that these women could more than hold their own in the so-called man's world of the firearms industry. The rapid growth of the outdoors group in Harris's magazine empire is in no small measure due to the grit and skills of the Harris's Angels team. Virginia Commander joined the group in the 1980s; her hunting and shooting experience rivals that of more than 99 percent of her peers in the world of firearms.

A champion shotgunner in the field or at competitions, Nina Rumbough was a member of the Ruger Sporting Clay's Professional Lady's Shooting Team, and for several years directed advertising and public relations for Holland & Holland, Ltd., New York. A regular gun in driven shoots in the United Kingdom, she and her husband, Jan Roosenburg, a retired vice president of H & H, New York, are on a shoot at *bottom right*.

Facing page: Two of the Harris's Angels team: Parker Gentry (*above* Model 70 Sporting Rifle by Damen Connolly of Australia) and, *below,* Shirley Steffen. A banker's daughter and southern belle, Gentry was understudy to Ginny Commander, became a stalwart on Ruger Sporting Clay's Professional Lady's Shooting Team, and has extensive hunting experience in the Western Hemisphere, Europe, the United Kingdom, and Africa. After living in the United Kingdom for several years, she returned to New York in 2000, and became an account executive with Emap Petersen Publications. Shirley Steffen joined Harris in the 1990s, and is presently executive publisher of the outdoor group. She, too, has a savvy and experience in shooting sports. Collection of gun industry patches from Al Cubeta.

MISS GUSSIE L. KENYON
Firing Position

MISS MILDRED HARKER, BALTIMORE, MD.
An Expert with Rifle, Revolver and Pistol

MISS ARLAYNE BROWN, ST. LOUIS, MO.
An Expert with Rifle, Revolver and Pistol

MRS. J. H. FITZGERALD
Firing Position

Irene Aitken, with her husband, Russell Barnett Aitken, at
Newport, Rhode Island. Clare Boothe Luce with wild turkeys and
side-by-side shotgun (likely a Purdey) at the Mepkin estate.
Beautifully hatted competitor Miss Lesle, of Guernsey, at Bisley
range, England, early twentieth century. Revolver shooters from
J. H. FitzGerald's *Shooting,* all recognized champion shots from
the 1920s to 1930s. Markswoman, *top center,* in India, firing
military-style rifle. Shotgunner from the 1930s in pigeon-shooting
ring.

Russ's first wife, Annie Laurie, was also a shooter. Before she met Russ, she had been on safari in Africa, and was quite an accomplished sportswoman. These pursuits were the great attraction between them. Russ had a special aptitude for teaching others, and he must have helped to add to her shotgunning skills.

I think of fine guns as works of art. That is why I was drawn to them so strongly. Russ began actively collecting in the 1950s, and was helped by early dealers, at a time when collecting was based on genuine interest, rather than as investments.

I really began looking at Russ's collection at the time of the Christie's/Metropolitan Museum of Art Arms & Armor Department charity auction of October 1985. That event offered the opportunity to meet a lot of the people with the Met and from the field of arms collecting. Not long after, when Russ became ill, we had to do a lot of renovation in our East Side apartment. At that time the entire collection was moved off the walls, and in the process I began to study these objects, and realized fully how incredible they are.

When Peter Hawkins came from Christie's London office to view the collection, Mrs. Aitken requested his help in cataloging them. The project required several visits, involving the inventory of pieces from the Aitken residences in Newport, Rhode Island, as well as on the East and West Sides of New York.

Detail from a tribute to Lord and Lady Mountbatten, by Holland & Holland, Ltd. Concept developed by Malcolm Lyell, for many years managing director.

269

Lower left, conservation staff and visiting antiquarians in the Department of Metalwork at the Victoria & Albert Museum, London, on the occasion of the study trip by the Arms and Armor Visiting Committee, Metropolitan Museum of Art (October 2001). Mughal saddle ax held by Simon Metcalf, senior metalwork conservator of the Metalwork Conservation Department, was recently treated in the laboratory. From *left,* Annie Hall, Joanna Whalley, Donna Stevens, Sophia Wills, visitors Anne Brockinton and Bernice Zwanger, Diana Heath (head of the conservation section), Vivian Lam (another visitor), and Metcalfe. *Top left,* Annie Hall, with Persian helmet. *Top right,* conservators at the Royal Armouries Museum, Leeds, with some of their current projects. From *left,* Alison Draper, Kate Stockwell, and Suzanne Kitto. *Bottom right,* in front of the Royal Armouries Museum; from left, Thom Richardson and Graeme Rimer of the Armouries, Stuart Pyhrr, Arthur Ochs and Allison Sulzberger, Donald LaRocca, and the author. Photographer: Dean Boorman, president of the Armor and Arms Club, and a participant in the tour.

Several women hold significant positions in various museums visited: the Royal Armouries Museum (Ann Green, board of directors), London's Wallace Collection (director Roslind Savill), the Tower of London (Bridget Clifford, assistant to curator Christopher Gravet), the British Museum (Dora Thornton, curatorial department of medieval and later European art).

The Sables Reflection

Official Publication for the Members of Safari Club International Foundation Sables

2001 Spring/Summer

A.W.L.S.
AMERICAN WILDERNESS LEADERSHIP

Membership Special!!
2 For the price of 1

FAMILY VALUES include
HUNTING
CONSERVATION
& SPORTSMANSHIP

Each gun was disassembled and every lock removed. The interiors were checked for numbers and other markings. We organized the provenance, and I then put all the files together. Harvey Murton and the late Bob Carroll—for many years armorers at the Metropolitan Museum of Art—also helped. The pieces were cleaned and, when appropriate, carefully restored. The mounting and displaying of objects was executed masterfully.

Mrs. Aitken continues to expand the collection.

I'm still acquiring pieces from time to time. The most recent—from the Rothschild Collection sale at Christie's in 1999—were a magnificent support for a regal matchlock, and a miniature sword made on order of Catherine the Great for her grandson.

Most of my friends know that when we're in a great city, at some point I'm going to wander off and see the arms and armor collections. Once we were at Windsor Castle, and with the curator of the Queen's collections. As soon as the tour was over my friends were off to do something, and I went to see the Armory.

Some of my friends say they can understand why I am fascinated with these arms; they are truly exquisite. Others will see the collection, and sort of say, ooh, firearms. That reaction I just ignore; failing to recognize beauty and elegance is rather ridiculous; I look at firearms the same way that I do at any work of art. I love to look at a masterpiece of French furniture, take it apart, look inside the drawers, and study all aspects. The same with a firearm. It is very important when you love a work of decorative art that you look at it completely, and examine it, and understand how it's put together, and what made it such a special object.

Russ had a lot of friends who were great shots, among them Carola Mandel, of Chicago and Palm Beach, Clare Boothe Luce, and Dorothy Hutton—widow of E. F. Hutton. Russ loved women that shot. I would have encouraged him to teach me; had his health stood up, we would have been on a lot of shooting trips. He loved those house party shoots. I don't think there's any place in Europe where Russ had not shot. He was also president of the Explorers Club; that was very much a shooting group; a lot of women were members there as well.

Guns were just the great, great love of his life, as they are of mine.[7]

Women in Hunting and Conservation

Following in the footsteps of the pioneering women who braved resistance from men and disapproval from other women to become hunters, today's women at arms are taking positions of leadership and advocacy to promote responsible hunting and conservation—as well as earning respect for their skills in the field.

The Sables—Women's Arm of Safari Club International

Safari Club International, founded by big game hunter and sportsman C. J. McElroy in 1972 and headquartered in Tucson, Arizona, boasts nearly fifty thousand members. Made up largely of individuals who can afford to hunt around the world, professional hunters are also a strong contingent of the membership, as are manufacturers of firearms and accessories, hunt outfitters, and professionals in the world of conservation and wildlife management. The organization's programs are targeted toward promoting the sport of hunting, and to encourage the best in sportsmanship and outdoor adventure. Over the years the organization has become one of the most effective advocates of the hunter's ethic.

Ranked high among the SCI's assets is the women's program, known as the Sables. Members commit time, money, and energy to the

American Wilderness Leadership School, to Hunters Against Hunger, to Becoming an Outdoorswoman, and to a number of other activities. One member, Janet D. Nyce, was raised in the suburbs and "always loved the outdoors, and was happy sleeping in the backyard in a tent or climbing trees." Her husband, Jim, was raised on a farm, and came from a family with a hunting and fishing tradition:

Upon marriage I discovered my husband's change of character as his face glowed with anticipation of the upcoming hunting season. I felt left out. Then my father told me, "You can sit home and pout, or you can get out there and see what this is all about." So I did. I had no experience with firearms. In those days [c. 1966] there weren't outdoor workshops and camps where you could learn. My first shooting instruction was short. Put this on your shoulder. Look down this ridge. Point it. Pull the trigger.

As my hunting life evolved, I moved from squirrels and birds to deer. One of my first deer seasons I harvested a doe. It wasn't the cleanest of shots and it changed my life forever. No one ever told me how responsible I would feel when the doe lifted its head and looked me in the eye. I vowed I would learn to shoot swift and clean before I harvested another animal. I took shooting lessons, read books, and asked many questions about the hunter's role.

Before long, Nyce had joined several pro-hunting groups and was assisting her husband, an officer of an SCI chapter. She became the first female SCI chapter president, in Pennsylvania, and the first woman to hold such SCI positions as regional representative and director at large. Among other duties she chairs the SCI Foundation Education Committee, and is the Sables' treasurer.

I found that one of the ways I can encourage more people to start their own personal safaris in the outdoors is to teach. Jim and I spent countless hours in the forest with our young family, teaching our children about the wonders of nature. Now, I'm proud to say our children are nurturing a love for the outdoors in their children. It's a family tradition to be

Facing page: Reflecting the energetic and broad-based activities of the Sables, participants are generally widely experienced huntresses, in addition to their charity efforts advocating programs oriented toward women. Governing board at *right*, beneath heading for *The Sables Reflection*, for 2000 (*bottom*) and 2001 (*top*). President Barbara Strawberry at *right*, with roe deer, beneath invitation to Third Annual Sables Rep Appreciation Tea. Former president Mary K. Parker at *left*, bottle-feeding elk calf. Yet another former president, Janet D. Nyce, at *left center*, with husband, Jim, and his white wolf, taken in Yellowknife, Northwest Territory.

Poster star since the late 1980s for Sturm, Ruger & Co., Kelly Glenn-Kimbro has appeared in dozens of company advertisements. Western photographer Jay Dusard took test pictures that launched the series. Selection from more than thirty-five images comprising the complete collection; new issues appear at least on an annual basis. Her appearances at trade shows, such as for SHOT and the NRA, attract innumerable admirers, who are rewarded with hunting insights and signed posters.

Kelly Glenn-Kimbro shown
with the new Ruger PC-9
9x19mm Carbine.

RUGER®

ARMS MAKERS FOR RESPONSIBLE CITIZENS

RUGER

GOLD LABEL
SIDE-BY-SIDE SHOTGUN

273

Educational programs of the National Shooting Sports Foundation, under direction of Doug Painter, have broadened the base of firearms and shooting interests since the group's pioneering work in the 1960s and 1970s. From the beginning, women have played a vital role in developing and administering programs. In addition to a selection of its educational publications and videos, at *lower right,* is the "About Country Sports" monograph, prepared by the Countryside Foundation, primarily for distribution to schools in the United Kingdom.

accomplished, ethical, and respectful hunters. While our five grandchildren don't yet completely understand what it means to be good stewards of wildlife for their generation, they are coming along and through them others will learn to appreciate the rich hunting heritage enjoyed by millions of sporting enthusiasts.

Several years ago, I started attending a camp for women called "Becoming an Outdoorswoman." About 25,000 women a year now attend these workshops nationwide, in which I regularly serve as a camp instructor. As a member of the National BOW Advisory Board, a mother, a grandmother, and a huntress, I'm passionate about teaching women and youth.

My personal safari is a journey that has taken me to the Pennsylvania and U.S. legislatures. I have come to know some very fine men and women who work tirelessly to help safeguard our outdoor heritage through politics. I've also met some dedicated men and women who disagree with our hunting tradition.

No one ever told me how hunting would change my life. My next goal is to help set the standards to preserve access to the outdoors in my own state of Pennsylvania, either as a game commissioner or legislator.[8]

Kelly Glenn-Kimbro, Mountain Lion Hunting Guide and Ruger Poster Star

In 1988 Sturm, Ruger & Company vice president Tom Ruger was searching for a model who knew how to use a gun, for a series of company posters. Tom Pew, of Ruger's advertising agency, Merlin, Inc., recommended Kelly Glenn, a professional mountain lion hunter from Arizona. She has been the Ruger poster star ever since.

Born in 1961 to a family of cattle ranchers on the Mexican border, she is the fifth generation of settlers who came from Texas in 1896. During years when ranching was unprofitable, they sustained themselves as professional hunting guides for mountain lion, desert mule deer, Coues deer, and javelina. Glenn recalls:

My grandpa, Marvin Glenn, started hunting mountain lions in the 1940s, to protect his stock. He

275

One of the most exquisite shotguns ever made, Betty Lou Sheerin's 28-gauge over-and-under by James Purdey & Sons, London. Gold inlaying, engraving, and damascening by master engraver K. C. Hunt. Motifs of Western scenes, foliage, flowers, and brands embellish the receiver, top lever, triggerguard, fore end, as well as the muzzle and the barrel breech. Note stylish inlay of name on bottom of stock (page 173). Serial number 28059, with 27-inch barrels, 2¾-inch chambers, and single trigger.

Right: Colt Model 1862 Police presentation to Carolyn Carter, now president, Grey Advertising, U.K., Europe, Africa, and the Middle East. She has admired firearms for their artistry and craftsmanship since her introduction to the subject by her husband, enthusiast Dr. Jeffrey Starr.

turned it into a guiding profession and in 1944, my dad, Warner, at the age of eight, started helping with the guide business.

In the late '60s and the '70s, my brother Cody and I helped my Grandma Margaret and my mom, Wendy, with the ranching and hunting chores. Occasionally we would go hunting, school permitting. But, there were dog pens to be cleaned, dogs and mules to be watered and fed, lunches to be made for the next day's hunt, and camps in need of cooked meals.

As Glenn and her brother grew older, they became more active in the business, and her "love for the lifestyle grew." Following graduation from high school she "jumped into the ranch and hunting life with both feet." Completing

college studies in 1984, she became a full-time professional guide and rancher.

I had become a part of a team. I was being taught by who many considered the best in the sport of hunting mountain lions on dry ground. We rarely had snow so the men (and myself) and the hounds hunted these elusive creatures by trailing them through country that ranged from oak grasslands and gentle rolling hills, to rim rocks and cliffs, to pine-top mountains, and desert country filled with cactus and brush.

We hunted in extremes ranging from one-hundred-degree heat to days that never reached over forty degrees. Some mornings it would be zero degrees when we rode out. We hunted through rain and high winds, dust storms and scorching heat. But because of our location geographically, we saw many perfect days . . . cool to mild, no wind, moisture in the

ground from recent rains making trailing better, and sunshine.

Our mountain lion hunts have always been carried out on horse- or muleback (mostly mule).

For the hounds, known as Walkers, Glenn holds a special affection and respect. The dogs were trained

primarily to trail mountain lion, and to leave alone the occasional bear, coatimundi, Coues deer, or javelina. My dad and Grandpa Marvin bred them to have a lighter body weight and smaller feet than many of their ancestors. There were usually enough trained hounds so that they could be split into packs of four to six each; one pack could hunt a day and then rest two or three days while other packs were hunting.

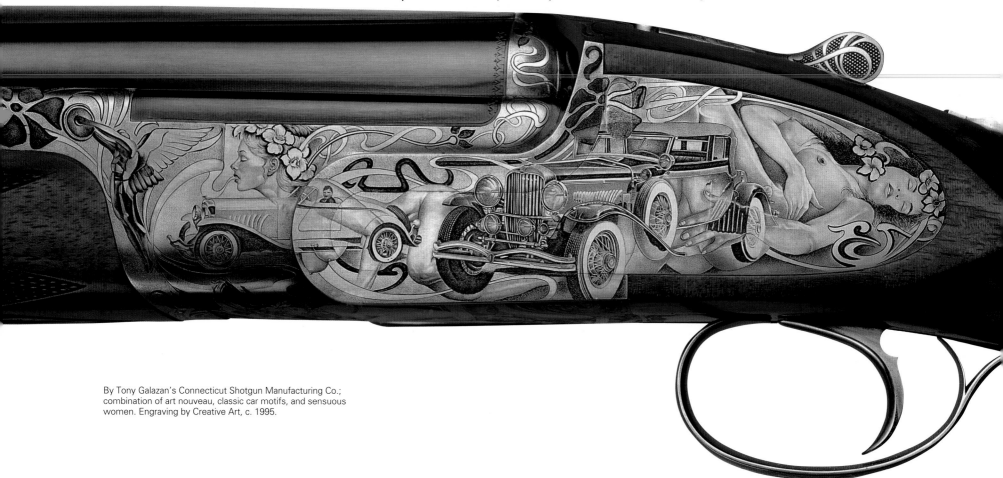

By Tony Galazan's Connecticut Shotgun Manufacturing Co.; combination of art nouveau, classic car motifs, and sensuous women. Engraving by Creative Art, c. 1995.

Seven-year-old Diane Wildenstein (*top left*) proudly holds her Chipmunk .22 rimfire rifle, and trophy for the pot, taken in Kenya, at the family ranch, Ol Jogi. *Right center,* documentary filmmaker Riva Freifeld discussing her Annie Oakley project with Kevin James (*top*), Tweed Roosevelt, the author, and Richard Isaacs, at book launch party. At *bottom right,* former Tiffany & Co. archivist Janet Zapata chats with her coauthor of *The Arms of Tiffany & Co.,* a

work in progress. To *left,* Tiffany chairman William R. Chaney, with his wife, Carolyn, and author at launch of *Steel Canvas.* To their left, gun engraver K. C. Hunt, with his wife, Sheila, and children Allison and Marcus—both now engravers in the British firearms trade. *Lower left,* Leslie Citreon, on safari in Botswana, 1987, with professional hunter Gux Merkides. *Lower right,* Ellen Enzler-Herring at signing of *Theodore Roosevelt: Outdoorsman,*

published by Trophy Room Books. *Center right,* Nancy Goldberg and Kevin James, on the occasion of firing Theodore Roosevelt's .500/.450 H & H elephant rifle. *Top right,* author's agent, Peter Riva, with wife (and archery and shotgun shooter), Sandra. *Center left,* author's mentor at Royal Armouries, William Reid, and elegant arms-and-armor-savvy wife, Nina.

I hereby certify that Inger Illum, known as " the goosegirl " shot two full-grown - tigers on the evening of 24th April 1934, in - the East Kalibhit Range of Nimar Forest - Division, Central Provinces, India. She - was waiting for the tigers alone in the jungle, over a buffalo killed by them. Both the tigers were dead on the spot.

S. A. Vahid

Khandwa, C. P.   Divisional Forest Officer,
6th May 1934.   Nimar Division.

Glenn learned to find lion tracks on dry ground, how to identify the age of the track, the sex of the animal, measure its stride, and help the hounds as they dealt with the rough conditions. She was taught to "decipher the baying of the hounds, from cold trailing, to pursuit, to barking treed."

When, in 1991, her grandfather died, it was a devastating blow:

We had lost our leader, our friend, our mentor. His hounds and his mules knew he was gone. He had been a legend. His smile was etched in our minds and we never broke stride, we moved ahead with the ranching and hunting.

It is now 2001. My dad is sixty-five years old, I am forty. We still guide a couple of deer hunts in the fall, and then we start lion hunting, guiding booked hunts, December through April. Throughout the years, the mountain lion population has increased in many areas of the United States, including our desert southwest. This has brought an increase in the number of stock killers. Ranchers from all over southeast Arizona and southwest New Mexico call us year-round to respond to calf, sheep, or colt kills. We respond immediately and try to catch the particular lion that killed the livestock.

So, between the booked hunts and the livestock-killing lions, Dad and I hunt about three-quarters of the year. Any day that we are not hunting, we are cattle ranching.

I shoot several Model 77 Ruger rifles, and for handguns I carry a Ruger GP100 .357 Magnum or a SP101 in .357 Magnum.

The driving force behind the scenes is Glenn's mother. It is she who books the hunts, looks after the accounting, the cooking, and general details. Further, she feeds the animals, and runs the ranch while Glenn, her father, and her brother are afield. Glenn's mother is also the caregiver for her ten-year-old daughter, Mackenzie, "the light of my life": "She has learned to ride, and speak Spanish. She loves animals and the ranch, and has been on a short lion hunt and loved it. I hope to convey my love of ranching, hunting, and nature to her and have no doubt she will love it as much."

Guns as Storytellers

Carolyn Carter Starr's interest in arms was sparked by stories of the American West. That interest "grew as I discovered the real allure of guns—that they don't just tell stories of events, but unique stories of individuals."

Those that are great storytellers are uniquely personal. That's what makes the special engraving so fascinating. Some people believe the unique charisma of the owner is somehow passed into these fabulous firearms. I certainly felt that when I fired Theodore Roosevelt's Holland & Holland elephant rifle.

Most of the women I know who have personal guns are uniquely charismatic. In many cases, their guns are an expression of themselves—of their personal style and independent spirit.

"Silk and steel" captures the paradox of seduction and strength that's true both of great guns and great ladies.[9]

A Professional Hunter in Africa—Natasha Illum Berg

Natasha Benedikte Illum Berg is a rarity in Africa. For the last eight of her thirty-one years she has been one of only a handful of female professional hunting guides. Her ancestors are Danish and Swedish, and her grandmother was the accomplished huntress and outdoorswoman Inger Illum Berg.[10]

Born in Sweden, Natasha Illum Berg frequently visited the family's hunting estate, Eriksberg, in Blekinge, along the coast deep in the south. Blanketed with forests and populated with red deer, sika deer, roe deer, fallow deer, vicent (European bison), wild boar, mufflon sheep, and a wide variety of ducks and geese, the country fostered her love of nature and hunting.

I am a professional hunter and an author, currently hunting in Tanzania and writing my second book, a novel set between Europe and Africa.

Animals and their behaviour, conservation, and hunting were part of my life since I was born. (So much that when I, aged four, heard a male opera singer for the first time, I asked my mother whether he was rutting.)

At eighteen, having completed high school, Illum Berg made her first trip to South Africa. After a year, however, she was called home: "Do what you want, but get an education first," she was told. After four years studying forestry, she took advantage of an opportunity to work for a hunting company in Tanzania as an apprentice professional hunter.

I had never been to East Africa before. I invited my darling mother for lunch at our favourite restaurant in Copenhagen and told her, "Mother, I am moving to Africa and I will probably never move back to Scandinavia again." I don't recall her as being surprised in any way. Being my mother, she had probably known long before I, that my nature was not that of comfort and security, but was craving for adventure, big challenges, and raw beauty.

She was surprised with the reaction to her new career, especially from women, who couldn't understand her desire to live the hunter's life—and did not hesitate to tell her so.

Many despised me (some still do). I don't think that it is so much because they hate hunting, many of their husbands love hunting, [but] more because I am a woman who hunts. . . . Almost as if they regard men to be from a different world, and therefore accept their strange customs as a matter of course, but can't accept it in someone of their own tribe.

There is also a bit of chauvinism lurking in the

Facing page: Inger Illum and her two trophy tigers, taken in the Indian jungle. She also pursued dangerous game in Africa. Granddaughter Natasha Illum Berg is one of a handful of women professional hunters in Africa. Cape buffalo taken by her in full charge. An accomplished writer, her memoirs—based on several years in the bush—have been published in Danish; other language editions are to follow.

African bush, but I don't see much of a future for this defenseless animal.

I grew up believing that hunting is conservation if done the right way. I know that it is.

Illum Berg's view that some who call themselves hunters are in fact "killers" is disturbing: "Those are people who have never heard of hunting ethics, have no respect for the game or the very delicate patterns of ecological balance." She voices the concern that the distinction between hunters and killers needs to be made to the public, for the sake of the future of the sport.

It is true that all the killing humans do of animals, except for those few hungry peoples left who have no other choice, is for pleasure. I laugh when I listen to Westerners who are against hunting if they eat meat of any kind. The pleasure of filling their spoilt stomachs with the pink limbs of a suckling pig, or the pleasure of hunting a buffalo is morally the same when it comes to the justification of taking the life of an animal. We all know that eating pigs is nothing that anybody needs to survive, more than I need to hunt a buffalo to survive.

The difference, however, is that I try to create a better life for the buffalos in general, by shooting one of them, where they try to create a miserable life for pigs in general, by eating one of them.

Wildlife conservation in Africa—or anywhere—is about land and people, not about animals, she says.

Conservationists and nature lovers in general should focus on getting rid of killers who pretend to be hunters; they would be silly to try to get rid of hunters. Discarding the hunter is throwing a fine-tuned instrument out the window, just because you don't know how to use it.[11]

"Women Make Exceptionally Good Hunters and Usually Shoot Better Than Men"—Robin Hurt, Safari Hunter

Robin Hurt is internationally recognized as the hunter's hunter, today's successor to the line of British professionals with lineage back to Philip Percival himself. Hurt had taken the "big five" (elephant, rhinoceros, lion, leopard, and Cape buffalo) of Africa by his thirteenth birthday, and has been a professional guide for over thirty-nine years. He holds a deep respect for women who hunt:

I have always said that women make exceptionally good hunters and usually shoot better than men. The reason for this is straightforward. Hunting is perceived to be a man's sport, and therefore women who take up hunting and shooting wish to excel. Often, women start this activity later in life than most men. Women listen more carefully to instructions. They are willing to learn. They do not have bad habits that they are unwilling to change. In short, women are much easier to instruct in hunting and shooting than men are, resulting in excellence. A lot of men think they know it all, and hate to be instructed!

Some of the most outstanding women shots I have had the pleasure of hunting with on safari include Mrs. Olive Kleberg, Mrs. Janelle Kleberg, the Alexander sisters Helen and Emory, all brilliant shots and all from the King Ranch, Texas. Mrs. Lynn Foster, Mrs. Mollie van Devender, Mrs. Katrin Henkel, are all experienced safari hunters and superb rifle shots. My daughter Hilary can shoot a rifle as well as any man and her success comes from a childhood where she used to hunt for doves and pigeons with an open-sighted .177 caliber air rifle. Hilary was deadly with this air rifle and we enjoyed many a good pigeon pie.

But the best shot of all was a young Canadian girl, Catherine Eaton. On Catherine's first safari, she collected fourteen big game animals including leopard and lion, with a total of fifteen shots. I have never seen anyone shoot so well, male or female, in nearly forty years of safari hunting. I believe Catherine's record is a unique achievement. Her trigger control was perfect. She learned how to squeeze a trigger, the most important element of rifle shooting. She had never shot a single animal prior to coming on safari![12]

Fashion and Film

For decades, film stars have been drawn to hunting and shooting, some from a need to learn as part of an upcoming role, others through association with avid hunters and sportsmen. Many learned their skills from other celebrities like author Ernest Hemingway.

Today's young female actors are no exception. An article in *Style* magazine, February 2001,[13] entitled "Shooting *de Rigueur* Among the Stars" shows that the sport has not lost its glamorous appeal. The magazine's hip readers were told "why all the shooting stars are wild about Scotland": "Once the domain of the tweedy country buffer, shooting is now *de rigueur* among the stars. Models Naomi Campbell, Ines Sastre, and Elle Macpherson have been seen in moleskin trousers, while Madonna has had lessons on how to hit a flying target—lock, stock and two smoking barrels."

The most popular spot was Drynachan Lodge, "set within 30,000 acres of moorland [in the Drynachan valley]," by the river Findhorn, near Inverness, Scotland, on the "historic Cawdor Estate" with "60 miles of tracks, picnic huts etched with 19th-century drawings, and a secluded lodge dating back to 1828." Among the guests

who have rolled in its heather include Posh and Becks, Bryan Ferry, Richard Branson, David Linley, Philip Treacy, and Isabella Blow. It has also hosted the other kind of shoot for photographers Ellen von Unwerth, Mario Testino, and Patrick Demarchelier, and models Stella Tennant, Amber Valetta, and Kirsty Hume. Staff ensure that guests don't lift a finger except to pull a trigger, and a top chef cooks your meals from local organic ingredients, such as partridge, duck, grouse, crab, langoustine, and wild mushrooms and berries. . . .

"Gun-Toting Madonna Has Taste for Hunting"—New York Post, November 24, 2001

The British press carried several articles about actress and pop singer Madonna, her film-director husband, Guy Ritchie, a British gentleman and outdoorsman, and the shooting party held on the occasion of their marriage in Scotland, in December 2000. Madonna's love for English country sports became widely known among British shooters, not a few of whom were already familiar with the keen interest of Ritchie. One of his films, *Lock, Stock and Two Smoking Barrels,* employed an expensive pair of fine British shotguns within the plot line. Further, he has stated that when growing up, his ambition was to be either an officer in the British Army (like his Victoria Cross–winning grandfather) or a gamekeeper. It was Ritchie who introduced Madonna to bird shooting.

An article in the New York *Post* confirmed that Mrs. Ritchie was indeed a countryside convert:

> Madonna isn't crying fowl when it comes to shooting wildlife for sport and food.
> The superstar songbird revealed yesterday she has developed a hearty appetite for traditional English blood sports, especially pheasant shooting.
> She says she and her British film director-husband, Guy Ritchie, often stage shoots on the grounds of their sprawling English country estate, Ashcombe House.
> "I wear leather shoes, I eat fish, I eat chicken and I eat game. I like knowing what I'm eating, and knowing the process," she added.[14]

This piece—and several others in magazines, newspapers, and on television—was based on an interview with the forty-three-year-old star, broadcast on BBC Radio One.[15]

Women at Arms for the Future

Pressure from activists against guns and shooting has been instrumental in a banding together of gunmakers, retailers, shooters, and collectors to promote shooting sports, as well as to advocate safety and responsibility. Companies like Ruger, whose motto is "gunmakers for respon-

sible citizens," actively promote educational programs for gun owners. Every new gun sold is accompanied by safety information. Product catalogs tout careful handling of guns. Every single hunting/conservation group in America—all thirty-five of them at this writing—offer programs addressed to women.

On August 7–10, 2000, a summit meeting of these groups was held, under auspices of the Boone & Crockett Club. Those attending were Bear Trust International, the Camp Fire Club of America (and its Conservation Fund), Conservation Force, the Dallas Safari Club, Ducks Unlimited, the Foundation for North American Wild Sheep, the International Association of Fish & Wildlife Agencies, the International Hunter Education Association, the Izaak Walton League, the National Rifle Association, the National Shooting Sports Foundation, the National Trappers Association, the National Wild Turkey Federation, Orion—the Hunter's Institute, Pheasants Forever, Inc., Pope and Young Club, Quail Unlimited, Inc., the Rocky Mountain Elk Foundation, Safari Club International, the Shikar Safari Club, the Texas Wildlife Association, the Theodore Roosevelt Conservation Alliance, the Conservation Fund, the Mule Deer Foundation, the Ruffed Grouse Society, the Wildlife Society, Wildlife Forever, the Wildlife Habitat Council, the Wildlife Legislative Fund of America, and the Wildlife Management Institute.

The meeting was held to develop unity and a vision for wildlife for the future, and to recommend a wildlife conservation agenda for the Bush administration. Collectively, these groups represent a constituency of more than 5.3 million individuals.

Considering the concern of the majority of the female population for public health and welfare, for safety—particularly of children, for reduction in crime, for better communities and a sta-

ble, protected environment, matters such as the availability of firearms are of particular consequence.

Simply put, the future of the magical world of firearms rests in the hands and hearts of women—particularly those in the United States. As men become more sensitive and understanding, and much more willing to share their love of firearms and shooting, the participation by women and girls will continue to escalate. At the same time, the firearms industry does not need to push gun sales to women. The impetus comes largely from the women themselves, and thus it is they who are coming to the business as potentially enthusiastic participants. More than any other constituency, and for several reasons, the future of firearms in America is in the hands of women.

Women as shooters, collectors, gunmakers, or simply arms enthusiasts are realizing that this is the best period in history to have an interest in firearms and the shooting sports. More programs are available, as are more coaches keen to demonstrate the hows and the whys, and there are more opportunities to shoot and to hunt. At the same time, the gun itself stands at its technological peak.

Will the ratio of men to women in the world of firearms ever become even? That remains unlikely. But the fact that the dynamic has changed, is changing, and will continue to change is a certainty.

At *center,* Jamie Zagrodnik—with Ruger bolt-action Express rifle in .416 Rigby, and Winchester 101 with custom stocks—and faithful pet dachshund, Stanley. She is flanked by Mimi Towbis, armed with a Colt Combat Commander and Desert Eagle in .44 Magnum. The latter pictures were taken for posting in her City Fitness boutique in San Francisco, to convince clients to shut off their cell phones before entering. Photographer John Adrain specializes in wildlife and portraits of striking women.

APPENDIX A

Female Gunmakers from the London Gun Trade, 1851

From Appendix IX of Blackmore's *London Gunmakers, 1350–1850*, the following intriguing listing:

Age Groups of London Gunmakers, 1851

Age	Gunsmiths Male	Engaged in Gunmaking	
		Male	Female
10	9	2	1
15	166	5	4
20	195	8	5
25	191	4	5
30	142	5	5
35	111	6	7
40	89	5	3
45	58	2	9
50	87	5	7
55	71	3	1
60	38	4	5
65	31	-	1
70	24	4	2
75	9	2	-
80	2	1	-
	1,223	56	55

APPENDIX B

Starting to Shoot, and What to Wear:
An Article by Annie Oakley

Why Ladies Should Learn to Shoot

There are many reasons why Ladies should go in for both Trap and Field shooting. After thirty-one years of nearly continuous shooting, I can truthfully say I know of no other recreation that will do so much towards keeping a woman in good health and perfect figure than a few hours spent occasionally at trap shooting and as I am learning new stunts nearly every week, I am quite sure that providing a woman has fairly good health and eyesight, she is never too old to learn.

Either shooting clay targets or game in the field, there is just enough exercise to do good, not to say anything about the fresh air you breathe.

Many ladies are afraid to start shooting on account of the gun kicking. If the gun is heavy enough, not overloaded and fits you properly, you will find little if any recoil. I would, however, suggest using a rubber recoil pad, fitted to the end of the stock. I heard a gentleman say a short time since that he was going to buy his wife a twenty bore and start her at the traps. He wouldn't think of using such a light gun himself and he couldn't have given her a worse handicap to begin with, for while a twenty bore is a pleasure to use on game in the field, a twelve gauge, full choke (not less than 7¼) is what is needed for trap shooting.

At first you should have some of your gentleman friends who know how it should be done give you some instructions. If you do not care to go to some gun club, have him buy a hand trap and throw the targets easy until you learn to break some and gain confidence. As to dress, something loose so that your every movement will be free; your shoes should have a low, flat heel, so as not to throw you forward. The hat should be wide enough to shade the eyes and fit snugly, but comfortably on the head. All your clothing while at the trap should feel part of yourself.

When you are going after a target, concentration means everything.

After the first few weeks you will find yourself looking forward to your afternoon at the gun club, where judging from my personal experience I can safely say you will be a Welcome Guest.

Cambridge, Md.   ANNIE OAKLEY.

APPENDIX C

Women in British Munitions Plants, World War I

During the employment of women in the munitions industry in World War I, the British Government was concerned with their welfare. A special ten-page report was drawn up to consider the matter, printed by His Majesty's Stationery Office, by Harrison and Sons, London. It was entitled:

Ministry of Munitions.
Health of Munition Workers Committee.
Memorandum No. 4.
EMPLOYMENT OF WOMEN
Presented to both Houses of Parliament by
Command of His Majesty
1916

The memorandum concluded with:

25. Finally, the Committee desire to state that, in their opinion, if the present long hours, the lack of helpful and sympathetic oversight, the inability to obtain good, wholesome food, and the great difficulties of traveling are allowed to continue, it will be impracticable to secure or maintain for an extended period the high maximum output of which women are undoubtedly capable. The Committee recognize that emergency conditions must obtain in many cases, but they are satisfied that every effort should be made to organize women's labour effectively and promptly. It may be that in the entanglement of problems new and old, the coming of the new and their imperative claim for solution will help the solving of the old. There is impulse now as there was impulse long ago when the cause of the children in the cotton mills of Lancashire won the early Factory Acts for the generations that followed. There is need now as there was need then. There is need for the work of women in industry; there is need also for safeguarding that service. Happily there is manifest a public spirit and a devotion able to overcome difficulties and solve problems. There is a also a fuller recognition of the claims of women and of their children and of their vital importance to the State, which is reward for the sacrifice and courage of those women now working steadfastly in the ranks of labour.

APPENDIX D

Women's Participation in the Shooting Sports

The National Shooting Sports Foundation has commissioned surveys on female shooting and hunting participation since 1989. The results of the study covering the years 2000 and 2001, augmented by data from the National Sporting Goods Association (NSGA) and the Sporting Goods Manufacturers Association (SGMA),* includes the following:

2000

According to the SGMA, sports participation by females (age six and older) included:

Camping: 22.9 million (46.9 percent of total number of campers)

Fishing (freshwater): 14.3 million (32.4 percent of total number fisherman)

Target shooting: 3.4 million (22.7 percent of total number shooters)

Hunting with firearms: 2.5 million (13.0 percent female)

Archery (target): .8 million (17.6 percent female)

Hunting with bow and arrow: .3 million (6.1 percent female)

Muzzleloading: .2 million (6.1 percent female)

* The 2002 Entertainment, Sports and Leisure Market Research Handbook

2001

From *Superstudy of Sports participation*, volume III:

Shooting—Sporting Clays

485,000 female participants

Average age: 26.4 years

Average annual income: $56,600 (male and female)

Shooting—Trap and Skeet

579,000 female participants

Average age: 30.3 years

Average annual income: $58,900 (male and female)

Shotgun Shooters (all types)

867,000 female participants

Average age: 28.4 years

Average annual income: $58,400 (male and female)

Target Shooting (with rifle)

2,808,000 female participants

Average age: 28.5 years

Average annual income: $56,300 (male and female)

Target Shooting (with pistol)

2,553,000 female participants

Average age: 32.7 years

Average annual income: $58,100 (male and female)

Target Shooting (all types)

4,039,000 female participants

Average age: 30.7 years

Average annual income: $56,800 (male and female)

Shooting (all types)

4,352,000 female participants

Ages 6–11: 397,000

Ages 12–17: 568,000

Ages 18–24: 893,000

Ages 25–34: 879,000

Ages 35–44: 669,000

Ages 45–54: 673,000

Ages 55–64: 134,000

Ages 65+: 140,000

Average age 30.7 years

Average annual income: $57,200 (male and female)

Participants of women per 100 people: 7.8

APPENDIX E

Statistics of Firearms and Shooting

Firearms in Japan—and the Numbers of Female Owners, December 1999

According to the Department of Firearms Control of the National Police of Japan, the total number of legal firearms owners in Japan as of December 1999 was as follows: 221,282, of which number 3,908 were female (1.77 percent of all gun owners). Each owner may have one or more firearms. The number was broken down further:

Shotgun only:	164,257
Shotgun and rifle:	23,299
Shotgun, rifle and airgun:	2,964
Shotgun and air rifle:	14,334
Rifle:	2,133
Rifle and air rifle:	1,679
Air rifle:	12,616

The total of shotgun owners, from the above groupings, comes to 204,854, the total of rifle owners to 30,075, and that of air rifles to 31,593.

Although the number of female gun owners in Japan is quite limited, the number of firearms and the total of those who own them are surprising figures. It is likely that in time, as is happening in the United States, the percentage of women gun owners in Japan will increase. That prospect will have a lot to do, however, with the advancements of women in that culture, in terms of independence and self-reliance.

APPENDIX F

Oh! How Those Women Could Shoot

Published for many years in Baltimore, Maryland, *The American Shooter* was directed primarily at the world of trap. The column "Oh! How Those Women Could Shoot" was intended to encourage women's participation in the sport, and was written by Harriet D. Hammond. In the issue of January 15, 1916, she recommended trapshooting as "The Ideal Sport for Women":

The sport of trapshooting, by reason of its fascinations and wonderful health benefits, is fast becoming one of the most popular sports among the outdoor sport-loving women of the country. It is not nearly so strenuous as golf and tennis, and the improvement in the manufacture of ammunition and guns has been so truly wonderful in the last few years that there is no longer need for any fear or dread of the shotgun. The so-called "kick" is a thing of the past, and it is now possible for the most refined and sensitive woman or girl to learn to shoot without the slightest injury or shock to her nervous system.

Trapshooting, which combines sport with fresh air and sunshine, has brought the roses to the cheeks of many pale, delicate women. It stirs up the circulation, strengthens the nerves, quickens the eye and brings all the muscles into play; in fact, an afternoon at the traps is the next best thing to an osteopathic or massage treatment, it is so wonderfully invigorating and refreshing. Women physicians and trained nurses are most enthusiastic over the sport and strongly endorse it as a most healthful sport for women.

Of course, the well-fitting gun plays an important part in the sport of trapshooting, and when a beginner is taken out for her first try at the flying clays, care should be taken that she does not attempt to use a gun that is too long in the stock for her. The stock of her gun should be short enough to fit comfortably and easily against her chest, and not out on her arm, where the slightest bit of recoil will bruise the soft muscular tissues and cause a black and blue spot that is not at all dangerous, but looks very formidable to the novice.

Until the muscles of her arms become accustomed to the weight of her gun, it would be well for the beginner to start with a small-bore shotgun, preferably a 20 gauge. A well-balanced little gun of this bore will shoot just as easily as the standard 12 gauge trap gun, and will be much easier for the beginner to handle. In a few months' time she will have become so accustomed to the weight of this little gun that it will seem like a toy to her and she will ask to be promoted to the larger bore gun used by her more experienced sisters.

Every novice should have individual instruction. Give her all the time she wants and make sure that she assumes a correct position and knows her gun perfectly before you allow her to shoot. This may seem to take up a lot of time at first, but it will pay in the long run, and the first rules of trapshooting correctly learned will follow the shooter all through her trapshooting career and she always will be master of herself and of her gun no matter what kind of a tournament she may take part in. She won't hold the men back and make them wish she was anywhere but in their squad, for when they find out that she always lives up to rules and can shoot just as fast as they can, they will not only be glad, but proud to have her line up with them at the traps.

Women are no longer content to stay in the house every afternoon and sew or crochet. The spirit of sport has gotten into their blood, and they want to get out and drink in the fresh air and sunshine and do something to develop their muscles and make them stronger mentally and physically. And there is no better sport in the world for just this sort of development than trapshooting.

Nancy Floyd—*Stopping Power,* a Work in Progress

Launched in 1993, *Stopping Power* is an ongoing project in text and photographs, examining the evolution of female firearms owners in America. The study examines the many reasons women choose to arm themselves, and "how their controversial choice alters current gun debates."

Further quoting from Floyd's project description:

> The idea still persists in society that men will protect women when they are in danger. However, facts contradict this assumption. All too often when a woman is attacked in a parking lot or beaten up by her spouse, no one rushes to her rescue. Although women use various methods for dealing with violence, the most controversial choice they can make is to arm themselves. *Stopping Power* documents the social, political and historical implications of female gun ownership.
>
> The project consists of three components which are addressed concurrently:
>
> Documentation of individual women gun owners . . . a series of photographs and interviews . . . along with a portrait of each person is a statement describing, in her own words, why she owns a gun and how she feels about it. . . .
>
> Examination of contemporary social and political aspects . . . staged and documentary photographs illustrate women's changing attitudes towards gun ownership, including both positive and negative aspects . . . sports shooting and personal defense classes . . .
>
> Analysis of the history of women gun owners . . . examining how women have been historically represented by the media, by the gun industry and by various gun groups . . . interviews with prominent people in the gun world, including anti-gun advocates, as well as research on women gun owners from the mid-1800s to the present . . . [plus] researching various photographic archives for photographs of women with guns.
>
> I am not interested in making a statement about whether gun ownership is right or wrong. Rather, I am interested in the social and cultural implications of a society where women appear to be arming themselves in record numbers. I'm also interested in the evolution of women gun owners in America; how these women represent themselves and how they are represented by others. By looking at women gun owners from the past, as well as by interviewing contemporary gun owners, *Stopping Power* becomes a relevant, critical study of the women who choose to enter the gun debate.

NOTES

Chapter 1: Aristocratic Shooters and Collectors
from Queen Elizabeth I to Queen Elizabeth II

1. Barbara Ehrenreich, "She Got Game," *Ms.,*
   June–July 1999.
2. *Ibid.*
3. Work in progress on deer hunting.
4. Taken from Charles Alexandre Francois
   Felix, Comte d'Hezeques, and Baron de
   Mailly's account of court life prior to the
   Revolution, "Recollections of a Page," p.
   389.
5. John F. Hayward, *The Art of the
   Gunmaker,* volume I.
6. Heribert Seitz, "Prinsessa Pa Jakt," volume
   XIII, no. 6, 1974.
7. Possibly from N. Kutepov, *The Royal Hunt
   in Russia,* published 1902 and 1911.
8. "Pair of Ivory-Stocked Flintlock Pistols of
   Empress Catherine the Great." *Recent
   Acquisitions: A Selection, 1986–1987,*
   Metropolitan Museum of Art, 1987.
9. *Memoirs of the Duke of Saint-Simon on
   the Reign of Louis XIV and the Regency,*
   volume 3.
10. D. Hart-Davis, *Monarchs of the Glen,*
    1978; further quotations also from that
    source.
11. *The Big Shots;* further quotations also from
    that source.
12. "Sabretache," written under a pseudonym,
    1948.

Chapter 2: Women at War

1. The World Wide Web has a growing
   number of sites that recognize the role of
   women in warfare through the ages. One
   of the best of these is the Lothene
   Archaeology Group's "Women as
   Warriors" pages (compiled by Nicky
   Saunders of Edinburgh, Scotland)
   (www.lothene.demon.co.uk/
   others/women.html); others include
   (reachable through links on the Lothene
   site): www.gendergap
   .com/military/Warriors.htm,
   www.undelete.org/
   military.html, http://userpages.aug.com/
   captbarb/.
2. Donna M. Lucey, *I Dwell in Possibility:
   Women Build a Nation, 1600–1920,* p. 26.
3. *Ibid.,* p. 28.
4. *Ibid.,* p. 72.
5. *Ibid.,* p. 73.
6. *Ibid.,* p. 73.
7. *Ibid.,* p. 61.
8. This is a story that has been retold over the
   years, contributing to some confusion.
   Partially quoted and paraphrased by E.
   Merton Coulter, "Nancy Hart, Georgia
   Heroine of the Revolution: The Story of
   the Growth of a Tradition," *The Georgia
   Historical Quarterly,* volume xxxix, June

1955, number 2, Georgia Historical Society, Savannah. The date of the Milledgeville piece was "condensed from the Milledgeville *Recorder*" of 1825, according to historian Lucian Lamar Knight, 1913.

9. Lucey, pp. 92–93.

10. Reverend Dr. Robert O. Neff, "Mrs. Johnson's Rifles (A Woman's Part in Arming the Earliest Confederate Marylanders)," *The Gun Report,* May 1983.

11. Weidenfeld and Nicolson, 1981, p. 88.

12. Dorothy Laird, *Queen Elizabeth: The Queen Mother,* Hodder and Stoughton, 1966.

13. On the Internet, see www.gendergap.com/military/Warriors.htm and www.lothene.demon.co.uk/others/women.htm.

14. As told in Alison Owings, *Frauen German Women Recall the Third Reich,* pp. 266–83.

15. Correspondence from Mrs. Ezell.

16. J. David Truby, *Women at War: A Deadly Species.*

17. See www.gendergap.com/military/Warriors.htm.

Chapter 3: America's Unique Firearms Experience

1. *Public Records of Connecticut,* 1:455–56.

2. William C. Smith, *Indiana Miscellany* (Cincinnati: Poe & Hitchcock, 1867; reprinted Chicago: Library Resources, 1970), pp. 77–78.

3. Henry Rowe Schoolcraft, *Rude Pursuits and Rugged Peaks: Schoolcraft's Ozark Journal, 1818–1819.*

4. Correspondence with Clayton Cramer.

5. Lucey, *I Dwell in Possibility.*

6. Dwight B. Demeritt, Jr., *Maine Made Guns and Their Makers.*

7. Based on Richard Rattenbury's "A Winchester for All Seasons," *Man at Arms,* September–October 1986.

8. Quoted from her memoirs in Rattenbury, "A Winchester for All Seasons."

9. From Rattenbury, "A Winchester for All Seasons."

10. These and other citations as quoted in Penelope Bodry-Sanders, *African Obsession: The Life and Legacy of Carl Akeley,* 1991.

11. Yet another woman of distinction has emerged from relative obscurity through publication of Barbara R. Stein's *On Her Own Terms: Annie Montague Alexander and the Rise of Science in the American West* (Berkeley: University of California Press, 2001). Alexander, whose family resided in Oakland, California, collected specimens of game, including antelope, zebra, and elephant, on a 1904 hunt in East Africa. Her father, Samuel T. Alexander, created a Hawaiian fortune based on sugar. He was so confident of her skills in the bush that he wrote if his gun bearer "cannot handle the lion I know that Annie will sieze [*sic*] it by the tail and sling it 20 ft away." On another occasion he wrote: "Should Annie meet a lion by herself, I don't think that she would hesitate to open fire on it. She is made of good stuff." And "[Annie] has become a woman of blood, enamored of firearms and the chase!" Tragically, Samuel Alexander died while father and daughter were on a side trip to Victoria Falls. As a memorial to her father, she founded the Museum of Vertebrate Zoology at the University of California, Berkeley, in 1908. In 1906, 1907, and 1908 Alexander collected specimens in Alaska on expeditions she financed herself. Seeking a variety of fauna and flora, including brown and grizzly bear, she also took sheep and small game. Alexander's companion during forty-two years of expeditions was yet another accomplished outdoorswoman and deadly shot, Louise Kellogg, also of Oakland.

12. James L. Clark, *Good Hunting.*

13. Roy Chapman Andrews, *Born Under a Lucky Star.*

14. Lucille Parsons Vanderbilt, *Safari Some Fun! SOME FUN! Seventeen Letters to Her Mother, January to March 1935.*

15. This article was copyrighted in 1971 by Mary Hemingway.

16. Quoted in *The Best of Jimmy Robinson,* John R. Meyer, 1980.

17. Leigh Perkins, with Geoffrey Norman, *A Sportsman's Life: How I Built Orvis by Mixing Business and Sport.*

Chapter 4: Lady Gunmakers and Engravers, Collectors, and Antiquarians

1. A compilation of women, and a few girls, who were London gunmakers and sword cutlers, drawn from Howard L. Blackmore's *Gunmakers of London, 1350–1850,* totals more than 135. Over the centuries, the two major gunmaking cities in England have been London and Birmingham. See Appendix A. The author compiled an up-to-date computer listing,

based primarily on Banta's research, and has turned over the disks to allow the monograph *Lady Gunmakers, 1350–2001* to be published, by S. James Gooding's Museum Restoration Service.

2. Marco E. Nobili, *Lebeau-Courally: Guns & Rifles Maker Since 1865.*
3. Correspondence with Mrs. Moermans.
4. March 3, 2001.
5. John G. W. Dillin, *The Kentucky Rifle,* 1993.
6. *Virginia Genealogist* 3 (1957) 3 at 109.
7. *Proceedings of the Northumberland County Historical Society,* 1935, volume vii, pp. 70–76.
8. Dr. Linda DePaun, *Remember the Ladies— Women in America, 1750–1812.*
9. Elizabeth P. Bentley, *Passenger Arrivals at the Port of Baltimore, 1820–34,* (Baltimore: Genealogical Publishing Co., 1982).
10. For firsthand information on the Colt Cartridge Works see *United States Magazine,* March 1857, "A Day at the Armory of Colt's Patent Fire Arms Manufacturing Company, Hartford, Connecticut."
11. Household Worlds, chapter 5, volume IX; the publication was a weekly journal.
12. *The Sporting Goods Dealer,* May 1904.
13. Peter H. Johnson, *Parker: America's Finest Shotgun.*
14. Designers of submachine gun and assault rifles.
15. Based on correspondence with Mrs. Geschickter.
16. *American Rifleman,* February 1990.
17. Based on the obituary tribute by Stuart W. Phyrr, A. O. Sulzberger Curator,

Department of Arms and Armor, the Metropolitan Museum of Art.
18. Memoir from correspondence with Diana Keith Neal.
19. Correspondence from Diana Keith Neal.
20. Correspondence from Kathleen Hoyt.

Chapter 5: Annie Oakley—Shooting's Heroine: "A Little Lady Made of Steel Wires"
1. Charles Lancaster, *An Illustrated Treatise on the Art of Shooting,* 1906.
2. *Ibid.,* p. 224.
3. For Miss Oakley's comments on coaching women shooters, see Appendix B.
4. For Miss Oakley's views on the ability of women as shooters, see Appendix B.
5. *The Sporting Goods Dealer,* undated article from the Oakley-Butler scrapbooks, Buffalo Bill Historical Center, Cody, Wyoming.

Chapter 6: Wild West Shows and Exhibition Shooters
1. For an excellent study of Lillian Smith and her times, see Michael Wallis's *The Real Wild West: The 101 Ranch and the Creation of the American West.*
2. *The Rifle,* March 1887.
3. Dick Baldwin, "The Road to Yesterday," *Trap & Field,* November 2000.
4. Based on an article by Prunella Hall, "Urges Women to Take Up Shooting," believed to have run in the *Boston Globe,* c. 1950.
5. See Gary Kieft, *Beyond the Wild Bunch,* chapter 10: "Shooting Events 'On the Side.'"

Chapter 7: The Sporting Tradition
1. Translated from *Hunting and Women, Argernis Jagc?*
2. Correspondence with Professor Stange.
3. *Woman the Hunter.*
4. Stange's estimate; figures from other experts vary somewhat.
5. *Woman the Hunter.*
6. *Ibid.*
7. *Ibid.*
8. *Ibid.*
9. A book based on this thesis is in preparation by Stange.
10. Correspondence with Professor Stange.
11. *The American Field,* August 16, 1884.
12. *Ibid.,* July 24, 1886.
13. Excerpt from manuscript of *With Rifle and Petticoat.*
14. See March 15, 2000, article by Doug Pike, cited on the HoustonChronicle.com website.
15. Correspondence with Susan Campbell Reneau.
16. Correspondence with Wayne Anthony Ross.
17. This and other quotations from correspondence with Alisha Rosenbruch.
18. Anthony Dyer, *Men for All Seasons: The Hunters and Pioneers.*
19. Letters furnished to the author by Lens Illum.

Chapter 8: Target Shooting—the Precise Science and Demanding Sport
1. See Appendix E.
2. Colonel William C. Church, *Army and Navy Journal,* August 12, 1871.
3. Purchased by the NRA in 1872.

4. "Mania Has Seized the Markswomen of New England," *The Rifle*, May 1888.

5. *American Single Shot Rifle News*, September–October 1990.

6. *American Rifleman*, January 1988.

7. "Big Shot from the Big Sky Country," *American Rifleman*, March 1991.

8. Interview with Mrs. King.

9. *Ibid*.

10. Interview with Ms. LeGate.

11. *Insights*, December 1996.

12. Boxed birds versus thrown birds—a variation of the sport practiced in Mexico and some other countries in which professional handlers throw the birds aloft when called for by the shooter.

13. Interview with Ms. Revitz.

14. Nick Sisley, "High Level Shooting Tips," *Sporting Clays Magazine*, November 1997.

15. Marion Maneker, "Shooting Party," *New York*, October 11, 1999.

Chapter 9: The World of Make-Believe

1. From the Oakley-Butler scrapbooks, Buffalo Bill Historical Center, Cody, Wyoming. Uncited and undated news clipping, but likely a U.S. newspaper, from c. 1889.

2. Miss Bernhardt was fond of the United States, saying, "I adore this country, where women reign."

3. William F. "Buffalo Bill" Cody had met and was greatly admired by Miss Bernhardt.

4. According to Leider, in about 1938 "West [greeted] her bodyguards at a train station, [and] famously asked one of them, 'Is that a gun in your pocket, or are you just happy to see me?' The line resurfaced often, and made its way into *Sextette* more than forty years later." *Becoming Mae West* (New York: Da Capo Press, 2000), pp. 243, 289.

5. Thell Reed is yet another Hollywood shooting coach known to have taught a number of performers, both male and female. Among women he has coached are Ellen Barkin (Calamity Jane in the film *Wild Bill*) and Sharon Stone (for *The Quick and the Dead*).

6. March 23, 2002.

7. Correspondence with Ms. Rittgers.

8. Interview with Ms. Freifeld.

9. Interview with Ms. Kaiser.

Chapter 10: Women at Arms: Today and Tomorrow

1. Based on an interview by Pamela Des Barres in *The Independent on Sunday*, London, June 10, 2001.

2. Interview with Ms. Hammer.

3. Interview with Ms. Froman.

4. Philip Sherwell, *The Sunday Telegraph*, October 28, 2001.

5. Susan H. Greenberg, with Gregory Beals, Pat Wingert, Debra Rosenberg, Karen Springen, Patrick Crowley, and Ed Caram, "'Get Out of My Way,' Women Soldiers, Making Quiet Progress, Now Hold Dangerous Combat Positions," *Newsweek*, October 29, 2001.

6. Michael Their, "A Female Captain in Policing's Male World," *Newsday*, September 21, 2001.

7. Interview with Mrs. Aitken.

8. Interview with Ms. Nyce. See also James Barron, "A-Hunting She Will Go," *The New York Times*, November 26, 1997, which discusses the phenomenon of women entering the ranks of hunters.

9. Correspondence with Mrs. Starr.

10. See chapter 7, pp. 204 to 205.

11. Interview with Ms. Berg.

12. Letter to the author, November 7, 2001.

13. See also Janine King, "Insight: Annie Oakley Is Alive and Living Next Door," *Elle*, September 1991.

14. Adam Miller, New York *Post*, November 24, 2001.

15. For a photograph of Coco Chanel on a wild boar hunt with Winston Churchill, see *Fashions of the Time*, *The New York Times*, February 24, 2002, "The Power Behind the Cologne."

In his nearly seven-page-long list of some three hundred pseudonyms "of various authors in the allied fields of sporting and shooting," Ray Riling (*Guns and Shooting: A Selected Chronological Bibliography*) identified but eight women: Mrs. Elinor (Pruitt) Stewart, whose pseudonym was "A Woman Homesteader"; Mrs. H. C. Brown, published as "Beryl"; Mrs. Dean Atkinson ("Duncan Fife"); Mrs. E. A. Moriarity ("Ellen Alice"); Mary Emma Dart Thompson ("Mary Dart"); Margaret H. Mather ("Morgan Herbert"); Mrs. Courtivey Lewis Letts ("Mrs. John Borden"); and Mrs. Nellie Blanchan Doubleday ("Neltje Blanchan").

So rare were women writers on these subjects that Riling's statement at the end of his introduction to the listing concludes with the observation that "the following list, believed to be the largest specifically on pen-names in the field of guns and shooting, has been prepared to reveal the *men* behind the pen." (Italics mine.) Among those he missed, and one of the most important: Paulina Brandreth, published under the name of Paul Brandreth.

Of particular value in compiling this bibliography is the listing supplied the author by Kenneth Czech, the result of years of research on hunting books. His work *An Annotated Bibliography of African Big Game Hunting Books, 1785–1950* also proved an indispensable source.

General Titles

Blee, Kathleen. *Inside Organized Racism: Women in the Hate Movement.* Sacramento: University of California Press, 2002.

———. *Women of the Klan: Racism and Gender in the 1920's.* Sacramento: University of California Press, 1991.

Coles, C., and A. Vandervell. *Game and the English Landscape.* New York: Viking Press, 1980.

Czech, Kenneth P. *An Annotated Bibliography of African Big Game Hunting Books, 1785–1950.* St. Cloud, MN: Land's Edge Press, 1999.

Deuchar, S. *Sporting Art in Eighteenth Century England.* New Haven: Yale University Press, 1988.

Riling, Ray. *Guns and Shooting: A Selected Chronological Bibliography.* New York: Greenberg, 1951.

Siltzer, F. *The Story of British Sporting Prints.* London: Hutchinson and Co., 1925.

Silve, S. *Dutch Painting, 1600–1800.* New Haven: Yale University Press, 1995.

Strong, R. *Artists of the Tudor Court.* London: The Victoria and Albert Museum, 1983.

Trefethen, James B. *Americans and Their Guns.* James E. Serven, ed. Harrisburg, PA: Stackpole Books, 1967.

Walker, S. A. *Sporting Art. England 1700–1900.* New York: Clarkson N. Potter, 1972.

American West

Adams, Ramon F. *Six-Guns and Saddle Leather.* Norman: University of Oklahoma Press, 1969.

Brown, Dee. *The Gentle Tamers: Women of the Old West.* Lincoln: University of Nebraska Press, 1958.

Crandall, Judy. *Cowgirls: Early Images and Collectibles.* Atglen, PA: Schiffer Publishing Ltd., 1994.

Flood, Elizabeth Clair. Photography by William Manns. *Cowgirls: Women of the Wild West.* Santa Fe, NM: Zon International Publishing Co., 2000.

Hunter, J. Marvin, and Noah H. Rose. *The Album of Gunfighters.* Bandera, TX: J. Marvin Hunter, 1951.

Lamar, Howard R. *The New Encyclopedia of the American West.* New Haven and London: Yale University Press, 1998.

Manns, William, and Elizabeth Clair Flood. *Cowboys: The Trappings of the Old West.* Santa Fe, NM: Zon International Publishing Co., 1997.

Stratton, Joanna L. *Pioneer Women: Voices from the Kansas Frontier.* New York: Simon & Schuster, 1981.

Archery

Burke, E. *The History of Archery.* London: Heinemann, 1958.

Hansard, G. A. *The Book of Archery.* Lyon: Derrydale Press, 1994.

Hardy, R. *Longbow, A Social and Military History.* London: Patrick Stephens Ltd., 1995.

Longman, C. J., and H. Walrond. *The Badminton Library of Sports and Pastimes: Archery.* London: Longmans, 1894.

Aristocrats, Socialites

Aschan, Ulf. *The Man Women Loved: The Life of Bror Blixen.* New York: St. Martin's Press, 1987.

Beaumont, Richard. *Purdey's: The Guns and the Family.* London: David & Charles, 1984.

Campan, Mme. J. L. H. *The Private Life of Marie Antoinette, Queen of France and Navarre,* vols. 1 and 2. London: Bentley, 1884.

Morby, J. E. *The Wordsworth Handbook of Kings and Queens.* Ware: Wordsworth Editions Ltd., 1989.

Orleans, Charlotte-Elizabeth. *Secret Memoirs of the Court of Louis XIV.* London: G. and W. B. Whittaker, 1824.

"Sabretache." *Monarchy and the Chase.* London: Eyre and Spottiswood, 1948.

Saint-Simon, Claude Henri de Rouvroy, Comte de. *The Memoirs of the Duke of Saint-Simon on the Reign of Louis XIV and the Regency,* vols. 1–3. London: Macmillan, 1900.

Southerland, D. *The Yellow Earl: Hugh Lowther, 5th Earl of Lonsdale.* London: Castle, 1965.

Watson, A. E. T. *King Edward VII as a Sportsman.* London: Longmans, 1911.

Wolf, J. B. *Louis XIV.* London: Gallancz, 1968.

Collecting, History of Arms, Memorabilia

Akehurst, R. *Sporting Guns.* London: Weidenfeld and Nicolson, 1968.

Baker, David J. *The Royal Gunroom at Sandringham.* Oxford: Phaidon-Christie's, 1989.

Benitez-Johannot, Purissima, and Jean-Paul Barbier. *Shields: Africa, Southeast Asia and Oceania.* London: Prestel, 2000.

Berman, V., ed. *Masterpieces of Tula Gun-Makers.* Moscow: Planeta Publishers, 1981.

Blackmore, Howard L. *Firearms.* London: Studio Vista Limited, and New York: E. P. Dutton and Co., Inc., 1964.

———. *Hunting Weapons.* London: Barrie Jenkins, 1971.

Braun, Anne. *Historical Targets.* London: Roydon Publishing Co., 1983.

Bull, S. *An Historical Guide to Arms and Armour.* London: Studio Editions, 1991.

Dolinek, V., and J. Durdik. *The Encyclopedia of European Historical Weapons.* London: Hamlyn, 1993.

Frohnhaus, Gabriele, B. Grotkamp-Schepers, and Renate Philipp, ed. *Schwert in Frauenhand Weibliche Bewaffnung.* Solingen: Bleichstellungsstelle, 1998.

Gamber, O., H. Schedelmann, and Bruno Thomas. *Arms and Armour.* London: Thames and Hudson, 1964.

Grancsay, Stephen V. *Arms & Armor: Essays by Stephen V. Grancsay from the Metropolitan Museum of Art Bulletin, 1920–1964.* New York: Metropolitan Museum of Art, 1986.

Hardy, R. *Longbow: A Social and Military History.* London: Patrick Stephens Ltd., 1995.

Hart, H. H., ed. *Weapons and Armour.* New York: Dover, 1978.

Houze, Herbert G. *Winchester Repeating Arms Company: Its History & Development from 1865 to 1981.* Iola, WI: Kruase Publications, 1994.

Mann, Sir James. *European Arms and Armour.* Wallace Collection Catalogues: vol. 2. London: William Clowes and Sons, 1962.

Nickel, Helmut, Stuart W. Pyhrr, and Leonid Tarassuk. *The Art of Chivalry.* New York: Metropolitan Museum of Art and American Federation of Arts, 1982.

Pope, Dudley. *Guns.* London: Spring Books, 1965.

Strauss, Bob, and Beverly Strauss. *American Sporting Advertising: Gun and Powder Company Posters and Calendars,* vol. 1. Jefferson, ME, and Spring, TX: Circus Promotions Corporation, 1987.

———. *American Sporting Advertising: Hunting and Fishing Posters, Calendars, Cartridge Boards,* volume 2. Jefferson, ME, and Spring, TX: Circus Promotions Corporation, 1990.

Tarassuk, Leonid. *Antique European and American Firearms at the Hermitage Museum.* Leningrad: Hermitage Museum, 1971.

Wilson, Guy M. *Treasures of the Tower, Crossbows.* London: HM Stationery Office, 1975.

Conservation

Elting, Kathy. *Cougar Attacks: Encounters of the Worst Kind.* Guilford, CT: The Lyons Press, 2001.

Gordon, Rue E., ed., Jamie N. Anderson, asst. ed. *Conservation Directory: A Guide to Worldwide Environmental Organizations.* Vienna, Virginia: National Wildlife Federation, 2000. Annual publication.

Reiger, John F. *American Sportsmen and the Origins of Conservation.* New York: Winchester Press, 1975.

Crossbows

Payne-Gallwey, Sir Ralph. *The Crossbow.* London: Holland Press, 1990.

Wilson, G., ed. *European Crossbows: A Survey by Joseph Alm.* London: Royal Armouries Press, 1994.

Dueling

Freeman, Joanne B. *Affairs of Honor.* New Haven: Yale University Press, 2001.

Kiernan, V. G. *The Duel in European History: Honor and the Reign of Aristocracy.* Oxford: Oxford University Press, 1986.

Entertainment, Exhibition Shooters, Wild West Shows

Buscombe, Edward, ed. *The BFI Companion to the Western.* New York: Atheneum, 1988.

Kieft, Gary. *Beyond the Wild Bunch: The Fast-Growing Sport of Cowboy Action Shooting.* Scottsdale, AZ: Dillon Precision Products, Inc., 1999.

Laws, Susan (Aimless Annie). *Cowgirl Action Shooting.* Wimberley, TX: Aimless Enterprises, 2000.

Wallis, Michael. *The Real Wild West.* New York: St. Martin's Press, 1999.

Wilson, R. L., with Greg Martin. *Buffalo Bill's Wild West: An American Legend.* New York: Random House, 1998.

Expeditions

Adams, W. H. Davenport. *Celebrated Women Travellers of the Nineteenth Century.* London: W. Swan Sonnenschein, 1883.

Akeley, Carl, and Mary Jobe Akeley. *Adventures in the African Jungle.* New York: Dodd, Mead & Co., 1930.

Akeley, Delia J. *Jungle Portraits.* New York: Macmillan Company, 1930.

Baker, Florence. *Morning Star: Florence Baker's Diary of the Expedition to Put Down the Slave Trade on the Nile, 1870–73.* Edited by Ann Baker. London: William Kimber, 1972.

Birkett, Dea. *Spinsters Abroad: Victorian Lady Explorers.* New York: Lasil Blackwell, 1989.

Bodry-Sanders, Penelope. *African Obsession: The Life and Legacy of Carl Akeley.* Jacksonville, FL: Batax Museum Publishing, 1991.

Delpar, Helen, ed. *The Discoverers: An Encyclopedia of Explorers and Exploration.* New York: McGraw-Hill, 1980.

Gallenkamp, Charles. *Dragon Hunter: Roy Chapman Andrews and the Central Asiatic Expeditions.* New York: Viking, 2001.

Middleton, Dorothy. *Victorian Lady Travellers.* New York: E. P. Dutton, 1965.

Polk, Milbry, and Mary Tiegreen. *Women of Discovery.* New York: Clarkson Potter, 2001.

Preston, Douglas J. *Dinosaurs in the Attic: An Excursion into the American Museum of Natural History.* New York: St. Martin's Press, 1986.

Robinson, Jane, ed. *Unsuitable for Ladies: An Anthology of Women Travellers.* Oxford: Oxford University Press, 1995.

———, ed. *Wayward Women: A Guide to Women Travellers.* Oxford: Oxford University Press, 1990.

Root, Nina J., ed. *Catalog of the American Museum of Natural History Film Archives.* New York and London: Garland Publishing, 1987.

Savory, Isabel. *A Sportswoman in India: Personal Adventures and Experiences of Travel in Known and Unknown India.* London: Hutchinson & Co., 1900.

Speedy, Mrs. *My Wanderings in the Soudan.* London: Richard Bentley, 1884.

Stevenson, Catherine Barnes. *Victorian Women Travel Writers in Africa.* Boston: Twayne Publishers, 1982.

Tinling, Marion. *Women into the Unknown: A Sourcebook on Women Explorers and Travelers.* Westport, CT: Greenwood, 1989.

Falconry

Cummins, J. *The Hound and the Hawk: The Art of Mediaeval Hunting.* London: Weidenfeld and Nicolson, 1989.

Feminism, Guns, and Hunting

Stange, Mary Zeiss. *Woman the Hunter*. Boston: Beacon Press, 1997.

Strange, Mary Zeiss, and Carol K. Oyster. *Gun Women: Firearms, and Feminism in Contemporary America*. New York and London: New York University Press, 2000.

Gun Culture

Carr, Patrick, and George W. Gardner. *Gun People*. Garden City, NY: Doubleday, 1985.

Gunmakers, Engravers, Knifemakers, Stockmakers

Austyn, Christopher. *Gun Engraving*. Huntington Beach, California: Safari Press, 1996.

Bailey, DeWitt, and Douglas A. Nie. *English Gunmakers: The Birmingham and Provincial Gun Trade in the 18th and 19th Century*. New York: Arco Publishing Co., 1978.

Blackmore, Howard L. *Gunmakers of London, 1350–1850*. York, Pennsylvania: George Shumway Publisher, 1986.

———. *Gunmakers of London, 1350–1850: The Supplement*. Bloomfield, Ontario: Museum Restoration Service, 1999.

Boothroyd, Geoffrey, and Susan M. Boothroyd. *Boothroyd's Directory of British Gunmakers*. Amity, OR: Sand Lake Press, 1994.

Buigne, Jean-Jacques, Pierre Jarlier, *et al. Le "Qui est qui" de l'arme en France de 1350 à 1970*. La Tour du Pin: Editions du Portail, 2001. Two vols.

E. I. Du Pont de Nemours Powder Co. *Diana of the Traps*. Wilmington, DE, 1915.

Forissier, Maurice, with Christian Friedrich. *Gravure Moderne de Saint-Etienne*. Biarritz: Editions du Pecari, 1998.

Grancsay, Stephen V. *Master French Gunsmith's Designs of the XVII–XIX Centuries*. New York: Winchester Press, 1970.

Groeneworld, J. *Quackenbush Guns*. Mundelein: John Groeneworld, 2000.

Hayward, John F. *The Art of the Gunmaker*, vol. 1. London: Barrie and Rockliff, 1962.

———. *The Art of the Gunmaker*, vol. II. London: Barrie and Rockliff, 1963.

Herr, Eugen. *Der Neue Støckel*. Schwäbisch-Gemund: Verlag Journal Schwend. Three vols: 1978, 1979, 1982.

Howard, Robert A., and E. Alvin Gerhardt, Jr. *Mary Patton: Powder Maker of the Revolution*. Rocky Mount Historical Association, 1980.

King, Peter. *The Shooting Field: One Hundred Fifty Years with Holland & Holland*. London: Quiller Press, 1985.

Lavin, James D. *A History of Spanish Firearms*. London: Herbert Jenkins Ltd., 1965.

Mann, Sir James. *Wallace Collection Catalogues: European Arms and Armour*, vol. 2. London: William Clowes and Sons, 1962.

Newland, M. A. *Gun and Gun Part Makers of Staffordshire*. England: privately printed, 2000.

Oakley, Annie. *Powders I Have Used*. Wilmington, DE: E. I. Du Pont de Nemours Powder Co., 1914.

Tweedale, G. *The Sheffield Knife Book*. Sheffield: Hallamshire Press, 1996.

Washer, Richard. *The Sheffield Bowie and Pocket Knife Makers, 1825–1925*. Nottingham: T. A. Vinall, 1974.

Webb, Cliff. *London Apprentices: Gunmakers' Company, 1656–1800*, vol. 8. London: Society of Genealogists, 1997.

Hunting

Baillie, Mrs. W. W. *Days and Nights of Shikar*. London: John Lane, 1921.

Beaufort, Duke of, and M. Morris. *The Badminton Library: Hunting*. London: Longmans, Green and Co., 1886.

Bluchel, Kurt G. *Game & Hunting*. Cologne: Konemann Verlags Gesellschaft, GmbH, 1997.

Borden, Courtney (Mrs. John Borden). *Adventures in a Man's World: The Initiation of a Sportsman's Wife*. New York: Macmillan, 1933.

Boyce, Joyce. *My Farm in Lion Country*. New York: Frederick Stokes, 1933.

Bradley, Mary Hastings. *Trailing the Tiger*. New York: D. Appleton and Co., 1929.

Brander, Michael. *The Big Game Hunters*. London: Sportsman's Press, 1988.

———. *Hunting and Shooting*. London: Weidenfeld and Nicolson, 1971.

Brandreth, Paul (Paulina). *Trails of Enchantment*. 1930.

Breadalbane, Alma G. *The High Tops of Black Mount*. Blackwood, 1907.

Brown, Delores Cline. *Yukon Trophy Trails*. Sidney, B.C.: Gray's Publishing Ltd., 1971.

Brusewitz, G. *Hunting*. London: George Allen and Unwin, 1969.

Burke, R. St.G., and Norah Burke. *Jungle Days: A Book of Big-Game Hunting*. London: Stanley Paul & Co., 1935.

Coffrey, Leora S. *Wilds of Alaska: Big Game Hunting*. New York: Vantage Press, 1963.

Colville, Mrs. Arthur. *1,000 Miles in a Machilla: Travel and Sport in Nyyasaland, Angoniland, &*

Rhodesia, with Some Account of the Resources of These Countries; and Chapters on Sport by Colon Colville. London: Walter Scott Publishing Co., 1911.

Cummins, J. *The Hound and the Hawk: The Art of Medieval Hunting.* London: Weidenfeld and Nicolson, 1989.

De Watteville, Vivienne. *Out in the Blue.* London: Methuen and Co., 1937.

Dinesen, Isak [Karen Blixen]. *Out of Africa.* New York: Random House, 1938.

Dixie, Lady Florence. *The Horrors of Sport.* London: Arthur Pearson, 1910.

Douglas, Gertrude M. *Rifle Shooting for Ladies.* London: Arthur Pearson, 1910.

Fischer, Helen. *Peril Is My Companion.* London: Robert Hale, 1957.

Gardner, Mrs. Alan. *Rifle and Spear with the Rajpoots: Being the Narrative of a Winter's Travel and Sport in Northern India by Mrs. Alan Gardner.* London: Chatto and Windus, 1895.

Gasset, José Ortega y. *Meditations on Hunting.* Bozeman, MT: Wilderness Adventures Press, 1995.

Greville, Lady, ed. *Ladies in the Field: Sketches of Sports.* New York: D. Appleton and Co., 1894.

Hart-Davis, D. *Monarchs of the Glen. A History of Deer-Stalking in the Scottish Highlands.* London: Jonathan Cape, 1978.

Harvey, Lieut. Col. J. R. *Deer Hunting in Norfolk.* Norwich: Norwich Mercury Co. Ltd., 1910.

Henderson, Kathleen C. T. *The Sporting Adventures of a Memsahib.* Madras: privately printed, 1918.

Herbert, Agnes. *Casuals in the Caucasus: The Diary of a Sporting Holiday.* London: John Lane, 1912.

———. *Two Dianas in Alaska.* London: John Loane, 1909.

———. *Two Dianas in Somaliland: The Record of a Shooting Trip.* London: John Lane, 1907.

Hobusch, E. *Fair Game.* New York: Arco Publishing, 1980.

Houston, Pam, ed. *Women on Hunting.* Hopewell, NJ: Ecco Press, n.d.

Jenkins, Lady. *Sport and Travel in Both Tibets.* London: Blades, East & Blades, 1910.

Johnson, D. E. *Victorian Shooting Days.* Woodbridge: Boydell Press, 1981.

Kemp, Michael. *Shooting Game.* London: Adam & Charles Black, 1972.

King, Mrs. E. L. *Hunting Big Game in Africa.* Winona, MN: privately printed, 1926.

Kist, J. B., J. P. Puype, W. Van Der Mark, and R. B. F. Van Der Soot. *Dutch Muskets and Pistols.* London: Arms and Armour Press, 1974.

Knaur, Droemer. *Jagdschätze im Schloss Fuschl.* 1974.

McConnaughey, Lucille Harris. *Woman Afield.* New York: Vantage Press, 1987.

MacDonald, Sheila. *Tanganyikan Safari.* Sydney: Angus & Robertson, 1948.

Martin, Brian P. *Tales of the Old Gamekeepers.* London: David & Charles, Ltd., 1989.

Menkes, Suzy. *Queen & Country.* London: HarperCollins, 1992.

Morden, Florence H. *From the Field Notebook of Florence H. Morden.* Concord, NH: Rumford Press, 1940.

Morden, William, and Irene Morden. *Our African Adventure.* London: Seeley, Service, 1954.

Nickerson, Joseph. *A Shooting Man's Creed.* London: Sitdgwick & Jackson, Ltd., 1989.

Parker, E., ed. *The Lonsdale Library of Sports, Games and Pastimes: Shooting by Moor, Field and Shore.* London: Seeley, Service and Co., Ltd., 1929.

Perkins, Leigh, with Geoffrey Norman. *A Sportsman's Life: How I Built Orvis by Mixing Business and Pleasure.* New York: Atlantic Monthly Press, 1999.

Prescott, Marjorie Wiggin. *Tales of a Sportswoman's Wife.* Boston: Merrymount Press, 1936.

Roberts, Brian. *Ladies of the Veldt.* London: John Murray, 1965.

Ruffer, J. E. M. *The Big Shots: Edwardian Shooting Parties.* New York: Viking Press, 1978.

———. *Good Shooting.* London: David & Charles, 1980.

St. Maur, Mrs. Algernon. *Impressions of a Tenderfoot, During a Journey in Search of Sport in the Far West.* London: John Murray, 1890.

Schroder, Piffa, *Bags and Baggage: A Visitor's Guide.* Timothy Jaques, illus. London: Gun Room Publishing, 1997.

———. *Banging on a Bird's Eye View of Country Sport.* London: Gun Room Publishing, 1995.

———. *Bird's Eye View.* London: Gun Room Publishing, 1995.

———. *Fair Game: A Lady's Guide to Shooting Etiquette.* 1995.

Seton, Grace Gallatin. *Nimrod's Wife.* New York: Doubleday, Page & Company, 1907.

Shaughnessy, Patrick, and Diane Swingle. *Hard Hunting.* New York: Winchester Press, 1978.

Sheehan, Laurence, with Carol Sama Sheehan and Kathryn George. *The Sporting Life: A Passion for Hunting and Fishing.* New York: Clarkson Potter Publishers, 1992.

Slaughter, Frances, ed. *Sportswoman's Library*. London: Archibald Constable, 1898.

Strutt, J. *Sports and Pastimes of the People of England*. London: Thomas Tegg, 1838.

Swan, James A. *In Defense of Hunting*. San Francisco: HarperSan Francisco, 1995.

Turbeville, G. *The Noble Art of Venerie or Hunting*. London: Thomas Purfoot, 1611.

Tyacke, Mrs. R. H. *How I Shot My Bears; or, Two Years' Tent Life in Kullu and Lahoul*. London: Sampson Low, Marston and Co., 1893.

Vanderbilt, Lucille Parsons. *Safari. Some Fun! SOME FUN!* Sands Point, N.Y.: privately printed, 1936.

Watson, J. N. P. *Victorian and Edwardian Field Sports*. London: B. T. Batsford, 1978.

Wheatley, Harriet. *Lady Angler: Fishing, Hunting and Camping in Wilderness Areas of North America*. San Antonio: Naylor, 1952.

Whitaker, J. *Deer-Parks and Paddocks of England*. London: Ballantyne, Hanson and Co., 1892.

Legislative

Halbrook, Stephen P. *That Every Man Be Armed*. San Francisco: Liberty Tree Press, 1984.

Kates, Donald B., ed. *The Great American Gun Debate*. San Francisco: Pacific Research Institute for Public Policy, 1997.

———. *Targeting Guns: Firearms and Their Control*. New York: Aldine, 1997.

Kleck, Gary. *Point Blank: Guns and Violence in America*. New York: Aldine de Gruyter, 1991.

Kleck, Gary and Don B. Kates, Jr. *Armed: New Perspectives on Gun Control*. Amherst, NY: Prometheus, 2001.

Kopel, David B. *The Samurai, the Mountie, and the Cowboy*. Amherst, NY: Prometheus, 1992.

Lott, John R., Jr. *More Guns, Less Crime*. Chicago: University of Chicago Press, 1998.

Malcolm, Joyce Lee. *To Keep and Bear Arms*. Cambridge: Harvard University Press, 1994.

Poe, Richard. *The Seven Myths of Gun Control*. Roseville, CA: Forum, 2001.

Marksmanship

Cornfield, S. *The Queen's Prize*. London: Pelham Books Ltd., 1987.

Cottesloe, Colonel Lord. *The Englishman and the Rifle*. London: Herbert Jenkins Ltd., 1945.

Davies, Ken. *The Better Shot: Step-by-Step Shotgun Technique with Holland & Holland*. London: Quiller Press, 1996.

Winans, Walter. *The Art of Revolver Shooting*. New York and London: G. P. Putnam's Sons, Knickerbocker Press, 1911.

———. *Shooting for Ladies*. New York: G. P. Putnam's Sons, 1911.

Various. *Bisley: The National Shooting Centre*. National Rifle Association, 1994.

Self-Defense

Lucey, Donna M. *I Dwell in Possibility: Women Build a Nation, 1600–1920*. Washington, DC: National Geographic, 2001.

Metaska, Tanya K. *Safe, Not Sorry: Keeping Yourself and Your Family Safe in a Violent Age*. New York: Regan Books, 1997.

Quigley, Paxton. *Armed and Female*. New York: St. Martin's Press, 1990.

———. *Not an Easy Target*. New York: Simon & Schuster, 1995.

Wright, James D., Peter H. Rossi, and Kathleen Daly. *Under the Gun: Weapons, Crime and Violence in America*. Hawthorne, NY: Aldine, 1983.

Shotgun Shooting, Game and Competitive

Lancaster, C. *An Illustrated Treatise on the Art of Shooting*. London: Charles Lancaster, 1906.

Robinson, Jimmy. *The Best of Jimmy Robinson*. Detroit Lakes, MN: John R. Meyer, 1980.

Tournaments

Barber, R., and J. Barker. *Tournaments*. Woodbridge: Boydell Press, 1989.

Barker, J. R. V. *The Tournament in England, 1100–1400*. Woodbridge: Boydell Press, 1986.

Gravett, C. *Knights at Tournament*. London: Osprey, 1988.

Young, A. *Tudor and Jacobean Tournaments*. London: George Philip, 1987.

Women at War

Beevor, Antony. *Stalingrad: The Fateful Siege, 1942–1943*. New York: Penguin Books, 1999.

Campbell, John M., and Donna Campbell. *War Paint: Fighter Nose Art from WWII and Korea*. Osceola, WI: Motorbooks International, 1990.

Craig, William. *Enemy at the Gates: The Battle for Stalingrad*. New York: Penguin Books, 2001.

Downey, Fairfax. *Cannonade: Great Artillery Actions of History, the Famous Cannons and the Master Gunners*. Garden City, NY: Doubleday, 1966.

Ethell, Jeffrey L., and Clarence Simonsen. *The History of Aircraft Nose Art, WWI to Today*. Osceola, WI: Motorbooks International, 1991.

Jones, David E. *Women Warriors: A History*. London and Washington, DC: David E. Brassey's, 1997.

Kimball, Jeannine Davis, with Mona Behan. *Warrior Women: An Archaeologist's Search for History's Hidden Heroines.* New York: Warner Books, 2002.

Owings, Alison. *Frauen: German Women Recall the Third Reich.* New Brunswick, NJ: Rutgers University Press, 1993.

Paret, Peter, Beth Irwin Lewis, and Paul Paret. *Persuasive Images: Posters of War and Revolution from the Hoover Institution Archives.* Princeton, NJ: Princeton University Press, 1992.

Truby, J. David. *Women at War: A Deadly Species.* Boulder, CO: Paladin Press, 1977.

Valderano, Duke of. *The Owl and the Pussycat.* London: Minerva Press, 1998.

Werner, Harold. *Fighting Back: A Memoir of Jewish Resistance in World War II.* New York: Columbia University Press, 1992.

Wistrich, Robert. *Who's Who in Nazi Germany.* New York: Bonanza Books, 1982.

Writers/Photographers

Johnson, Martin. *Lion: African Adventure with the King of Beasts.* New York: Blue Ribbon Books, 1929.

———. *Safari: A Saga of African Adventure.* New York: Grosset and Dunlap, 1928.

Johnson, Osa. *Four Years in Paradise.* Garden City, NY: Garden City Publishing Co., 1941.

———. *I Married Adventure: The Lives and Adventures of Martin and Osa Johnson.* New York: J. B. Lippincott Co., 1940.

Lasson, Frans, and Clara Svendsen. *The Life and Destiny of Isak Dinesen.* Chicago and London: University of Chicago Press, 1976.

Catalogs

Schuyler, Hartley, and Graham Schuyler. *Military Goods, Guns, Pistols and Fancy Goods.* New York, 1864.

Miscellaneous auction catalogs, various companies, including Sotheby's; Christie's; Butterfield's; David Condon, Inc.; J. C. Devine, Inc.; Wm. "Pete" Harvey; James D. Julia, Inc.; Little John's; Greg Martin Auctions; and Rock Island Auction Co.

Monographs

Anon., National Rifle Association. *Bisley, the National Shooting Centre.* Brokwood, Woking, Surrey: Bisley Camp, 1994.

Cole, Howard N., and Robin Fulton. *The Story of Bisley: A Short History of the National Rifle Association and Bisley Camp.* Guildford and King's Lynn: Biddles Ltd., 1990.

Jones, Major William. *Twelve Months with Tito's Partisans.* Bedford, England: Bedford Books, Ltd., 1946.

Periodicals

Miscellaneous copies of more than one hundred periodicals from the United States, United Kingdom, and Continental Europe were consulted, dating back to the nineteenth century.

The Rifle, vol. I, May 1885–April 1886; vol. II, May 1886–April 1887. Reprint edition by Broadfoot Publishing Co., Wilmington, NC: Tom Rowe Books, 1990.

The Rifle, vol. III, May 1887–April 1888; vol. IV, May 1888–June 1888. Reprint edition by Broadfoot Publishing Co., Wilmington, NC: Tom Rowe Books, 1990.

National Rifle Association of America: all periodicals published by the organization, from its inception in 1871 to mid-2001.

Articles in Periodicals and Other Sources

Barron, James. "A-Hunting She Will Go," *The New York Times,* November 26, 1997.

Christensenk, Maureen. "A Gun in Her Hands: Women in Firearms Advertising, 1900–1920," *Armax,* vol. V, 1995.

Credland, A. G. "The Grand National Archery Meetings 1844–1994 and the Progress of Women in Archery," *Journal of the Society of Archer Antiquaries* 43 (2000).

Donato, F. Di. "Did Eneolithic Women in the Po Valley Shoot the Bow?" *Journal of the Society of Archer Antiquaries* 43 (2000).

Ehrenreich, Barbara. "She Got Game," *Ms.,* June–July 1999. Interview with Professor Mary Zeiss Stange.

Freedman, Alix M. "Tinier, Deadlier Pocket Pistols Are in Vogue," *The Wall Street Journal,* September 12, 1996.

Garlington, W. M. "Hail the Riflewoman," *American Rifleman,* January 1931.

Gibson, G. "The Mystery of the Amazons," *Journal of the Society of Archer Antiquaries* 19 (1976).

Gooding, S. James. "The London Gun Trade, 1850–1900," *The Canadian Journal of Arms Collecting,* vol. 18, no. 3.

———. "Sarah and Richard Walker and Their Capmaking Enterprises at Birmingham," *Arms Collecting,* vol. 28, no. 4.

Harper, John A., Jr. "Distaff Pistol Training," *American Rifleman,* December 1966.

Ingraham, Laura. "Why Feminists Should Be Trigger Happy," *The Wall Street Journal,* May 13, 1996.

King, Janine. "Insight: Annie Oakley Is Alive and Living Next Door: Janine King Considers the Rise of the American Gunwoman," *Elle,* September 1991.

Lake, F. "The Early History of Ladies Target Archery," *Journal of the Society of Archer Antiquaries* 9 (1966).

Larish, Inge Anna. "Why Annie Can't Get Her Gun: A Feminist Perspective on the Second Amendment," *University of Illinois Law Review,* 1996.

Larkin, Joseph A., C.P.L. "The Quest for the Guns of Martin & Osa Johnson," unpublished manuscript.

Lister, Ronald. "Sarah Bernhardt's Revolver," *The Gun Report,* November 1977.

Lopez, Liselotte. "Schutzenliesl Beer Steins," *American Single Shot Rifle News,* September–October 1990.

O'Neill, Molly. "Smart Set's Latest Accessory Is a Real Pistol," *The New York Times,* January 4, 1993.

Schroder, Patricia. [Miscellaneous articles on rifle shooting from *Shooting Gazette* magazine, and from *Bisley* magazine].

Stange, Mary Zeiss. "Disarmed by Fear," *American Rifleman,* March 1992.

Topperwein, Mrs. Adolph. "Shooting as a Sport for Women," *Recreation,* March 1909.

Wiltsey, Norman. "Ad Topperwein . . . a Shooting Legend," *Guns & Ammo,* October 1961.

Videos

"Annie Oakley: Little Sure Shot." Riva Productions. Program in progress.

"Women and Guns." Greystone Productions for the A & E Network. Program number 3613 in the series *Tales of the Gun.* Series produced c. 1998–2000, with this sequence from the first thirteen programs, done c. 1998. The series was broadcast primarily on the History Channel.

ACKNOWLEDGMENTS

Never before has the author experienced such enthusiastic responses to requests for information and illustrations as in the research for *Silk and Steel*. The data and images—still coming in at this writing—were more helpful than could ever be imagined, pouring in from all over the United States, from Europe, and from other parts of the world. Quickly, this book took on a life of its own.

And when Peter Beard came to Hadlyme for a week's time to do the principal photography, as always, his insights were right on the mark. In the process of creating the key collages that would bring visual life to the book, the project evolved on several levels. When the week was over, we had what the author regards as the most striking collection of images from any of our previous collaborations—and more than enough to ignite the walls in the forthcoming loan exhibition based on *Silk and Steel*.

In preparing the following list, it should be noted that several persons have already been credited, within the text, often with quotations from the person herself—or sometimes, but not often, himself—or with credit for sharing extensive research holdings.

In grateful appreciation:

To Guy Wilson, former director, Royal Armouries Museum, and master of the armouries, H.M. Tower of London, for his incisive foreword, and for his vital role in launching the exhibition and its related components. And to the chairman of the Royal Armouries Museum board of trustees, Sir Blair Stewart-Wilson, formerly equerry to H.M. the Queen (1976–94). And to other members of the board of trustees, particularly Ann Green.

To Graeme Rimer, keeper of weapons, for suggestions and counsel. To J. S. Ivinson, who kindly devoted an entire month to searching the Royal Armouries Library, as well as pursuing numerous other sources. To Thomas Costello, U.S. representative for the Royal Armouries Museum, and consultant to arts and cultural institutions.

Further, several museums, libraries, and historical societies in the United States and Europe shared images and objects from their collections. The author is most particularly indebted to:

American Museum of Natural History, Barbara Mathé, senior special collections librarian, Department of Library Services.

Musée de l'Armée, Liège, Belgium, Claude Gaier, director and president, International Association of Museums of Arms and Military History.

Musée de l'Armée, Paris, Aleth Depaz, Service Photographique.

The Adirondack Museum, Blue Mountain Lake, New York, Caroline Welsh, curator, and Jim Meehan, Photographic Archives.

The Denver Public Library, Western History/ Genealogy Department, Josephine O. Teodosijeva.

The Georgia Historical Society, Jewell Anderson Dalyrymple, reference coordinator, and Nelson Morgan, Hargrett Rare Book and Manuscript Library.

The John Fitzgerald Kennedy Library, James B. Hill, Audiovisual Archives.

The Martin and Osa Johnson Safari Museum, Conrad G. Froehlich, director, and staff.

The Metropolitan Museum of Art, Stuart Phyrr, Arthur Ochs Sulzberger Curator of Arms and Armor, and Donald LaRocca, curator in charge.

N.R.A. Museum, Bisley Camp, England, N.E.C. Molyneux, honorary curator.

Museum of Hunting and Fishing, Bernd E. Ergert, director, Munich, Germany.

Monticello, Thomas Jefferson Memorial Foundation, Charlottesville, Virginia, Susan R. Stein, curator.

Imperial War Museum, London, Angela Godwin, manager, communications, and David Penn, curator.

National Cowgirl Museum and Hall of Fame, Fort Worth, Elizabeth Clair Flood, consultant.

National Cowboy and Western Heritage Museum, Oklahoma City, Richard Rattenbury, curator of history.

Franklin D. Roosevelt Library-Museum, Hyde Park, New York, Mark Renovitch.

Sophienburg Museum and Archives, New Braunfels, Texas, Michelle Oatman, executive director.

Yale Center for British Art, New Haven, Connecticut, Patrick McCaughey, director.

Further thanks are extended to:

Cubeta's, particularly Garry Terra, who supplied all the props and equipment crucial for the principle photography session, even coming by the site to help, and taking some of the candid 35mm shots with his Nikon.

Various members of the staff of the National Rifle Association, for assistance on numerous subjects. Past president Marion Hammer, Sandra Froman, Sue King, Craig Sandler, H. Wayne Sheets, Mary Sue Faulkner, Mark Keefe, IV, John Robbins, and Stephanie Henson, as well as to others noted elsewhere.

Shari LeGate, executive director, Women's Shooting Sports Foundation, for illustrations, information, and a lengthy interview.

Robert Delfay, executive director, National Shooting Sports Foundation, for assistance on several matters.

Barbara Strawberry, president, Sables, Safari Club International, for images and information, and for arranging for Mary K. Parker and Janet Nyce to provide additional material.

Nicky Saunders of the Lothene Archaeology Group, Edinburgh, Scotland, who has compiled an excellent and exhaustively detailed website recognizing women warriors through the ages.

Rudy Prusok, archivist, American Single Shot Rifle Association.

To Jeffrey and Carolyn Carter Starr; it was Carolyn who suggested the title for this book.

Mrs. Irene Roosevelt Aitken, for her cooperation in both interview and photography.

Dietrich Apel and the German Gun Collectors Association, for numerous leads, and for assistance with translations and images.

Faye Boyer, crack rifle shooter.

John and Anne Brent, for the makings of a sportswoman's collage.

Alec Wildenstein, and his assistant, Eva Malinow, for images and data on the Marie Antoinette fowling piece.

Brooke Chilvers and Rudy Lubin, Haut Chinko Safaris, for researching sources in France, Germany, and Austria, and locating rare and important images.

Kristian Davies, whose art research gave the project an early boost, for images of women and firearms in the fine arts.

John Delph and John J. Malloy, for assistance with historic advertising art, particularly of the period c. 1890 to 1920.

Peter de Rose, for arranging a full day's photography of selections from his extraordinary collection.

Richard Alan Dow, whose expert editorial assistance is greatly appreciated, as on previous—increasingly complex—projects.

Mrs. Virginia Ezell, for guidance on women at war.

Jim Herring and Ellen Enzler-Herring, Trophy Room Books, for suggestions and images.

Norm and Ruth Flayderman, for research data and images, including on the little-known subject of American almanacs.

The O. K. Harris Gallery, New York, and artist Mary M. Mazziotti.

Harris Publications: Stanley Harris, president, Virginia Commander, executive publisher, Shirley Steffen, group publisher, and Parker Gentry—all of the Outdoor Group.

Herbert G. Houze, for illustrations, insights, and suggestions.

Roy G. Jinks, for devoting time and resources to the photography session in Northampton, and for plumbing his vast knowledge for insights on several themes.

Martin J. Lane, Martin Lane Historical Americana, whose advice and counsel have been crucial in bringing this project to fruition.

Joseph A. Larkin, who assisted in research on Osa Johnson, and the firearms of the Johnsons, and kindly sent books and other materials.

Robert M. Lee, founder and president emeritus, Hunting World, Inc., and Anne Brockinton, for numerous aids, and hospitality.

Carol Lueder, Fair Chase, Inc., for assistance with the bibliography of hunting, and specific quotations on the subject.

Priscilla Martel, of All About Food, for marshaling innumerable sources in the search for cookbooks, memorabilia, and photographs for the section on game cuisine.

Holly A. Miller of the *American Rifleman* staff, whose thorough research discovered innumerable images, articles, and notes that were helpful throughout the project.

Jerry and Ruth Murphey, of the 101 Ranch Association, for their guidance and images on Princess Wenona/Lillian Smith.

Leigh Perkins, president, Orvis, for information and illustrations on his introduction to guns, hunting, and fishing.

Frankie Preston, for providing a veritable library of important source material.

Paxton Quigley, for her expertise on women and self-defense.

Frau Professor Monika Reiterer, for sending a copy of her book, with translations, and for other assistance and insights.

Kim Rhode, Olympic champion shooter, and her father, Richard, for numerous images, and for offering to assist in the project's marketing.

305

Dr. Kenneth Robbins and Professor Barbara N. Ramusack, for their assistance with huntresses, photographs, and art from India.

Patricia L. M. Schroder, for assistance in both photography and research, and for insights on the shooting sports in the United Kingdom.

Rob Senkel, Bo Koster, and Raymond Bridgers, Greystone Productions, for sharing data from their research for the video *Women and Guns* in the *Tales of the Gun* series.

Larry and Betty Lou Sheerin, for sending the priceless Purdey over-and-under, and a collection of photographs.

Phil and Linda Spangenberger, for insights on movies, television, reenactments, and cowboy action shooting.

Professor Mary Zeiss Stange, Ph.D., for her insights into the world of women and hunting.

Bruce Stern, for allowing photography of selections from his extraordinary military arms collection.

Peggy Tartaro, executive editor, and Karen MacNutt and Sheila Link, contributing editors, *Women & Guns* magazine.

Paul Warden and staff, America Remembers, for their support with special-issue firearms commemorating women.

Chris and Louise Litke Wilkinson, for their assistance with the Evans rifle collage, and data on the 1st Battery, Connecticut Light Artillery.

Numerous enthusiasts of arms, who generously helped to assist the author in collecting information and illustrations: Richard A. Baldwin, Richard Blow, Bill and Suzie Brewster, Jeff Brown (Aspen Hills Books), Jim and Linda Carmichel, Clayton Cramer, Kenneth P. Czech, Ken Elliott, Judi Glover, J. Kevin Graffagnino (executive director, Kentucky Historical Society), Thomas E. Henshaw, Peter Horn II (vice president, Beretta, USA), Greg Jones (Swarovski), John and Linda Jones (Collectors Arms International, Inc.), James D. Lavin, Ph.D., Ken Levin (Bismuth Cartridge Co.), John McWilliams, Virginia Mallon (Pheasant Ridge Hunting and Conservation Club), Greg and Petra Martin, David Mead, Roger Mitchell (vice chairman, Holland & Holland, Ltd.), Tim Newark (editor, *Military Illustrated*), James Nottage, Jeffrey K. Reh (vice president and general counsel, Beretta USA), Susan Campbell Reneau, Alisha and Jim Rosenbruch, Mrs. Ray (Ethel) Saign, David Saltman, Max and Virginia Scheller, Tony Seth-Smith, Lee Silva (Greg Silva Memorial, Old West Archives), Joseph W. Snell, Dr. Jeffrey Starr and Carolyn Carter Starr, Richard R. Wagner, Jr., Ken Waite, Robert Wegner, Ph.D., and David Winks.

Rosemarie Parady, Deborah Parady Nelson, Suzanne O'Sullivan, and Barbara Cromeenes, and Mrs. Suzanne Noyes Brussel, whose help was crucial throughout the project.

Gary Reynolds, who, as always, played a key role in keeping the author focused on the project at hand.

Matthew K. Beatman, in appreciation of his spirited assistance, and in dealing with sundry annoyances.

The many women who sent photographs and information, often describing an array of competitions, shooting expeditions, and other experiences, the compilation of which has been crucial to the spirit and content of this book.

Peter and Sandy Riva, who have come through yet again, and assisted in innumerable ways.

And finally to my family: Heidi, Neal, and Nicholas Valk; Peter, Heather, and Brier Rose Werner; Christopher and Stephen Wilson; who again exercised restraint and patience, as yet another project required time and energy that should have been devoted to them.

Peter Beard in composition of collage frontispiece to chapter 9, at author's residence, Hadlyme, Connecticut.

Photograph Credits

Most of the photography, including collage material, was shot by G. Allan Brown, using a 4 × 5 View Camera, with Kodak Ektachrome film (either daylight for outdoors or tungsten for studio work). Brown was often assisted by his associate Bob Label. The exposed film was developed in the laboratory of R. J. Phil, East Hampton, Connecticut. Peter Beard was responsible for creative design and layout for several of the color illustrations—particularly the most critical ones—although the majority of collages were laid out by the author.

To Alexander's Photo Center, Ltd., for images of Marie Krautzky Grant's trophies.

To Keith Buckingham, Christie's, London, for images on behalf of Peter Hawkins.

To Robbie George, for triathlete images.

To Sammy Gold, Corpus Christi, Texas, for the images of the Princess Wenona guns and memorabilia from the Jerry and Ruth Murphey Collection.

To Sherman Hines, for images of hunters afield.

To Nic Hutchings, of Bonham's, London, for the images of Mrs. Patricia Schroder's trophies.

To Bruce Pendleton, for several images from the Merrill Lindsay Archives.

To Sean Riva, for the images of Irene Roosevelt Aitken and the author.

To Douglas Sandberg, for several images.

To T. Shubart, for images of Natasha Illum Berg.

To James A. Swan, Ph.D., for covering the Hollywood Celebrity Shoot.

To Ann Y. Smith, of *Shooting Sports USA* and *In Sights* magazines.

To the many who sent snapshots of their shooting and hunting adventures, most often taken by friends.

OWNER AND COLLECTION CREDITS

H.M. Queen Elizabeth II, 21 (*right, top*), 25; Adirondack Museum, 83 (*right*), 216 (*left*); John Adrain, 282; America Remembers, 151, 171; American Museum of Natural History (New York), 88, 93; Mrs. Irene Roosevelt Aitken, 6–7; author's library, 53, 59 (documents), 79 (*left*), 80 (selected photographs), 82 (selected photographs), 117, 119, 130, 150, 161, 179, 210; John Banta, 34; Bayerisches Nationalmuseum (Munich), 5 (*right*); Natasha Illum Berg, 202; Berkeley Castle (Gloucestershire, UK), 14; James U. and Lesia Blanchard III, 127; Nancy Bollman, 185; Anne Brent, 189; Bridgeman Art Library, xiv, 23 (Wimpole Hall), 30, 35 (Musée de la Ville de Paris, Musée Carnavalet, Paris); British Library (London), 4; Anne Brockinton, 185; Buffalo Bill Historical Center, 80 (miscellaneous photographs), 84, 179; Buxtun, 46, 61; Butterfield's, 20 (*left*), 71 (*right*), 72 (*center*), 74, 143 (*left*); Al Cali, 74 (*right*); Jim and Linda Carmichel, 184, 187; Castle Rosenborg, (Copenhagen), 12 (*top*); Brooke Ann ChilversLubin, 187; Christie's, 17 (*bottom, left*); Cubeta's (Middletown, Connecticut), 177, 184, 187, 192 (*right*); Julie Culver, 191; Ken Czech, 91; Michael Del Castello, 141, 144, 149; Denver Public Library, Photographic and Manuscripts Division, 76, 80 (selected photographs); Peter de Rose, 73, 78, 93 (*left*), 121; Douglas Eberhart, 77 (*left*); Jim and Ellen Enzler-Herring, 98, 178 (*right*), 179 (*top*), 198; Annie Bianco Ellett, 168; Stephen and Marge Elliott, 82; Joel Etchen, 164 (*top*); Virginia (Mrs. Edward) Ezell, 49 (photograph), 55, 59 (book); Stephano Fausti, 115 (*right*); Kate Feduccia, 192 (*right*); Claude Gaier, Musée de l'Armée (Liege), 112; Frans Hals Museum, 9; Parker Gentry, 188; O. K. Harris Gallery, 83 (*left center*); Peter Hawkins, 2, 11, 196; Historisches Museum (Dresden), 13 (*top*); Holland & Holland, Ltd., 26, 196; Deborah Langley Horn, 197; Peter Horn II (Beretta Gallery, New York), 21 (*bottom*); Herbert G. Houze, 20 (*right*); Jennifer Hunter, 83; Hunting World, Inc., 117; Imperial War Museum (postcard collection, brochures), 43, 44; Thomas Jefferson Memorial Foundation (Monticello), 110; Roy G. Jinks, 121; John F. Kennedy Presidential Library, 98; Peter King (*The Shooting Field*), 26; Labeau-Courally, 113; Martin J. Lane, 118; Susan Laws, 169; Kenneth Levin, 179; Carol Leuder, 89, 91, 94, 97, 174; Leupold-Stevens, 128; Liechtenstein Collection, 17 (*left, center*); John McWilliams, 39 (*left*); Priscilla Martel, 180–181; Greg Martin, 71 (*left*), 72 (*right*), 127, 131; Greg Martin Auctions, 75 (*bottom left*), 105 (revolver), 144; Martin and Osa Johnson Safari Museum, 91–92; the Metropolitan Museum of Art, 15; Ruth and Jerry L. Murphey, 154, 157; Dr. Joseph A. Murphy, 18–19; Musée de l'Armée (Paris), 3, 12 (*bottom*); Musée Carnavalet (Paris), 35; Musée de la Chasse (Chambord), 16 (*left*); Musée de la Chasse (Chateau de Gien, *right*), 16; Musée de la Ville de Paris, 35; National Cowboy Hall of Fame and Western Heritage Center, 79 (*right*), 211 (*right*); Virgil Mylin, 140, 145, 147, 152, 156, 158–160, 164 (*bottom*), 166; National Firearms Museum, 66 (*top*); National Rifle Association of America, 85; Diana Keith Neal, 124, 125, 127; Herb Peck, Jr., 72 (*left*), 75 (*right*), 155; Leigh Perkins, 102–103; Robert E. Petersen Guns & Ammo Collection, 107; Rose L. Piroeff, 185; Wesley Powers, 105; Suzette Rattenbury, 115 (*left center*); Danielle Reed, 185; Jeffrey K. Reh, 80 (revolver photo); Penny Reneson, 192 (*left*); Gastinne Renette, 23; Gary Reynolds, 28 (bolt-action rifle), 59 (knife), 98 (shotgun); Rijksmuseum (Amsterdam), 8; Peter Riva (Marlene Dietrich image), 41; Teal Rodgers-Henkel, 170; President Franklin Delano Roosevelt Memorial Library, 104; Alisha Rosenbruch, 194–195; Tom Rowe I, 1; Royal Military College of Canada (Douglas Arms Collection, Kingston, Ontario), 41; Sables, Safari Club International, 183, 187, 200; Diane Scarlese, 114; Max and Virginia Scheller, 100–101, 207; Mrs. Patricia L. M. Schroeder, 206, 211 (*left* and *center*); Theresa Shafer, 82; Betty Lou Sheerin, 173, 190, 275; Carter Short, 77 (*right*); Staatliche Kunstsammlungen, Dresden, 8, 10, 13 (*left*); Professor Mary Zeiss Stange, 175; Bruce Stern, 37, 47, 48, 49, 51, 57, 58; Tiffany & Co., 134; Tombstone Western Heritage Museum, 81; Maria Laura Uberti, 112; Richard and Diane Ulbrich, 32, 64, 66 (*center* and *right*), 67, 69–70, 74 (*left*), 137–138, 143 (*right*), 146, 161 (*right*); University of Georgia Libraries (Hargrett Rare Book and Manuscript Library), 68; Jacques Vettier, 201; Ken Waite, 83 (*left, bottom*), 106, 108, 136, 163, 172, 176, 178, 208–209; Dayna Wenzel, 185; Alec Wildenstein, 17 (*right*); Chris and Louise Litke Wilkinson, 42, 76 (Evans rifles); Wimpole Hall (Bridgeman Art Library), 23; Winchester Mystery House (San Jose), 119; Women on Target (NRA), 186; Woolaroc Museum (Bartlesville, Oklahoma), 82; Michael Zomber, 148.

INDEX

NOTE: *Italicized* page numbers refer to picture captions.

312

315

317

ABOUT THE AUTHOR

R. L. WILSON has authored more than forty books and three hundred articles in a career that has spanned four decades. A son, nephew, and grandson of Presbyterian ministers, his dedication to the world of arms and armor began in his boyhood in Minnesota, followed by internships at the Corcoran Gallery of Art, the Armouries, H.M. Tower of London, and the Wadsworth Atheneum, where he was appointed curator of firearms at the age of twenty-three.

He resides in San Francisco, but his consultancies with private collectors and institutions such as the Autry Museum of Western Heritage, Cody Firearms Museum, the Royal Armouries Museum (Leeds), the National Firearms Museum, and the Metropolitan Museum of Art keep him continually traveling.

Left back endpaper: 7mm Remington Magnum Model 70 rifle of Eleanor Bradford Barry O'Connor, accompanied by three photos in the field (beneath grip of rifle; serial no. 569788, .30-06 caliber, with Weaver K3 scope). Though only five feet, two inches tall and weighing 110 pounds, Eleanor O'Connor outshot her famous husband, Jack—the most distinguished firearms writer of his day. She did so while making it clear to his sizeable audience that women could hold their own with men in the hunting and shooting world. When she died at age seventy (in 1978), she could look back on a life in which she had no knowledge or interest in hunting until taught to do so by her Arizona-born husband. On O'Connor's innumerable expeditions, Eleanor was often present, and regularly hunted herself. She was his assistant and secretary, and mother to their four children. In *The Best of Jack O'Connor* (1977), he fondly wrote:

On many of my hunts my wife went with me. She has always been my favorite hunting companion. She is a magnificent camp cook and a very fine shot. If I had to stand off a battalion of man-eating tigers I cannot think of anyone I'd rather have beside me than my wife.*

Girl holding Valley quail and shotgun, fifteen-year-old daughter Caroline. To *right* and *below*, professional guide Karen Le Count on mule and with Coues deer (operated in Arizona, Utah; specialty: mountain lion). Girl with shotgun holding chukar, Christina Gindt; to *left*, with two shotguns and dog, Hope Buckner (wife of rifle owner, Eldon Buckner.)

At *top*, Catherine Eaton, on Tanzania safari, with guide Robin Hurt; who was astounded by her phenomenal shooting prowess. *Top right*, and encircling much of collage, Californian Renee Snider, one of the most dedicated and experienced of contemporary big game hunters; images include lion group from extraordinary trophy room, shared with husband Paul. *Left* and *lower center*, Mona Model, on safari in Tanzania, and with stag taken in Scotland; conservationist husband, Robert, current president of historic Boone & Crockett Club—which now includes women members. *Center*, ten-year-old Greta Martin (with pet cat Momo, and parents Greg and Petra; the wild boar taken by latter on Salinas, California, ranch of Tony Lombardo); lifetime hunting license issued to Greta at age nine. *Lower center*, family of Texans Calvin and Marge Bentsen, on family ranch, La Coma, in Red Gate, Texas—including total of eight daughters and granddaughters—all hunters. Conservationist Bentsen's black rhinos now at Disney World's Safari Park, Orlando. *Lower right*, big game hunter and Colt collector Kitten Blickhan with various trophies, taken while on safari in Africa with husband John; some of hunting done with antique Colt double rifle. *Right center*, the shooting Priores, on their Kenyon, Minnesota, farm; Harriet and Charles, with daughters Anna and Caroline, help their father in handloading ammunition, and dealing with local varmint population; African guide Natasha Illum Berg with client and trophies, Tanzania, 2002.

Bottom, from *left*, late-nineteenth-century women, first with Quackenbush air rifle and bonnet; next, huntress Mrs. A. G. Wallihaw with Remington rolling block rifle and mule deer, each taken with single shot at 180 yards; third, Stagecoach Mary with Model 1876 Winchester carbine; and fourth, Arizona pioneer

*Nancy L. Lewis, "Eleanor O'Connor," *Arizona Wildlife Trophies*. Mesa: Arizona Wildlife Federation, 2000.

Sharlot Hall in bonnet, with Winchester Model 1866 carbine; former Tiffany & Co. archivist Janet Zapata, with Colt Peacemaker, standing by historic rampant colt of cast and gilt zinc—it was atop Colt factory dome, Hartford, from c. 1867–1990s. Margie Petersen, with husband Robert E., founder of Petersen Publishing Co. (purchased c. 2001 by Primedia); key associate Ken Elliott holding commemorative Model 21 Winchester made by Tony Galazan's Connecticut Shotgun Mfg. Co., taken at Safari Club International convention, 2003; Mrs. Petersen a widely experienced international huntress. Brigitte Siatos on safari in Botswana, in the Okavonga Delta, with husband Tom, retired executive publisher and vice president of Petersen Publishing; the Southern impala taken at 210 yards. Through Siatos's contacts in the shooting world, Brigitte became an accomplished shotgun, handgun, and rifle shot. On hunting big game she "never takes a shot unless it will be perfect." Proud of earned nickname: "One-Shot Sue". Next, Kitten Blickhan, with Grant's gazelle taken on African safari; *far right*, lady professional hunting guide Mrs. Brun, from Namibia, with gentleman client and trophy wildebeest.

Right back endpaper: Huntress Eleanor O'Connor's Model 70 Winchester rifle, stocked by Lenard Brownell, and shot by her on innumerable hunts; among trophies with this rifle: two tigers (India, 1965), a lion, and an elephant (Zambia, 1969). *Top left*, Sandanista revolutionary in candid picture by Dwayne Newton, 1990s; Schuetzenfest items from *Alte Scheibenwaffen* book (1999), which documents women in the Germanic shooting festivals and competitions. *Top center* and *below* buttstock and floorplate, family of Kurt and Billy Jean Vogel, with Monica and Teddy, from shooting family of gunmakers William B. Ruger, Sr., and Jr. Billy Jean's Single Action Shooting Society moniker is Lacey Belle. To *left* of New Jersey competitive skeet shooter and huntress Betty Roschen is May Mickelsen with Model 52 Winchester target rifle; set several national smallbore rifle records and was first female to win varsity letter on University of Arizona Rifle Team (1965). *Top right*, model and firearms enthusiast Joey Davis, with rare Colt Single Actions consigned to Greg Martin Auctions, San Francisco. *To right*, Beverly Haines, Kathleen Hoyt and Amy Navitsky, of Colt's Manufacturing Co., at Colt Collectors Association show, Austin, Texas. Ann and Morris Hallowell, formerly of Greenwich, Connecticut, now enjoying their firearms-based business in Montana. *Far left*, Ursula Kepler, served as pistol-packing medical technician in World War II and was taught to hunt and shoot by father; from distinguished pioneer Wyoming family. *Women's Outlook* first published 2003; initial print run of 200,000 copies; immediately became foremost periodical focusing on women and the shooting sports. *Left*, the historic Stagecoach Mary. Beneath rifle's forend, Electra Havemeyer Webb, with trophy Caribou, on Alaska hunt (c. 1929); to *right*, Kate Jennings Webb (Mrs. Harry Havemeyer Webb), with trophy brown bear, Alaska (c. 1947); several descendents carry on family outdoors tradition. *Lower left*, Medallion d'Oro indicating exclusive honorary membership in the Club de Tiro, Canto Blanco, Madrid, awarded to champion competitive pigeon shooter Laura Revitz, September 7, 2002; club president don Arturo Fernandez officiated at the ceremony, honoring Revitz's contributions to the sport, and her distinguished achievements in competition. *Above medal* and at *center*, Sharlott Hall, Arizona pioneer and widely respected shooter. *Beneath* triggerguard, distinguished markswoman Alice Bull. *Bottom center*, Linda Swan of Colorado, arms collector and

experienced huntress. Coleen Klineburger, member of distinguished hunting family, went on innumerable expeditions worldwide; passed away in 2003, and was eulogized in Safari Club International publications. At *bottom*, from *left*, dust jacket from DeAnne Blanton and Lauren M. Cook, *They Fought Like Demons, Women Soldiers in the American Civil War*. Superb portraits of women stars from *Dallas* TV show engraved on star Larry Hagman's deluxe commemorative Holland & Holland 12-bore side-by-side shotgun; Victoria Principal (Pamela Ewing), Charlene Tilton (Lucy Ewing), Barbara Bel Geddes (Ellie Ewing), and Linda Gray (Sue Ellen Ewing). Sturm, Ruger & Co. ladies from the front office, Newport, New Hampshire; from *left*, Carol Twyon, executive secretary to William B. Ruger, Sr., for some seventeen years; Brenda L. Walsh, executive secretary to William B. Ruger, Jr.; Kathy Graham and Patti Dustin, both of the accounts payable department. Russian Army beauty queen entrants ("Beauty in Epaulets") with Kalashnikov AK-47 rifles, by Associated Press, in *The New York Times*, March 7, 2003. Minnesota huntress Emily Bakko, daughter of St. Olaf College Natural Science Professor Gene Bakko, with Winnie and Bailey and ring-tailed pheasant; Lauri Duffy and father Jim, with four of favorite pistols, hail from Rhode Island and Cody, Wyoming; Texan Mrs. Marge Bentsen, with favorite Winchester Model 21 shotgun; Nancy Bollman of Michigan, with superb zebra, and zebra-striped Ruger .44 magnum carbine; three black-and-white formal portraits of armed women with favorite guns, by Warren Hukill, Emeryville, California (San Francisco Bay area) photographer, from his book in progress, with working title *Women and Their Guns*. Three-year-old Anna Priore and father, on family range in Kenyon, Minnesota, with M1 Garand rifle, and other shooting paraphernalia. With Thompson Center single shot rifle, Karen Mehall, editor, *Women's Outlook* magazine, and trophy white-tail deer; Kate Murphy Riggs with son Hudson, at two months, grandson of arms collector Joseph Murphy and wife Martha; note holstered miniature Colt Six-Shooter, from a matched pair, by Aldo Uberti, from Joel Morrow's Imperial Russian Armory.